BLACK BRAZIL

UCLA Latin American Studies
Volume 86

BLACK BRAZIL

Culture, Identity,
and Social Mobilization

Edited by
Larry Crook and Randal Johnson

UCLA Latin American Center Publications
University of California, Los Angeles

UCLA Latin American Center Publications
University of California
Los Angeles, CA 90095-1447

Cover design: Linda M. Robertson

Cover art: Painting of a Candomblé ceremony (1993) by Brazilian artist Terciliano Jr. Reproduced with permission of the artist. Photo by Henry John Drewel.

Library of Congress Cataloging-in-Publication Data

Black Brazil : culture, identity, and social mobilization / edited by
    Larry Crook and Randal Johnson.
        p.   cm. — (UCLA Latin American studies ; v. 86)
    Includes bibliographical references and index.
    ISBN 0-87903-087-9
    1. Blacks—Brazil.   2. Blacks—Race identity—Brazil.   3. Brazil—Relations—
Africa.   4. Africa—Relations—Brazil.   5. Blacks—Brazil—Religion.
6. Blacks in mass media.   7. Social structure—Brazil.   8. Brazil—Race
relations.   I. Crook, Larry.   II. Johnson, Randal, 1948–   . III. Series.
F2659.N4B53   1999
305.896081—dc21   99–33770

Contents

PREFACE   ix

INTRODUCTION
  Larry Crook and Randal Johnson   1

PART ONE. Voices from the Black Movement   15

1   Race and Politics in Brazil
  Benedita da Silva   17

2   The Black Movement: Without Identity There Is
  No Consciousness or Struggle
  Thereza Santos   23

3   Where Are the Blacks?
  Antônio Pitanga   31

4   Olodum and the Black Struggle in Brazil
  João Jorge Santos Rodrigues   43

5   Candomblé and Community
  Maria José do Espírito Santo França   53

PART TWO. Perspectives on Race, Class, and Culture   59

6   Perspectives on Race and Class in Brazil
  Carlos Hasenbalg   61

7   Blacks in Salvador: Racial Paths
  Jeferson Bacelar   85

PART THREE. Brazil/Africa   103

8   Africa-Brazil: "Ex Africa Semper Aliquid Novi"?
  Anani Dzidzienyo   105

9   Art History, Agency, and Identity: Yorùbá
     Transcultural Currents in the Making of
     Black Brazil
          Henry John Drewal   143

10   Black Brazil: African Notes on a New Negritude
          Femi Ojo-Ade   175

PART FOUR. Religions, Culture, and Resistance   199

11   Candomblé in Bahia: Repression and Resistance
          Júlio Braga   201

12   Power, Invention, and the Politics of Race:
     Umbanda Past and Future
          Diana DeG. Brown   213

13   The Fall of a Black Prophet: Pentecostalism and
     the Rhetoric of Race in Urban Brazil
          John Burdick   237

PART FIVE. Music, Carnival, and Identity   247

14   Carnival: The Colors of Change
          Antônio Risério   249

15   The Multiplicity of Black Identities in Brazilian
     Popular Music
          José Jorge de Carvalho   261

16   The Rise of Bumba-meu-Boi in Maranhão:
     Resilience of African-Brazilian Cultural Identity
          Kazadi wa Mukuna   297

PART SIX. Blacks in the Visual Media   311

17   The Flash of Spirit: Cinematic Representations of
     Afro-Brazilian Religion
          Robert Stam   313

18   The Drama of Modernity: Color and Symbolic
     Exclusion in the Brazilian *Telenovela*
           Denise Ferreira da Silva   339

19   The Representation of Blacks on Commercial
     Television in Brazil: Some Cultivation Effects
           Michael Leslie   363

     CONTRIBUTORS   377
     INDEX   381

Preface

The essays brought together in this volume were first presented at a conference held on the campus of the University of Florida in April 1993. The idea of the conference was to explore multiple dimensions of Afro-Brazilian culture with a special focus on the construction of identities and the ways cultural expressions and formations are embedded in and give rise to processes of social organization and mobilization. To this end, the conference was divided into sessions similar to the groupings of essays in this book. In their planning of the conference, the organizers sought, first, to provide an overview of the current situation of race relations, the changing paradigms of racial thought, and the relationships among race, class, and culture in Brazil before shifting to more specific areas such as the historical, cultural, and political relationships between Brazil and Africa, the role and representation of blacks in media and culture, Afro-Brazilian religions, music, and identity, and links between cultural and political aspects of the contemporary black movement.

Major funding for the conference was provided by the North-South Center and the United States Department of Education (Title VI) through the Center for Latin American Studies. Various academic units and cultural organizations at the University of Florida participated in making the conference a success, and to them we owe a debt of gratitude: the Center for Latin American Studies, the College of Fine Arts, the College of Liberal Arts and Sciences, the College of Journalism and Communications, the Center for African Studies, the Department of Music, the Department of Romance Languages and Literatures, the Department of African and Asian Languages and Literatures, the Harn Museum of Art, the Grinter Galleries, the Center for Performing Arts, the J. Wayne Reitz Union Program Council, and the Florida/Brazil Institute. We would also like to express our gratitude to the Brazilian Consulate General in Miami and the Centro de Estudos Norte-Americanos of the Conjunto Universitário Cândido Mendes for their support.

Many people contributed to the conference's success, and to them we express our sincere thanks: Ambassador Rubens Ricupero, Consul-General in Miami Vera Machado, University of Florida President John V. Lombardi, Provost and Vice President Andrew Sorensen, Dean Willard W. Harrison, Dean Donald E. McGlothlin, Associate Dean David Colburn, International Studies and Programs Director Uma Lele, Center for Latin American Studies Director Terry McCoy, Center for Latin American Studies Associate Director Debbie Pacini-Hernández, plus Bira de Almeida and Corpo Santo, George Reid Andrews, Gerard Béhague, Tara Boonstra, Brazilian Music Ensemble Jacaré, Bryan Byrne, Sylvia Crook, Brooke Deratany, Ken Dossar, Raymond Gay-Crosier, Marvin Harris, Ali Hersi, Cida Johnson, Elizabeth Lowe, Tony Meola and Bragadá, Kerry Oliver-Smith, Charles A. Perrone, Mark Read, Eduardo Romero, Helen Safá, Peter Schmidt, Mary Ubersax, Adão Ventura, Olabiyi Babalola Yai, and Naná Vasconcelos.

Introduction

LARRY CROOK and RANDAL JOHNSON

Like the United States, Brazilian society comprises a complex ethnic, racial, and cultural mix. The oft-repeated notion of the three "races"— European, Amerindian, and African—scarcely accounts for the multiplicity of cultural forms coexisting in the Brazilian melting pot. Today's Brazil is a pluriethnic and multiracial society with substantial Japanese, German, Italian, Slavic, Jewish, and Arabic communities. Brazilians of African descent constitute nearly half of the country's population and have had a major influence on virtually all aspects of Brazilian society.

The African influence in Brazil is embedded in many different facets of daily life, ranging from language, music, dance, religion, art, and cuisine to more intangible ways of feeling, seeing, laughing, and being. Deriving initially from highly diverse African civilizations—including Sudanese (Yoruba, Ewe, Fon, Fanti-Ashanti), Bantu (Abunda, Cabinda, Benguela), and Islamicized (Hausa, Mandingo, Nupe) civilizations—this influence has over time been adapted, dispersed, and transformed into cultural practices now seen as characteristically Brazilian (e.g., Bahian cuisine and the samba). These cultural practices and Afro-Brazilian identities have resisted, survived, and evolved—and new forms have been created—in the face of political and social repression and economic marginalization both during and after slavery. They have also persisted under paternalistic state-supported processes of folklorization and commercial appropriation as well as under the racial discrimination which faces Brazilians of African ancestry throughout social life.

In response to the contemporary social, economic, political, and cultural situation of Afro-Brazilians in the country, an unprecedented black consciousness movement began to form in the early 1970s at the

1

confluence of numerous factors. First, the movement's emergence occurred at a crucial moment in Brazilian history when the military regime began to lose both social legitimacy and political control and civil society showed new signs of life, leading to the long process of political "re-democratization" and the eventual restoration of civilian rule in 1985. Voices which were previously repressed could finally be heard. A second significant factor was the politicization of black college-educated professionals who had realized that their exclusion from middle-class positions and thus from socioeconomic advancement and upward mobility was due primarily to their race (Andrews 1991:166–180; Hanchard 1994:111). Additional factors were the influence of liberation movements in Lusophone Africa, Latin America, and the Caribbean, and the impact of the U.S. black movement, in both political and cultural terms.

This renewed consciousness became very clear during the centenary of abolition in 1988. Official and unofficial commemorations marking the event were often characterized less by consensus concerning the importance of abolition, which did in fact occur peacefully in 1888, than by conflicting interpretations and contested visions of the significance and legacy of abolition (Maggie 1989). In fact, many Afro-Brazilian groups questioned whether the event should be celebrated at all, especially in light of what they saw as the unfulfilled promises of abolition, the permanence of deep-seated racial discrimination in the country, and the lack of equal opportunities for Brazil's non-white population. In the most significant racial protests since the activities of the Frente Negra Brasileira (Black Brazilian Front) in the 1930s, a number of black organizations boycotted festivities on May 13 itself, preferring to sponsor counter-marches prior to that day. In Rio de Janeiro, a protest march held on May 11 was violently repressed by military police (Hanchard 1994:149–150). In Salvador, the most "African" city of Brazil, the government canceled official celebrations under pressure from carnival organizations, and the only commemoration was a march and public demonstration on May 12 with the theme "cem anos sem abolição" ("100 years without abolition"). Others chose to express their concerns by calling for discussions of abolition in a critical, rather than celebratory, fashion, focusing specifically on abolition's meaning for contemporary Afro-Brazilians (Andrews 1991:218–233).

The events of 1988 dramatically illustrate the emergence of a new racial dynamics based less on the apparent quiescence that has long characterized official versions of race relations in the country than by denunciations of deeply engrained racial discrimination and contested interpretations of racial identities and stereotypes. Along with the multiple and diverse manifestations of a renewed Afro-Brazilian consciousness, the events of 1988 also exemplify a changing racial order in contemporary Brazil. Evidence of this changing order has led a number of social scientists to call for the development of new paradigms—or a critical reexamination of existing ones—for the discussion of race in contemporary Brazilian society.

Previously dominant theories of race and race relations in Brazil—scientific racism in the nineteenth century, the ideology of racial "whitening," the notion of Brazil's racial "exceptionalism" (Hanchard 1994:43–47), the myth of a harmonious "racial democracy," codified by Gilberto Freyre in the 1930s, Degler's "mulatto escape hatch," and analyses of race and racism as reducible (and secondary) to class-related issues—have tended to neglect or minimize the importance of race in the structuring and perpetuation of social inequalities. While contemporary analyses have focused on structural aspects of racial inequality and discrimination and some have attempted to understand the linkage of inequality to ideology, they have generally downplayed or denied the importance and the complexity of modes of cultural expression and practice, which may be forms of both resistance and accommodation. Recent events in Brazilian race relations underscore the need to conceptualize race itself as a contested terrain where struggles between different and often contradictory visions of society take place. A critical examination of race relations in Brazil must assess the role of cultural expression and identity formation within the process of social mobilization.

One of the most contentious disputes within the black movement has been between those activists and groups engaged in explicitly political activity and those, often pejoratively called "culturalists," whose primary focus is, at least initially, on cultural practice. Michael Hanchard, for example, has recently argued that culturalism, "the excessive valorization and reification of cultural production," has functioned as an impediment to the development of a strong, national, politically effective black organization in Brazil (1994:9, 98–141). Cultural expression per se, extracted from its social context and reified or, in some cases, appropriated by commercial or elite interests, no doubt contributes little to the formation of the kind of black organization or movement of which Hanchard speaks. Nevertheless, as we will see below and throughout this volume, cultural groups, organizations, and movements have in fact been of crucial importance in the formation of the contemporary black movement in Brazil. The multiple perspectives presented in this volume seek to explore the dynamic relationship between cultural practice and social mobilization.

The volume editors have been guided by two important underlying presuppositions. The first is that notions of race are socially and historically constructed. As such, they constitute discourses which are relative and subject to conflictive interpretations. In other words, race is "a phenomenon whose meaning is contested throughout social life" by different groups, individuals, and institutions (Winant 1992:183). Consequently, racial and ethnic identities change and are frequently conflictual. They are, in short, stakes in a struggle between different and often contradictory visions of society.

To give but one obvious example, it is well known that Brazil's system of racial classification is much more complex and ambiguous than the dichotomous (black/white) system of the United States. In the 1980 census, Brazilians offered 136 color and racial labels to describe their color; respondents in the 1976 National Household Survey provided nearly 200 such terms (Andrews 1991:249). The census itself used four categories (Table 1) to describe race: white (*branco*), black (*preto*), brown or mulatto (*pardo*), and yellow (*amarelo*, indicating Brazilians of Asian ancestry).

Recognizing the numerical significance of the combined black and brown populations, the black movement rejected the tripartite black/

TABLE 1

Brazilian Racial Composition, 1940–1980, by Decade

(%)

Year	White	Brown	Black
1940	63.5	21.2	14.7
1950	61.7	26.5	11.0
1960	61.0	29.5	8.7
1980	54.8	38.4	5.9

a. Because of their small numbers, "yellows" have not been included in this table.

Source: Jan Fiola, *Race Relations in Brazil: A Reassessment of the "Racial Democracy" Thesis.* Program in Latin American Studies: Occasional Papers Series, no. 24 (University of Massachusetts, Amherst, 1990).

brown/white system of classification in favor of a bipartite black/white system similar to that used in the United States, a system that better reflects the socioeconomic reality of race relations in Brazil.[1] In relation to the 1990 census the movement encouraged Afro-Brazilians to record their racial category accurately, using the slogan "Não deixe a sua cor passar em branco" ("Don't let your color go blank" or "Don't let your color go down as white"). It is clearly in the interest of the black movement to promote such a dichotomous system, since blacks and browns combined account for nearly half of Brazil's population, just as it is in the interest of the white elite to insist on a system using multiple levels of classification in the continued defense of the myth of racial democracy and racial hegemony. Racial classification, one aspect of racial thought, is clearly a stake in a broader struggle for social equality and political democracy.

A second assumption, which derives from the first, is that cultural expressions involving questions of identity are inseparable from broader political processes, even when the connections are not rendered explicit. As a form of identity politics, cultural practice may ultimately have a more profound and lasting impact than some kinds of more specifically political activities. Rather than being expressions of an "innocuous non-conformity" (Fernandes 1976) or manifestations of a questionable "culturalism," cultural practices which lead to the emergence of a new consciousness, even when in an apparently dispersive manner, may well be a necessary step in the development of more explicitly political organizations by helping to shape political and social awareness. If for whatever reason *pardos* do not identify themselves as black, it will be very difficult for them to be mobilized by or to support fully the political objectives of the black movement. Cultural practice may help develop the necessary identification. J. Michael Turner (1985), for example, has noted the seminal influence of the Black Soul movement on the changing racial attitudes of Afro-Brazilian university students in what he calls their shift "from brown to black." Bahian *blocos afro* (African blocs) such as Ilê Aiyê and Olodum have had a similar impact.

The contemporary Brazilian black consciousness movement has taken many forms. Some organizations like the Movimento Negro Unificado (MNU; Unified Black Movement), SOS Racismo, and the Centro de Articulação de Populações Marginalizadas (CEAP; Center for the Articulation of Marginalized Populations) have combined explicitly political, anti-racist agendas in their struggle for the social, economic, and cultural emancipation of Brazil's black population (Gonzalez

1985:126; Andrews:1991:193–194; Hanchard 1994:119–129). Others, such as GELEDES, a black women's organization founded in São Paulo in 1990, are more issue-specific, focusing, in this case, on reproductive rights, health issues, and racial discrimination in the Brazilian labor market (Hanchard 1994:131). Although the impact of such organizations has been visible in the incorporation of black issues into the platforms of Brazil's political parties and their bringing attention to issues of racism and race relations in Brazil, black representation and real political power are still minimal at local, state, and national levels. Additionally, such activist organizations have suffered from ideological fragmentation, an inability to organize nationally, and from the large gulf between their actual members and the mass majority of black Brazilians who remain largely unaware of their activities.

Unlike their more activist political counterparts, the cultural components of the black movement are, in general, more integrated into the daily fabric of black Brazilian life. One of the first manifestations of a revitalized black consciousness in Brazil occurred in the early 1970s in the working-class suburbs of Rio de Janeiro and São Paulo. What has become known as Black Soul drew inspiration from and assumed many of the superficial accoutrements of the black movement in the United States, especially its music and modes of dress and behavior (Afro hairstyles, dashikis, elaborate handshakes). In short, their participants adopted a posture that rooted Afro-Brazilian identity in the black body.

Black Soul espoused no specific political ideology, but its very existence challenged conventional views of race by asserting a unique black identity within Brazilian society. By rejecting such traditional Afro-Brazilian practices as samba, which was held to have been corrupted by commercialism and white cultural dominance, and by adopting instead cultural forms frequently associated with the angry militancy of the Black Power movement in the United States, Black Soul's participants aligned themselves with a transnational assertion of black identity. For this its participants were harshly criticized as "un-Brazilian" by left intellectuals (including some black intellectuals) and, on the right, by the military. By calling attention to blacks *as* blacks with their own identity, Black Soul implicitly challenged the official ideology of racial democracy and harmony and represented, as Michael Hanchard has put it, "a threat to the national project" (Hanchard 1994:111–119; also Mitchell 1985; Turner 1985; Winant 1992).

Traditional Afro-Brazilian cultural organizations have often concerned themselves with reclaiming and upholding Brazil's rich African heritage, reestablishing aesthetic relations with contemporary Africa and the African diaspora, and redefining what it means to be black in Brazil. Long-standing Afro-Brazilian religious (e.g., Candomblé, Xangô, Tambor de Mina) and secular traditions (e.g., *capoeira,* Bumba-meu-Boi, *maracatu, afoxé*) provide important loci for the perpetuation and reproduction of African-derived social practices. At the same time, they have also been used as "binding elements of a social homeostasis that benefits elites" in the construction of a national "consensus culture" (Yúdice 1994). Traditional Afro-Brazilian cultural practices have often been romanticized and folklorized by official Brazil and analyzed as the relics of a tribal Africa. This process helped construct the image of a "frozen" Africa safely distanced from the contemporary realities of blacks in Brazil. Thus constructed, these frozen practices could function as mechanisms of elite social control and racial hegemony. They could also be appropriated by the economic interests of a tourist industry dealing in "exotic" culture (the commercialization of Rio's *escolas de samba* [samba organizations] and carnival is a prime example).

But these same traditions in Brazil have also served as mechanisms of resistance and as resources for blacks to construct their own identities. Marginalized black populations throughout Brazil have used tradition as a tool for interpreting and acting on their world. As Mukuna's essay in this volume points out, rather than an ossified relic of the past, Bumba-meu-Boi served as a dynamic site of black cultural resistance in Maranhão both during and after slavery. Similarly, Júlio Braga demonstrates that Bahian Candomblé has been a site of community identity and resistance for Salvador's black population for over a hundred years despite— perhaps in reaction to—official and unofficial discriminations. Thus, rather than representing only a frozen mythical Africa, even the most "traditional" Afro-Brazilian cultural practices may also be a means of constructing dynamic relationships both with Africa and with the contemporary Afro-Brazilian community. Traditions are not static historical facts but are "socially constructed arrangements of behavior that can be reinterpreted, developed, or even 'invented' " (Erlmann 1991:11). Afro-Brazilian traditions can and have been used as strategic resources by competing social forces within the society in their contest for power.

The black community's self-awareness of both the historical trajectory and contemporary relevance of cultural practices to the social and political mobilization of blacks in Brazil has greatly increased since the 1970s. Recently formed black cultural organizations have become aware of their social and political roles and consciously attempt to raise racial consciousness and combat racial discrimination and oppression at the grass-roots level through cultural activism and the politics of identity. Black carnival organizations from Bahia known as blocos afro are arguably the most dynamic and socially committed cultural associations of the black movement in Brazil, extending their cultural activity to social, political, and economic arenas (see comments by João Jorge Santos Rodrigues in this volume). Emerging in the 1970s, they formed one of the initial manifestations of the new black consciousness, heralded the "re-Africanization" of Bahian carnival (Risério 1981), and predated the formation of the MNU. Constituted as recreational cultural organizations, these groups are committed to the struggle against racial discrimination and economic inequality. Since the founding of Ilê Aiyê (the first bloco afro) in 1974 and the remarkable success of Olodum in the 1980s, the bloco afro model has taken over the Bahian carnival and has spread to Brazil's other major cities as well.

Other cultural manifestations of the new black consciousness include the Black Soul/funk movement of the 1970s and 1980s, the popularity of reggae and Rastafarianism, and the more recent explosion of Brazilian rap. Two extremely interesting and related aspects of these youth-oriented phenomena (as well as of the bloco afro movement) are their connection to mass media technology and their pan-African/diasporic nature. Emerging in a Brazil connected to world events via the mass media, these movements—unlike those of previous generations—exploit media and technology at many levels. This has allowed them to transcend Brazil's geopolitical boundaries and folkloric stereotypes about African tradition. Precisely because most if not all of these cultural practices cannot be circumscribed neatly within Brazil's geopolitical-cultural boundaries, they have been extremely useful in articulating transnational and transcultural perspectives.

Black Brazil now defines itself as part of a diaspora. Nowhere is this more evident than in popular culture, especially in the field of popular music. This has important implications for the renewed significance of "race" in Brazil. The political and social potential of these movements centered on music should not be ignored nor dismissed as merely supporting an imperialist U.S.–based cultural hegemony. In the case of the blocos afro, the construction and manipulation of symbols highly charged with "Africanness" from diverse sources (reggae and Rastafarianism from Jamaica, Candomblé and slave revolts from Brazil, civil rights struggles from the United States, and mythical and contemporary Africa) have led to the articulation of a pan-African identity. This has been carried into the mainstream culture industry via a new genre of popular music known as *axé* music. By making aesthetic connections to black populations throughout the world, these movements establish new forms of identity that challenge the nature of the traditional hegemonic Brazilian national identity.

Black Brazil's cultural practices are not only necessary in order for Brazil to become truly democratic, but they are also absolutely essential in order to mobilize the mass population of Afro-Brazilians with divergent social, economic, and ideological backgrounds. Culture, writes Stuart Hall, "is a sort of constant battlefield . . . where no once-for-all victories are obtained but where there are always strategic positions to be won and lost" (1981:233). It is frequently a contested terrain, located at the center of social and political life, where struggles occur to link specific practices and forms to values and identities and where consciousness and the formation of group identities intersect social and political power. In this sense cultural practice can be simultaneously a site of domination and resistance, of hegemony and counter-hegemony. Nowhere has this process been more evident than in the Brazil of the last two decades with respect to the growing racial and political consciousness of its black population. As evidenced in the essays in this volume, cultural practices, racial formation, and social mobilization are linked to one another in a nexus with social and political power within Brazil. In various ways the contributions reflect the idea that racial and ethnic identities are not static categories but evolve, change, and frequently involve conflictual processes.

Afro-Brazilians have utilized cultural expressions both to construct unique identities within Brazil and to resist various forms of domination, as well as to articulate racial self-identification with other peoples of the African diaspora. As a form of identity politics, cultural practice has a profound and lasting impact on social and political formation in Brazil. But the role of culture continues to be particularly problematic in Brazil owing to the historically pervasive racial hegemony which has promoted an image of racial harmony while concurrently reproducing a system of racial inequalities and discriminations. It is undeniable that, in the service of this hegemony, Afro-Brazilian cultural practices (folklore, religion, music, dance, etc.) have been paternalistically glorified, com-modified, and converted into symbols of Brazilian national identity, stripped of racial and political implications.

Michael Hanchard has recently argued that Afro-Brazilian intellec-tual activists of the 1970s attempted to subvert this process by "infusing new meanings into old Afro-Brazilian symbols and cultural practices" but that this "resulted in the use and appropriation of cultural practices as ends in themselves rather than as means to broader, more compre-hensive ethico-political activities" (1993:59). Treating cultural practice as merely a means to "broader, more comprehensive ethico-political activi-ties," however, runs the risk of not only denigrating the values of the bearers of those cultural traditions (the very people needed to be mobi-lized) but also of failing to take advantage of the organic relationship between cultural practice and political action. One of the reasons why such activity has not been translated into greater mass mobilization of black Brazil is that cultural practices are often conceptualized—from an elite and privileged perspective—as merely the means to an end. What has been lacking is an appreciation of both the efficacy and the every-dayness of the expressive aesthetics of black Brazil's cultural practices.

Rather than being fetishized as sacred cultural artifacts or dis-missed as merely emasculated relics, cultural practices should be con-ceptualized as inseparable from contemporary social and political processes. The cultural consequences of this include both opportunities for gain and possibilities of loss. Cultural processes and products of sub-ordinate groups will always be subject to appropriation and rearticula-tion by the dominant group within society (to wit the marketing of axé music). But through appropriation and rearticulation, the dominant class must adjust itself by incorporating features of the subordinate group in order for its core values not to be threatened (Meintjes 1990). In this light, the aesthetic sensibilities rooted in contemporary black Brazil-ian experience and now spread via mass media may do more than aes-thetically transform Brazil; they may help reformulate its core values. However important the formation of racial identity and consciousness, the impact of the cultural dimension in black Brazil's struggle for equal-ity must also be gauged against changes in economic, social, and politi-cal power. As João Jorge, president of Bahia's leading bloco afro Olodum, notes in this volume, "the struggle for culture has to bring wealth to the community." This is an extremely important consideration and one that social analysts continue to debate. Can (and will) the identity politics embedded in cultural expression increase access to the social, economic, and political sources of power for Brazil's black community? Is one possible without the other? There may be no easy answer to either of these questions.

This volume brings together the diverse perspectives of scholars, politicians, and cultural activists who assembled in April 1993 for the 42nd Annual Conference of the University of Florida's Center for Latin American Studies. For the conference (titled "Black Brazil: Culture, Identity, and Social Mobilization") participants were asked to present papers exploring the multiple dimensions of Afro-Brazilian culture, focusing specifically on the construction of identities and the ways grassroots cultural expressions are linked to social organization and mobilization. All of the participants shared a common concern with locating black Brazil in its historic and contemporary social and cultural realities. In preparing the papers of that conference for publication, the editors faced several problems. In order to preserve the diversity of contributing voices, the editors have attempted to provide stylistic consistency without imposing a single disciplinary model. Indeed, contributors include participants in Brazil's contemporary black movement (the first black woman to be elected to congress in Brazil, an actor turned politician, the intellectual leader of one of the most dynamic Afro-Brazilian cultural organizations in the country, a longtime militant who has worked on cultural and political fronts, a Candomblé initiate), a journalist, poet, and lyricist, anthropologists, sociologists, ethnomusicologists, literary critics, and film, television, and communications scholars. The contributors also represent diverse national origins: Argentina, Brazil, Congo (Zaire), Ghana, Nigeria, and the United States. The multiplicity of perspectives focusing on a common underlying theme allows for the emergence of a clear pattern of arguments about the perpetuation of racial discrimination in Brazil and the diversity of ongoing forms of struggle and resistance against it.

We open the volume with statements from five active participants in Brazil's contemporary black movement. As frontline protagonists of the struggle for equality and the fight against racial discrimination, we believe their voices deserve to be foregrounded. We have not attempted to squeeze their comments into an academic mold, since their intention is to give a sense of their own lived experience and the political viewpoints that derive from that experience. They make no pretense at scholarly interpretations (indeed, in debates at the Black Brazil conference

some of them expressed skepticism about scholarly interpretation itself).
By the same token, we have tried, where possible, to respect the diverse
styles, discourses, and opinions of the contributors, speaking as they do
from different disciplinary, and in some cases ideological, perspectives.
For example, because of its Afrocentrist approach and pan-Africanist
stand, Femi Ojo-Ade's essay differs in methodology and style from other
scholarly articles in the volume. John Burdick's piece is highly personal
and almost informal in style, without ceasing to be analytical, while
Antônio Risério's contribution is essayistic and journalistic rather than
academic. Finally, some authors, like Carlos Hasenbalg and Michael
Leslie, rely heavily on quantification, while others, such as José Jorge de
Carvalho, Robert Stam, and Denise Ferreira da Silva, base their interpretations on more subjective forms of analysis. The multiplicity of voices,
discourses, and styles allows *Black Brazil: Culture, Identity, and Social
Mobilization* to contribute to the discussion of the issues facing Brazil
and its contemporary black movement in a spirit of open and democratic debate.

NOTE

1. Since the 1950s, numerous scholars and researchers have concluded that
mulattos suffer virtually the same discrimination as blacks in the labor market
and other key areas of Brazilian society. According to their conclusions, the significant racial dividing line is between whites and "non-whites." This analysis
refutes the thesis of the "mulatto escape hatch" proposed by Carl Degler. See
Andrews (1991:249–258). Rather than use the arguably racist category "non-
white," the editors have used, interchangeably, the terms "black" and "Afro-
Brazilian" to refer to both blacks and "browns."

REFERENCES

Andrews, George Reid. 1991. *Blacks and Whites in São Paulo, Brazil: 1888–1988.*
    Madison: University of Wisconsin Press.

Erlmann, Veit. 1991. *African Stars: Studies in South African Performance.*
    Chicago: University of Chicago Press.

Fernandes, Florestan. 1976. *Circuito fechado: quatro ensaios sobre o "poder insti-
    tucional."* São Paulo: Hucitec.

Fiola, Jan. 1990. *Race Relations in Brazil: A Reassessment of the "Racial Democracy" Thesis*. Program in Latin American Studies: Occasional Papers Series, no. 24. University of Massachusetts, Amherst.

Gonzalez, Lélia. 1985. "The Unified Black Movement: A New Stage in Black Political Mobilization." In Pierre-Michel Fontaine, ed., *Race, Class, and Power in Brazil*. Los Angeles: Center for Afro-American Studies, UCLA.

Hall, Stuart. 1981. "Notes on Deconstructing 'The Popular.' " In Raphael Samuel, ed., *People's History and Socialist Theory*, pp. 227–240. London: Routledge.

Hanchard, Michael George. 1993. "Culturalism Versus Cultural Politics: Movimento Negro in Rio de Janeiro and São Paulo, Brazil." In Kay B. Warren, ed., *The Violence Within: Cultural and Political Opposition in Divided Nations*, pp. 57–85. Boulder, Colo.: Westview Press.

————. 1994. *Orpheus and Power: The Movimento Negro of Rio de Janeiro and São Paulo, Brazil, 1945–1988*. Princeton: Princeton University Press.

Maggie, Yvonne, ed. 1989. *Catálogo: centenário da abolição*. Rio de Janeiro: Centro Interdisciplinar de Estudos Contemporâneos, Universidade Federal do Rio de Janeiro.

Meintjes, Louise. 1990. "Paul Simon's Graceland, South Africa, and the Mediation of Musical Meaning." *Ethnomusicology* 34(1):37–74.

Mitchell, Michael. 1985. "Blacks and the *Abertura Democrática*." In Pierre-Michel Fontaine, ed., *Race, Class, and Power in Brazil*, pp. 95–119. Los Angeles: Center for Afro-American Studies, UCLA.

Risério, Antônio. 1981. *Carnaval Ijexá: notas sobre afoxés e blocos do novo carnaval afrobaiano*. Salvador: Corrupio.

Turner, J. Michael. 1985. "Brown into Black: Changing Racial Attitudes of Afro-Brazilian University Students." In Pierre-Michel Fontaine, ed., *Race, Class, and Power in Brazil*, pp. 73–94. Los Angeles: Center for Afro-American Studies, UCLA.

Winant, Howard. 1992. "Rethinking Race in Brazil." *Journal of Latin American Studies* 24(1):173–192.

Yúdice, George. 1994. "The Funkification of Rio." In Tricia Rose and Andrew Ross, eds., *Microphone Friends: Youth Music and Youth Culture*. New York: Routledge.

Part One | VOICES FROM THE BLACK MOVEMENT

D iscussions of race in Brazil have often involved academic debates over diverse theoretical positions and disputes between militants and culturalists. But the importance of racial identification is felt by everyone in Brazil. For Brazilians who identify themselves as members of the Black Movement race is a particularly salient concept. The voices heard in this section include a black politician (Benedita da Silva), a militant leader and intellectual of the Black Movement (Thereza Santos), an actor/director/politician (Antônio Pitanga), a cultural activist and leader of Olodum (João Jorge Santos Rodrigues), and a Candomblé initiate and social activist (Maria José do Espírito Santo França). Together, these voices speak of Brazil as a historically racist and unjust society. But each, in his or her own way, indicates a belief in the ability and responsibility of black Brazilians to resist, to struggle, and eventually to construct a just society.

Benedita da Silva's contribution is the personal account of a black woman, a *favelada* slum-dweller, who suffered all of the social, economic, and racial injustices of Brazil's poorest black segment of society but who, despite it all, rose to be the first black congresswoman elected in Brazil. At the time of the conference (April 1993) in which she gave the keynote address, she was the only black woman in the Brazilian congress. In 1994 she was elected to the senate. Her key message is one of empowerment for the disenfranchised of Brazilian society: women, the poor, and the black. Thereza Santos has been active in the Black Movement for more than twenty-five years and her essay recounts both accomplishments and failures of the movement. She is particularly critical of individuals within the movement who have no commitment to social transformation and

15

racial struggle but who subvert the objectives of the Black Movement for their personal gain.

Antônio Pitanga, who was elected to Rio de Janeiro's City Council in 1992 on the Workers' Party (PT) ticket, is well known to Brazilian audiences through the many films in which he has appeared. His contribution provides a history of black Brazil in the twentieth century and especially the importance of its cultural and artistic manifestations. João Jorge Santos Rodrigues presents a Bahian perspective and tells of the evolution of racial identity in the city of Salvador da Bahia. Key in this evolution was the emergence of the *blocos afro* (African blocs) carnival associations of the 1970s, 1980s, and 1990s which highlighted black pride and social commitment. João Jorge, president of the bloco-afro Olodum, emphasizes the political and economic dimensions of Olodum and its continuing struggle against racism. For international audiences who know Olodum only via its recordings (including musical collaborations with Paul Simon and Michael Jackson), he provides a glimpse into the social and political importance the group commands within Brazil. João Jorge's account, like the others in this section, combines firsthand knowledge with the rich oral history of a black community. Finally, Maria José do Espírito Santo França's brief contribution discusses Candomblé as a site of community, resistance, social cohesion, and knowledge.

1 | Race and Politics in Brazil

BENEDITA DA SILVA

I have just come from a conference in Mexico where we talked about the relationship between the state, social movements, and political parties. There, the question of race in Latin America was present in every discussion and in every inference. At no time were the state, social movements, political parties or even the situation in the Third World as a whole mentioned where the issue of race was not evident. Race is not only a concern of Brazil and the United States, but also of everyone who knows world history and who understands the difference between being a man or a woman, being poor or rich, being black or white.

Brazil was the first colony in the Americas to use black slave labor. Historical data indicate that at the end of the eighteenth century more than half of the new colony's population was made up of black slaves. Starting in 1530 and continuing throughout the next four centuries, European colonizers, with unbridled greed, practiced the most inhuman model of human slavery. Captured in a brutal manner, primarily in the coastal region between Guinea-Bissau and Angola, the first blacks, our ancestors, were brought to colonial Brazil to serve the interests of a European bourgeois elite seeking rapid wealth. Brazil, the recently occupied new colony, became the economic rearguard of Europe, and slave "trade" (read "contraband") became one more element in their profit. Before sailing to the colony with their ships' galleys empty, traders began to transport a new kind of "merchandise"—black people to be sold or rented after surviving the fifty-day voyage from Angola to Rio de Janeiro.

As in any place where blacks became slaves, in Brazil the question of labor was fundamental to justifying the presence of blacks in Brazilian society in order to support economically the bourgeois elite of Europe. In reality, two ethnic groups were slaves in Brazil, blacks and the Amerindians. Slavery exists today in Brazil, only the instruments have changed, because the elite remain in power, and the ideas of the colonizer remain the same. Their defense mechanisms have changed, but the objectives remain the same. Why? Because in the colonial period, black slaves were simply commodities used to produce profit. Economically speaking, black hands helped to make the nation grow and create wealth. However, blacks lost not only their identity, but also their culture in a process of acculturation through which customs, traditions, dialects, speech, and patterns of beauty disappeared. The instruments of domination used at that time identified the black slave as such. Today, things are much more disguised.

Brazil is a country that still has—has always had—low salaries. The minimum wage is less than a hundred dollars a month. Moreover, when inflation increases in Brazil, poverty also increases, and the Brazilian population's purchasing power decreases. In addition to widespread poverty, Brazil also has to live with the myth of racial democracy. It is said that there is poverty but not racism in Brazil. In fact, the two coexist. Racism and poverty both exist. We cannot confuse the two.

Brazilian blacks, a majority in the country, have many names: mulatto, *moreninho* (little dark one), *feijãozinho* (little black bean), *crioulinho* (little creole), *amarelinho* (little yellow one). It seems that everything but the number of blacks is "little" (*-inho*). The use of these identifiers causes a serious loss of identity. Since we are a majority and we are poor, people tend to identify poverty with race. However, there is social prejudice and there is racial prejudice. This distinction is important because we are talking about a considerable portion of the population in both quantitative and qualitative terms. Brazilian society owes blacks social justice, political participation, economic opportunity, and cultural emancipation.

Our rights are constantly violated, and we face this form of domination because the power elite has never possessed the humanity to perceive the full ramifications of what they are doing. The rate of child mortality, hunger, and misery in the country is staggering. There are 38 million impoverished children, and their number increases every day. Many are on extermination lists. Statistical data on race from the morgue show that a disproportionate number of blacks are being murdered. But official documents do not indicate that they are black. The recent census does not numerically reflect the fact that the Brazilian population is mostly black. These are ways to eliminate this population. Laws, behaviors, and attitudes constitute the process of whitening the population.

A certain confusion exists between poverty and ethnicity, which we export easily and with tranquility because we have the best carnival in the world, we have Pelé, and we also have the great mulattas—but we do not have only that. We have more than coffee, Pelé, and carnival. We have a population that is discriminated against and marginalized, yet contributes to the country's economy to make it tenth in the world. The majority of the population resists the powerful who write the laws. Let me cite a few examples: the Law of the Free Womb (1871) freed children of slaves, that is, it freed them to continue being slaves, to be one less mouth for the colonizer to feed, to leave the family domain, to be street children, and, later, to be exterminated. Today things are the same; they have not changed. Today there is a law that protects these children and states that they are a national priority. Nevertheless, children are dying of hunger and working in prostitution. The Law of the Sexagenarians (1885) freed slaves when they reached the age of sixty. Freed them to do what? To die on the cold sidewalk with no income or support. In other words, they were free to continue being slaves. The Golden Law, which officially abolished slavery in 1888, said we were all free. But is that really the case?

I am the only black woman in the Brazilian Parliament. I am the only black woman out of 503 representatives in the Brazilian congress. Why do I point this out? To make these facts real so that you will understand the situation of blacks in Brazil today. What place do blacks truly occupy in Brazil? Where are the blacks? In prisons, in slums, on sidewalks. They fill the ranks of the unemployed and the illiterate. You need to know that this situation exists in Brazil. I do not want to be responsible for promoting the image of a different Brazil, when in fact we must join hands and change not only Brazil, but also the world, to create a more human relationship between men and women, whether they are Chinese, French, American, or Brazilian. We Brazilians must also accept this challenge, one that faces us daily. To accept this challenge as a means of resistance, we must struggle to determine Brazil's image. I do not represent the image of Brazil—the face of the Brazilian people—that many consider suitable for holding the position of representative. We must struggle to change this image, to dignify all Brazilian people, guarantee their rights, and defend their deepest moral values.

It is important for all of us to be aware that our culture is a millennial culture which survived the cruelest of all discriminations, which from the eighteenth century until today insists on seeing Africa and its people through the lens of racial supremacy. As we reflect on the culture, identity, and social mobilization of Brazilian blacks, it is fundamental that we be aware that our dances, food, religion, and traditions are not folklore, but rather the indisputable affirmation of the citizenship of a people. Our culture is a culture of resistance, and this resistance is growing day by day in black organizations and other entities concerned with social mobilization.

Redeeming our culture and our character is important, and that is why we want to invest, we want to have our turn and our voice. But we want much more than that. We want the whole Brazilian nation to change—this pluriethnic nation that lives the myth of racial democracy, that was born out of violence, that was built by violence. Slavery is violence, rape is violence. Brazilian society was born of rape. When the colonizers arrived, they raped black and Indian women—that is how Brazilian society was born. We want Brazil's ethnic reality to be preserved in tenderness, in kindness, in rebellion, in desire, with the will to change and with justice. It is not only our will, nor a question that faces only Latin America. I don't believe in any society, capitalist or not, that does not have social justice and economic equality, where people go hungry, where they do not all have a place to live, and they do not all have a job.

In race relations alone this achievement would not be enough for me because we want the image of every nation to project the same equality. I no longer want to be the only black female representative of my country in the national congress. I don't want to be the only one who travels around Brazil saying, "There are blacks in our national congress." I don't want to because I come from a social class in Brazil where I grew up hungry, cold, thirsty, and sleeping on the sidewalks. I was a street child in Brazil. I am an exception to every rule. I stand here today because of a consciousness of the desperate situation of blacks and the poor, the consciousness that made me understand that we must have justice. We cannot tolerate this deceit forever. My country is beautiful, it is wonderful. I love my country, and I talk to my country.

Recently I was a candidate for mayor of the city of Rio de Janeiro. For the first time in Brazil, a black woman ran for mayor of this great capital city, and I had to face all the contradictions of Brazilian society. It was not a municipal campaign; it was a national and even an international campaign. Like a thermometer, I could measure our advances—and the achievements of blacks, of women, and of the poor—as well as our setbacks. I had never so closely faced and so deeply felt the meaning of machismo and racism as I did in that campaign. It was unbearable, even after fifty-one years of struggle, even after having lived through cold, thirst, misery, hunger, unemployment, the loss of children, to see that Brazil was not ready to have a black mayor in a major city, even though we are a majority of the population.

This is but one more piece of evidence that it is not enough to go to college if you are black in Brazil; it is not enough to have knowledge if you are black in Brazil; it is not enough to be honest if you are black in Brazil. We are not identified with the beauty of knowledge and with administrative ability. And even *we* are not accustomed to administering with so much injustice. Our breasts fed the children of the masters in Brazil. But today our children are the ones living on the sidewalks in Brazil, making many forget or fail to protect our image, not only in public institutions, but with dignity for being black and feeling proud of our city.

It is painful to know that the skin color of the children who wander the streets, of the majority of those who are in prison, and of those who live in slums is black. But, following the example of South Africa, we know that the challenge is to make the masses discover their value and to exercise true political power. I have dedicated myself to this end, confronting prejudice and fighting for freedom. I hope that this conference and the participation of all Brazilians will help us achieve this goal.

I am sure that everyone here, including all who came from Brazil, will make a contribution so that all of you will know the other side of Brazil, the side that is not written about in books, is not on television, is not shown in movies. You may not know this Brazil, but those of us who are here, who have come here from the struggle, who have risen from the mud on the ground to the plateau, we know perfectly well what we are saying, and we need no further proof. It will be enough for you to hear from us during these days to understand that we are telling the truth.

2 | The Black Movement: Without Identity There Is No Consciousness or Struggle

THEREZA SANTOS

Brazilian society taught me how to be a black woman. Every day I thank that profoundly racist society for the opportunity to discover myself as a person. And I discovered that as a black woman I am different in society. I discovered that the official literature gives me nothing other than the dominant sectors' perspective which allows them to dominate blacks more thoroughly. I thus began to search for myself.

My struggle is not mine alone. I cannot undertake my struggle individually. I want all people to join in my struggle: blacks, whites, women, men, the physically impaired, and so forth. For this reason I was able to become a person free of all prejudice as well as an internationalist person. I am a Carioca who lives in São Paulo. I did not go there by choice, I was forced in that direction. I have no vocation to be a heroine, and when the police thought it was time for me to be behind bars, I had to flee, and the only road I knew led to São Paulo. So I went to São Paulo and fell in love with the city, so much so that I spent five years in Africa, then returned to São Paulo, not to Rio.

Some things bother me a lot. For example, I work with an *escola de samba* (samba organization). I am a person of Afro-Brazilian religion, and in São Paulo I constantly discuss the fight between Rio's samba and São Paulo's samba. Recently a singer named Eliana de Lima and a group called Raça Negra appeared in São Paulo. Carioca artists had always made their money in São Paulo because São Paulo is the greatest industrial center of Latin America. It is also the most racist and right-wing state in Brazil. Our artists, many of whom are my personal friends for whom I have the highest admiration, kept feeding the fight between São Paulo and Rio because suddenly the hen with the golden eggs had begun

23

to feed its own chicks. During the last carnival the fight was between Rio de Janeiro and Bahia. Unfortunately, the people of Rio de Janeiro elected a peacock as their mayor, and this peacock determined that Rio is a shopwindow and provoked a terribly divisive fight.

In this samba struggle, between Rio's carnival and São Paulo's carnival, I took the position that was for me coherent. I do not want to live in a country that is constantly divided. We blacks have the obligation to know that we cannot play the game created by Brazilian society which sees our culture as something compartmentalized. When people speak of black culture in Brazil, they talk about Candomblé, *capoeira,* and samba. We must realize that this is a Judeo-Christian concept and that it is in the interest of the dominant classes to defend this concept and not develop a concept of culture that expresses the essence of human beings.

When Brazil discovers this, it will have to accept itself as a country with a very strong influence of black culture. It is important that blacks not commit this kind of mistake. We have to stop thinking that the samba of one place is better than that of another, that the culture of one city is better than that of another. We have to know that human beings are the essence of culture, and that our participation as blacks in Brazil has been too great to be limited to only one state or to one space.

In speaking about the Black Movement, my position is based on my commitment, as a militant, to search for new roads to follow. I am a militant in the Black Movement, taking pride in and acknowledging all the errors which that implies. But that's all right because war is war. As militants we take responsibility for our mistakes, but we also know that we must have the courage to reshape our function and actions.

To understand the Black Movement one must understand the discriminatory mechanisms developed by the dominant powers to destroy the racial and cultural identity of blacks. The destruction of identity generates subordination and reinforces the idea of the black as a negative type who is ethnically and culturally inferior. Therefore, since blacks are accepted socially to the extent that they approach white values, they are led to accept the symbolic mechanisms of domination and, consequently, their racial identity and consciousness are forgotten or marginalized. The discriminatory values that see blacks as inferior and whites as superior, based on Judeo-Christian values, deny and clash with black religious values in which there is no dichotomy between good and bad, superior and inferior.

To discuss the Black Movement is to discuss the definition of the face of Brazil. Official data from the IBGE (Instituto Brasileiro de Geografia e Estatística; Brazilian Institute of Geography and Statistics), according to the latest survey taken, which was only recently published, reveal that the Brazilian population is 5 percent "black," 55 percent "white," and 39 percent something called "brown" (*pardo*). This strange category called brown is also called mulatto, a corrupted form of "mule." In 1990 the official black population was, according to the IBGE, 6 percent. This information leads us to conclude that Brazil is whitening its population with startling velocity. The reality is that besides official efforts at whitening, using the methodology of self-classification, we must also struggle with the precariousness of data on blacks. As if this were not enough, built into the official census is what we call *deformation*—part of the political and ideological inculcation of the black population which has determined its invisibility in the different spheres of national life.

A part of this strategy is the prevalence of arbitrary designations in relation to the item "color" which seek, fundamentally, to establish fissures in the identity of blacks through their separation into *preto, mulato, pardo, moreno, café com leite, canela*, and so on. This differentiation has been a factor in the obfuscation of the numerical importance of blacks in Brazilian society as a whole, and as an element in the fragmentation of racial identity.

Yet another part of the strategy developed by the dominant ideology is the myth of "racial democracy," constructed to obfuscate a conflictive, discriminatory, and separatist social reality. The stereotype developed from this concept has led blacks to assume their pseudo-incapacity for socioeconomic evolution, thus removing them from the process of consciousness-raising and destroying whatever is left of their racial identity and their most basic rights of citizenship.

The Black Movement

The Black Movement in Brazil was created by, and has as participants, blacks who have gone through this process of destruction of racial identity, but who have also assimilated and incorporated all of the paradigms developed in society in relation to individual blacks, with fundamental deformations. A fully elaborated consciousness is lacking, and this takes many away from what should be the objectives of racial struggle. Also resulting from this process is the unconscious desire for whitening as a form of social acceptance. For these reasons, the primary objective often becomes individual economic and social ascension, with black identity and the much celebrated struggle on behalf of blacks frequently serving simply as a lever for personal projects, often using black cultural identities to raise funds that end up not being used to benefit the cause that was initially proposed. As a result, we have a Black Movement, which is by and large immobile, acephalous, and unable to meet the most basic needs of the Afro-Brazilian community, which means a total absence of conditions for fulfilling the role for which it was created.

In truth, some blacks have no commitment to what should be the primary objective of the Black Movement, but rather view blacks as an object of study—the same view held by the racist society—and practice what was previously a motive of criticism of social scientists. In practice they do not seek any kind of relationship or approximation with the Afro-Brazilian community, yet they are "specialists" in the production of academic journals where blacks, as an object of study, are merely a means to guarantee funding from international organizations. They are more concerned with a pseudo-study of blacks than with social integration.

One thing moves and irritates me. We had elections last November. It is unnecessary to say that there were practically no blacks elected even to city councils in Brazil. A few in cities in the interior of São Paulo, Antônio Pitanga in Rio de Janeiro. One comrade of the PCdoB (Partido Comunista do Brasil; Communist Party of Brazil) was elected, but, beside this, blacks were barely visible in the electoral process. But what angers me and makes me seek a solution, knowing that my position is not generally accepted by the Black Movement, has to do with Benedita da Silva's candidacy for mayor of Rio de Janeiro. Because of the profound deformation I referred to earlier, blacks in Brazil unfortunately were unable to see that for the first time—and I hope it's the last—we lost the opportunity to rediscover our history and take our destiny in our own hands.

You may respond that I placed all of my hope in Benedita da Silva because she is a black person. It matters little. If people have only black skin, if they have no commitment to racial struggle, if they have no commitment to social transformation, skin color is not enough. Every black person in Brazil knows what Benedita da Silva has done. I am not a member of Benedita da Silva's party. But when we do not have the political consciousness to elect this woman to transform the face of Brazil, I am truly ashamed to be black. The revolt that has been developing inside me since the elections is that we blacks, and not Benedita da Silva, lost the election by slightly over 100,000 votes. I hope this situation changes in the future and that there is finally an election in which blacks can raise their heads and say: today I have a place in Brazil, I have regained my right to citizenship.

Black Movement, Black Women

Despite the historical role of black women as the economic mainstay of black men and in the struggle for resistance, black women's participation has been relegated to that of servant, a consequence of the machista ideology that has always permeated the Black Movement. Another important element in this relationship results from the process of alienation expressed in the manifest preference of black men for white women and the super-valorization of white aesthetic values. Oliveira Porcaro and Araújo Costa, in *Repensando a mulher negra*, show that as the educational level and income of black men increase, an expressive proportion of them marry white women: around 36.9 percent of those with between eight and ten years of schooling and 43.2 percent of those with more than eleven years of schooling.

Although aware of this reality, one must not suppose a feminist perspective for the movement of black women, that is, opposition or distancing from the Black Movement as a whole, but it is necessary to stress the perverse effects that machista ideology has for the Black Movement, even to the point of contributing to the fragmentation of racial identity. As a consequence of the consciousness attained by black women, the relationship between the movement of black women and the Black Movement has begun to change, but the difficulties of this relationship have slowed the emergence of politically active black women since the Black Movement needs them, resulting, consequently, in the weakening of the Black Movement.

Objectives

One of the primary objectives of the Black Movement is the systematic denunciation and struggle against the genocide practiced against blacks in its different forms: the murders committed by the police; the subhuman conditions generated by the total lack of access to the most elementary conditions of survival; the sterilization of black women; the mental genocide practiced through the stigmas and prototypes that destroy blacks' self-esteem and dignity. Racism and discrimination are common facts, yet the Black Movement has not achieved a cohesive organization that would prepare it for oppositional action in defense of the black community.

Black Movement and Political Action

Political parties long ago discovered the potential of the black vote, at first with a view of blacks as an object for use: the cost of the black vote was a bottle of rum. At most it might be worth a soccer T-shirt. With the exception of the PT (Workers' Party), on learning of the Black Movement, they have understood the importance of "coloring" their bases with a few black figures, not to elect black candidates, who by and large receive no financial support for the campaign, but rather in search of the black vote for the party ticket.

The political parties suppose that they discovered the Black Movement, but they put party action above black militancy, just as they confuse party politics and political action. This deformed vision of its role contributes to the disaggregation of the Black Movement. The most visible face of this reality are the public meetings that attract no more than twenty people because they are transformed into party events. The Black Movement thus loses the opportunity to transform the demands of the black struggle into acts of strength and thereby gain the respect of the population, including that of the black population.

I would like to share a news item with you. I have no opinion on the matter, but I think it is very important. It reads as follows:

Blacks Allege that Throne Belongs to Zumbi

Manifesto delivered to the Supreme Electoral Tribunal
claims the right to the Brazilian crown

Brasília. The royal family Orleans de Bragança has an adversary in the dispute for the Brazilian crown. In a manifesto delivered to the Supreme Electoral Tribunal, the Center for Black Resistance Zumbi dos Palmares announced its candidacy in the monarchical campaign. Signed by Ogã Neninho do Baluolê, the document exalts the experience of the reign of Zumbi dos Palmares. "Why not relive the kingdom of Palmares, which had as much legitimacy as the Brazilian empires," asks Neninho do Baluolê. The manifesto emphasizes that the launching of the campaign is not a separatist initiative; the intention, Neninho stresses, is to find a solution to national problems and insert blacks in the discussion of electoral disputes in an organized manner. The administration of public monies, attention to the needs of children and adolescents, respect for the family, and the restoration of the dignity of the Indian population, are all part of the Center for Resistance's platform. They also defended renewed investments in the cultural arena.

This document generated all sorts of responses throughout Brazil. We have been called "King Zulu," "King Zumbu." In other words, it has been a real party. But this has everything to do with our commitment to struggle.

Allow me to share another news item. This one is about a black woman, Marli, who became famous a decade ago. Marli wrote a book in which she declares, "I am afraid of cockroaches, not the police." This woman's brother was murdered by the police, a normal occurrence in Brazil. The difference is that this woman had the courage to struggle and to seek the arrest of the policemen who committed the murder. Of course, of the eight policemen who participated in the murder, only one was arrested, but that is already a giant step forward in Brazil.

Two months ago, Marli's sixteen-year-old son was also murdered by the police. Ten years ago, when she took her stand, numerous international and national organizations, including many whites, supported her struggle. Now, everyone is silent. After all, she protested when they killed her brother, so why does she have to protest now that they have killed her son? People pay no attention and do nothing. But I don't question the fact that *they* do nothing, I question the fact that *we* do nothing. My concern has to do with blacks because I think that when we start to do something, whites will obligatorily act with us.

Conclusion—Future Directions?

Only the Black Movement has the potential to undertake concrete actions to meet the Afro-Brazilian community's needs and aspirations for freedom and dignity. Because of its experience with racism and prejudice, which caused many to suffer all sorts of violence, the Movement will be able to participate in the dialectical process of knowledge, which will result in the elaboration, based on social practice, of a project that will lead Afro-Brazilians to reassume their destroyed identity and seek effective participation in Brazilian society. It will, however, be necessary to have the courage to commit suicide as the "Other" in order to reemerge entirely identified with the race and class to which they belong.

Then they will discover that the right to citizenship depends on us, through the organization, action, and revindications that come from the awareness of our human condition and that depend on our political action and the transformation of society. Society will then be obligated to undertake the integration and social transformation of Brazil.

3 | Where Are the Blacks?

ANTÔNIO PITANGA

Where are the blacks? As a person who works in the media, as an actor and director, I once constructed a character called the observer. An observer arriving in Brazil—a foreign observer, obviously—with even the slightest concern with understanding race relations in the country would immediately ask this question: where are the blacks? Starting in the airplane, this observer would probably not be surrounded by black Brazilian men and women. In Brazil it is difficult to find a black flight crewmember or even a black airplane passenger. On arriving at the airport in Rio de Janeiro, it is unlikely that the hypothetical observer would be waited on by a black attendant, except the baggage carrier or perhaps the taxi driver. Arriving at the five-star hotel where he will stay, our observer would almost certainly not be in the company of black Brazilians in the swimming pool or the restaurant. But it would not be impossible for him to find a black musician playing background music in the piano bar.

Picking up a magazine to read in his room, the observer will look for a photograph of a black model, but will not find one. The obstinate observer will flip through more and more magazines and will find a photograph of a black person only if there is an article about crime. Hopping from one television channel to another, he will not find a single black host or anchorperson. Our observer, in fact, will have only minimal chances of seeing images of blacks on television, and these chances are even more remote in terms of advertising or any other communications vehicle. Leaving his hotel to go to a nearby bar, the observer will begin to see more blacks in the streets near the hotel. His first contact will inevitably be with the children who wander the streets at all hours and who will almost certainly ask for spare change or something to eat.

The social contrasts in our country mirror its racial contrasts. Intrigued by his first glance at Brazil's racial inequalities, the next day our imaginary character decides to visit the *favelas* that surround the high-rent district where he is staying, and there it becomes difficult for him to find white faces. In every passageway of the favelas he visits, he observes that almost all of the people are either black or brown (*pardo*). The hotel's ratio has been inverted.

Walking through the streets of the city, our observer will begin to think that the much-acclaimed Brazilian racial democracy is a fallacy. The faces he sees on the sidewalks are mostly black and brown, but when he stops at a magazine stand, the photos he sees are almost all of European men and women. The contrast between the faces he sees on television, in magazines, in films and those he sees in the streets becomes even more accentuated when he goes to Rio de Janeiro's central rail station where people catch the train for the suburbs. The observer may then realize that there are two Brazils: the one that is shown on television, and the one in the streets. In the latter are the blacks and browns. In the former, almost exclusively whites.

Unhappy with what he has seen, our observer goes to the Instituto de Pesquisa das Culturas Negras (Institute for Research on Black Cultures) to ask how blacks view the Brazilian racial democracy that has been so widely publicized by the country's authorities for decades on end. Sitting down with participants of the Black Movement, our observer will learn that Brazilian racial democracy is a farce, a farce that was unmasked in the streets during the Centenary of Abolition. What abolition?

Brazil was the last country to end slave traffic and to abolish colonial slavery itself. The capital accumulated by slave labor permitted Brazilian authorities to finance a large campaign of European migration for the express purpose of whitening Brazilian society. In the second half of the nineteenth century, black slaves were gradually replaced by European immigrants—particularly Italians—on the large coffee plantations of the state of São Paulo. These immigrants largely worked as tenant farmers.

The Golden Law (Lei Aurea), which abolished slavery, concomitantly abolished the former slaves' job opportunities. Former slaves received no reparations for the forced labor of several generations that enriched the white oligarchies; to the contrary, slave owners demanded reparations for the losses caused by the law that freed their slaves![1] This was due in large part to the fact that the Golden Law was an ordinary law and not a constitutional amendment. The ordinary law respects acquired rights, which is not demanded of constitutional amendments.

Without reparations of any sort, those who were freed from colonial slavery still had to face the fact that European immigrants, especially in the South and Southeast, held almost all of the jobs in a growing free labor market. This fact owed much to the racist thought consciously elaborated by the intellectuals of the First Republic, which attributed the country's technological backwardness to black and Amerindian labor. In other words, the abolition of slavery, in the form it took place, did not really have the goal of freeing black workers. Its true purpose was to free white elites from a society in which blacks and browns would become an unquestionable majority. Within this logic it would be difficult to understand abolition without the importation of European labor.

From slavery to marginalization, from the beginning of the Republic, blacks began to amass in the hovels and, later, the favelas of large cities. Their cultural and religious manifestations, which had been persecuted during slavery, continued to be persecuted during the Republic.

The initial decades of free labor in Brazil were marked by an interethnic dispute between European and Asian immigrants and by severe discrimination against descendants of Africans and Amerindians. In several cities in the interior of São Paulo, blacks could walk on only certain streets and sidewalks. By the same token, blacks were prohibited from frequenting whites' clubs and social events. Many companies would not accept black labor, and discrimination was evident even in public service.

This marginalization and humiliation could not go on without a political response. In the 1920s a vigorous black press emerged, and in the 1930s there appeared the Frente Negra Brasileira (FNB; Black Brazilian Front), which led mass demonstrations against racism and the social exclusion of the Afro-Brazilian community. The FNB was the largest organization of the Black Movement in the Republican period, and it spread throughout Brazil with more than 70,000 members. The FNB had a strong impact, and thanks to its struggle the integration of blacks in the free labor society began, albeit timidly. The activities of the Frente Negra, among whose directors was the poet Solano Trindade, were curtailed by the Estado Novo dictatorship. In the following decade, playwright Abdias do Nascimento created the Teatro Experimental do Negro (Black Experimental Theater) in Rio de Janeiro. Solano Trindade, following another path, created the Teatro Popular do Negro (Black Popular Theater). Black protest began to take place in the form of cultural expression.

With the process of industrialization in the 1940s and 1950s, Brazilian capitalism suffered profound transformations. The racial discrimination of the first decades of the century, which took the form of the exclusion of black labor from the job market, would take on different characteristics. Capitalism, unable to do without black and northeastern labor, began absorbing it in unprecedented quantities, albeit selectively; that is, a specific, low-status place was found for blacks in the labor market.

The role of women in the social reproduction of the black community in the first two decades of the century must be emphasized. Exclusion from the job market occurred primarily in relation to black men. The white families of the turn of the century would never give up the domestic and culinary service of the black woman. During slavery there was a differentiated relationship between seignorial families and the male and female slaves who worked in the owner's house or mansion. House slaves were treated much better than those who worked in the fields, the so-called shanty slaves. Both in the period before and after abolition, the black families in charge of the domestic service for the white aristocracy were treated more paternalistically, and in many cases black families were considered almost as an appendage of the white family. These domestic and family relationships are of fundamental importance for understanding what has become known as the myth of Brazilian racial democracy.

The presence of black women in white families' kitchens was a determinant factor both for the material reproduction of the black community, since it was there that women received food for their children, and for the paternalistic relationship between white families and black families. The donation of food, used clothing, and other items that were no longer needed contributed greatly to the belief on the part of white Brazilian families, especially Catholic families, that they were not racists. Also contributing to this perception was the fact that black adolescent girls frequently served as the first sexual experience for the sons of white families. In this way the process of the Brazilian population's miscegenation began, leading intellectuals of the stature of Gilberto Freyre to believe that there would never be racial conflict in Brazil, but rather the integration of blacks and whites, both of whom would in the future be surpassed by a vast generation of miscegenates.

The myth of racial democracy was further reinforced by the fact that for many decades blacks and whites did not compete for the same place in the labor market. The expansion of dependent capitalism, especially after World War II, revolutionized Brazilian society, which witnessed the emergence and expansion of new technical occupations brought about by industrialization. At the same time the working class grew rapidly and began to have a certain political influence through its unions. The growth of civil construction in the Southeast and the unprecedented expansion of the industrial working class modified race relations. Development in the 1940s, 1950s, and early 1960s, the "golden years," was able to absorb the labor force coming from the countryside to the city, attenuating the problem of marginalization in the large urban centers. Blacks effectively began to integrate the urban proletariat and have access to diverse social programs, the most important of which was basic education.

Blacks and whites began to occupy rather well defined social and geographical spaces in Brazilian society. The "brown" population grew enormously with interregional migration, especially from the Northeast to the Southeast. The elites' space of power and control, however, was not miscegenated. Miscegenation did not alter the racial concentration of patrimony, income, power, and social prestige. The doctrinary influence of the Brazilian Communist Party among leftist intellectuals, as well as among union and popular leaders, was determinant in a "reductionism" of Brazilian social contrasts. In other words, for the Communist Party, the Brazilian social contrast reduced to the rich on the one hand and the poor on the other. The physical and ethnic identification of rich and poor was always an expendable factor for the Brazilian left. In this sense, the Marxist influence also contributed to strengthening the myth of racial democracy. The Brazilian racial problem, therefore, would be absent from the reflections of intellectuals of all ideological stripes. Concomitantly, however, it would be constantly present in the daily life of the black population.

In the second half of the 1970s, with the exhaustion of the so-called economic miracle, the Brazilian model of development collapsed without being able to respond to the demands that it itself had created. On the one hand, the recession no longer permitted the absorption of the labor force that the Brazilian structure of land ownership and agricultural production continued to expel from the country to the city. On the other, the amplification of the educational system put poor blacks and whites in competition for the same places in the labor market. During this period a greater number of blacks entered liberal professions such as law, education, and medicine, which was complemented by the expressive presence of blacks in sports and the arts. In this social context in which blacks threatened to leave the traditional place Brazilian society had reserved for them, racist practices began to reemerge. At the same time, black organizations began to proliferate throughout Brazil on a scale compared only to the first decades of the Republic.

The crisis of the Brazilian economic miracle was accompanied by the political crisis of the military regime. The student movement and workers' movement took to the streets in large protest marches and strikes against the dictatorship's economic policy. The profile of Brazil's social movements also changed. Reality would surpass the thesis of the Communist Party that Brazilian social conflicts would involve management and labor or, in a broader sense, rich and poor.

The new social movements became well established and began to divide political space among students and union members. Neighborhood organizations, movements in the poor suburbs and slums, began to demand urban improvements and to question the model of our cities. Women, in turn, formed several autonomous organizations, which they themselves represented in political rallies, and began to raise specific issues that would have to be added to issues of general concern.

In 1978 two black athletes were barred from working out in the Clube de Regatas Tietê in São Paulo. Shortly thereafter, a group of young black people who were leaving a dance in the poor suburbs (*periferia*) of São Paulo took, as a prank, a bottle of milk from a residence. For that offense, one of them was murdered in a police station. The next day, in July 1978, a public protest against these cases of racism took place on the steps of São Paulo's Municipal Theater. This event marked the formation of a new black organization, the Movimento Negro Unificado (MNU; Unified Black Movement). The first national movement since the Frente Negra Brasileira, the MNU began to unite the struggles of all black organizations in Brazil. Playwright and economist Abdias do Nascimento, then in the United States, returned to Brazil with the specific goal of founding this movement before returning to the United States to complete his academic responsibilities and to undertake an international mission for the MNU. Also charged with disseminating information about MNU's struggle in international forums was sociologist Lélia Gonzalez, who kept the MNU informed about black movements in other parts of the world.

The most common accusation against the MNU was that it would divide the workers' struggle. These accusations, coming from the traditional left, did not impede specific protests of blacks against racism nor the participation of blacks in broader struggles, such as the memorable "Diretas-Já" campaign, in which the black movement had its own presence in the rally that attracted more than a million people in Rio de Janeiro.

The myth of racial democracy suffered a profound blow and lost its intellectual support among both conservative and progressive intellectuals. Social indicators concerning blacks and whites began to be disseminated, embarrassing the country. Once again, however, Brazilian elites came up with a peculiar solution. If statistics on race provided evidence of deep racial inequalities and, therefore, of the existence of racism in a country that had always claimed that it did not exist, then such data should not be collected. In a move entirely coherent with this position, Brazilian authorities removed the item "color" from the ten-year census, which makes the quantification of blacks and their social indicators difficult, at best.

The most recent data on social indicators for blacks and whites in Brazil are from 1976, based on the National Household Survey of the IBGE (Instituto Brasileiro de Geografia e Estatística; Brazilian Institute of Geography and Statistics). Compiled by researchers Lúcia Helena Garcia de Oliveira, Rosa Maria Porcaro, and Tereza Cristina de Araújo, this study, published by the IBGE itself, is sufficient to reveal racial inequalities in Brazil. Nonetheless, with regard to race, we do not have reliable data because in IBGE's methodology skin color is indicated by the respondent and not by the surveyor according to scientific parameters. The ideology of whitening, which is strongly inculcated in the population, makes the shame of being black or mulatto interfere in the responses, distorting the sample's data. In other words, in Brazil, blacks say they are brown (pardo), browns say they are white, and so on. Nevertheless, let us examine the data.

In 1976 the active labor force (workers with a defined professional occupation) in Brazil numbered 39 million people. Of these 39 million, 57 percent were white, 30 percent brown, and just 9 percent black. These figures in themselves indicate the marginalization of blacks in relation to the active labor force. Of the total of white workers, 8.5 percent were engaged in high-level occupations. Only 1.1 percent of blacks and 2.7 percent of browns held similar positions. Of the total of high-level occupations, whites comprise 82.4 percent, browns 14 percent, and blacks a mere 1.7 percent. For the sake of economy, we are not including the small percentage of "yellows," or workers of Asian descent. Among the professionals in high-level positions, the average income of whites was Cr$ 10,200 per month while that of blacks at the same level was just Cr$ 3,700 and that of browns, Cr$ 5,000. No racial democracy can withstand such numbers! (Data are from Pesquisa Nacional por Amostra de Domicílios, Instituto Brasileiro de Geografia e Estatística, 1976.)

In relation to education, the IBGE has published more recent data concerning social indicators. In 1987 the white population between 30 and 39 years of age had an average of 5.9 years of schooling, while the black population of the same age had but 2.8 years of formal education.

The negative effects of racism cannot be understood by statistics alone, but must also be seen in its violence to the personality and identity of people and social groups. Racism corrodes that which is most precious in human beings, self-esteem and self-love. People who do not love themselves cannot understand the pain of others and become incapable of solidarity within their own social group. Each person has a self-image that is given to him or her by others. If many people tell a child that he or she is ugly or inept, the child will believe it.

Racism consists in telling a whole collectivity that it is ugly and inept, and that its defects offend the other part of society which is pretty, good, and capable. It is not by chance that black consciousness movements normally start with the affirmation of Afro-Brazilian beauty and culture. First blacks say to themselves that they are beautiful and that their culture is wonderful. Later they try to show this to whites, and even later engage in the struggle for their civil rights.

The Black Movement converted the Centenary of Abolition into a broad national debate about racism. Brazilian society, for at least one year, focused on the open sores of racism and the negative effects of the Brazilian abolitionist process. On May 13, 1988, the 100th anniversary of the Golden Law, a march of more than five thousand blacks, called "March against the Farce of Abolition," was stopped in the streets of Rio de Janeiro by the Brazilian army.

The Brazilian Black Movement celebrates November 20, proclaimed by the MNU as the National Day of Black Consciousness, in honor of the death of Zumbi, the leader of the Quilombo de Palmares and the greatest historical point of reference for the Afro-Brazilian community.

The national debate about racism and the protests that marked the centenary of the Golden Law had a positive political impact for the antiracist struggle in the country. The movement of cultural affirmation of the *blocos afro* in Salvador began to transform that city's carnival into huge protests against racism and all forms of oppression. And this was done in a joyous, delightful, entertaining, Brazilian manner. It was the pleasure of struggling against racism. If he were alive, Bob Marley would certainly want to become familiar with the new reign of the antiracist reggae in which Salvador has been transformed. Jimmy Cliff spends carnival in Bahia every year in honor of the *tupiniquim* Rastafarian movement and to explore the fantastic rhythm that has been baptized as the samba-reggae. Nevertheless, the blocos afro in Bahia are not limited to carnival. Since the 1980s Olodum in Pelourinho and Ilê Aiyê in Curuzu have been engaged in the struggle against apartheid and for the liberation of Nelson Mandela. Throughout the year Olodum develops programs to help street children.

Axé music, as samba-reggae has become known, is today the most important movement of the cultural affirmation of Brazilian blacks, and it has already achieved wide exposure in media throughout the country. Through axé-music and Bahian carnival-axé, negritude is more present in the media than it was during the Centenary of Abolition.

In 1990, just two years after the debates of the Centenary, the population elected three black governors. Until then there was not a single black governor in the federation's 22 states. Of special note is the case of Espírito Santo, where racist jokes and an electorate with a large number of European immigrants were not enough to keep black engineer Albuino Azeredo from occupying the highest position in the state.

Four years after the Centenary, Federal Deputy Benedita da Silva, a black woman and a *favelada*, ran for mayor of Rio de Janeiro and came very close to winning, which is one more demonstration that the consciousness of the black community is growing at an accelerated pace. Political parties can no longer ignore the electoral potential of the black community. Whether for seats in congress or on city councils, governorships, or even the presidency, parties that turn their back on that potential may pay a dear price.

Today the Black Movement in Brazil comprises more than two hundred organizations throughout the country. The struggle of Brazilian blacks is not and cannot be isolated. It must be added to the struggle of all oppressed segments in the country. Above all, the struggle of Brazilian blacks is part of the struggles that are taking place everywhere to make the planet a better place for all, struggles that authoritarian ideologies are trying to impede. For this reason, black Brazilian organizations participated actively in the Global Forum of Nongovernmental Organizations during the World Environmental Conference in Rio de Janeiro. Also for this reason, Brazilian blacks are interested in a closer relationship with their African American brothers.

Many times in our pacifist struggle, we Brazilian blacks are forced to make concessions and even accept a number of things that we don't like. But what we will never do is accept racism and cease participating in our country's future destiny.

It is necessary to say all of this in order to show how difficult it is being black in Brazil. To discuss blacks in a limited time frame is very difficult because a black man's mind is a crazy thing. I speak as a man of the media, a person who participated in a group—Cinema Novo—that created a new language, a person who has acted in more than 80 films in Brazil, with the lead role in more than 60 films. How does this need to participate arise in a person who had no access to universities or libraries, but who felt the need to protest from a very young age? I always felt that the protest had to occur through books, through images, through collective action.

When I was a young man my group of friends included Glauber Rocha, Jorge Amado (who still had black hair), Antônio Carlos Magalhães, who is today governor of Bahia, Calasans Neto, Manuel Araújo, Roberto Pires, Oscar Santana, Santos Caldafé, Carybé. And from these friends there emerged a group that wanted to make a kind of cinema that would show the country's true face. Thirty-odd years later, Cazuza wrote a song called "Brazil, Show Your Face." But we were already singing the song in 1958, through films such as *Barravento* (The Turning Wind), *A Grande Feira* (The Great Market), *Tocaia no Asfalto* (Ambush on the Asphalt), and even *Pagador de Promessas* (The Given Word).

I was part of Cinema Novo, but it's kind of funny that I was the only black person in the group. And God, who acts in mysterious ways, had it that the only participant who had not gone to a university was Antônio Pitanga. But I was the only one who could speak the language of my people and my race. I was the only actor. All the others were directors, intellectuals, but they always had to come through me, through my emotion, through my heart and guts, to reach the grandeur and the response of my people. And it is funny because today I don't belong to any movement. I belong to all movements because as an artist I traveled on the wings of all the birds I could see and catch. No single movement could limit my discussion and the discussion of my people. That was how Cinema Novo was born.

When I say that our foreign observer walking through Brazil will not find blacks, we all know that it is true. When I was a child, we were the majority, and I am able to pass this story along to my children only because our history, our culture has always been by word of mouth. A nineteenth-century politician and statesman, Rui Barbosa, "the eagle of The Hague," in order to cleanse the black stain from the country, burned all the documents telling of the origin of the slave families. During the dictatorship I was forced to leave the country. But being forced to do so was good because I spent two years traveling through Africa trying to find where I had come from. And through the food, the dialect, the fabrics, I was able to compare what I saw with what I had learned from my mother. I found myself in Dahomey, and I have passed this along to my children.

I said that when I was a child we were a majority. Two decades ago we were 35 percent of the population. More recently, some eight years ago, blacks were 15 percent of the population. Yesterday, a friend who came with me on the airplane said, "Pitanga, we are only 5 percent." The story of father to son remains. We see our children grow, and we get smaller. The situation of blacks seems to be the same. Not long ago the *mãe de santo* was black, the *pai de santo* was black, the soccer coach and players were largely black. The samba school director was black, the *bicheiro* was black. Today they are all white. And sometimes I ask myself, what kind of artist, what capability is this to be able to photograph your race? But you have to try. I think that this moment is unique, and because it is unique it is signaling to us, helping us signal. This race that is so oppressed, destroyed, has its heart in the soul, a love capable of understanding that it is possible to change, that it is possible for other races to understand the grandeur of the black people.

It is very strange to talk about blacks. It gives me the impression that we are a species on the verge of extinction. This discussion cannot remain between four walls. Blacks and whites allied together can understand. I am certain that, with our heads uplifted and our eyes on the future, we are the future, but always with the reference point of our history. As a man of the cinema, I have much to show what kind of country this is, what kind of Brazil this is, but I am absolutely certain that no black man who looks to the future is tied solely to the past. We have our memory as our historical reference, but we are the future. And I want to thank you in the name of the future, in the name of my children, in the name of a Brazil that we have to rescue, because it is almost disappearing, culturally speaking. I want to return here one day with other images, another discourse, and, I hope, with my children. I want to be sitting here listening to them. It is not a utopia because this Brazil has already seen what happened in 1635, in the Serra da Barriga, with Zumbi dos Palmares. Up in the hills was Brazil, down below the Dutch and the Portuguese. Up there were whites, blacks, and Indians working in the fields, the economy, commerce. This Brazil that really existed is capable of all things. Everything is large when the soul isn't small.

NOTE

1. Along similar lines, in every city in Brazil there is a street called Voluntários da Pátria (Volunteers for the Fatherland). These volunteers were not the blacks who fought in the Paraguayan war, ceded by their owners. The volunteers for the fatherland, rather, were the owners themselves who let their slaves go to war. The owners became volunteers without having ever been to war.

4 | Olodum and the Black Struggle in Brazil

JOÃO JORGE SANTOS RODRIGUES

I will speak of the history, the struggle, and the trajectory of blacks in Brazil. I want to explain what black culture in Brazil is all about and what it means to be black in Brazil. And I would like to describe the resistance and the struggle of black Brazilians in their attempt to construct a just, pluriracial, multireligious, and wealthy society.

The process of reAfricanization in Brazil, especially in Bahia, has had an important role in raising the consciousness of a significant segment of the white population that needed to abandon the hypocritical posture of following a Marxist position without ever having supported the full integration of blacks and indigenous Brazilians into the future society they imagined. But reAfricanization has had an even greater impact on the white, conservative elite of the Brazilian right, which has seen its seemingly eternal power of manipulation and misinformation shaken by a radical, tough, and implacable movement of black consciousness.

The stage for the contemporary reAfricanization of Brazil could not have been located in a more appropriate city than Salvador, Bahia. Ten years after Salvador was founded in 1549 as the first capital of Brazil, the first *quilombos* (maroon societies) were already being formed by black Africans from Guinea, Mozambique, Angola, and the Gold Coast. These early quilombos were called Pirajá, Monte Serrat, Boa Viagem, and Pernambués. From that time on, the history of Bahia has been marked by rebellions and conspiracies among African slaves, black Brazilians, mestizos, the Tupinambá population, and poor whites. The accumulation of these events differentiates Bahia from all other Brazilian states including São Paulo, Rio de Janeiro, Maranhão, and Pernambuco.

In Bahia a war of independence was fought which culminated on July 2, 1823, with the expulsion of the Portuguese colonial troops. While in São Paulo the Portuguese Emperor, Pedro I, declared Brazil's independence, in Bahia black blood was shed because slaves had been told that as soon as the Portuguese left, they would be free. The indigenous community was also told that as soon as the Portuguese invaders left, their land would be returned. Led by slave owners from the surrounding area, a liberation army entered the city of Salvador on July 1, 1823. On July 2 this army of blacks, slaves, Indians, and the disinherited occupied the municipal square of Salvador and proclaimed Brazil's true independence. At the same time, the Portuguese colonial armada, the largest in the Americas until that time and which had anchored in the Brazilian Northeast to keep it from being free, was sailing out of the Bay of All Saints. A year earlier, Rio and São Paulo had commemorated Brazil's independence with formal balls.

At that painful moment, the city of Salvador realized that the Bahian elites were not going to free the slaves or give land back to the Indians, but that they would have to continue fighting. The impact of having had guns in their hands, of hearing the concept of freedom for all, profoundly marked the black community in Salvador for the remainder of the nineteenth century.

Twelve years later, in 1835, the infamous revolt of the Malês occurred. Dressed in blue and white clothes covered with Arabic inscriptions, Islamicized blacks attacked the jails and attempted to establish an Islamic state in Bahia. Repression was swift and cruel. Four blacks were executed at the Campo da Pólvora, and an absolute silence fell over their descendants. Blacks were subsequently prohibited from wearing rings and certain kinds of clothes. They were also not allowed to utter phrases that even remotely suggested that they were Muslim or Malê. The mere suspicion that someone might have had something to do with the rebellion was cause for arrest. The revolt failed because the followers of Candomblé feared that Islamic proselytism would destroy other African religious groups.

Something unusual happened on execution day. It was determined that the rebels would not be shot, but hung, because it was thought that bullets would not kill blacks. But not a single hangman could be found to execute the leaders of the revolt and someone was paid to shoot them. Despite the official proclamation of a great celebration on the day of the execution, few people attended the execution. Official history has erased the names of Pacífico Licutã and Sanni but oral history ensured that their story would endure.

In light of the accumulation of such events, the reAfricanization of Brazil, even with the prefix "re-", can be seen as positive because it has allowed us to encounter our own history. In the twentieth century, the persecution of Candomblé, of the *afoxés*, produced a new kind of black person in the city of Salvador—the fearful black who would wear dark clothes (navy blue or brown) to diminish his blackness. Hair was cut as short as possible and no rings or bracelets were worn. Candomblé beads were hidden. He would not parade in carnival groups that made reference to Africa. But despite its shortcomings, this generation of the 1930s, 1940s, and 1950s studied hard and educated itself. In the 1960s there were at least five excellent black doctors in Salvador, two excellent black architects, and four excellent black judges. For this reason Salvador was called the land of the *preto doutor* (the black doctor).[1]

Our parents from this generation transmitted something very important to us, despite their fear of being and acting black in a repressive society. They transmitted dignity, and they transmitted our history. They told us how the police used to invade black neighborhoods and order everyone into the streets dressed in their underwear to find out who was who. They also told us how the authorities invaded the *terreiros* of Candomblé and took sacred instruments to the police station where they would be placed alongside guns that had been used to commit crimes. Our parents' generation, afraid to be black, miraculously passed along the oral tradition of our African heritage. They passed on respect for elders, the strength of culture, and the knowledge that wisdom could be conveyed in spoken as well as written form.

In the early 1960s, many of us thought that by studying we could be successful in Brazilian society. But the 1964 military coup destroyed that idea for the black community. The white opposition elite left the country in exile or because of the impossibility of continuing to live in Brazil. We stayed in Salvador, in Rio, in São Paulo, in São Luís, Maranhão, facing authoritarian regimes, facing the repression of ideas, facing educational inequalities. But we survived and culture became the road to follow. We could not go to the university, we could not join political parties, we could not do anything except reconstruct our black identity.

We went to Rio de Janeiro and discovered a carnival organization called Cacique de Ramos which became our reference point in the 1960s and inspired poor blacks and mestizos from various neighborhoods in Salvador to form their own *blocos índios*.[2] In 1969, in the neighborhood of Garcia, the group Cacique do Garcia was created. In 1970 the Apache do Tororó was formed, followed by 13 large blocos índios whose participants were largely blacks and mestizos, the poor people in Salvador. These blocos índios took over the city's festival with hegemonic strength and Bahia's carnival soon witnessed an escalation of violence. The press labeled these groups "inciters of violence." In 1972 Apache do Tororó's 5,000 members, inspired by the Apache nation, paraded through the streets with their wood tomahawks. That same year, a carnival group called Lá Vem Elas, formed by white women, registered a complaint with the police accusing members of Apache do Tororó with rape. The complaint was sufficient reason for 3,000 people to be arrested in a single night. Anyone wearing Apache costuming—white and red pants, a white and red headdress, or stripes of white face paint—was subject to arrest. Many members discarded their clothes to avoid arrest. From that moment on, the Apaches carried the stigma of violence.

Salvador's black community involved in the blocos índios wanted something more, something stronger and more intense. It no longer wanted to be identified with American Indians. In 1974 the *bloco afro* Ilê Aiyê was formed. The creation of Ilê Aiyê in the area of Liberdade known as Curuzu was a milestone of contemporary Brazilian negritude and the struggle against racism. Ilê Aiyê was formed with an exclusively black membership. Its blacks only policy was initially criticized as racist. But gradually Ilê Aiyê began conquering its own space and by 1977 it was one of the largest carnival organizations in Salvador. Then followed an aesthetic musical revolution within Bahian carnival when the *afoxé* Badauê began using a sound truck to amplify its songs of negritude and included women in leadership roles.

In this process some people stood out—Vovô, Apolônio, Moa—community leaders who acted as organic intellectuals uniting the community.[3] In the Liberdade and Engenho Velho de Brotas neighborhoods, black consciousness grew fervently. Books of African literature in Portuguese circulated from hand to hand like rare coins. The ideas of Amílcar Cabral, Samora Machel, and Agostinho Neto and the role of the MPLA, PAIGC, and FRELIMO were very important.[4] We went to an extreme viewpoint: whites are worthless, blacks are good. Africa is God, Europe is the Devil.

We created our own binary oppositions, helped a great deal by a Bahian intelligentsia that reinforced Nagô-centrism and intensified our limited vision. These intellectuals patted us on the back saying

> That's the path to follow, you must create a space for blacks in carnival. During the rest of the year, we will talk, we will interpret, we will do research, and we will tell you what you should do. But during the three days of carnival you will make your presence felt in the streets. We will demonstrate that we are not racists, since you know exactly when and in which districts you should parade and what you should do during these three days. During the three days of carnival we, the Bahian intellectuals, will not talk about blacks on television, in the newspapers, or on radio, you yourselves will. But from Ash Wednesday on, you can leave the talking to us.

This process was useful because no one expected much and something strange occurred. In Pelourinho, the city's historical district, a group called Olodum was born. Olodum is a Yoruba word that means the moment of creation, of being in Orum, the supreme deity, conceived by other religions as God. It is a powerful force. Olodum was founded in 1979 by prostitutes, homosexuals, people associated with the *jogo do bicho,* dope smokers, bohemian lawyers, and intellectuals. The group was known by only a few during its initial years. During the 1983 carnival season Olodum did not even parade but underwent an internal reorganization. Under the leadership of a new directorship in 1983 Olodum began to take steps to avoid the past errors of Ilê Aiyê, Badauê, Apache, the Filhos do Gandhi, Candomblé terreiros, political party members, Protestant church members, and members of the Catholic Church's Black Pastoral. And in so doing Olodum fulfilled an extremely important political role and wrote an important page in the history of Bahian music, culture, and negritude.

The first thing we did was to admit whites and mestizos as members. Olodum would be made up of blacks, whites, and mestizos. The second thing we did was to insert ourselves into the political struggle. We knew that participating in Candomblé was good, that being a black artist or cultural producer was good. But something was missing. Previous revolutions and rebellions had taught us that it is not enough to acknowledge the value of our blackness and to say that we were beautiful. Above all we had to be strong. We had to have institutionalized strength and Olodum would fulfill this organizational role.

In 1983 the black elites in Bahia associated with the wealthy black carnival organizations thought that Olodum would never amount to anything because it was made up of whores, queers, and thieves. At that time, I was a member of Ilê Aiyê, but I left Ilê Aiyê because I disagreed with the culturalist vision that was being implemented at the time. My sister was elected president of Olodum, and she called on me to help in the cultural area. That was ten years ago. At Olodum we followed a path that had two primary influences: (1) the North American black movement, the Black Panthers, the nonviolence of Martin Luther King Jr., the verbal violence of Malcolm X; and (2) an extremely diverse African influence. We were never able to focus on only one part of Africa. We were unable to locate the mythical Africa we had imagined. We realized that we were from different places in Africa, and therefore we absorbed the ideas of Kwame Nkrumah, Sekou Toure, Amílcar Cabral, Agostinho Neto, Samora Machel, Cheikh Anta Diop, and Frantz Fanon. It was our mission to take the ideas of these thinkers out of the classroom and lecture halls and to share them with people who had been beaten by the police many times.

One of Olodum's directors, Lazinho, had both arms broken by the police. We asked him what he would do with the ideas of Malcolm X. He responded that he would make a revolution. Another director, Carlos Cardoso, was shot twice by the state military police early one morning in 1990 while he was waiting for a taxi to take him to the airport. We asked him what he would do with the ideas of Mahatma Gandhi. He said he would make a revolution. In January of this year, another of our directors, Gilmar, received two bullets from a military policeman. We asked him what he would do with the ideas of Kwame Nkrumah. He answered that he would make a revolution.

No matter how much we were attacked and assaulted, we harbored no pain or hatred; we didn't lament our past or cry about our situation. Through it all we have constructed and are still constructing a patrimony that has not been given to us by any politician. We have established our independence from the jogo do bicho and from drug traffickers. It has not been easy because we have encountered many enemies, both black and white. Our work has been based on self-esteem, on telling our history through carnival music. This is the history of Africa and the African diaspora. It is the history of humanity. Our work is based on principles of nonviolence. No matter how much we are attacked, we respond only with the violence of ideas. Olodum's work is a form of nonviolent guerrilla warfare. At all moments we are engaged in politics. At all moments we are articulating the taking of power. At all moments we are thinking about taking power in order to create the concrete conditions for us to share the wealth of a country that has gold, petroleum, cacao, coffee, sisal, plenty of land, plenty of water, and plenty of air.

Our primary international banner has been the struggle against apartheid. In this arena, Olodum's first priority was to talk about the release of Nelson Mandela. Now, with his release, our international priority is to talk about the war in Angola. Olodum also writes and performs music. The *samba reggae* was created by master Neguinho do Samba. But in addition to music, Olodum has a theater and dance company and operates the Olodum Creative School.

In the area of human rights we have fought against police violence in Bahia, especially in the Maciel-Pelourinho neighborhood. The shootings I referred to earlier are related to this. The military police in Bahia hate us and attribute to us the extensive freedom of the black community to circulate in Maciel-Pelourinho, to smoke marijuana, and to use other drugs. But we were behind the current restoration of the historical center of Salvador. When everyone else wanted to forget Maciel-Pelourinho, we identified ourselves as a bloco afro from Maciel-Pelourinho. The state government has recently inaugurated the restoration of the historical center of the Pelourinho at a cost of $12 million dollars. This is the concrete result of the national and international action of Olodum. It is not a gift from the governor to the city. It is the result of pressure, a collection of past debts, on the level of civil rights, so that the taxes we paid would restore this historical patrimony of humanity.

Olodum is composed of 7 executive directors, 17 administrative directors, and 13 advisors; the band has 200 members, 9 singers; and the organization has 3,100 associates. We correspond with institutions in Africa, Europe, the United States, and Japan. We produce our own records and have already made six records in Brazil, the latest of which is titled *A Música de Olodum*.[5] And we publish 5,000 copies of our own biweekly newspaper, which provides information and the lyrics to our songs. We have also published a songbook, which was released during our festival. We have our own boutique, where we sell Olodum products such as hats and T-shirts.

Many people ask us why we do this. One thing we have learned from American blacks is that money circulates just once in the ghetto, whereas it circulates ten times in other districts. When we only spoke about culture and let others produce these things, our community continued to be poor. The struggle for culture has to bring wealth to the community. We may have beautiful music, but we cannot continue to be hungry, miserable, and impoverished. So we wanted to develop a project that would absorb part of the unemployed labor force of our community. We wanted to expand out institution beyond its educational activities to include jobs. Olodum's boutique was created specifically for this purpose. Our men and women now make products which are sold both nationally and internationally. We produce Olodum's shows in Brazil and abroad. The concrete result of reAfricanization is that today we have considerable sums of money at our disposal.

But we are not Africans, we are Brazilians. As Brazilians, we have to provide an example. This is not an individual struggle and I am not the only person in Olodum. I am speaking by delegation. I would like to mention a few names: Nego, Cristina, Eusébio, Lazinho, Tom, and Petú. These are Olodum's executive directors. They are the personalities of Olodum. Master Neguinho do Samba, Rita, Dora, Zulu, Marcelo Gentil, and a large number of people are collectively constructing an identity of concrete alternatives. In Olodum's headquarters there are almost 200 posters of the worldwide black struggle, but not a single photo of a director. We do not want to have a chest full of our own pictures or a house glorifying individual achievements. We want a house that breathes the life of a dynamic culture. We want the children who go there every day to have responsibility for their own future and to be proud that they are black.

I am proud to be black. I am proud to be a man. I am proud to be a human being. I am not going to say that Brazilian racism is worse than American racism, but you need to know that American racism is the father and mother of racism in other parts of the world. If Americans are not sensitized to the extent of creating cooperative networks to put an end to racism here and in other parts of the world, you will not have a future either. Because the poor people of the world will come here to try to work, and if they can't find a job, they will kill your children and grandchildren and take your house and car. That is what is happening today in many countries of Europe, in Brazil, and in South Africa. Racism is the great evil of the end of this century. It is no longer communism and it is not AIDS. It is the fact that people and nations continue to attribute to themselves the right to say who is good, who is bad, who should work, who should not work, who has the right to have a house, food, and education.

NOTES

1. The term "doutor" is used quite freely in Brazil for university-trained professionals. It is also a term of respect used frequently by working-class people when addressing a male adult of the middle and upper classes.—Ed.

2. *Blocos índios* are Bahian carnival organizations that utilize Amerindian (primarily North American) symbolism.—Ed.

3. Vovô (Antonio Carlos dos Santos) and Apolônio (Apolônio de Jesus Filho) were leaders of the bloco afro Ilê Aiyê; Moa (Moa do Catendê) led the afoxé group Badauê.—Ed.

4. MPLA (Movimento Popular de Libertação de Angola; Popular Movement for the Liberation of Angola); PAIGC (Partido Africano da Independência da Guiné e Cabo Verde; African Independence Party of Guinea and Cape Verde); FRELIMO (Frente de Libertação de Moçambique; Front for the Liberation of Mozambique).—Ed.

5. As of February 1997 Olodum has completed ten recordings.—Ed.

5 | Candomblé and Community

MARIA JOSÉ DO ESPÍRITO SANTO FRANÇA

Before entering into the theme of my talk, I would like to greet all of you, your *orixás* (deities), and your ancestors. My name is Maria José do Espírito Santo. I am a daughter of Nambucó, initiated into the Keto nation in the *terreiro* of Ilê Iyá Omin Axé Iyá Massê, the terreiro of Mãe Menininha do Gantois. I am a *filha-de-santo* (initiate) of Maria Escolástica de Nazaré, Mãe Menininha. I was initiated into this passage, in this current life, on 13 December 1971. I am the successor and promised one to the position of *iyalorixá* of the terreiro Ilê Axé Omin Dá, led by Dem do Zamborim do Espírito Santo, my mother, and Jetonir, who was also initiated in the Gantois terreiro.

I fulfill my mission with the tremendous pride of being the promised one, of representing such illustrious *mães* who have known how to resist and overcome life's obstacles with great wisdom. With these women—the heroines of resistance who gave birth to the heroes of resistance—I learned the meaning of life: who I am, where I came from, what I came to do, how I will do it, to what end, and why I will do it. There is no "for whom" because the higher order is to work for all. There is also no "where" because that doesn't matter either, as long as I continue to fulfill my mission. These women's example of life and struggle is our motto. They did not raise us with paternalism. In the same way, we raise our own children to value what we are, what we have, how we value life and living. How sad it would be if there were no victories. We would have nothing to tell. We are daughters of maids, washerwomen, *fateiras*,[1] *baianas* who sell *acarajé*.[2] I am a baiana de acarajé. Because of acarajé I was able to pay for my undergraduate and graduate education. I received a Ph.D. with a dissertation on domestic labor in honor of my mother.

53

My generation of initiates is preparing itself to occupy one of the most sublime positions, that of *iyalorixá* (cult priestess; literally, "mother of the gods"). Our joint efforts and the efforts of our mothers have allowed us to attain this goal and objective. The first step of the process was initiation, when we received *axé*, that is, the ability to communicate with the orixás as a holy being. Then we were led to scientific knowledge, as our mothers say. They were unable to sit on the bench of science, but they knew it was necessary for us to do so. They gave us this opportunity, so we went to school to learn more than they were able to learn.

Today I want to talk about the construction of identity and social mobilization in the *terreiros*. When they were transported to Brazil, African religions formed part of the cultural patterns of the ethnic groups enslaved by the colonizer—supported by the ideological apparatus of domination—who considered them to be barbaric practices. The colonizer later came to see these religions as a form of ideological, social, and cultural resistance. Thus the persecution of our religion by the repressive apparatus, which even today refers to it with such derogatory terms as fetishistic, exotic, pathological, animist, white magic, a system of superstitions, low spiritism, and so forth. Unlike other religions which have been incorporated into mainstream institutional frameworks, Afro-Brazilian religions have survived as a nucleus of cultural resistance in the process of democratization of Brazilian society, seeking the construction of self-determination through total freedom of practice and expression.

Attempts to destroy the cosmogonic, philosophical, scientific, and aesthetic universe of Candomblé, which are structures of identity and forms of social and individual behavior, were unable to impede the emergence of other organizations, institutions, groups, and entities which struggle for participation and for greater freedom in society. Gêge-Nagô culture has a strong presence in many states, complementing the cultural process of the communities of Bantu origin which strengthen cultural identity by opening spaces in the new socioeconomic context.

Although oppressed and discriminated against, Afro-Brazilians, as the majority segment of society, represent a threat to the dominant classes. As superstructures Afro-Brazilian religions exist and develop without serving sociopolitical and cultural domination. The terreiro communities have always been seen as sites of racial and social danger, leading to the creation of numerous stereotypes used to justify actions against their operation. The creation of stereotypes, the importation of foreign cultural standards and fashions, and the attempt to destroy their cultural values are some of the factors responsible for the loss of cultural identity and the resulting fragmentation of our personality.

The terreiro communities are autonomous, independent spaces which are appropriate for reflection, allowing us to know and analyze our own reality in such a way that our action will be committed to fulfilling our aspirations in a conscious, efficient, and responsible manner. Their organization is endogenous, allowing for objective political action in a process of development based on Afro-Brazilian models. Located primarily in outlying areas, the terreiro communities act as a means to limit marginalization and social mistreatment, structuring defense mechanisms in the process of social dynamics and poliethnic interaction, concomitantly divided into classes and strata with conflictive and antagonistic interests, subordinated to policies of the foreign metropolis, which vigilantly watches the growth of popular organizations in all Latin American countries.

The ever greater concern with problems of survival and the transformation of living conditions permits concrete reflection—not abstract and subjective reflection—about misery, public calamity, hunger, the lack of dignified housing (which is increasing day by day), the alarming rate of disease, viruses, the sterility of black women, the extermination of children and adolescents, the alarming influence of drug traffickers, the invasion of schools, the rate of illiteracy, education which is disassociated from our reality, the impunity of elites, racism, violence in its diverse forms, unemployment, and other issues that touch us and that have been the motive for many discussions and for the adoption of means of struggle. In cultural sectors, these discussions and forms of struggle have expanded with considerable success into music, dance, poetry, painting, sculpture, and literature. Nevertheless, the terrible policy of deculturation and discrimination has been unable to achieve the objectives of the state apparatus.

The folklorization of Afro-Brazilian religious cults still forms part of the strategies of the apparatus of domination. Those who insist on this practice in order to favor the cash register of tourism insist on presenting us as followers of a canned, outdated religion with no function, serving merely as a spectacle or an example of how free blacks expressed their beliefs.

Blacks have been marginalized from the political and productive process. The increasing rate of marginalization has provoked so-called criminality. Thus, blacks are dominant in the prisons, the unemployment lines, and the hardest and poorest paid jobs. Through its conservative function, education—the school as a state ideological apparatus—and its textbooks, especially at the elementary level, deal primarily with subjective themes such as the fatherland, the family, and moral values. Texts provide only vague and imprecise ideas and information about blacks, presenting them as passive and humble, serving as an unspecialized labor force. The Brazilian educational system is elitist par excellence. The system is not interested in providing individuals with the means that would allow them to reflect on their reality or to develop a critical consciousness. Strategically, this hegemony is used to keep us disunited and disorganized as a group.

The rules of this game have changed greatly in these last few years with the emergence of organizations such as Olodum, which do not permit the interference of politicians or of paternalism. They are composed of highly capable young people who are politically aware and astute and who represent new, emergent forces in solidarity, concerned with a new social and political project that will build a more just and egalitarian society. The terreiro communities are also involved and allied with the process that challenges dominant theoretical, psychological, and educational currents, emphasizing the role played by both genders.

The media and the ideological and repressive apparatuses invest heavily in social alienation. They spend millions to shape an image of a prosperous consumer society, unattainable by those who live desperately on the margin of society, in the periphery of large cities, where the situation is critical.

Those who are less privileged remain at the mercy of the false prophets who think they are the spokesmen of Eden.[3] They take advantage of the total disdain of those in power to prescribe eternal consolation, collecting tithes for services rendered. They see themselves as messengers of faith who were designated to bring balsam to soothe the people's suffering. Worse yet, they use our religion as a point of attack. With their followers, they promote false trance sessions, and when the pastor asks who has been possessed, they respond that an orixá is an *exu*, whom they consider to be the devil. The churches are open to anyone who believes that the pastor is an emissary of their God. They give him money, which could be used to buy food for their children, and they listen to his sermons as truly maladjusted people who scream and cry. Everything the pastor says is transmitted over loudspeakers and recorded to be broadcast on radio and television programs. In Brazil, the number of followers is so great that they bought several radio and television stations. And the poor are ever more distant from their own reality.

Sustaining themselves on their pedestal of wealth—their great wisdom—the terreiro communities grow qualitatively day after day. Scholars from all over the world visit terreiros, which are increasingly diversified. The presence of professionals from all fields—sociologists, anthropologists, filmmakers, writers—and their identification with our religion favors interaction and the exchange of ideas among its followers, while at the same time leading to the adoption of positions vis-à-vis their socioeconomic situation. Attracted by the magnitude of the orixás, which fulfill an enormous spiritual role, they also take on the responsibility of supporting our social role and function.

The physical space of the terreiro communities is used for diverse cultural events such as lectures, book releases, video exhibitions, the formation of dance, music, and theater groups, auditions, meetings, workshops, adult literacy classes, and a variety of other activities which permit a greater participation of the community in which the terreiro is situated. There are terreiros which have their own archive, which are constantly visited and consulted. The objective of all these activities is the recovery of an autonomous dignity, the nonassimilation of the thought patterns of the dominant so as not to use the same weapons they use. All of this assumes acceptance of and taking responsibility for our own destiny, our history, and our culture in the fight for the preservation of spaces and for the recovery of Afro-Brazilian identity in the struggle for the right to full citizenship. Our practice goes beyond the immediate concern with studying. We cannot cease, for a moment, to be intellectuals, to go to the university and become specialists in many different areas. Many have even received advanced degrees.

I would like to close with some general considerations from Moacir Gadotti:

> If ideals are necessary to give life to our practice, they may be insufficient to generate change. To place all responsibility for change on society or the state is merely to create an alibi to justify our weakness or our inertia. If we are conscious of the positions we take in relation to a society divided in classes, if we have a class consciousness, we know for whom and against whom we are working and we certainly create an organic link with the class we defend. As an educator I cannot educate those who ignore the moment in which they live.

NOTES

1. Women who sell animal viscera.—Ed.

2. Bean cakes fried in palm oil (*dendê*), cut open, and filled with a spicy mix of shrimp, onions, and peppers.—Ed.

3. The reference here is to forms of evangelical Protestantism which have grown so rapidly in Brazil during the last few decades.—Ed.

| Part | PERSPECTIVES ON RACE, CLASS, |
| Two | AND CULTURE |

In this section, Carlos Hasenbalg and Jeferson Bacelar offer sociological and historical analyses of the relationships among race, class, and culture in post-abolition Brazilian society. Hasenbalg, an Argentine-born sociologist who directs the Centro de Estudos Afro-Asiáticos in Rio de Janeiro, presents empirical evidence of the distributive inequalities and discriminations in Brazil's social structure and class system. He focuses specifically on the differential allocation of groups of color and gender/color in the labor market and occupational structure, correlating that allocation with the unequal distribution of education and income disparities. Hasenbalg concludes that economic growth and modernization have not led to a decrease in the socioeconomic distance between the country's racial groups, but rather that racial discrimination in the labor market has in fact increased in recent years, with blacks and browns continuing to be concentrated at the base of the social hierarchy.

Bacelar, an anthropologist and director of the Centro de Estudos Afro-Orientais of the Universidade Federal da Bahia, focuses on the city of Salvador. In the first part of his essay, Bacelar discusses the occupational and social situation of the city's majority black population in the preindustrial period following the abolition of slavery in 1888. He shows how racism and racial discrimination were built into the social structure as the primary factor of stratification, with blacks occupying the lowest levels of the occupational structure and the social hierarchy. Bacelar then turns toward the more recent period, post-1950, when the city witnessed an economic and social transformation, especially with the development of modern industrial centers, which did not, however, transform the negative stereotypes the dominant sectors had of Afro-Brazilians, nor their objective position in the labor market. He then traces the revival of *afoxés* and the emergence of the *blocos afro*, pointing out both positive and problematic aspects of these important components of black Brazil's cultural affirmation.

6 Perspectives on Race and Class in Brazil

CARLOS HASENBALG

Historical Aspects

The growing volume and sophistication of historiography dealing with slavery in Brazil contrasts starkly with the number of studies on the social history of blacks after abolition. The participation of former slaves and free blacks in the urban industrial society which developed in the years following abolition, as well as in the period's agricultural systems, has not been fully studied.

The scant attention that historians have dedicated to this subject is due in part to the absence of data concerning the color of the population in demographic censuses from 1890 until 1940. At the same time, the analytical focus of the majority of studies on the beginning of industrialization in the country—emphasizing the emergence of new relations of production and a free labor market—led them to give priority to the formation of the working class and the labor movement in São Paulo and, to a lesser degree, Rio de Janeiro. This analytical option left the majority of the emerging subaltern urban classes on the margins of history.

One of the consequences of this omission in relation to the integration of blacks and mulattos in the class structures that formed after the end of slavery has been the inappropriate generalization of processes that took place in São Paulo, the most studied regional case, to the rest of the country (Bastide and Fernandes 1959; Fernandes 1965). In the decades following abolition black workers in São Paulo were displaced by European immigrants not only on coffee plantations but also in the urban centers that were then in a phase of rapid economic development and industrialization. Blacks and mulattos were thus excluded from the most dynamic employment sectors and relegated to subsistence agriculture in rural areas or to non-specialized services in urban centers.

As Andrews has correctly noted, what gives the Paulista experience a special character and differentiates it from other regions of the country is the official promotion and subsidy of foreign immigration from the 1880s until the second half of the 1920s.

> The labor market in São Paulo did not reveal any of the rigid racial controls imposed by the state and used, for example, in the segregationist systems of South Africa and the southern United States during this same period. Nevertheless, the labor market was powerfully affected by the state's direct intervention, which inevitably produced results loaded with racial implications: the inundation of the local labor market with a flood of European immigrants. (Andrews 1988:493)

Revising Florestan Fernandes's interpretation, Andrews shows that the exclusion of blacks from the first stage of Paulista industrialization until 1930 was more the result of state immigration policies than of a lack of preparation, ability, or the social disorganization of former slaves. The entrance of black workers in São Paulo's industrial proletariat would begin only with the revalorization of the national worker throughout the 1920s and the interruption of the flow of immigrants at the end of the decade. Thus, during the period between 1888 and 1930 in no other part of the country were white immigrants so clearly the winners and blacks the losers in the economic development and prosperity generated by the coffee boom and industrialization. And it was precisely the São Paulo experience, characterized by competition with immigrants and the marginalization of blacks from the labor market, that would be generalized for the country as a whole.

In Rio de Janeiro, things occurred differently. This city, which at the end of the last century had the greatest concentration of urban blacks in the country, had received a great number of foreign immigrants during the second half of the nineteenth century. In the decades following abolition this immigration flow continued, but it did not have the volume or demographic impact equal to that of São Paulo. Besides, immigration to Rio was more spontaneous and was not subsidized. Although there was competition between blacks and immigrants, with results favorable to the latter, the displacement of the black population did not have the same dimensions as in São Paulo. The census of 1890 indicated a high concentration of blacks and mulattos in non-specialized jobs outside of the dynamic employment sectors. Even so, 17 percent of blacks and mulattos were employed in industry and made up 30 percent of the labor force in this sector. This fact indicates an incipient process of the proletarization of blacks in Rio de Janeiro, anticipating what would occur in the rest of the Southeast starting with the interruption of the flow of immigrants in 1930.

The situation of other regions of the country with a high concentration of the black population, like the Northeast and Minas Gerais, has not been studied. Nevertheless, the impact of foreign immigration in them was negligible, and it is possible that blacks participated from the beginning in the peripheral industrialization that took place there.

In general, in the decades following abolition, the majority of the black population continued to work in agriculture. The transition from slave labor to formally free labor did not mean the generalization of wage labor in Brazilian agriculture. In fact, the formation of a capitalist labor market in rural Brazil occurred in a more complete manner only in Paulista coffee production.

As Eisenberg (1977) has suggested, the forms of free labor were differentiated from slave labor merely by the basic freedom to abandon one's job. Labor relations in Brazilian agriculture during the period were characterized by a low degree of contract labor and a predominance of non-monetary forms of remuneration. In the Northeast, where the transition to free labor was already rather advanced at the time of abolition, the former slaves joined the ranks of tenant farmers, day laborers, and peasants in traditional labor relations characterized by seignorial dependency. Andrade (1983:74), analyzing the transition to free labor in the Northeast, notes that wage labor as such became the general rule in sugar agriculture only after the 1960s as a result of the application of the Estatuto do Trabalhador Rural (Rural Worker Law).

Demographic census data for 1940 and 1950 permit a description of the employment situation of whites, blacks, and mulattos after more than fifty years had passed since abolition (Table 1).

The situation in São Paulo in 1940 is characterized by the predominant association of blacks and browns with agricultural work (71.2 percent). In that year, only 39,000 non-whites, or 12 percent of the total, worked in the secondary sector, which corroborates the delayed entrance of blacks and mulattos in the industrial proletariat in that state. Between 1940 and 1950 São Paulo's occupational structure experienced rapid urbanization, particularly among the non-white population. The

TABLE 1

Sectoral Structure of Employment of Color Groups,
Selected Regions of Brazil, 1940 and 1950[a]

(%)

Sector	São Paulo		Distrito Federal and Rio de Janeiro		Others[b]		Brazil	
	W	NW	W	NW	W	NW	W	NW
				1940				
Primary	56.3	71.2	25.2	44.9	76.6	81.3	65.9	77.4
Secondary	17.5	12.0	19.8	21.7	6.2	7.0	10.9	8.6
Tertiary	26.2	16.8	55.0	33.4	17.2	11.7	23.2	14.0
Total	100.0	100.0	100.0	100.0	100.0	100.0	100.0	100.0
				1950				
Primary	42.0	48.9	17.0	23.0	70.4	75.6	55.8	68.7
Secondary	24.3	20.5	23.1	23.1	7.3	8.0	14.6	10.6
Tertiary	33.7	30.6	59.9	53.9	22.3	16.4	29.6	20.7
Total	100.0	100.0	100.0	100.0	100.0	100.0	100.0	100.0

a. W = Whites; NW = non-whites. NW includes blacks and browns and excludes yellows
and those who did not declare their color.
b. Excludes states in Southern Brazil.

proportion working in agriculture fell from 71.2 percent to 48.9 percent
between these two dates. In 1950 the relative participation of blacks and
browns in the secondary sector increased to 20.5 percent, still less than
the 24.3 percent of whites. Nonetheless, it was in this decade that, for the
first time, industrial employment of blacks and browns grew more
rapidly than that of whites, increasing from 39,000 to 86,000 people in
this sector.

In 1940 what is today the state of Rio de Janeiro (the Federal District plus the city of Rio de Janeiro) was the most urbanized and indus-
trialized region of the country. The relative presence of blacks and
mulattos in the primary sector was greater than that of whites, 45 percent
and 25 percent, respectively. But the proportion of non-whites employed
in industry also surpassed that of whites (21.7 percent and 19.8 percent),
and this was more accentuated in the Federal District, where 34 percent of the non-whites and only 23.3 percent of the whites worked in

industry. This fact also seems to confirm that the entrance of blacks and mulattos into the industrial working class in Rio de Janeiro preceded that of other regions, particularly São Paulo. Through the 1940s the urbanization of Rio de Janeiro's occupational structure was accelerated, particularly in the case of the non-white population, whose participation in the primary sector decreased to only 23 percent in 1950. In that same year the proportional presence of whites and non-whites in industry was equal at 23 percent.

In the rest of the country (excluding the three states of the South), which includes the least developed regions, whites as well as blacks and mulattos remained primarily linked to agriculture in 1940 and 1950. The low degree of industrialization in these regions is reflected in the small proportion of people employed in the secondary sector, where non-whites have a relative participation slightly superior to that of whites, who were better represented in the tertiary sector of the economy. The slight changes in the sectoral employment structure between 1940 and 1950 are also indicative of the region's less dynamic economic activity.

Finally, in Brazil as a whole, which combines these divergent regional processes, one notes the disproportionate representation of blacks and browns in agricultural work: 77.4 percent in 1940 and 68.7 percent in 1950. The late incorporation of this group into the urban working class is visible in the proportion of whites and non-whites employed in industry in these two years: 10.9 percent and 8.6 percent in 1940 and 14.6 and 10.6 percent in 1950, respectively. Whether it is because it competed from a disadvantaged position with immigrant workers in the most industrially advanced regions, or because it remained more concentrated in less economically dynamic regions, in the decades following abolition the black and mestizo population was incorporated belatedly into the developing urban-industrial world.

Race and Class at the Centenary of Abolition

The period between 1950 and 1980 was not prodigious in official statistics concerning the race and color of the Brazilian population. The 1960 census had serious technical problems, its final results were only available more than ten years after their collection, and the published information refers to groups of color only by sex and age. The census of 1970 simply omitted questions about color, which were reincorporated only in the 1980 census.

It was in this same period that Brazil, together with the other countries of Latin America, experienced a rapid structural transition from an agrarian society to a class society in a capitalist mold, following a general process known as "conservative modernization" (CEPAL 1986). The motor of this transition was the rapid economic growth and diffusion of capitalist modes of production that occurred between the second postwar period and the economic crisis of the 1980s. One of the basic axes of the changes in the social structures which occurred in this period was the rapid transformation of occupational structures, resulting in increased occupational mobility which provided the social logic of the model of growth.

> In this social logic, the combination of increases in capital investments and improvements in the level of specialization of the labor force permitted the absorption of growing proportions of the active population in activities and occupations of greater productivity, income and social status. (CEPAL 1986:17)

Of all South American countries, Brazil had the most rapid economic growth between 1950 and 1980, when the growth rate of the per capita gross national product was 351 percent, or an annual rate of 4.3 percent. This expansion occurred despite the high rhythm of demographic growth during this same period.

In the sectoral employment structure, the economically active population in the primary sector declined from 60 percent in 1950 to 30 percent in 1980, and there occurred a transfer of the labor force to industry and modern services. Between 1960 and 1980, when the structural transformations accelerated, the total number of people working in the secondary sector grew from 2,940,000 to 10,675,000, increasing its relative participation from 12.9 percent to 24.4 percent. During the same period, the proportion of people occupied in the tertiary sector went from 33.1 percent to 45.7 percent.

Another aspect of the structural transition is provided by the expansion of middle-range occupational strata. To have a precise idea of this expansion, it suffices to recall that the number of people in administrative and technical-scientific occupations—the proxy of the so-called new middle class—increased from 2.5 million in 1960 to 8.2 million in 1980.

Even maintaining a pattern of accentuated social and economic inequalities, these changes in per capita product and income, in the employment structure, and in the specialization and productivity of the labor force translated into an increase in the well-being of important sectors of the population. The structural transition was experienced by a significant portion of individuals and families as upward social mobility. A study based on the 1973 Pesquisa Nacional por Amostra de Domicílios (PNAD; Household Survey) indicated that the proportion of socially mobile individuals, that is, individuals who engaged in an occupation socially superior to that of their parents, reached approximately 46 percent of the cases of the sample. The individuals in the inverse situation, in a position inferior to that of their parents, constituted but 13 percent of the sample (Hasenbalg and Silva 1988:ch. 1).

To complete this brief description of social changes in the decades prior to 1980, when the model of growth entered a crisis, we should also note the rapidity of the process of urbanization, the expansion of wage labor in the work force, the demographic transition evidenced in the decrease in fertility and in the deceleration of population growth, and the increase of the participation of women in the labor force.

In sum, the economic and social crisis of the 1980s occurred at the moment when Brazil found itself, in relation to other Latin American countries, in a relatively advanced phase of transition toward a class society in a capitalist mold. It is only then that the return of a systematic collection of data about the color of the population in censuses and household surveys permits an evaluation of the insertion of racial groups in the class structure and in the system of social stratification. We have chosen to work with data from the PNAD of 1988, since they permit a description of the situation of the black and mestizo population exactly a century after the end of slavery in Brazil.

Before analyzing the differentiated insertion of racial groups, it is important to point out the more general characteristics of the system of classes and social stratification in contemporary Brazil. The strong inequalities embedded in Brazil's social structure and class system represent the first aspect to be noted. These inequalities can be illustrated in relation to the distribution of education and income.

In terms of the first of these dimensions of inequality—education—it is well known that Brazil's educational performance is weak, if one considers the level of per capita income, and that education is unevenly distributed in the labor force. The last column of Table 4, which registers average years schooling of different groups or occupational categories, permits empirical verification of this fact. The average schooling of the occupational strata varies from approximately 17 years of study among the liberal professions to merely 2 years for rural workers. Furthermore, the schooling of non-manual occupational groups, with the exception of self-employed small businessmen, is almost twice that of urban manual laborers. In addition to Brazil's unequally distributed education, the salary profile of the educational groups is also strongly slanted. Recent studies (Camargo and Gianbiagi 1991; World Bank 1992) point toward educational distribution as the most important explanatory factor in the unequal distribution of income.

The inequalities in the second distributive dimension, income, may be verified in the last column of Table 5. One notes, for example, that the average income of liberal professionals is more than twenty times greater than that of rural workers and domestic service employees. In 1989 the Gini coefficient of per capita family income distribution in Brazil was 0.633; the poorest 20 percent received 2.1 percent of the income, while the wealthiest 10 percent received 51.3 percent. The same Gini coefficient for individual distribution of income among workers was 0.625 (World Bank 1992). These coefficients are not only the highest in Latin America and the Caribbean, but also of all the countries in the world that have statistics on income distribution.

The second aspect to be emphasized concerns the weight—already diminished in relation to preceding decades—of the rural sector in the structure of classes and occupational strata. In 1988 the agricultural sector absorbed approximately one fourth (25.5 percent) of the country's total labor force. Despite modernization, capitalization, and the increase in technology that occurred in Brazilian agriculture in the last 25 or 30 years, the class structure of the country's rural areas remains extremely polarized between a small group of agricultural landowners and a large mass of autonomous small-scale agricultural producers and manual rural workers. At the base of this polarization is the continued high concentration of land ownership. In historical terms, the lack of any significant form of agrarian reform explains the absence in Brazil of an independent peasantry and a rural middle class. The widespread poverty of the country's rural population (with the possible exception of the Southern states) is causally linked to the flux of rural-urban migration, the accelerated rhythm of urbanization, and the strong pressures on the labor supply in the urban labor market.

Third, the categories of urban manual workers include the majority of the economically active population (46.6 percent), while the industrial working class constitutes a minority (13 percent) of the economically active urban population. As CEPAL has noted:

> The proletariat, in the strict sense of manual wage laborers in the manufacturing industry, does not constitute nor will it constitute a great popular mass that is the motor of history in Latin America, less because of a weak process of industrialization (which has not been inconsiderable in many countries of the region), but rather because of the non-intensive character of its labor force and of the worldwide expansion of the service economy in recent years. (CEPAL 1986:71)

The counterpart of the minority position of the industrial proletariat is the increasing expansion of the urban working class in the tertiary sector. To it belong the categories of manual workers employed in services (11.5 percent) and a vast and heterogeneous group of manual workers in the informal sector (22 percent).

Fourth is the sector of non-manual workers, which absorbed 27.9 percent of the working population in 1988. Within this sector one can distinguish a portion that corresponds to the old middle sectors, comprising autonomous liberal professionals, small employers in industry, commerce, and service, and self-employed small entrepreneurs who account for approximately 6 percent of the economically active population. Strictly speaking, the group of self-employed small businessmen who do not employ other people occupies an ambiguous position between the petite bourgeoisie and the urban informal sector. The remaining sectors of non-manual employment can be assimilated into the new middle class, a product of recent capitalist development. These occupational strata are characterized by the predominance of wage labor; they have grown and become differentiated in the last few decades and have experienced the impact of the expansion of women's employment. The feminization of employment is particularly notable in the low non-manual sector, where women hold 50 percent of the jobs.

In material terms, the situation of some low non-manual occupational groups does not differ substantially from the manual strata that are more favorably positioned in the labor market. Thus, for example, the average income of employees in the routine and office worker non-manual category is inferior to that of manual workers in modern industry and to some manual workers in the informal sector. If one considers the low non-manual worker as belonging to the set of occupations typical of the new middle class, one should not forget that his market

TABLE 2

Occupational Distribution of Population Ten Years of Age and Older,
According to Color and Gender in Brazil,[a] 1988[b]

Occupation	W	NW	WM	WF	NWM	NWF	Total
High non-manual	9.0	2.9	9.0	8.9	2.8	2.8	6.3
Petite bourgeoisie	7.2	3.9	8.6	4.7	4.3	3.2	5.8
Low non-manual	19.0	11.6	14.9	26.7	9.0	16.1	15.8
Industrial working class	12.9	13.3	16.0	7.4	17.4	5.7	13.1
Service working class	11.8	10.8	13.1	9.6	12.6	8.5	11.5
Informal sector	19.4	25.7	13.0	30.7	15.0	44.8	22.0
Agricultural owners	1.0	0.5	1.4	0.1	0.7	0.1	0.7
Agricultural workers	19.7	31.3	24.0	11.9	38.2	18.8	24.8
Total	100.0	100.0	100.0	100.0	100.0	100.0	100.0

a. Excludes persons described as "yellow" or without declaration of color, which represent less than 1 percent of the working population.
b. W = whites; NW = non-whites; M = male; F = female.

Source: Special tabulations of PNAD, 1988.

situation and well-being are superposed to those of the better paid sectors of the urban working class.

Table 2 shows the distribution of groups of color and gender in a
hierarchized set of occupational strata.[1] Persons designated as black
or brown, as defined by the census, were grouped in the category of
non-white.

These large occupational strata, which indicate differentiated positions within the class structure and the labor market, were constructed
by aggregating of the most frequently used categories of Table 3.[2]

Racial groups are unequally distributed in this set of large occupational categories. Clearly, non-whites (blacks and browns) are dispro-
portionately represented among agricultural workers and in urban
manual categories. Inversely, blacks and browns are underrepresented at
the top of the occupational hierarchy, in non-manual sectors. Almost a
third of non-whites (31.3 percent) are farm workers, while the percentage of whites in these jobs is less than 20 percent. Practically half of the
non-whites (49.8 percent) work in urban manual occupations, as
opposed to 44.1 percent of whites. The greatest inequality in the occupational distribution is found in the non-manual categories, where the proportion of whites (32.2 percent) is almost twice that of non-whites (18.4
percent). Using the eight occupational strata of Table 2, one can calculate

TABLE 3

Occupational Distribution of Groups of Color and Gender in Brazil, 1988[a]

(%)

Occupation	W	NW	WM	WF	NWM	NWF	Total
Liberal professionals	0.5	0.1	0.7	0.3	0.1	—	0.3
Employed liberal professionals	1.3	0.3	1.5	0.8	0.3	0.2	0.8
Directors and administrators	4.3	1.6	4.8	3.5	1.7	1.4	3.2
Other professionals	2.9	0.9	2.0	4.3	0.7	1.2	2.0
Owner-employees	3.8	1.0	4.8	1.9	1.4	0.4	2.6
Administrative/executive	3.2	1.4	3.3	3.2	1.3	1.5	2.4
Technicians/artists/supervisors	7.8	5.9	5.9	11.2	4.3	8.6	7.0
Self-employed businessmen	3.4	2.9	3.8	2.8	2.9	2.8	3.2
Routine non-manual	8.0	4.3	5.7	12.3	3.4	6.0	6.4
Working-class modern industry	3.3	2.6	4.8	0.7	3.7	0.5	3.0
Working-class traditional industry	9.6	10.7	11.2	6.7	13.7	5.2	10.1
Working-class services	11.8	10.8	13.1	9.6	12.6	8.5	11.5
Self-employed manual	7.9	8.0	7.3	8.8	7.7	8.2	7.9
Domestic services	9.6	15.4	4.0	19.7	5.3	33.9	12.1
Ambulatory vendors	1.9	2.3	1.7	2.2	2.0	2.7	2.0
Agricultural owners	1.0	0.5	1.4	0.1	0.7	0.1	0.7
Agricultural technicians and administrators	0.8	0.8	1.3	—	1.3	0.1	0.9
Autonomous agricultural producers	6.4	8.3	9.4	1.0	11.5	2.4	7.2
Rural manual labor	12.5	22.2	13.3	10.9	25.4	16.3	16.7
Total	100.0	100.0	100.0	100.0	100.0	100.0	100.0

a. W = whites; NW = non-whites; M = male; F = female.

Source: Special tabulations of PNAD, 1988.

an index of dissimilarity in distribution of 0.183, indicating that 18.3 percent of the non-whites would have to change strata in order for the occupational distribution of the two racial groups to be equal.

The data in Tables 3, 4, and 5 complement the information in Table 2, providing the distribution of groups of color and gender/color in the more unaggregated categories which form the strata of Table 2 and the educational level and average income of these categories.

In the rural sector, blacks and browns have a relatively higher participation than whites both among autonomous agricultural producers and among rural manual workers, groups where poverty is much higher. The average schooling of these groups, around two complete years,

TABLE 4

Average Schooling by Occupational Strata
According to Groups of Color and Gender in Brazil, 1988[a]

(Years)

Occupation	W	NW	WM	WF	NWM	NWF	Total
Liberal professionals	17.0	16.7	17.0	16.9	16.7	—	17.0
Employed liberal professionals	16.8	15.9	17.0	16.3	14.7	14.7	16.7
Directors and administrators	11.7	9.9	11.6	11.8	9.5	10.6	11.3
Other professionals	14.8	13.2	14.8	15.2	12.0	14.1	14.7
Owner-employees	9.5	7.1	9.3	10.5	6.8	8.7	9.1
Administrative/executive	11.1	9.8	10.7	11.8	9.2	10.6	10.8
Technicians/artists/supervisors	10.3	8.9	9.4	11.2	8.0	8.7	9.8
Self-employed businessmen	6.3	4.0	6.2	6.4	4.0	3.8	5.4
Routine non-manual	10.0	9.1	9.3	10.5	8.5	9.8	9.7
Working-class modern industry	6.1	5.5	6.1	6.0	5.4	6.4	5.9
Working-class traditional industry	4.4	3.7	4.2	5.1	3.4	5.0	4.1
Working-class services	6.2	5.2	5.9	6.8	5.1	5.6	5.1
Self-employed manual	5.1	3.9	5.0	5.3	3.7	4.1	4.6
Domestic services	3.6	3.2	3.7	3.6	3.3	3.1	3.4
Ambulatory vendors	5.2	4.5	4.6	5.9	3.1	4.4	4.4
Agricultural owners	6.0	2.9	5.8	7.3	2.9	3.2	5.2
Agricultural technicians and administrators	4.8	3.3	4.8	4.8	3.2	7.1	4.2
Autonomous agricultural producers	2.9	1.1	3.0	2.4	1.2	1.0	2.1
Rural manual labor	2.8	1.4	2.8	2.9	1.4	1.3	2.0
Total	6.6	4.0	6.2	7.3	3.7	4.6	5.5

a. W = whites; NW = non-whites; M = male; F = female.

Source: Special tabulations of PNAD, 1988.

would classify these workers as illiterates and semi-illiterates. In terms of income, self-employed agricultural workers have a considerable advantage over rural wage laborers, Cr$ 36,000 and Cr$ 19,000, respectively. Nonetheless, these two groups receive average incomes inferior to those of all categories of urban workers, with the exception of domestic workers. From this one may conclude that rural-urban migration does not necessarily imply a dislocation of rural poverty to the cities (CEPAL 1986). The migrant worker of rural origin not only finds in the city better access to the educational system and social services, but also encounters a labor market with better paying jobs than those in agriculture.

TABLE 5

Average Income of Occupational Strata
According to Groups of Color and Gender in Brazil, 1988

(Cr$ 1,000)

Occupation	W	NW	WM	WF	NWM	NWF	Total
Liberal professionals	369	320	421	192	320	—	363
Employed liberal professionals	439	320	483	310	384	173	424
Directors and administrators	249	151	292	142	177	96	229
Other professionals	221	148	309	149	201	102	208
Owner-employees	270	196	290	179	195	204	257
Administrative/executive	165	106	187	127	123	80	152
Technicians/artists/supervisors	94	59	127	64	80	40	82
Self-employed businessmen	95	62	107	67	72	44	83
Routine non-manual	71	57	79	65	68	46	67
Working-class modern industry	92	69	95	57	71	40	84
Working-class traditional industry	48	32	45	31	33	27	38
Working-class services	50	40	57	36	46	27	46
Self-employed manual	64	42	83	29	51	18	54
Domestic services	24	18	43	17	34	14	21
Ambulatory vendors	54	32	65	39	33	30	44
Agricultural owners	240	138	237	292	139	106	213
Agricultural technicians and administrators	60	44	60	58	44	106	54
Autonomous agricultural producers	45	26	46	31	28	15	36
Rural manual labor	21	17	23	15	19	10	19
Total	88	41	107	58	50	28	70

Source: Special tabulations of PNAD, 1988.

In Tables 4 and 5, one notes that whites in these two categories of rural workers present a significant advantage in terms of educational level and average income. These advantages perhaps have less to do with race than with the unequal geographic distribution of color groups. In effect, 71 percent of these white workers are employed in the more modern and developed agriculture in the Southeast and South of the country, something that occurs with only 30 percent of the blacks and browns occupied in agriculture.

The category of agricultural technicians and administrators occupies an intermediary position in the rural class structure and employs slightly less than 1 percent of the total economically active population.

The group is almost entirely masculine, with the relatively low educational level of 4.2 years and income that does not exceed that of the better paid urban workers. Blacks and browns in this category are also less educated and have lower incomes than those of their white peers.

Agricultural owners represent only 0.7 percent of the economically active population and constitute a group with a low level of formal education, an average of 5.2 years of schooling. Nevertheless, land ownership gives them a relatively privileged position in the distribution of income; the average income of CR$ 213,000 puts them in a situation that is slightly inferior to that of urban entrepreneurial employers. The mechanisms of acquisition and transmission of property ownership benefit men almost exclusively; white and non-white women are virtually excluded from the category of rural property owners. As one might expect, blacks and browns have limited participation in this category of owners: the proportional representation of non-whites in this class is half that of whites, 0.5 percent to 1.0 percent, respectively. The resources of non-white rural property owners are inferior to those of whites, a fact suggested by average years of schooling (2.9 and 6 years of study, respectively) and the average income, which is only 57 percent that of whites.

In relation to urban manual strata, Table 2 indicates that, unlike what occurred in the first half of this century, in 1988 blacks and browns had already equaled and had even slightly surpassed whites in their relative participation in the industrial working class. The percentages of wage-earning manual laborers in industry are 12.9 percent for whites and 13.3 percent for non-whites. This parity occurs when two significant circumstances are present. The first is that competition for access to occupations of greater social status shifts to jobs in the non-manual category (Andrews 1991). The second is that relative weight of the industrial working class in the class structure begins to decrease both as an effect of the economic crisis which began in the early 1980s and continues until today and because of the global tendency toward the rapid expansion of the tertiary sector of the economy.

Tables 3, 4, and 5 complement the information about the pattern of participation of racial groups in the industrial working class. Table 3 shows that whites have a slight advantage over non-whites in modern industries, with 3.3 percent and 2.6 percent, respectively. The counterpart of this is a relatively greater presence of non-whites in traditional industries, which present average salary levels much inferior to those of modern industries. This is due in part to the greater numeric presence of non-whites in the civil construction industry, which absorbs non-specialized and poorly paid workers (Hasenbalg 1992).

Tables 4 and 5, which provide information on schooling and average income, reveal a pattern that will be repeated in other occupational strata. Non-white industrial workers have educational levels and incomes inferior to those of whites, with educational differences smaller than those of income. In modern industries, the average education of non-whites is 90 percent that of whites and their income level is only 75 percent that of whites. The same percentages in traditional industries are 84 percent and 67 percent. Two factors explain this pattern. The first has to do with the existence of salary discrimination, through which workers who are equally productive receive different salaries because of attributes such as race and gender, which are unrelated to productivity. The second factor is related to the greater numerical presence of white workers in the industries of the more developed regions of the country, which pay higher wages.

It should be added that women, both white and non-white, have a reduced participation in the industrial working class, particularly in modern industries. Despite the fact that women workers are more highly educated than the men, they receive lower wages in both traditional and modern industries. Because of their race and gender, black and brown women hold the lowest paid industrial jobs.

The working class in services is composed of manual wage laborers in the tertiary sector of the economy and absorbs 11.5 percent of the total labor force. The relative participation of whites in this sector of urban employment is 11.8 percent, slightly superior to the 10.8 percent of non-whites. The average education of workers in this category, 5.1 years of schooling, surpasses that of workers in modern industry by one year and is 0.8 years less than that of workers in modern industry. The average income of the category, Cr$ 46,000, surpasses the Cr$ 38,000 of traditional industry but is much less than the Cr$ 84,000 of modern industry. The educational and income differences between racial groups in this category are moderate; non-whites have 84 percent of the education and 80 percent of the income of whites. This suggests, on the one hand, that occupational and wage discrimination based on race is not accentuated in this occupational stratum. On the other hand, the differentials between genders are strong in the category. As is the case throughout the labor force, women employed in this category are more educated than men within each color group, while their income is substantially inferior to that of men. This is due in part to wage discrimination based on gender, but possibly the differential follows to a great degree the unequal distribution of men and women within the occupations of this stratum. Thus, for example, women are largely excluded from the better-paid occupations of transports and are concentrated in jobs of personal, non-domestic services.

As defined here, the urban informal sector encompasses self-employed manual workers, workers in domestic service, and street ped-dlers. These three categories account for 22 percent of the total economically active population and constitute almost half of the people who work in urban manual strata.

The category of self-employed manual workers includes almost 8 percent of the economically active population, with an almost equal proportional participation of whites and non-whites. The average level of education in this category, 4.6 years of study, surpasses that of work-ers in traditional industry and their average income is greater than those of this category and those of the service working class. This is an indica-tion that the urban informal sector is heterogeneous and cannot be totally assimilated to the condition of poverty and low qualification of workers. The group of self-employed manual laborers is characterized by its internal stratification, which is suggested by the strong differentials of income according to race and gender. This income oscillates from an average of Cr$ 83,000 for white men to just Cr$ 18,000 for non-white women. Thus, the white men in this category enjoy a market situation, as indicated by income, that is relatively good within the sector of urban manual jobs, being surpassed only by workers in modern industry. Since they are self-employed workers, who do not sell their labor power, the strong differentials in color and gender cannot be explained by occupa-tional and wage discrimination based on these criteria. Race and gender discrimination can act only indirectly in this case, impeding access to the best jobs in the formal sector for non-whites and women. Inequalities in income between groups of color and gender in this stratum are probably related to the unequal resources of these self-employed workers: levels of formal education and skills learned previously in the labor market, levels of savings and capitalization, and facility of access to markets of goods and services offered by the informal sector.

The category of workers in domestic service forms the lowest seg-ment of the urban labor market, congregating the least educated (3.4 years of study) and lowest paid (Cr$ 21,100) individuals. Historically, this employment sector has always been large in Brazil and it continues to be voluminous today: in 1988 it employed 6.7 million people, equivalent to 12.1 percent of the total labor force. Traditionally the category absorbs people of rural origin and low educational levels. It is a predominantly feminine sector, where women represent 75.5 percent of those employed. Even absorbing almost a fifth of the employed white women, this category is characterized as being the primary occupational enclave of non-white women, congregating 34 percent of them. This occupational concentration in domestic services reached the unprecedented level of 47.6 percent of black working women.

The category of ambulatory workers who, together with domestic employment, can be seen as a residual of a preindustrial labor market absorbs 2 percent of the total of employed persons, with an equal representation of men and women, whites and non-whites. Traditionally composed of market vendors, fruit and candy vendors, and vendors of newspapers and magazines, this category today includes, because of the economic crisis, a growing number of *camelôs* or street vendors who populate the country's large cities.

Leaving aside the popular urban world, we will now move to an examination of race and gender groups in the non-manual occupational strata, beginning with the categories comprising the high non-manual stratum.

In terms of the two central variables of social stratification studied here, education and income, the autonomous and employed liberal professionals are found at the top of the occupational hierarchy. These two categories are formed by the traditional professions of high prestige and status: engineers, architects, doctors, economists, and lawyers, including solicitors and magistrates. Two processes have characterized the evolution of these occupations in recent years. The first is the massification of these professions, accompanying the expansion of the system of higher education in Brazil since the 1960s. The second is the growing salaried employment of this group of professionals, seen in the relative participation of each of the categories: whereas the autonomous liberal professionals form 0.3 percent of the economically active population, salaried professionals make up 0.8 percent of the total number of employed individuals.

Groups of gender and color have a differentiated participation in these two higher-level occupational strata. While white women have increased their participation in this male occupational redoubt and have reached the level of 1.1 percent in these categories (half of the 2.2 percent of white males), non-whites, men and women, experience a much greater degree of exclusion, represented by only 0.4 percent.

The third high non-manual stratum is that of public and private sector directors and administrators. This group includes individuals ranging from the highest levels of public administration (ministers of state, for example), to directors and aides, to managers in public service. Administrators of businesses in all branches of economic activity—with the exception of agriculture—also form part of this group, including managers and those in charge of the administrative section of these enterprises. It is, therefore, an internally stratified group, covering both leadership and management positions in public and private organizations. This internal stratification and diversification is corroborated by the average income of the category (Cr$ 229,000), inferior to that of the liberal professionals. The average level of education of this stratum, 11.3 years of study, also indicates that a higher education diploma is not a requirement for access to many of these occupational positions.

Again, the degrees of exclusion of this stratum based on ascriptive criteria of race and gender are different. While white women are represented with 3.5 percent in these occupations (a proportion less than that of the 4.8 percent of white males), the non-whites have a relative participation of only 1.6 percent. Here barriers that tend to impede non-whites from occupying positions of authority over whites in bureaucratic and organizational hierarchies certainly come into play. This is consistent with the observation that is commonly made about the absence of non-whites in the highest levels of all institutional areas in Brazilian society, except those of sports and show business, where maximum mobility is possible for some black celebrities. The few non-whites who enter this category do so through the lowest steps in this set of occupations, as is suggested by their average income, which represents only 61 percent of that of whites employed in the sector.

To suggest that racial exclusion in this stratum is more accentuated than exclusion based on gender does not mean that women are not discriminated against in these occupations. We have only to observe that white women in this stratum are more educated than white men but have incomes slightly inferior to half of the men. This indicates that women also face barriers to entering the hierarchically superior occupations of this category.

The fourth and last high non-manual category is that of other professionals. It includes all the other professions, besides liberal professions, for whose exercise a university diploma is required. The category includes a group of older professions of less prestige than the liberal professions, such as accountants, dentists, and pharmacists, as well as a set of new professions that are the product of the division of labor inherent in the most recent phase of economic development. Unlike the liberal professions, these new occupations do not pass through a historical phase characterized by the autonomous exercise of the profession; they are already born as typically salaried occupations.

The pattern of racial exclusion is repeated in this stratum, albeit in a somewhat less accentuated manner. The relative participation of whites and non-whites is 2.9 percent and 0.9 percent, respectively. White women are present in this set of less prestigious professions in proportions superior to white males, with 4.3 percent and 2 percent, respectively. The high representation of white women (and even the not inconsiderable presence of 1.2 percent of non-white women) is due to the great numeric weight of careers such as social assistants, registered nurses, and secondary and some higher-level primary teachers, which are characterized by being almost totally feminized and devalued in terms of salary. In short, this stratum can be characterized by racial exclusion and occupational segregation by gender.

The four high non-manual strata include positions from which power is exercised in Brazilian society, as well as occupations which are subsidiary to the exercise of this power. Social prestige and high income are the rewards of these positions in symbolic and material terms. It is in this set of occupations that non-white Brazilians suffer the greatest degree of exclusion. Just 3 out of 100 blacks and browns have access to these positions. This leads one to consider in more detail the motives of the exclusion of non-whites from the top of the occupational hierarchy.

At first glance it could seem that this is purely a question of racial discrimination in the labor market. This would be the case in which racial ascription limits recruitment for certain occupations or obstructs promotion or career mobility within these occupations. This kind of discrimination has been well documented (Silva 1985; Lovell 1989, 1992). Nonetheless, there is another factor that permits one to explain the scant presence of non-whites in the high non-manual stratum and which is related to education as a mediator of occupational mobility. One should recall that with the partial exception of the stratum of directors and administrators, a university diploma is almost by definition a requirement for recruitment in the high non-manual occupations. This consideration relates to the restricted access of blacks and browns to higher education and the consequent limitation of the number who are in a position to become candidates for jobs that require university degrees. Data published by PNAD in 1987 estimated at 4.3 million the number of people with a complete higher education in Brazil. Of this total, only 485,000 were black or brown. In this same year, among people ten years of age and older, 6.2 percent of whites and only 1.1 percent of blacks and browns had completed higher education. We should add further that this unequal access to university credentials is not likely to be corrected in the short or medium run, as indicated by the distribution of groups of color in university enrollments. Of a total of almost 1.5 million students who attended universities in that year, blacks and browns, who represent 44 percent of the total population, comprised only 16 percent of the country's university students.

One can conclude, therefore, that the lack of access by non-whites to the highest levels of the occupational structure is related to: (1) discriminatory processes that operate in phases of life prior to entrance into the job market, limiting the acquisition of a formal education, and (2) racial discrimination in the job market. The potential for social mobility among non-whites is restricted by discrimination and actions in the pre–job-market phase and in the job market itself. This situation is rather different from that of women, since they have already surpassed men in educational terms, but they face fundamental discriminatory barriers in the job market.

The next step consists in the examination of the participation of groups of color and gender/color in the two strata that compose the petite bourgeoisie. The category of owner-employers is composed basically of small and middle-sized businessmen in the diverse sectors of the urban economy who possess a level of capitalization such that it permits them to contract other people as employees. Demographic censuses and household surveys do not provide information about the number of people employed by these businessmen, and it is thus impossible to use this criterion as an indication of the size of their businesses. Nonetheless, there is no separation between ownership and control in most of these businesses. Self-employed entrepreneurs present a level of capitalization that impedes their contracting other people, mobilizing to the maximum the labor force of family members for the enterprise.

Compared with whites, non-whites are less represented among owner-employers (3.8 percent and 1 percent, respectively) and are almost on the same level of self-employed entrepreneurs (3.4 percent and 2.9 percent). The small participation of blacks and browns among small owners and entrepreneurs, particularly in the first category of employers, has less to do with discriminatory barriers than with the level of capitalization required in these occupations. Historically, the position of the non-white population in the social structure has not been favorable to obtaining the resources necessary for entrance into this kind of activity: formal education, levels of income and savings, and socialization in the practices of the small and medium-sized economic undertakings. One should further note the diminished participation of women of the two racial groups in the category of owner-employers. Their participation increases when one moves from the stratum of small-scale enterprises to that of self-employed businessmen.

Finally, the low non-manual stratum is composed of executive administrative functions, technical and artistic occupations, positions of supervision of manual labor, routine non-manual labor, and office work. The stratum absorbs 15.8 percent of the total employed population, includes a large female contingent, and is formed by a vast set of white-collar occupations, predominantly salaried, which are found in the middle range and low steps of the bureaucratic hierarchy of public and private organizations. These occupations demand the mastering of the symbolic codes of writing and basic mathematical skills, as suggested by the average educational level of these categories, which is around ten years of study and is clearly superior to that of manual occupations. If the administrative, technical, and artistic occupations still allow some degree of initiative and decision-making, the routine, non-manual occupations are characterized tendentially by the repetitive nature of the jobs.

In this stratum is located the natural border between the world of white-collar labor and manual labor, which is relevant from the perspective of the distribution of prestige and social honor. For women who belong to middle sector families, this set of occupations functions as a form of legitimation of the social status of the class of origin. At the same time, these occupations are the destination of many socially ascendant individuals originally from urban popular sectors. As already noted, in material terms these occupations are not greatly differentiated from specialized manual labor, as is the case with workers in modern industry, whose average income surpasses that of the last two categories of low non-manual labor.

Even when they experience a lesser degree of exclusion than in the high non-manual category, blacks and browns are also underrepresented in the low non-manual categories. Their relative participation in this stratum, 11.6 percent, is notoriously inferior to that of whites, which reaches 19 percent. On the one hand, the lower level of average schooling of the non-whites employed in the low non-manual stratum suggests that the educational deficit of this segment of the population limits the number of candidates qualified for this kind of job. On the other hand, the income differentials between whites and non-whites within each of the low non-manual categories, proportionately greater than the educational differences, suggest the existence of occupational and salary discrimination (career mobility) based on racial ascription.

The differential allocation of groups of color and gender/color in the labor market and the occupational structure reflects the patterns of social hierarchization in force in Brazilian society and is manifested in accentuated distributive inequalities. The unequal valorization of labor offered by these groups is elegantly captured by the difference between their average incomes. White women earn only 54 percent of white males' income, non-white men earn 47 percent, and black and brown women earn only 26 percent of this same amount.

A century after the end of slavery, manual labor continues to be the place reserved for the majority of descendants of slaves in Brazil. Contradicting what theories modernization might lead one to believe, the structural transition propitiated by the rapid economic growth of the last decades does not seem to have significantly decreased the socioeconomic distance between the racial segments of the population. The little available evidence concerning the situation of racial groups across time indicates that there has been an increase of racial discrimination in the labor market in recent years (Lovell 1992).

The disproportionate presence of blacks and browns at the base of the social hierarchy is due in part to their greater numerical concentration in the less developed regions in Brazil. Besides this locational disadvantage, the effects of racist practices are felt in all aspects of the life of non-whites (Silva and Hasenbalg 1992). It is in the stages of this cycle that precede the entrance into the labor force that blacks and browns have their educational opportunities limited. To less education, a resource that is increasingly important in competition for spaces in the occupational structure, one should add the results of racial discrimination in the labor market itself, closing the vicious circle that confines blacks and browns in subordinate social positions.

NOTES

[Ed. Note: As indicated in the Introduction to this volume, the Brazilian census includes four categories for indicating color: *branco* (white), *preto* (black), *pardo* (brown), and *amarelo* (yellow). Hasenbalg groups pretos and pardos in the category "non-white." In the translation, pardo has often been rendered as "mulatto."]

1. The only group found outside of the hierarchical order is that of agricultural owner, as the choice was made to keep agricultural and non-agricultural sectors of the economy separate.

2. The high non-manual category comprises autonomous liberal professionals, employed liberal professionals, public and private sector directors and administrators, and other high-level professionals. The petite bourgeoisie includes owner-employees in industry, commerce, and services and self-employed small businessmen. The low non-manual category includes administrative functions; technical and artistic occupations and supervisors of manual labor; and routine non-manual occupations and office workers. The industrial working class encompasses wage-earning manual workers in modern and traditional industries. The service working class includes all manual wage laborers in the tertiary sector. The informal sector comprises all self-employed manual workers, workers in domestic services, and ambulatory vendors. Finally, in the rural sector, one must distinguish the strata of agricultural owners and workers, which encompasses a reduced group of agricultural technicians and administrators plus autonomous agricultural producers and rural manual workers.

REFERENCES

Andrade, M. C. de. 1983. "Transição do trabalho escravo para o trabalho livre no nordeste açucareiro: 1850/1888." *Estudos Econômicos* 13:1.

Andrews, George Reid. 1988. "Black and White Workers: São Paulo, Brazil, 1888–1928." *Hispanic American Historical Review* 68:3.

_____. 1991. *Blacks and Whites in São Paulo, Brazil, 1888–1988.* Madison: University of Wisconsin Press.

Bastide, R., and F. Fernandes. 1959. *Brancos e negros em São Paulo*. São Paulo: Companhia Editora Nacional.

Camargo, J. M., and F. Gianbiagi, eds. 1991. *Distribuição de renda no Brasil*. Rio de Janeiro: Paz e Terra.

CEPAL. 1986. "Transición estructural, movilidad ocupacional y crisis social en América Latina, 1960–1983." (Mimeograph).

Eisenberg, P. L. 1977. *Modernização sem mudança: a indústria açucareira em Pernambuco, 1840–1910*. Rio de Janeiro: Paz e Terra.

Fernandes, Florestan. 1965. *A integração do negro na sociedade de classes*. 2 vols. São Paulo: Domus.

Hasenbalg, Carlos. 1992. "O negro na indústria: proletarização tardia e desigual." In *Relações raciais no Brasil contemporâneo*. N. V. Silva and C. Hasenbalg, eds. Rio de Janeiro: Rio Fundo Editora.

Hasenbalg, C., and N. V. Silva. 1988. *Estrutura social, mobilidade e raça*. São Paulo: Vértice.

Lovell, P. 1989. "Racial Inequality and the Brazilian Labor Market." Ph.D. dissertation, University of Florida.

———. 1992. "Raça, classe, gênero e discriminação salarial no Brasil." *Estudos Afro-Asiáticos* 22.

Silva, Nelson do Valle. 1985. "Updating the Cost of Not Being White in Brazil." In Pierre-Michel Fontaine, ed., *Race, Class, and Power in Brazil*. Los Angeles: Center for Afro-American Studies, UCLA.

Silva, N. V., and C. Hasenbalg. 1992. *Relações raciais no Brasil contemporâneo*. Rio de Janeiro: Rio Fundo Editora.

World Bank. 1992. *Poverty and Income Distribution in Latin America: The Story of the 1980s*. Report no. 27.

7 | Blacks in Salvador: Racial Paths

JEFERSON BACELAR

This essay has certain limitations and advantages in terms of understanding the trajectory of the black population in Brazil. Limitations because although Brazil is an immense country, with considerable variation in its historical, economic, social, and regional circumstances, the essay deals only with a single Northeastern city, Salvador, which obviously hinders possible generalizations. The study focuses on blacks in two distinct time frames and social settings: (1) the preindustrial society of the years that preceded abolition and (2) the modern, capitalist society of the 1960s to the present. The essay also has certain advantages because the specific situation of blacks in Salvador is not substantially different from the more general condition of blacks in Brazilian society as a whole: extreme privation of the elementary forms of existence, inequality in the labor market and the world of consumption, and the constant and marked presence of racism and racial discrimination.[1]

Blacks in the First Republic

Salvador emerged from slavery (1888) and the Empire (1889) without major alterations in its social and economic order, which remained largely the same throughout the First Republic (1889–1930). A new bourgeois order was not constituted, there was no large demographic growth, nor was there a large number of foreign immigrants. Blacks and mestizos made up the majority of the population, as they do today.

The city remained faithful to its function as a port city and its mercantile vocation, based primarily on the export of agricultural products. The industry that did exist was an activity "in involution," with a low level of capitalization and largely dependent on the mercantile sector. The city's economy was controlled by the high commerce of the export of primary goods (especially cacao, but also sugar, tobacco, salt, and leather) and by the wholesale business, which imported merchandise from other countries or states to attend to the needs of local consumption. Political power remained in the hands of the rural oligarchies, even when their representatives lived in the city.

Bahia was a stratified society in which traditional families of large landholders, wealthy merchants, high-level government employees, and politicians composed the central nucleus of the dominant sector. Formed almost exclusively by whites of European descent, the rare mestizos who reached the dominant sector conformed to the established hierarchy by "whitening" themselves. At the other extreme of society were the masses, predominantly black and working class, forming what was called the "little people" and the "riff-raff." Between the two was an intermediate sector including small and middle-sized merchants, liberal professionals, public servants, and employees in commerce. This middle sector included many mestizos, who identified with the dominant groups through their loyalty and solidarity.

Limited social mobility did exist, and, in general, ascension was possible within the sector itself, although it was almost impossible to penetrate the higher sector. Hierarchically defined social distances were maintained and reinforced by the traditional codes of treatment and behavior emanating from the dominant groups. They were the ones who established private power and solidified that power through personal relations, supplanting or becoming synonymous with the public order. These relations were characterized by the use of favors and concessions in exchange for subservience and an unequal extension of power based on the hierarchies and controls established by the "holders of power."

Despite the existence of free labor, there was no labor market. Workers were contracted not because of their professional qualifications or capacity for work, but above all because of their personal and moral situation. They should be "obedient, moderate, and good mannered." Forms of remuneration were always mixed—money plus food, housing, loans, and so forth—which reinforced the primacy of personal relationships. This is the society that reminded Donald Pierson of medieval Europe because of its order and stability (it is a shame that Pierson did not also think of feudal lords). And, not surprisingly, the dominant groups were not interested in change.

Still in the heat of the celebration—or in the drying of tears—of abolition, on May 16, 1888, the president of the province proposed the creation of a May 13th Society which established the following prerogatives: (1) former slaver owners determined the remuneration or form of retribution of the labor force; (2) former slaves should fulfill the contract (generally verbal) with their employer even if it was a simple reproduction of slave relations; and (3) those who refused to submit to labor contracts would be criminally charged for vagrancy. The social order was thus maintained without substantial transformations, preserving a paternalistic outlook. The private sector continued to define labor relations with the support of public powers when coercion was needed.

With the advent of the Republic, slightly more than a year after abolition, changes began to be made in the power structure, causing clear repercussions among the working masses. The extension of the right to vote propitiated a multiplicity of party factions representing the interests of dominant groups. Struggles between those groups generated a climate of political effervescence in the city, with each party attempting to form bases of support among sectors previously excluded from participation.

However, the mobilization of the "people," unexpected events notwithstanding, further cemented the established structures rather than providing new representation for the subaltern populations. Political clientelism, an extension of the private order and of personal relationships in the public field, divided the working masses, making the constitution of organized and autonomous forms of participation in the world of politics virtually impossible. The generalized control and manipulation of the public sector became evident and was extended to labor relations. Since the Constitution of 1891 established that labor contracts were free, it became the state's responsibility only to assure that they were fulfilled.

This broad process of domination of the working masses clearly affected the black population since blacks were the demographic majority in the city. With startling examples of revolts in their past, it became fundamental for the dominant groups to impede their social organization.

After abolition and the establishment of the Republic, racism became a "natural" component of society, with its discriminatory practices built into the social structure itself and constituted as the basic principle of stratification. If, with abolition, nothing happened in relation to the racial question, with the Republic the situation changed somewhat. Starting at that moment, blacks would have rights and duties before the law and society just like anyone else, and their equality should be defended by all, with the dominant groups having the responsibility to protect and sanctify their new position in society. This was accomplished with propriety and efficacy: through indignation at police violence "against a poor old man"; by strongly reacting to Epitácio Pessoa's vote, in the Paris conference, for the inequality of races; through the encouragement of protests against the racial situation in the United States; and by saying that others—foreigners living in the city—were the true racists. Brazilian racial democracy was beginning to take shape.

Racist behavior was internalized, however, in the daily life and habits of blacks and whites throughout the city of Salvador and a "pact of silence" emerged. The situation of blacks in the labor market, where they occupied the lowest positions, was not discussed. They were allowed access to certain professional categories that did not require high levels of qualification, such as that of "stockboy" in the city's major stores and commercial establishments. It was not a question of segregation in public spaces, expressly delineated in the field of leisure. Also left undiscussed were unequal forms of treatment and relationships between blacks and whites—an inequality expressed with all cordiality, of course, as long as blacks stayed in their place.

In view of the dramatic framework of accommodation, in a society with consolidated strategies of domination, what was the situation of blacks and the mechanisms used for their affirmation in Salvador? According to occupational data found in Salvador's cemeteries in 1892 and gathered by Donald Pierson in 1936 (Tables 1 and 2), a uniform trend is observable even though the data come from two distinct and different historical moments. In both cases, blacks occupied the lowest categories of occupational stratification and, in a generalized sense, engaged in occupations dependent largely on physical strength or that required a low level of specialization.

In a society whose social and occupational structure was openly discriminatory, raising the racial question was seen as both an affront to a social order that considered blacks "equal" and as having the potential for uncontrollable consequences. The road would have to be another one. For blacks, as employees, the road would be the acceptance of various forms of subjection, including the creation of the figure of the "good worker." Many blacks adhered to this system and, under the protection of the "holders of power," obtained a certain occupational and economic stability. Nonetheless, many others rejected such a possibility.

The disciplinary and subservient character of the reigning standards of labor relations conflicted with blacks' desire for autonomy and political freedom. Blacks knew that they earned little in the time and effort dedicated to labor that produced wealth for others. They had already had the experience of freemen who, through autonomous labor, "on their own account," had managed to assemble a reasonable patrimony. In the occupational positions mentioned above, one of the essential strategies of blacks in the world of labor was configured: their insertion into activities that made autonomous labor possible. In the primary sector this included work in the fields and at sea; in the secondary sector it involved artisan activities and occupations; in the tertiary sector there was ambulatory commerce, the transportation of products and domestic service.

It would be in these activities, vital for the city's economy (e.g., the transportation of products) and for the existence of the dominant social sector (which did not work), that blacks would imprint their mark, creating their own rhythm and the amount of time allotted to production. This, evidently, conflicted totally with the disciplinary logic bosses wanted to impose on labor. Even worse, this rhythm extended to factories, commercial establishments, and public service. The political formulation, or form of resistance, without confrontations, that blacks established in relation to the world of labor was used to confer one more negative attribute on them: laziness.

From autonomous labor, as confirmed in the information gathered in the period's Wills and Inventories, there emerged the possibility for limited accumulation of capital and a patrimony, not to mention the significance of black women in the constitution of families and capital. Blacks maintained a symbolic, interactive, and dynamic field of activity in a society based on the time and economies deriving from the "culture of work." A black world persisted in Candomblé, carnival, religious and secular festivals, cuisine, popular medicine, cosmology, forms of treatment and solidarity, samba and *capoeira*, and familial matrifocality. Although certainly significant in the construction of the "black world," an additional element of reinforcement must be added to free time and money: the cultural practices of dominant groups.

The dominant sector desperately sought identification with European culture. They copied the fashions and modes from the advanced

TABLE 1

Occupational Stratification, Salvador, 1892

(Number and Percentage)

Profession	Black		Brown		White		Total	
	Number	%	Number	%	Number	%	Number	%
Farmhand	13	23.9	16	27.0	2	7.4	31	22.1
Laborer	10	18.2	4	6.8	1	3.7	15	10.7
Servant	4	7.3	11	18.6	3	11.1	18	12.8
Cook	4	7.3	2	3.4	1	3.7	7	5.1
Bricklayer	2	3.6	1	1.7	—	—	3	2.1
Worker	2	3.6	3	5.1	—	—	5	3.5
Cartman	2	3.6	—	—	—	—	2	1.4
Blacksmith	1	1.8	1	1.7	1	3.7	3	2.1
Seamstress	1	1.8	1	1.7	1	3.7	3	2.1
Painter	1	1.8	—	—	1	3.7	2	1.4
Artist	1	1.8	1	1.7	—	—	2	1.4
Washerwoman	1	1.8	1	1.7	—	—	2	1.4
Domestic servant	1	1.8	1	1.7	—	—	2	1.4
Raftsman	1	1.8	1	1.7	—	—	2	1.4
Seaman	1	1.8	—	—	—	—	1	0.7
Prospector	1	1.8	—	—	—	—	1	0.7
Fisherman	1	1.8	1	1.7	—	—	2	1.4
Soldier	3	5.5	6	10.2	3	11.1	12	8.7
Fruit vendor	1	1.8	—	—	—	—	1	0.7

TABLE 1 (Continued)

Profession	Black		Brown		White		Total	
	Number	%	Number	%	Number	%	Number	%
Street vendor	1	1.8	—	—	—	—	1	0.7
Handicraftsman	1	1.8	—	—	—	—	1	0.7
Coppersmith	1	1.8	—	—	—	—	1	0.7
Carpenter	1	1.8	—	—	1	3.7	2	1.4
Tailor	—	—	1	1.7	1	3.7	2	1.4
Cobbler	—	—	—	—	1	3.7	1	0.7
Gardener	—	—	2	3.4	—	—	2	1.4
Maid	—	—	—	—	1	3.7	1	0.7
Starcher	—	—	4	6.8	1	3.7	5	3.5
Boat pilot	—	—	—	—	1	3.7	1	0.7
Public scribe	—	—	—	—	1	3.7	1	0.7
Sailor	—	—	1	1.7	2	7.4	3	2.1
Clerk	—	—	—	—	1	3.7	1	0.7
Tradesman	—	—	—	—	2	7.4	2	1.4
Weaver	—	—	1	1.7	—	—	1	0.7
Priest	—	—	—	—	2	7.4	2	1.4
TOTAL	55	100	59	100	27	99.9	141	100
TOTAL		39.0		41.8		19.2		100

Source: Map of cadavers buried in the Quinta dos Lázaros, Campo Santo, Santíssima Trindade, Brotas, and N.S. de Escada cemeteries. Municipal Archive, 1892.

TABLE 2

Distribution of Occupations by Race, Salvador, 1936

(Number and Percentage)

Occupations in which blacks are dominant

Occupation	Number	Black	Mulatto	White	Cafuso	Total
Porter	100	93.0	7.0	0.0	0.0	100
Washerwoman	200	89.5	9.5	0.0	1.0	100
Cart man	100	83.0	15.0	0.0	2.0	100
Bricklayer	125	82.4	16.8	0.0	0.8	100
Stevedore	125	81.6	15.2	1.6	1.6	100
Domestic	250	78.8	18.8	0.8	1.6	100
Street worker	225	78.3	21.2	0.5	0.0	100
Candy peddler	100	77.0	21.0	1.0	1.0	100
Cobbler	70	74.4	22.8	2.8	0.0	100
Ambulatory sales	200	68.5	28.0	3.5	0.0	100
Day laborer	100	68.0	31.0	2.0	0.0	100
Shoeshine boy	50	60.0	32.5	5.0	2.5	100
Streetcar driver	80	60.0	32.5	5.0	2.5	100
Truck driver	150	44.7	43.3	10.7	1.3	100

TABLE 2 (Continued)

Occupations in which mulattos are more prevalent than blacks

Occupation	Number	Black	Mulatto	White	Cafuso	Total
Barber[a]	150	74.0	20.0	6.0	0.0	100
Band musician	98	68.4	23.5	8.1	0.0	100
Garbage collector	75	62.7	34.7	2.6	0.0	100
Streetcar inspector	50	62.0	24.0	10.0	4.0	100
Streetcar conductor	80	58.8	22.5	16.2	2.5	100
Fireman	100	58.0	32.0	9.0	1.0	100
Bus fare collector	90	54.5	30.0	12.2	3.3	100
Taxi driver	85	54.1	31.8	9.4	4.7	100
Civil guard	150	54.0	32.6	13.4	0.0	100
Bus driver	90	50.0	27.8	17.8	4.4	100
Soldier	750	48.1	40.5	11.1	0.3	100

a. In this category, mulattos were predominantly light-skinned.

Occupations in which mulattos are more prevalent than whites

Occupation	Sample	Mulatto	White	Black	Total
Police Officer					
High level	33	57.6[a]	42.4	0.0	100
Low level	38	47.4	34.2	15.8	100[b]
Clerk[c]	350	55.1[d]	44.6	0.3	100

a. There were only two dark mulattos.
b. Cafusos: 2.6%.

c. Office employees, tradespeople, cashiers, etc.
d. In this category, mulattos were largely light-colored.

TABLE 2 (Continued)

Occupations in which whites are most prevalent

Occupation	Number	White	Mulatto	Black	Light-skinned	Total
Bank clerk	125	84.0	2.4	0.0	13.6	100
Priest	50	76.0	8.0	0.0	16.0	100
Merchant	40	75.0	7.5	0.0	17.5	100
Cabaret dancer	26	73.1	11.5	0.0	15.5	100
University professor	232	70.3	14.2	0.0	15.5	100
Lawyer	413	67.1	9.7	1.7	15.2	100[a]
Politician	60	66.7	11.6	1.7	18.3	100[b]
Doctor	100	63.0	20.0	1.0	16.0	100
Teacher	58	57.0	24.1	3.4	15.5	100
Civil servant	250	45.2	32.8	5.6	16.0	100[c]
Tradesman	325	54.8	27.4	1.6	15.3	100[d]

a. Descendants of whites and Indians, 0.7%; descendants of Indians and blacks, 0.7%;
   descendants of whites, blacks, and Indians, 0.5%; incomplete data, 4.4%.
b. Mameluco (mixture of Indian and white), 1.7%.
c. Mameluco, 0.4%.
d. Mameluco, 0.3%.

Source: Donald Pierson, *Brancos e pretos na Bahia*, 2d ed. (São Paulo: Editora Nacional,
1971), pp. 227, 228, and 229.

countries of Europe and even rejected the Portuguese. This was evidently an ornamental culture, out of place and entirely inappropriate for the groups that composed our society. It was adopted, however, not just because of dependence on European values, nor because it came to constitute a common social repertoire. Europeanization represented, above all, the establishment and preservation of social distances through culture. Clearly, this meant that as long as blacks did not publicly violate European standards of behavior, they could do whatever they wanted to behind closed doors. And this opened the possibility for the formulation of an autonomous black Bahian world with roots in Africa.

Blacks in Modern Society

Starting in the 1950s and especially in the 1960s, Bahia witnessed a complete transformation of its society, with clear repercussions in the lives of blacks in Salvador. The new industrialization, an extension of the industrial development in the southwestern portion of the city, provoked profound changes in the physical layout of the city. The modern companies established themselves in the Aratu Industrial Center and later in the Camaçari Petrochemical Complex with a significant concentration of capital and oriented themselves toward production of intermediate goods. This area became the dynamic pole of the regional economy. With modern industrial development, which required a superabundance of labor, the city's demography was radically transformed by the influx of large numbers of people from rural zones.

Alternative modes of production were crushed—although they still persist—by the new industrialization and modern services. Self-employment became a means of mere survival, although it was increasingly used. Jobs and the demands of the "culture of work" could not be turned down since there were so many people available to accept the limited number of jobs. The urban landscape, in turn, was transformed with a significant expansion of the city and a devastating "peripheralization," without establishing the minimum requirements in terms of services and housing for the poor population. The city was enveloped by a large belt of poverty.

The city is structured in classes, with a local bourgeoisie identified with national and international interests; the middle sectors and the new working classes (associated with the dynamic pole of the economy) concerned with social and economic mobility; and the urban working classes (not incorporated into the affluent pole of the economy) nurtured by a feeling of belonging to a group of poor working co-inhabitants. The local bourgeoisie is made up of whites and light-skinned mestizos; blacks and mestizos appear in the middle sectors and the new working class, but with blacks in general occupying the least valued positions; and blacks constitute the clear majority of urban workers.

In Salvador's modern society racial discrimination against blacks continues through spatial, economic, and social "peripheralization," which is rapidly exacerbated in these heady and colorful times. Nevertheless, with the introduction of new dynamic areas of the city's economy, formulations about race relations have been altered. Individuals are now categorized according to their position vis-à-vis relations of production and consumption as well as according to the historical position of the diverse groups to which they belong in the broader context of Bahian society. Objectively, for the dominant groups and the ascendant social categories, blacks remain linked to the lowest positions in society and are negatively identified through images, stereotypes, and common expressions.

The myth of racial democracy is reinforced in an articulated and legitimizing, rather than contradictory, manner. Its permanence has a very old aspect, now endowed with a new function, as a base, that is, the numerical expressiveness of the black population. Thus, blacks seem to be fundamental elements in the maintenance and growth of capitalist relations of production, which, with their "subtle" mechanisms of selection in the labor market, do not provide reasons that justify open discrimination. Correlated with this is a concern with the danger that the exacerbation of racial conflict could provoke in the heart of Bahian society.

The state ideological apparatuses, in their multiple incarnations, emphasize the equality of relations between different individuals and groups and promote an idealized image of Bahian society as a model of racial coexistence and humanism. Associated closely with racial democracy is cultural democracy, that is, permitting blacks to cultivate their African heritage. The celebration and exaltation of Africa and foreign blacks, so much to the liking of Bahian intellectuals, emphasizes, as a counterpoint to racial democracy, the cultural equality of races in Salvador.

What are the mechanisms, at this new historical moment, for the affirmation of being black in Salvador? Attempts have been made in the political field, but all candidates who based their campaigns on racial issues have failed. The participation of blacks qua blacks in the new union movement has run directly into forms of corporatism oriented toward better salaries and privileges for organized workers. The black movement itself, because it comprises a sector of the black community that ascended socially and has an intellectualized perspective, does not attract the poor and largely illiterate black masses. Furthermore, the movement's polarized vision of the Bahian racial situation (divided rigidly into blacks versus whites), along with its position of radical political militancy, implies a reduction of social identity to color, which distances many blacks from their daily practices and customs. Urban social movements, in turn, associated with demands for the satisfaction of immediate and basic survival needs, see race as a secondary issue. Thus, numerous spaces continue to be closed to the affirmation of black identity.

Nonetheless, something has remained alive, with a solid foundation; it has survived slavery, has overcome political reaction for more than 40 years, and, even confronted with "new technologies," continues to exist. This something is the real and lived history, passed down through cultural practices in the social imagination, with Candomblé as its central axis.

Starting in 1970, Salvador's blacks elaborated a new proposal for carnival, reviving in a contemporary form the old *afoxés*. Ilê Aiyê was born as a form of reaction to white carnival and with the objective of celebrating the values of national and international black culture. It was created in the working-class Liberdade district, with an enormous black population and "with Candomblé at its doorstep." The sense of belonging for black urban workers took on a racial component through the new *bloco*. Culture became ideology and politics in the construction of the social identity of blacks in Salvador. Its power of attraction was enormous because of its proximity to the daily life of the black population. In a dynamic form, African roots were revived and a sense of negritude was created in the dreadlocks, rings, clothes, and music of Ilê Aiyê.

Starting with Ilê, other afoxés and blocos afro were created in the city with a number of variations, but all retained the perspective of negritude. It was in the 1980s, however, that their primacy among blacks was affirmed, with the accelerated expansion of the city. The affirmation of negritude spread through the social body, as vanity and pride in being black, as well as the creation of determinate "black spaces," such as

Liberdade and Pelourinho, "invaded" the city of Salvador. Composed primarily of young people, they were united, they had strength, and they had a capacity for identifying themselves as a group. They no longer needed to distance themselves from their color, since they now had their own spaces, and they finally recognized the possibility of exercising their citizenship as blacks.

However, despite these unique, extremely positive aspects of the culture of affirmation of being black in Salvador, we must see the other side of the story. Unlike in the past, the cultural production in capitalism has economics as its central axis; it obeys an expansionist and standardizing logic, with a definite political nature. The culture of the dominant groups not only maintains supremacy, but also traverses the entire social body, seeking its direction and control. Its authority and capacity for dissemination—through tastes, lifestyles, fashions, values—is reiterated through measures of the government itself, which seeks to control the market of symbolic goods. If we cannot forget the negative role of the culture of dominant groups in relation to the subaltern groups in the first phase, it has now become a totalizing and coercive element.

The character of domination, however, does not necessarily imply—and this is flagrant in the case of Bahian blacks—an absence of creativity among popular cultures. It is worth emphasizing that the striking inequality and discrimination in relation to blacks in Salvador make their culture, above all because of its roots and firm foundations in their daily life, a kind of "response" to the whites' manner of being. Relating and participating in a cultural whole of which it is an integral part, black culture, as an alternative mode of social experience, is reinforced under the prism of contrast.

In this context it makes little sense to discuss questions such as "authenticity," "purity," or "originality." What matters is understanding how the cultural elements deriving from other sources and groups are incorporated into black reality and its values. For example, whereas in the first decades of the Republic the higher strata were the importers of foreign culture, today, because of the enormous expansion of the means of mass communication, foreign influences have deeply penetrated subaltern categories among blacks. The fundamental thing to understand is that these elements—Latin American, American, African—are incorporated and "function" adequately in the black culture of Bahia.

In Salvador, in view of the creative expansion of blacks, the dominant groups appropriate their referent, attributing a new meaning to it. The intellectuals are substituted with new forms of cultural dissemination, the media, the commercialization of the exotic, the different. The cultural production of blacks, above all in music and dance, is transformed into "portraits of Bahian-ness" and inserted into the capitalist circuit of consumption of symbolic goods transmuted into commodities.

The year 1993 marked the national and international consecration of Bahian carnival, with the diverse channels of media exploiting this different, exotic society: "axé music," "timbalada," and the "song of the city" of its muse, Daniela Mercury, "the blackest little white girl of Bahia," as she has called herself. Defining carnival as a basically black product, the image of an egalitarian festivity, the *extraordinary expression* of racial and cultural democracy, has solidified itself.

In truth, the mythical, romanticized valorization of black culture qua product has achieved various things, among them racial segregation and a total lack of changes in the position of blacks in the class structure. In Bahian carnival, unlike the daily world of our lives which has been prevalent since the 1930s, free and equal, a system is structured that is deeply concerned with gradations and hierarchies. The official organization of the parade itself is structured along lines marked by social distinctions articulated with the racial criteria in the formation of groups: on one side, the "blocos de trios" (popularly known as blocos of "barons," of "whites"); on the other, the blocos of the poor and the black, that is, the afoxés, the blocos afro, the blocos de índios, and so on. Internal social gradations and separate forms of participation are established in each group within the parade's global composition.

All join together in the world's greatest carnival—everyone participates, "each in his or her place." There is no social interaction among the groups, and ropes mark the physical limits of each. In view of blacks' affirmation in carnival, the middle and upper classes, self-identified as whites, react by establishing rigid criteria of social and racial discrimination for participation in their own organizations. The more that black values take shape and gain space in carnival, the more distinguishing marks are solidified, ranging from phenotype, economic position, network of social relations, habits, behavior, and place of residence, to insertion into the "group of whites." To further cement barriers, they seek to stress the sense of "security behind walls" offered by the easily distinguishable protective barricades (ropes) which separate them from blacks. While blacks affirm their negritude, whites do not want to "mix."

Finally, in carnival, the position of blacks in the social hierarchy is poignantly rendered evident, with the clear and marked construction of "white walls" by groups who identify socially and racially with each other.

Carnival, the festivity, is not, in my view, an extraordinary moment, but rather the exacerbation of the ordinary, which makes *visible* our society's destiny. The "black face on the screen" and the appropriation of spaces—which become socially devalued, I should add—dedicated to the celebration of black life have generated as a response among whites, "in all cordiality," the perspective of "racial homogeneity," in the social world. The reality is the presence of condominiums and residential areas isolated from the "impurity" of the surrounding society and, in turn, the separation of social environments, restaurants, beaches, and other forms of coexistence. Might this not be the road toward an "apartheid à la Bahia?"

The transformation of black culture into a product of cultural industry also has a great impact on blacks themselves. The industry makes the selection, the choice of groups and individuals for insertion or ascension in the artistic and cultural world, generating divisions and disputes within the black community in relation to access to the capitalist market of symbolic goods. The status and prestige of individuals and blocos has begun to be measured by their acceptance, by the stage of co-optation in the world of the dominant.

Nevertheless, a more serious problem has emerged from the current situation in Bahia, and that is the perspective among blacks of the super-valorization of the limited economy that derives from culture, confusing it with the full participation of blacks in the labor market. The point is that, besides limited participation of the labor force in the cultural world, there has occurred a reaffirmation and consecration of "natural" characteristics of blacks. Among dominant groups the process of stigmatization is repeated along with attempts to definitively characterize blacks as incapable of reason in such a way as to justify their lack of mobility and ascension in society and the world of work.

Culture is life and danger, strength and temptation. Those who were familiar with Salvador in the 1950s and 1960s, when "blacks knew their place," however, know the advances that culture has provided and the significance of being able to say that one is black. It has been, and continues to be, the path of blacks in the construction of their racial identity in Salvador. What will come in the future, only God, that is, Ogum, knows. But clearly many have opened new paths so that blacks will no longer be forced to remain in the kitchen or to ride in the back seat.

NOTE

1. This text is a preliminary and simplified version of the introduction to a study titled "O negro na Primeira República em Salvador: a luta na liberdade," which is currently in progress in the Centro de Estudos Afro-Orientais with support from the Ford Foundation.

Part	BRAZIL/AFRICA
Three	

As noted in the introduction to this volume, the African influence in Brazil is pervasive. Some African cultural practices have been transformed and are now seen as characteristically Brazilian, whereas others have been exoticized and folklorized as remnants of a "primitive" legacy (when not brutally repressed, as noted by Júlio Braga in Chapter 11, Part Four). While revolutionary movements in Africa had an undeniable impact on the emergence of Brazil's black consciousness movement, at the same time some sectors of the movement have tended to develop an idealized or "mythologized" view of their true relationship with Africa (see comments by João Jorge Santos Rodrigues, Chapter 4, Part One). The essays in this section attempt to go beyond these limiting perspectives and treat historical and contemporary relationships between Brazil and Africa in both cultural and political terms.

First, Anani Dzidzienyo traces the recent development of diplomatic and economic relations between Brazil and Africa, focusing on some of the misunderstandings and problems that have characterized them. Dzidzienyo notes that Brazil has not accorded African countries the attention they deserve, while at the same time offering an idealized vision of African historical and cultural traditions still evident in Brazil as well as of Brazilian race relations. Examining multiple facets of a complex question, Dzidzienyo argues that the insertion of Afro-Brazilian concerns into diplomatic relations has the potential to transform those relations, but only after "official" Brazil comes to terms with Afro-Brazil.

Art historian Henry John Drewal then examines the pervasiveness and vitality of Yoruba "transatlantic transculturalism" in Brazil since the late eighteenth century. His primary focus is on the way Yoruba philo-sophical concepts, artistic forms, and cultural practices have contributed to the construction of black identities in Brazil, and he discusses how they have been used in the arts, architecture, religion, and contemporary carnival to confront or resist a frequently racist society. Arguments such as those outlined in Drewal's essay should serve, at the very least, as a word of caution to those who perhaps too quickly and simplistically denounce the "culturalism" of the black movement.

In his contribution, literary scholar, essayist, and creative writer Femi Ojo-Ade, writing from an African perspective, discusses the need for Brazil's black community (and diaspora communities everywhere) to construct a de-intellectualized "new negritude." Focusing on a wide range of cultural, intellectual, and political models and practices—most notably those of playwright/politician Abdias do Nascimento, poet Adão Ventura, and diverse manifestations in contemporary Bahia (religion, the blocos afro, and literature)—he argues that for the black movement to be truly successful in defending the interests of the Afro-Brazilian commu-nity, black consciousness first has to become real, "not *moreno* (brown), but *negro* (black)." In relation to Bahia, the author notes both the poten-tial and pitfalls of Brazilian negritude, which seemingly has vast num-bers of adherents, but whose adherence is not translated into political action or power. He concludes, however, that "If negritude is to have any meaning in the Brazilian setting, Bahia simply has to be the starting point, or the center of activism."

8 | Africa-Brazil: "Ex Africa Semper Aliquid Novi"?

ANANI DZIDZIENYO

Two tendencies may be noted in Brazil's relations with post-colonial Africa. At once contradictory and complimentary, they are invariably linked, irrespective of how they are conceptualized and articulated. One tendency is official Brazil's presentation of an exemplary system of race relations which, in contrast to other systems, is devoid of legally sanctioned overt and violent acts of discrimination against Afro-Brazilians. The other is that, having introduced the race factor into its relations with African countries, Brazilian officialdom often expresses surprise and even frustration when either Afro-Brazilians or continental Africans draw connections between official celebrations of the country's exemplary race relations and the actual predicament of Afro-Brazilians in Brazilian society.

In the view of many Afro-Brazilians, official Brazil offers Africans a sanitized image or package in which African historical, cultural, and religious traditions are extolled and presented as evidence of successful integration, while providing little evidence that present-day Afro-Brazilians are in any way real beneficiaries of the system of race relations. What is particularly troubling for Afro-Brazilians is the lack of interest in including them even symbolically in activities transcending the obligatory interfaces between official visitors from African countries and Afro-Brazilian cultural institutions.

In the final analysis, the test of Brazil's successes and failures in Africa is inexorably linked to changes in the position of Afro-Brazilians within Brazilian society. It would be serious enough if the above were the only complex factor in Africa-Brazil relations. But there is another dimension: the lack of identifiable policy (or even rhetorical) initiatives on the part of African countries dealing with Brazil. For those Africans who do visit Brazil—particularly that most African of Brazilian cities, Salvador, Bahia—certainly the initial impression positions Brazil as superior to the United States, with its globally known history of "poor" race relations. At the same time, however, it does not take long for the most casual African observer to notice the almost total absence of Afro-Brazilians from vital sectors of life and society, such as politics and the economy. The unchanging nature of this "absence" and the strained explanations or justifications provided when the question is raised continue to perplex.

The lack of recognition of the salience of race—or its perception by sectors outside Brazilian officialdom in assessing publicly articulated intentions—results in a certain perplexity for Brazilians. Not accustomed to factoring Afro-Brazilians into their policies except as festival participants, they are unable to comprehend fully both African questions when they are raised and Afro-Brazilian criticisms when they are voiced. The relative powerlessness of Afro-Brazilians within Brazilian society and their near absence from the domestic and external policy process are axiomatic. The nature of the foreign policy process in Brazil and the relative paucity of "voices" outside elite diplomatic and business circles account for the Afro-Brazilian absence.

The link between domestic race relations and international African policy becomes salient in specific situations when African visitors come to Brazil and when Brazilian delegations go to Africa. On these occasions, ritualized reassertions of historical and cultural linkages attempt to smooth the paths of present-day economic and political situations.

In the absence of clearly (or even vaguely) articulated policies, a close reading of published accounts provides invaluable opportunities for analysis. Comments of African envoys about the Afro-Brazilian predicament, for example, reveal the gap between interest in "solidarity" with this predicament and evidence of minimal understanding of it. On the Brazilian side, the invisibility of Afro-Brazilians in official circles makes it possible for both the governor of Bahia and the mayor of Salvador to publicly proclaim, during Nelson Mandela's visit (1991), the absence of racism at the very moment when Afro-Brazilian spokespersons and social scientists contradict such assertions. This essay, therefore, sees the (potential) centrality of Afro-Brazilians as inexorably linked to Brazilian activities in continental Africa for reasons that are not always comprehensible to Brazilians or Africans.

It is not a case of either privileging or underestimating history, culture, and religion, but rather of considering them as consequential in the foreign relations process. Having first raised the race relations banner, Brazil cannot easily extricate itself from its consequences. Unfortunately, African countries have not seen this opportunity for what it is.

This study explores the intersection of history, culture, and politics, their manipulation by the various parties involved in the relationship, and the position of Afro-Brazilians as both the weakest link (actually) and the strongest link (potentially) in the chain. By posing and attempting to answer some pertinent questions, it may be possible to transcend the rhetoric that has tended to obscure rather than illuminate African-Brazilian relations. Why should African-Brazilian relations attract anyone's attention, be they Africans, Brazilians, or others? What are the changes and perspectives that make these relations important? Are there differences in the way Africans and Brazilians approach these relations? What is the relationship between domestic race relations and, more specifically, the position of Afro-Brazilians vis-à-vis all of the above? Do Afro-Brazilians have a role to play in unscrambling the conundrum? Does the presence of a handful of high-profile Afro-Brazilians with continental African experience make a difference? To provide answers to these questions I examine public discussions from the Brazilian print media, focusing on state visits by African leaders and observations by Afro-Brazilians between the early 1960s and early 1993.

Race and Foreign Policy

Ince (1977) has noted that as long as race is a factor in international relations, states cannot conduct their foreign policies without race or ethnicity entering the picture at some stage, however minimal. Although this may have little or no applicability in interstate relationships among all white or all non-white states, it is most applicable in relationships between white and non-white states. According to Prieswerk (1970), there are four areas in which race and color are manifested in international relations: (1) relations between states of different races, (2) domestic racial conflicts as a threat to international peace, (3) internationalization of racially motivated movements, and (4) the impact of racial groups on foreign policy.

It was Brazil that highlighted the importance of race in Brazilian-African relations. Having initiated these relations by partly articulating them in terms of the historical and cultural connections between Brazil and Africa, direct attention was focused on black Brazilians or Brazilians of African descent. If Brazil enjoyed privileged standing in race relations, in comparison with other race relations systems, especially that of the United States, and if such privileged status was a function of Brazil's unique historical development from slavery to abolition, which had been marked by the absence of legal segregation and discrimination in the post-abolition period, it would be reasonable to project a discrimination-free and tension-free society with large numbers of blacks whose integration into the society was a testimony to exemplary race relations.

For the African consumers of this image, the major attraction was what appeared to be impressive evidence attesting to the endurance of readily identifiable African historical, cultural, and religious institutions that also contrasted sharply with existing knowledge about the United States. From the mid-1950s to the mid-1960s, international press coverage of race relations, racial violence, and civil rights struggles by black Americans contributed to the diffusion of an image of U.S. race relations in which black people were constantly under attack. If U.S. officials could not escape critical inquiry and strong criticism from sectors of African society, both because of negative reporting and actual testimonies of continental Africans with direct experience in the United States, Brazil did not have to face such difficulties. Brazil could afford to be a "friend of Africa" without being reminded of past colonialist misdeeds and ill repute or without being remembered as a country where people of African descent were lynched.

Brazil was not a logical destination for African travels and explorations, either metaphorically or practically, especially for Anglophone and Francophone Africans. Even for Lusophone Africans, Brazil was not easily accessible because of political and economic exigencies. The 1958 World Cup in Sweden—when pictures of the Brazilian football team revealed a number of black players who would later become household names—could be considered a landmark in African perceptions of Brazil. It was not that black athletes and performers from the United States were unknown to continental Africans; indeed, there existed a keen awareness of the adversarial and dangerous conditions under which they labored. The infamous racial segregation and discrimination which framed the perception of black life in the United States and which had been broadcast and printed around the world could not be more damning. Brazil did not labor under any such negative imagery. The treatment of black Brazilians offered a very marked contrast to the situation in the United States.

But if this combination of history, culture, and religious traditions constituted an unenviable asset at the beginning of Brazil's African diplomatic initiatives in post-colonial Africa, there was no guarantee of permanence over a long period. As continental Africans came into direct contact with Brazil and became more familiar with the realities of Brazilian society and the situation of black Brazilians, a gap appeared between the official rhetoric of privileged historical, cultural, and religious Africana as a basis for exemplary race relations, and the material economic, political, social, and cultural conditions of people of African descent in real life settings. Considering the relative paucity of unofficial African contacts with Brazil, further differences would emerge in perceptions and interpretations between Brazilian authorities and black Brazilians, on the one hand, and between official Brazil and official Africa on the other.

In the period from 1961 to 1993 there have been "high" and low points in Brazilian interest in Africa, coinciding with definitions of Brazil's global reach or its aspiration to (medium) power status as reflected in scholarly studies and the periodical literature, indicating occasional shifts in position on the part of public actors involved in or commenting on these relations. On the African side, the poverty of ideas and initiatives has been conspicuous. One way to alleviate this poverty is to recognize and come to terms with the contradictory position of Afro-Brazilians within Brazilian society. That could offer the first concrete opportunity for conceptualizing and critically assessing African-Brazilian relations within a framework where history and culture are not detached from the total universe of Brazilian society, politics, its idealized articulations, and the critiques of such articulations by scholars, Afro-Brazilian political, social, and cultural activists, and the Brazilian print media. Indispensable as they may be to any serious evaluation of Afro-Brazilian relations, the discussion of abolition, the return of Afro-Brazilians to specific continental African countries, or the tabulation and analysis of the volume of trade between Brazil and African countries are insufficient. The recent boom in the study of Afro-Braziliana by social scientists has not accorded even minimal attention to the interlocking relations between national, transnational, and reciprocal dimensions of Afro-Brazilian, Brazilian, and continental African relations.

African-Brazilian Relations

In 1961, at the time of his inauguration as first president of the republic of Nigeria, Nnamdi Azikiwe spoke of Nigerians' regard for all races of the human family as equals. He added that under no circumstances would his country and people accept the idea that the black race was inferior to any other. Furthermore, it would not be in Nigeria's national interest to fraternize with nations that practiced racial prejudice, nor should Nigerians acquiesce in such outrageous insults to the black race. Any nation with whom Nigeria maintained friendly relations could be deemed to be disrespectful to Nigeria if it indulged in any form of racial prejudice, no matter the manifestation (in Magubane 1989:199).

When Prime Minister Kwame Nkrumah addressed the All Africa Peoples Conference in the Ghanaian capital of Accra in December 1958, he spoke approvingly of the presence of African-Americans in the conference hall. He urged his audience not to forget that they were sons and daughters of Africa, the centuries of separation from the continent notwithstanding, and that the political emancipation movements under way on the continent augured well for the former's struggles for human dignity and citizenship in their own country, just as their struggles in the past in the service of Pan-Africanism had helped the continental struggle (in Magubane 1989:200). It is not accidental that both Azikiwe and Nkrumah graduated from a historic black institution in Pennsylvania, Lincoln University, and lived and thought about the African-American realities of the 1930s and 1940s, as well as about the linkage between them and the worldwide position of Africans and people of African descent.

Although the international relations and foreign policies of independent African countries have not been articulated in terms which have centered on the position of people of African descent, there is no denying that both sides recognize a form of dialectical relations between them, especially relations with those countries in the Americas with a history of slavery and a significant presence of black people. An African representative in the Americas who ignores the history and present-day situation of African-Americans/Brazilians/Cubans runs the real risk of living in incomprehension and a permanent state of confusion. An African-American who is unable to identify and comprehend the strengths or limitations of history, culture, and religion in explaining continental Africans' relative lack of interest in the plight of African-

Americans runs the corresponding risk of thinking or acting out of context, ignoring the critical connections between African nations as sovereign states and the cultural bridges individuals might traverse in unofficial capacities.

Speaking to the United Nations Fourth Committee (decolonization committee) on October 16, 1972, Amílcar Cabral recognized that some members were duty-bound to be obstructionist in dealing with issues pertaining to national liberation in Guinea and Cape Verde. It was difficult to believe that responsible men were fundamentally opposed to the legitimate aspirations of Africans who wanted to live in dignity, freedom, national independence, and progress. In the modern world it was not necessary to be courageous in order to support those suffering and fighting for their liberation; it was enough to be honest (1973:15–16).

He was fully aware, as were the U.N. and the African people, that irrespective of their moral and political value, the condemnations and resolutions would compel the Portuguese government to desist from its crime of "*lese humanité.*" Hence, there was no need to ask for more violent resolutions condemning Portuguese colonialism. Instead, he urged all member states of the U.N., in particular Portugal's allies, the Latin American countries, "and especially Brazil," to understand Guinea's position and to support African peoples' legitimate aspirations to freedom, independence, and progress (1973:37). The reference to Brazil was clearly to official Brazil.

Familial links between/among brothers entailed certain responsibilities with respect to a clear understanding of both the problems and the solutions beyond the primary condition of brotherhood. Herein enters comradeship, a matter of conscious choice. Appreciating the difficulties, problems, feelings, revolts, and hopes of the American brothers and sisters and seeing connections between their struggles and continental African struggles are proof of understanding contributing to mutual solutions.

> And we are very encouraged in our struggle by the fact that each day more of the African people born in America become conscious of their responsibilities to the struggle in Africa. Does that mean you have to leave here and go fight in Africa? We do not believe so. That is not being realistic in our opinion. History is a very strong chain. We have to accept the limits of history but not the limits imposed by the societies where we are living. (Cabral 1973:72)

While continental African policymakers and their representatives may not actively or routinely incorporate what Azikiwe and Nkrumah had delineated into their deliberations, the possibilities of fully insuring themselves and their fellow citizens against the manipulation of history, culture, and race by American countries is minimized, to the extent that they are cognizant of the differences between official rhetoric and actions affecting people of African descent in these countries. Even when such realities are recognized, there is little evidence to suggest that, individually or collectively, African diplomatic relations have benefited from serious academic or popular discussions of the nature of these ties. This is the background for exploring African-Brazilian relations.

The time frame for the following discussion of African-Brazilian relations is the period starting with the independence of continental African countries between 1957 and the present. Although there is a much longer historical relationship which dates back as far as the slave trade and slavery in Brazil (sixteenth to nineteenth centuries), important as this historical factor is, especially its cultural and religious permutations, such factors are not central to any determination of the real meaning of these relations today. As will be shown, Afro-Brazilian groups in particular can make important contributions to African-Brazilian relations—as in the example of Bahia, where the dominant role of cultural issues makes it impossible for Afro-Brazilians to eschew some form of cultural activism as part and parcel of political activity. Not to do so is to risk marginalization from the overall Afro-Bahian population.

It is of singular importance that some Afro-Brazilians (freed slaves) returned to West Africa starting in the nineteenth century, arriving at an imagined homeland where their tribulations would come to an end only to become "Negros Estrangeiros" (Black Foreigners) in the words of Manuela Carneiro da Cunha (1980). How this factors into mid- or late-twentieth-century international relations remains to be demonstrated. The irony is that *both* official and unofficial Brazil have correctly assessed the significance of history, culture, and religion in African-Brazilian relations today. It is the relationship between the remote past and the present, especially in its significance for Afro-Brazilians, that separates official and unofficial Brazil. The readiness with which Brazil has resorted to using parts of its history, culture, and religion—and the high visibility of a Pelé—are nowhere complimented by any serious exploration or recognition of either Afro-Brazilians or continental Africans which uses the same data to demonstrate the unreality of exceptional historical/cultural factors such as Pelé to contemporary Afro-Brazilian life and their participation in the national political economy. Serious as this Brazilian liability is, it pales in comparison with the even more conspicuous absence of even rudimentary discussions of policy initiatives or popular discussions of African-Brazilian relations in African countries.

Brazil's African Initiatives

This segment examines the twists and turns of Brazilian initiatives as well as intermittent African reactions that have been and continue to be just that, reactions. Over the last decade and a half there has been a noticeable Afro-Brazilian "entry" into the discussion, manifested in the ways Afro-Brazilians in different parts of Brazil have (re)discovered or imagined both the African past and its present. This development is beginning to receive the kind of scholarly and popular attention it deserves. Far from being a uniform process, there are different regional, class, and political differences which in themselves reflect the Afro-Brazilian pluriverse. The continuing evolution of Afro-Brazilians' cultural traditions and the increasing articulation of their role separate them from both their African genesis and their historic Afro-Brazilian past. This has thrown official and unofficial contradictions into bold relief, especially conflicting images of race relations.

The changes in Brazilian foreign policy in relation to Africa cannot be divided neatly into "progressive" and "non-progressive" periods exclusively in terms of civilian or military governments. The "progressive" era of 1961–1964 started with Jânio Quadros's "opening" to the Afro-Asian world (the "pre–Third World" Third World) and came to an end with the coup d'état which overthrew Quadros's successor, João Goulart. It was followed by a return to Brazil's traditional foreign policy: close alignment with the United States and Europe. Although new moves toward Africa were under way by 1972, during the Médici regime (1969–1974), the full shift occurred under President Geisel (1974–1979). As Nazário (1983:3) has written, what was distinctive about the foreign policy of Geisel and his foreign minister, Azevedo Silveira, was a refusal to be bound by loyalty to traditional allies or ideological considerations that could limit Brazil's access to needed resources and its room for maneuver. This new policy was characterized as universal in nature, and "pragmatic" and "ecumenical" in perspective. This "pragmatism" was much less idealistic than the previous Quadros/Goulart policy, which Selcher (1981) has characterized as "showy." Whatever the nomenclature, it is interesting to note that what one military regime removed, another restored.

Brazil's relations with African countries over the last three decades offer clear demonstration of its ability to structure, examine, and attempt to restructure these relations in the larger context of its traditional foreign policy stances, its close identification with the United States, and its efforts to establish some distance from this mode. But none of these moves takes place outside the parameters of the existing international system, in itself subject to fluctuations, although without major shifts, that is, before the collapse of the bi-polarity of U.S.–U.S.S.R. hegemony. If the early 1970s were characterized by what Selcher has called "heady ambitions of major power status" (1981:101), by the early 1980s, the frustrations of coping as a dependent power with limited room to maneuver in an international environment which offered only negative prospects for growth were evident. The international economic recession hit Brazil at a high point of its international trade, finance, and capital. There were two simultaneous developments, governmental acknowledgment of reduced space and less flexibility for operation, and the emergence of a more sophisticated global policy and greater global significance, which included engaging in a wider range of concerns and activities, including exports of manufactures, services, weapons, and military supplies (Selcher 1981:101–102).

Alexandre de S. C. Barros's discussion of Brazilian foreign policy and the role of the Ministry of External Relations (known informally as Itamaraty, after the palace which housed the ministry in Rio de Janeiro) provides valuable insights into why Afro-Brazilians have not figured and do not figure in Brazil's relations with African countries, thus separating Brazil from two other American republics with a conspicuous presence in Africa, namely Cuba and the United States (Barros 1984). Both of these countries have sent black diplomats and officials to African countries, which is extremely uncommon in Brazil.

Having historically carved a territory unto itself as a separate and highly successful training institute, which in Barros's analysis performs a dual function of training (preparation for diplomatic work abroad) and socialization, not even the military regimes of 1964–1985 succeeded in intervening in the formal functioning of Itamaraty. That is, it was spared intervention, a fate that other ministries suffered. This was partially because of the armed forces' high regard for Itamaraty. The heritage and mystique of its founder, José Maria da Silva Paranhos Júnior, Barão do

Rio Branco, like the quality of training and efficiency, made Itamaraty different from other government ministries. But Itamaraty's self-image of its ability to modernize and renew itself is in question, according to Barros, because of the changing nature of Brazilian diplomatic and commercial activities, which require the use of more (non-diplomatic) commercial personnel, who become the equivalent of second-class citizens within Itamaraty (Barros 1984:33–41).

The challenge was more complex where Africa was concerned because of the variable of race and the realities of domestic race relations in Brazil. Barros does not address this issue; but he does assess the price tag involved.

> In Brazil's opening to Africa, the political price was to decrease the importance of relations with South Africa, and to use as the bridgehead to Black Africa the former Portuguese colonies, under the assumption that by showing solidarity with them Brazil would conquer the hearts of other Black African countries. (Barros 1984:37)

Surprisingly, Barros does not hint at any possible links between black Africa and South Africa and the perceptions of them held singly or jointly by the domestic Afro-Brazilian population.

Monica Hirst pinpoints the racial variable in Brazil's African relations (Hirst 1984). In her discussion of foreign policy and the democratic transition, she notes that no significant bonds had been fostered between civilian society and foreign policy until the banner of racial equality was taken up as a topic in the process of democratization (1984: 225–227). Another insight provided by Hirst concerns the heightening of certain contradictions concomitant with the balancing act between ideological fidelity to the purported objectives of the 1964 "revolution" and the evolution of a novel or creative foreign policy, in Barros's words, by developing relations with countries whose domestic political ideologies could not be tolerated within Brazil society (Barros 1984:35).

Did it make sense to cultivate actively relations with revolutionary regimes in continental Africa (e.g., Angola) which were coming to power with Cuban and Soviet support and with the kind of politics which would have been condemned internally? Hirst cites General Hugo Abreu, former senior advisor to President Geisel, on some senior officers who could not comprehend negotiating with African communities, adding the "pragmatic" comment that, whatever they were in the eyes of Brazilians, they had to be understood within the context of their recent

historical evolution, the realities of external support available to them in
their struggle, and, above all, the fact that they were men of honor and
prestige in their own countries (Abreu cited in Hirst [1984:225–227]).

Could the doubters of the wisdom of supporting revolutionary leftists abroad, especially African ones, have imagined the remote possibility
of the domestic Afro-Brazilian population exploiting this development
in the service of its own struggles for political and socioeconomic
inclusion?

If we begin with the premise that there are no international relations
systems which can be properly characterized as natural based on historical, cultural, economic, and political factors, and that relations between
and among nations are primarily predicated on interests rather than any
real or imagined links of affection, we are in a position to free our discussion of African-Brazilian relations from historical and present-day
hyperbole which does little to strengthen such relations in any meaningful way. We must hasten to add, however, that it is impossible to ignore
specific historical factors which shape these relations, although we
should remember that this shaping is itself only a function of political
leverage in the decision-making process and is intimately linked with the
degree to which specific national groups or actions are privileged (or
not) within the sociopolitical and economic structures of states at home
and abroad.

Although people of African descent have been in Brazilian society
from the beginning of the country's existence, it is difficult to pinpoint
any time when they have been considered central to the formation of
domestic or foreign policies. Even when the major breach line between
slavery and abolition is recognized, a straight line linking those two periods and the post-abolition era can still reasonably be drawn. As Nazário
(1983) has noted, Africa was a forgotten entity in Brazilian foreign relations from the abolition of slavery in 1888 to the new foreign policy initiatives launched by the short-lived Quadros administration and
continued by Goulart.

A basic post-colonial reality in Africa's international relations must
be recognized: to a very large extent, these relations are framed by the
centrality of relations with Europe and the United States which take
precedence over any inter-African relations and relations with other
non–Euro-American countries. Such privileging is itself a result of
historical, economic, political, and cultural conjunctures dating back
to colonial days, acquiring a new, even stronger lease on life in the

post-colonial phase because of the realities of the international system into which newly independent African countries were inserted.

Brazil's African policies have been based on more or less clearly identified and articulated national interests and their pursuit through a highly respected professional foreign ministry, with its equally respected and admired training institute. But these advantages contained seeds of disadvantages and problem areas in terms of relations with African countries. African students in the Instituto Rio Branco quickly learned that they were virtually the only black faces in the Instituto and foreign ministry who were not confined to service sector activities. Since the late 1970s there have been a few exceptions, and it is increasingly possible to see blacks in positions that could not have been imagined two decades ago. Unlike the United States and Cuba, both of which have sent high-ranking officials to African countries and, in the case of the United States, where African-Americans can be seen in areas of society which could only be contemplated in a futuristic Brazil of the twenty-second century, Brazil, perhaps unintentionally, has reaped the whirlwind of the rhetorical storm about "racial democracy" so readily propagated both at home and abroad. Given that even high-ranking African representatives in Brazil end up being perceived and treated like any other black person by Brazil's dominant society and its agents (such as the police), it is somewhat useless to revert to the same historical and sociological explanations for lack of Afro-Brazilian's representation citing class, not race, without explaining how it came to pass that the two are unconnected or separable.

A direct link exists between domestic race relations and the perceptions and assessments of Brazil's foreign relations with African countries. Herein, perhaps, lies the genesis of both the official and unofficial emphasis on culture and history, as well as the description of Brazil as the "second largest community of blacks in the world after Nigeria." The seductiveness of Afro-Brazilian cultural/religious manifestations for continental Africans visiting or learning about Brazil is coupled with the imagining and articulation of an Africa with no cultural or political specificities or differences.

The challenge here is to recognize and appreciate the historical and cultural imaginings on both sides without permitting them to occlude existing sociopolitical and economic realities. To the extent that it is possible to undertake the most rudimentary (re)search about African countries and societies and their recent histories, it is insufficient to celebrate this imagined Africa without paying some attention to the political, economic, and social realities of present-day Africa.

On the continental African side, it is difficult to detect any consistent initiatives aimed at understanding the present state of Brazilian society and the position therein of Afro-Brazilians. There is a lack of appreciation of the sociopolitical and economic impediments against which Afro-Brazilians have had to (and continue to) struggle. How else could an African diplomat ask why Afro-Brazilians were not doing much about their sociopolitical integration into mainstream society?

It is perhaps noteworthy that no African country has an information center, office, or cultural center in Salvador, Bahia, forever cited as the African capital of Brazil. Nevertheless, continental African dignitaries or functionaries occasionally pass through the city, make the obligatory visit to Afro-Brazilian religious houses, watch a folklore show, participate in an official lunch replete with Afro-Brazilian menus, and then extol the marvels of seeing Africa in Brazil. But even in the course of such visits, there have been surprises deriving from that fundamental contradiction: the existence of visible and impressive blackness in public spaces and the equally impressive absence of blackness from offices in government and business. Considering this inescapable contradiction, the three participant groups—continental African visitors, official Brazil, and unofficial Afro-Brazil—are inexorably led to the genesis of existing African-Brazilian relations: the manipulation of history and culture as support for symbolic relations which have minimal chances of becoming reality, at least until a semblance of counter-initiatives materializes.

Could Brazil's relations with Lusophone Africa be the harbinger of a change in Africa-Brazil relations? First, continental African foreign relations would have to be re-centered, raising Portuguese to the same status as English and French. Such a move would not solve the problem, but it would at least expand the quantity of available information. Lusophone African countries could then serve as the bridge to more concrete relationships. The commonality of language, history, and past colonialism are insufficient grounds for conceptualizing and formulating policy, but they are inevitable starting points. A further complication relates to the peculiar circumstances surrounding "decolonization" in Angola and Mozambique and the subsequent civil wars which have not made for optimum conditions in which to formulate or execute domestic and foreign policies.

What, then, are the conditions under which these relations continue to exist and what are their future prospects? In a recent analysis, Dunn draws attention to a two-sided "reality" in the Africa-Brazil/Afro-Brazil–Brazil configurations, that is, what may seem incongruous to visiting ethnographers is very relevant and meaningful to the Afro-Bahian public (1992:12). The point is well made, but, which public? Or, which part of the public? One person's "meaningfulness" at the cost of another person's "misrepresentation" is an issue that has to be faced squarely to avoid begging the question, especially when there exist possibilities for *counter* checking "images." At what cost mythic prefiguration? Can people live by mythic prefiguration alone? Historical accuracy is not just an academic issue. There are incontrovertible political consequences. This reality could be more easily ignored were it strictly the case that such prefiguration was isolated from present-day Africa and Africans who in themselves manifest all the continent's contradictions. This does not mean that each and every Afro-Bahian celebrant or participant in Africana perforce becomes a historian of Africana, but rather that contemporary Africa is seen for what it is.

Particularly since the early 1970s, it has not been sufficient for Brazil to pursue an exclusively cultural strategy in its relations with postcolonial African countries. Simply put, "cultura (só) não pega" ("culture [alone] is not enough") because of continental Africans' interest in the political dimensions of the relationship, albeit generally on a formalistic plane. It made little sense to be regaled with culture, religion, and spirituality, emotionally significant and pleasing as they were, in the absence of Afro-Brazilian participation. This conspicuous absence of any convincing explanation continues to rankle and breed skepticism. All affirmations about the absence of systemic discriminations against Afro-Brazilians ring hollow. Carnival may very well be the occasion to assert Afro-Brazilian identity (Dunn 1992:18), but it raises even more fundamental questions, such as why only at carnival?

Writing about Africa in the collective memory of Haitians, for example, Guerin Montilus (1979) has noted that under continued oppression, Haitian blacks kept alive an almost perpetual nostalgia for the "African homeland," and that the memory of Africa pervades the most diverse aspects of Haitian popular culture. On the other side, St. Clair Drake (1975:3)[1] has observed that there were mixed bloods everywhere who deplored their African ancestry, and Richard Jackson

(1975:4–21) sees anti-African prejudice as a common denominator in race relations in both Anglo-America and Latin America.

In the Latin American context, what Irele has characterized as the "rehabilitation of Africa" is the salient part of black affirmation. This rehabilitation is a way of refurbishing the image of the black man, permitting an open and unashamed identification with continental Africa rather than essentializing Africa or positing some philosophical "negro essence" as an abstraction unrelated to concrete living situations and interactions. If this phenomenon becomes designated "negritude," as is often the case in Latin America, it cannot simply be dismissed because of the absence of any direct connection to the original negritude of Senghor, Césaire, Damas, and others. Because it is relational, its contact with colonial and racial experiences of domination was closely related to African nationalism and, in Latin America, to cultural and political affirmation (Irele 1965).

The lack of clarity in distinguishing between the continental African and a Latin American counterpart accounts for the confusion when issues are discussed at cross-purposes, as has been the case in African-Brazilian relations. Because each side draws from and manipulates history and culture for different reasons, it has been difficult to delineate the domestic and external consequences for either side of the usage. Even in this entangled situation, Brazil enjoys an advantage because it has been more the definer of the nature of the relationship, real or imagined, and it has shifted the premises of this definition according to assessments of advantages and disadvantages at specific historical junctures. This contrasts sharply with the intermittent spluttering from the African side.

Almost twenty years later, in 1993, Italo Zappa, a Brazilian diplomat who had been intimately involved in the (re)structuring of Brazil's African policies of the 1970s and 1980s, criticized his government's decision to scale down Brazil's diplomatic representation in Africa. It was odd that Brazil, which has described itself as the country with the largest number of citizens of African heritage outside continental Africa, was in danger of returning to an earlier period when there were more Brazilian diplomats in London alone than in the whole of continental Africa, a situation which might be good for the diplomats involved but terrible for the country. The role of the diplomat was to promote the global interests of the country and not to turn himself into a (mere) ambulatory salesperson. Without denying the importance of trade, it was flawed reasoning to justify the presence of an embassy exclusively on the grounds of commerce. No one had discussed closing down embassies in Africa for reasons of economy, but rather in order to shift priorities to Asian countries. The budget allocated to support the Brazilian diplomatic representation in Paris alone would be enough to run the embassies in continental Africa (Gryzinski 1993).

A *Jornal do Brasil* editorial endorsed Zappa's position ("Missão Política"), and others also joined in the debate. Responding to Zappa's criticisms, Ambassador Lampreia argued that relations exist between external policies and internal projects and that the history of Itamaraty and Brazilian diplomacy is intimately linked to the very formation of Brazilian nationality. The increasingly broad range of Brazilian diplomatic activities in a changing world carried a price. In 1982 the foreign ministry budget had been more than 2.34 percent of executive spending; it plunged to 1.37 percent in 1987, finally hitting bottom in 1992 at 0.3 percent. The high cost of maintaining foreign missions, especially in developed countries, is an incontrovertible fact since the dollar is the medium of conversion, and its vicissitudes have serious consequences for Brazilian diplomacy (Lampreia 1993).

In the wake of Foreign Minister Fernando Henrique Cardoso's declarations about the impending redefinition of Brazilian foreign policy, especially in relation to African countries, Afro-Brazilian Federal Deputy Wagner Nascimento (Minas Gerais) addressed the more promising, hence beneficial, prospects for trade in a speech in the Chamber of Deputies, arguing that it was yet another demonstration of the disrespectful manner in which Africa and people of African descent were treated by the dominant society and culture based on deep-rooted prejudice. He criticized the foreign minister's insinuations about policy toward Africa, suggesting that Brazil's eagerness to insert itself into the community of first world nations was contributing to ignoring the country's blackness. Instead of leaking information that was likely to prejudice relations with African countries, would it not have been more useful for the minister to have explored more positive measures for strengthening those relations (*Diário do Congresso Nacional*)?

In expressing hope for a peaceful resolution of the Angolan crisis, Deputy Fausto Rocha raised the rather curious possibility *(sic)* that Angolan leaders Agostinho Neto and Jonas Savimbi might soon reach an agreement. Considering the fact that Agostinho Neto, the father of Angolan independence and the country's first president, had been dead for over a decade, Deputy Rocha inadvertently supplied further evidence for Wagner Nascimento's allegations (*Diário do Congresso Nacional*).

Senghor in Brazil

In September 1964, six months after the military overthrew the government of João Goulart and in the heady early years of African independence, President Leopold Sedar Senghor, of Senegal, paid a state visit to Brazil. In the course of this visit, he suggested the creation of an Afro-Luso-Brazilian community ("Senghor sugere a criação . . ."). He praised Brazil's constitution for its liberalism and the careful enumeration of public liberties and the power which guaranteed their existence. The newspaper *Correio da Manhã* underscored the significance of Senghor's visit as symbolizing the desire to establish cultural, economic, social, and political bridges between Brazil and the sovereign states of Africa with whom Brazil shares borders in the South Atlantic. Common histories, shared ethnic background, and shared objectives about the improvement of material life and for spiritual progress were strong enough to obliterate myths and illusions in the building of a common front which would be the basis for dialogue ("Brasil-Senegal").

Nevertheless, there remained certain knotty problems, such as the crises in the Congo and South Africa, each of which would require specific policy initiatives. Brazilians had to recognize the existence of profound resentment on the part of Africans in the matter of Brazil's foreign policy toward Africa. On the one hand, Brazil proclaimed racial democracy; on the other hand, it continued to withhold support from Africans on one of the most emotion-laden questions in the continent, apartheid. There was a brief discussion of Carlos Lacerda's "lack of manners" and "disregard of protocol" during Senghor's visit and the suggestion that Lacerda should encourage Portugal to follow the example of other European colonial powers in Africa. Finally, it was hoped that the greater interests shared by Brazil and Senegal (and Africa) would survive "the intemperate arrogance of a fool" ("Senghor parte . . .").

The period following Senghor's visit and proposal were marked by Brazil's espousal of a firm commitment to the Western alliance and lack of identification with African liberation movements, especially in Portuguese-speaking Africa. Before President Médici's speech of August 12, 1971, the influential newspaper *O Estado de São Paulo* previewed its contents. There was likely to be an imminent shift in Brazil's policy toward black Africa and, consequently, in Brazil's relations with Portugal, especially in the tricky matter of the so-called overseas provinces. It became increasingly obvious that Brazil could not gain greater influence in black Africa while continuing to support Portugal unconditionally ("Médici fala . . .").

Two months later, in October 1971, observations made by Senegal's Ambassador Henri Senghor (nephew of President Senghor) in his farewell press interview became a subject of debate. After six years in the country, the ambassador observed that Brazil was on the verge of great change, including in the area of race relations. Though he did not notice racist behavior among the ordinary people, it nevertheless existed as a residue of socioeconomic factors. Noting that blacks were always found in menial and folkloric roles in newspapers, advertisements, and so forth, he suggested that education must be made accessible to all children, for this would be a good way to tackle the problem of social mobility for blacks and mulattos. He had arrived in Brazil thinking there were no racial problems, but his subsequent experiences in shops and elevators and an incident in Copacabana made him see another reality. He was leaving Brazil with a lasting impression, that of Brazilians as a generous people ("Henri Senghor's despedida").

Carlos Dushee de Abranches responded that the ambassador's observations could not pass without comment because they reflected the opinions and experiences of a cultivated man, with black skin, married to a white woman and with children exhibiting the combined parental racial features. The ambassador's family lived among Brazilians from different backgrounds and situations. That blacks were absent from higher levels of Brazilian life was not due to any discriminatory policy on the part of the government nor to any obstacles created by middle-class leaders in society, but rather to socioeconomic and educational factors (Abranches 1971). Bluntly stated, the ambassador's analysis was incorrect. Apparently, an African ambassador who had spent six years in Brazil was not entitled to his considered opinions based on specific observations and experiences. Perhaps Africans simply could not understand Brazilian race relations. If they had interpretations that contradicted the conventional position, they had to be convinced to the contrary. It was a duty Abranches took seriously.

The above contradiction—between realities of race relations for blacks, even black ambassadors, on the one hand, and, on the other, the frequency of assertions concerning the absence of any official policy of discrimination, which is tantamount to the negation of such practices—persists with impressive stubbornness. In early 1976, Africans would cause the issue to surface. Two Senegalese students enrolled in the Instituto Rio Branco. "These Africans will be treated the same way as any other students," observed an official of the institute. Although no legal objections existed, an article in the *Jornal do Brasil* commented that the Instituto had never enrolled black students, concluding that that was why Brazil had no black diplomats, despite the absence of racial discrimination in the country, which has always been invoked in official pronouncements as one of the virtues of Brazil's social system ("Rio Branco matricula dois africanos").

Rhetoric versus Reality

In 1968 Adalberto Camargo founded the Afro-Brazilian Chamber of Commerce, serving as its sole president. Camargo's primary interest was to make the Chamber the vehicle of closer economic and cultural relations between independent African countries and Afro-Brazil, drawing upon historical and cultural links in the service of commerce. By the early 1990s, because of Camargo's loss of his political power base and because the attendant clout was no longer there, the Chamber had much less access to official circles and direct participation in Brazil's relations with Africa.

On the occasion of the Chamber's twelfth anniversary symposium, in November 1980, Camargo spelled out the intersection of history, culture, and trade. He spoke not only in his capacity as Chamber president, but, "above all, as a Brazilian whose ancestors came from Africa and brought with them impressive cultural traits which have made a lasting contribution to Brazilian civilization." What had hitherto been a "timid," "Platonic" relationship between Africa and Brazil had to be made dynamic. Africa was not just Brazil's neighbor on the other side of the Atlantic, but also his family, the Afro-Brazilian family. Brazil's responsible pragmatism placed it on the same side as anti-racist African countries (Camargo 1980).

On the same occasion, Foreign Minister Ramiro Elysio Saraiva Guerreiro said that Africa had a special connotation for his generation and for the 120 million Brazilians. In all of Brazilian history, Africa had been very present in different ways, including the giving up of her youth to Brazil in the past, albeit involuntarily, for the construction of Brazil. But it was necessary to recognize Brazil's limitations for technical cooperation with Africa. This in no way undermined fundamental fraternal sentiments toward African countries and the maintenance of mutual respect in bilateral relations between Brazil and individual African countries. He was in no position to judge what the relevance of the Brazilian experience was for African countries because he could not be anybody's teacher. What happened in Brazil was a historical phenomenon. Brazil was not a racial paradise, nor merely a multiracial society, but rather a society in which individual circumstances of color or other such considerations are irrelevant because persons are what they are, individuals. Hence, he characterized Brazil as a "non-racial" society. Since he was neither a historian nor a sociologist, but rather a public servant, he could offer no explanations as to why Brazil became the way it was. He could only recognize this reality for the good that it is (Camargo 1980).

Also at the symposium, São Paulo mayor Paulo Maluf's memories were of whites, probably with "black souls," who, with absolutely generous intentions, brought many blacks to this blessed land of Brazil. Precisely on account of this, Brazil had no discrimination whatsoever based on race, religion, or color. What made him proud to be a Brazilian was not the gross national product, per capita income, or the material progress of the country. He was proud in the company of other Brazilians to live in a country where, above all else, there existed unity, brotherhood, and quality of life (Camargo 1980).

What constituted the real basis for Brazil's relations with African countries and what could be done to improve upon what was perceived to be a lack of fit between rhetoric and reality? Adalberto Camargo complained about the paternalism of Brazilians in their dealings with African countries. Furthermore, there was a lack of both political will and persistence on the part of Brazilians who have not been able to capitalize on the expressed needs of African leaders for Brazilian products, especially in the area of intermediate technology, potentially more appropriately adaptable to continental African conditions than Euro-American products. Brazil was in a good position to serve as a bridge between African and Latin American countries. For his own part, Camargo had been engaged in an effort to encourage Brazilians to see Africa with their own eyes instead of through Euro-American eyes. It was fundamental for Brazilians to remember their African roots and to abandon the practice of assuming that Africans were not intelligent or that they were perpetual children, for such attitudes were a source of irritation and anger among Africans (Rodrigues 1991a).

A comment from an African rankled official Brazil. Patrick Cole, former Nigerian ambassador to Brazil, compared the position of Brazilian blacks to those in South Africa, suggesting that "Apartheid is worse in Brazil than in South Africa" (Rodrigues 1991b). Negative reactions to the ambassador's comparison included (informal) suggestions that he disavow the whole statement and instead blame the inventive interpretations of a journalist for attributing the statement to him (*Correio Brasiliense*, May 1991).

Januário Garcia, former president of the Rio-based Institute for Research into Black Culture (IPCN; Instituto de Pesquisa da Cultura Negra), addressed the apartheid analogy in response to a question about social apartheid in Brazil. If he were walking through a *favela* there would be no need for him to have his identification papers ready for inspection because it would be assumed that he was in his "habitat." But were he to decide to go for a walk in Copacabana, there was a good chance the police would stop him and ask him to show his papers. In other words, he continued, the situation is similar to that of a black man in South Africa who is obliged to carry a pass on him in order to transit through white neighborhoods (Bernardes 1990:6–7).

As far back as the late 1960s, at the height of military repression, writer Jorge Amado had touched on the subject in his novel *Tent of Miracles*, describing a proposed seminar on apartheid and miscegenation as part of the centennial celebrations of the birth of a local writer and folklorist who had been treated as scum by the dominant society while alive but whose memory was rescued as a national historical figure because an American Nobel Laureate came searching for his books. Organizers touted the forthcoming seminar as the "most serious scientific event to take place in Brazil." The seminar had to be canceled in view of the fact that the authorities would take a dim view of this attack on South Africa at a time when Brazil was working out new relations with the apartheid regime (Amado 1978:139).

Not all Brazilians interested in relations with African countries articulated concerns about linking the domestic predicament of Afro-Brazilians to these relations. Fifty-four Brazilian companies, together with fourteen South African ones, were added to the list of Felício de Paula, who was interested in promoting commercial relations with

Southern African countries such as the Republic of South Africa, Zimbabwe, Angola, and Namibia. In view of the fact that only 6,000 kilometers separated them from Brazil, de Paula was surprised by the lack of dynamism in this area. He was simply serving as an intermediary between (potential) buyers and sellers on both sides, though he was not personally involved in the buying or selling of goods. He was fully aware of the importance of respecting Itamaraty's sanctions against South Africa, applicable at that time to trade in arms and oil. He had taken a number of Brazilian business representatives on tours of South Africa (Rodrigues 1991b).

Marcos Francisco Ananias can be fittingly described as the antithesis of image and reality in African-Brazilian relations. An Afro-Brazilian businessman in his early fifties, Ananias is vice-president of Plantel, a subsidiary of the Levy Organizations which publishes *Gazeta Mercantil*, Brazil's answer to the *Wall Street Journal*. Fluent in both English and French, Ananias also serves as honorary consul for the Republic of Togo in São Paulo. He has spoken of surprise on the part of Africans at the conspicuous lack of Afro-Brazilian representation at executive levels in Brazilian society. Africans do not understand how the much celebrated Freyrean "racial democracy," extolled for both domestic and foreign consumption, always appears to exclude blacks from positions of authority and influence. This invisibility could not escape Africans in Brazil or Africans viewing Brazilians in African countries. And since it was central to Brazil's activities in Africa, what was to be done to change this image? Arguing that a fundamental change in Brazilian attitudes in dealing with Africans was needed, he suggested that the sense of superiority Brazilians projected had to be abandoned, for this unjustified arrogance rankled Africans. Brazilians in Africa had to realize that they were not the only smart ones around (Rodrigues 1991c).

Speaking on the occasion of Ghana's independence day anniversary in Brasília in 1991, Ambassador Charles Kwami Hamenoo observed that Brazil did not appear to have the slightest interest in maintaining serious, mutually beneficial relations with African countries based on solid links of friendship and diplomatic and commercial exchanges. There was a certain abandon in the way Brazilians treated their own products in Africa. The ambassador revealed that the government of Ghana had been waiting for a response from some São Paulo companies regarding an order for 100 luxury buses for more than a year. It was not the Africans' fault that the volume of trade was small. Despite significant

efforts on Hamenoo's part, Ghana-Brazil relations had produced minimal results. He nevertheless remained committed to improving relations
with Brazil, whose only interest seemed to be nurturing its relations with
developed countries. He referred to U.S. President Bush's address to the
Brazilian legislature in the course of which he had noted Brazil's constant
desire to sit at the table of the rich, something the "rich nations" found
irritating. Furthermore, Ambassador Hamenoo opined that Brazil did
not seem to take cultural-historical linkages with Africa seriously. In the
matter of South Africa, he foresaw no détente with the regime as long as
apartheid remained in place (Rodrigues 1991d).

Brazil and Lusophone Africa

If relations between African countries and Brazil are never far
removed from the activities or inactivities of Portugal because of both
the recent and remote past, could we then look to relations between
Portuguese-speaking African countries and Portugal as special and
potentially indicative of a newly energized set of relations between Lusophone Africa and Brazil, the country with the largest number of Portuguese speakers (150 million)? A reasonable response to the question
involves disentangling historical facts, mythological and rhetorical discourse, and straightforward pursuit of national and international interests which are predicated upon unequal power relations mediated by
history and language.

Portuguese-speaking African countries stand in relation to Portugal somewhat the same way as Anglophone and Francophone countries
stand in their post-colonial relations to the United Kingdom and France,
respectively. The most obvious difference lies in the manner of the final
"rupture" with colonialism and the colonial power. Where there were
"negotiated" independence(s) in Anglophone and Francophone Africa,
with the sole exception of Algeria, and the special case of Guinea-
Conakry, where negotiations took place within the existing framework
of the British Commonwealth in which British hegemony remained
intact, and the corresponding French community in which French hegemony is even more conspicuous, these organizations nonetheless provided the semblance of sovereignty without seriously upturning the
political and economic foundations of the relationship between ex-
colonizer and ex-colonized.

Considering the circumstances surrounding the independence of Lusophone Africa, especially the hasty final "withdrawal" from Angola and Mozambique, complicated even further by the arrival of the *retornados* ("returnees") and their visibility in Portugal (not to mention the frame of mind of the leadership of the newly independent states), there was little likelihood of the formation of an "instant" post-colonial community like the Commonwealth or the French community. This backdrop in no way detracts from the reality of Portuguese-speaking African countries, but serves as a reminder of their emergence as one more variant, albeit a tardy one, of the re-articulation of post-colonial international relations between continental Africa and ex-colonial Europe.

For Portugal, Angola—the richest but also the most devastated ex-colony—tops the list in order of importance, followed by Mozambique, no less blessed with resources but also with significant British and Italian investments. Cape Verde is on a secondary plane, followed by São Tomé and Príncipe. Guinea Bissau is no less important but is considered to be on another level. Through its membership in the European Union (EU), Portugal has the potential to serve as a bridge between Africa and Europe, although EU interests at the moment are focused elsewhere (Duran 1993).

The possibility of forming a community of peoples who speak Portuguese was mentioned in June 1993, in an initiative attributed to Brazil. A motion of support for the idea had been adopted by the Brazilian Press Association. The objective for creating the community would be to strengthen links of friendship and promote events above and beyond formal diplomatic activities, in the area of cultural exchange and economic relations (*Notícias* [Maputo], June 2, 1993).

On March 7, 1993, *O Estado de São Paulo* published a supplement, *Africa Especial*, with the headline "Itamaraty aposta no futuro do continente" ("The Foreign Ministry Bets on the Continent's Future") (Rabinovici 1993). There are 21 major Brazilian projects in Angola, 11 in Nigeria. Angola constitutes Brazil's principal trading partner on the continent (US $59 million in 1992; in 1991 Brazil sold US $35 million, $143 million including oil). It was noted that some differences exist between Itamaraty's betting on the future of the continent and certain private sector perspectives. There are 17 Brazilian embassies, but some business people in the private sector complained about the lack of regular financing, making it difficult to capitalize on initiatives. Because of the civil war in Angola, companies such as Odebrecht and Pão de Açúcar have been forced to scale down their operations. Some noted the inability to compete effectively with South Koreans, Japanese, and Germans on the continent. One company, Cotia Trading, had sold everything, to the tune of US $50 million in exports in 1992, to Nigerian partners.

No special "supplement" in the Brazilian press on Africa and African-Brazilian relations would be complete without an article with a cultural-historical focus. Antônio Olinto's "África é a outra face do Brasil" (1993) summarized historical-cultural linkages, including the veneration of orixás and the eating of feijoada. He observed that strong cultural linkages had not found a counterpart in political relations. "Culturally united, we are politically separated or unknown."[2] He urged Brazilians to accept publicly the African component of their society, implying that such public recognition had not been forthcoming in the past.[3]

Could such a public recognition be inexorably linked to what Selcher (1981) described as "more actors and expanding agendas in Brazil's foreign policy," involving the drawing of more actors into the process of foreign policy formation? To the extent that Afro-Brazilians become more actively drawn into domestic political processes and decision-making and are subsequently regarded as key players not to be ignored or discounted, there is the possibility of spillover of this "influence" into Brazil's relations with Africa. Ultimately the final question becomes: is there a future which has no past?

Culture and Politics

The uses and abuses of Afro-Brazilian religion, history and society, and cultural traditions, including its most revered figures, by the "dominant" society were vividly demonstrated in the official and unofficial ceremonies following the death of Menininha de Gantois in 1986, at least in the view of Vera Felicidade, a psychotherapist and member of Ilê Axé Opó Afonja Candomblé. Writing in A Tarde she sought to contextualize the public ceremonies following Menininha's death. Here was this most revered Bahian mãe de santo, a descendant of Africans who had been labeled and persecuted as "animists." Her sacred terrain had been invaded and profaned in the past by the police. Now in death, her holy space is again invaded and profaned by crucifixes, signs of a religion which she, like all blacks, had adopted to save her skin and her authentic religion. Until 1976, Candomblés in Bahia could only operate with a police license. Furthermore, other immigrants in Bahia—Spaniards, Italians, Jews, and so forth—were considered more capable of contributing to the advancement of the national culture, unlike blacks, who were pollutants (Felicidade 1986).

Incredibly, she continued, some blacks, having imbibed some of the very mechanisms of abuse, and in order to ingratiate themselves with local authorities, openly contributed to the exploitation of Afro-Brazilian religion and customs as exemplified by the invitation which Egbé Oxossi extended to representatives of the local power structure to attend the seventh-day mass after Menininha's death. It is not the Afro-Bahian religious community that needed to "thank" the authorities by inviting them to attend mass at the Rosário dos Pretos Church.[4] At the national level, Senator Nelson Carneiro in his senate eulogy of August 14, 1986, talked about Mãe Menininha, "leaving behind a great lesson in humanity and the assurance that in Bahia religious faiths of different kinds are freely followed and practiced, contributing to the attraction of tourists to the city. . . . Mãe Menininha made a contribution to anthropological studies, thereby enriching Brazilian culture, especially with regard to race and black religions in Bahia" (Felicidade 1986).

Felicidade took exception to the above portrayal of Mãe Menininha as a poor black woman who was full of goodness, who lived and died in the mystical, folkloric, and tourist city of Salvador. Such characterization contributed to maintaining jaded stereotypes. In conclusion, she argued that lucid consciences are, of necessity, critical consciences. She and people like her were not so naive as to believe that firmly rooted prejudices were transformed overnight. There was a continuing need for struggle and vigilance (Felicidade 1986).

Jim Wafer and Hédimo Rodrigues Santana (1990) have explored the interconnections between culture, religion, and politics within the Afro-Brazilian universe and the meanings of Africa therein. "What is Africa?" they ask. They suggest that "answers to this question have to be understood in terms of the cultural politics—at local, national, and international levels—in which 'Africa' is the subject of definition." Brazilian perceptions of Africa have been the product of the interaction between two antithetical movements, one concerned with Brazilian national unity, the other with Brazilian cultural heterogeneity. An unintended consequence of such constructions is that, while often intended to combat racism, they have in fact contributed to the continuing disempowerment of black Brazilians. It is for this reason that the debate about Africa needs to be reconceptualized if it is to make any contribution to the course of justice for black Brazilians. As Wafer and Santana put it:

> One solution to this paradox would be to say that the Africa and the Brazil of the spirit world are mythological and therefore have an epistemological status different to that of the real Africa and the real Brazil. But we want to take a different tack. What we propose to do is to treat the "real Africa" and the "real Brazil" as themselves "imagined communities" . . . communities, moreover, that have been imagined differently at various periods of Brazilian history by various actors on the stage of Brazilian cultural politics. (Wafer and Santana 1990:99)

Once these communities have been imagined, do they continue to be merely imagined or do they take concrete shape in the minds and lives of those who inhabit them? And do we not then have to proceed beyond that which has been "imagined?" Otherwise, to adhere to the notion of nations being imagined communities becomes both conceptually and politically too restrictive (to a fault). Imagined or not, once they come into being as entities with political, economic, and other accoutrements, their imagined genesis is not a sufficient explanation.

When Ambassador Yaiyeola Joseph Lewu of Nigeria made an official visit to Salvador, Bahia, in July 1991, in order to get to know Bahia better, he set off a minor storm with pointed remarks directed at the Afro-Bahian community. He was disappointed to see the "brothers" in such lowly positions in this country. What was wrong with them? Why had they remained immobile instead of making significant contributions to the development of the country? They could not look to government to solve their problems. The answer lay in themselves. They needed to work hard and to vote for black candidates in elections ("Embaixador nigeriano . . .").

He made it quite clear that he was not advocating engaging in revolutionary activities to reach these objectives. His aim, he insisted, was to encourage blacks in Bahia to affirm their worth as human beings. His remarks were delivered on the premises of one of Bahia's historic black organizations, the Sociedade Protetora dos Válidos, founded in 1832 to help secure freedom for slaves and act as a mutual benefit association providing welfare for members and their dependents. By the early 1970s, the organization's membership was made up of senior citizens who were unlikely to be involved in the Movimento Negro, and for this reason the audience hearing the ambassador's remarks did not include younger representatives of the Movimento. In fact, a member of the Council of Black Organizations expressed indignation at the fact that none of their group had been invited to the session with the ambassador. State Secretary of Justice Maron Agle, representing Governor Antônio Carlos Magalhães, had not been there to welcome the ambassador: he actually walked in during the speech to polite hand clapping! Time limitations made it impossible for the ambassador to meet with members of the black organizations, but he suggested that they voice their opinions shortly thereafter when Nelson Mandela was scheduled to arrive in Salvador ("Embaixador nigeriano . . .").

Nelson Mandela in Brazil

It is arguable that in the annals of recent relations between Brazil and Africa no single event has succeeded in bringing to the Brazilian public the complex domestic and international variables, replete with contradictions, the uses and abuses of history and culture, official rhetoric, and actual performance in African-Brazilian relations as the visit of Nelson Mandela to Brazil in the summer of 1991. He was not, properly speaking, a head of state, but he was accorded all the honors reserved for heads of state. Since official visits and programs for visiting dignitaries are organized and implemented by senior officials in national, state, and local government in whose ranks Afro-Brazilians are conspicuous by their absence, it was not surprising that there would be a difference in expectation and access to Mandela between official representatives and the representatives of Afro-Brazilian groups who saw Mandela as a "brother" in struggle, an incontrovertible symbol for their own struggles in Brazil. News about his courage, endurance, and charisma had long preceded him. Afro-Brazilians had a special reason for celebrating his coming. As they increasingly sought to insert their predicament into a global comparative framework, the South African model of race relations—which was theoretically the polar opposite of Brazil's—had provided food for thought and Mandela as symbol and proof positive of resistance to racism was doubly inspirational.

When Mandela finally arrived, Afro-Brazilians found their access to him blocked by officialdom. Some Afro-Brazilians thought that official proclamations about pride in Africa's links to Brazil (historically and culturally) and the absence of "racial prejudice" in Brazil and pride in

Mandela's heroic status did not help them get close to Mandela or Africa. Salvador, Bahia, the "headquarters" of Africa in Brazil, lived through these contradictions during the eight hours of Mandela's visit to the most African of Brazilian cities.

In what may be characterized as a latter-day version of the expression, "para o inglês ver" (just for the British to see, or "just for show"), Mandela's Bahia visit was very much a case of "para o africano ver" (just for the African to see). Save for one picture of his hugging an elderly *baiana* at the Governor's Palace, there were no pictures of him in close contact with Afro-Bahians. Granted that the local black community had mobilized and been mobilized to travel to the airport with placards and drums to welcome the Great Brother from Africa, the most they could see, for security reasons, was a glimpse of Mandela as the limousine drove past (*Tribuna da Bahia*, August 2, 1991).

There was no doubt, however, that by the time he arrived in Bahia, he had overcome some of the initial misadventures which had characterized his initial arrival in Rio de Janeiro. He had praised Brazil's multiracial society, for example, holding it up as a model South Africa could emulate. Speaking about the lack of access Afro-Brazilians in Rio had to Mandela, Benedita da Silva, the Afro-Brazilian Workers' Party member of the Chamber of Deputies, had commented: "We live in a mythological racial democracy, but there is apartheid here." This was her response to the fact that a number of Afro-Brazilians were denied access at a reception for Mandela at the Governor's Palace in Rio de Janeiro. Many Afro-Brazilians and some other Brazilians in Rio had been astonished. Black organizations also protested the paucity of time allotted to them to meet with Mandela and blamed the government of Rio de Janeiro for this. Governor Brizola warned everyone to be mindful of Mandela's age and health (*Tribuna da Bahia* [Especial], August 2, 1991, p. 10).

Mandela's party arrived in Salvador in an "effervescent climate" described in press coverage as Salvador's reaffirmation of its "negritude." The city honored Mandela in several ways. For his part, he spoke forcefully in support of the black population and against all forms of racial discrimination. Salvador was described as the city with the third largest concentration of blacks in the world outside continental Africa, with no indication of which cities were ranked numbers one and two (*A Tarde*, August 3, 1991, p. 1).

But the visit, originally billed to last three days, was reduced to seven-and-a-half hours. José Lopes dos Santos is a 49-year-old printer nicknamed "Mandela" by colleagues because of his physical resemblance to Nelson Mandela. But this fact had not been sufficient motivation for him to learn more about the real Mandela. All he knew was that the African National Congress leader had been jailed for protecting blacks. With hopefulness, he contemplated how Mandela's coming to Bahia could work to his advantage in life's lottery. Perhaps he could be invited to play Mandela in an advertising campaign or a film (*A Tarde*, August 3, 1991, p. 3).

Mandela revealed that both Alceu Collares, governor of Rio Grande do Sul, and Brizola had openly admitted to him that racial prejudice existed in their states and that they were both committed to doing away with this problem. Mandela called Brazil a "brotherly country" and cited the victory of democracy over dictatorship by the Brazilian nation as an inspiration for Africa and all oppressed populations. Brazil had taken a step forward by inserting an anti-discrimination provision into the new constitution. However, he had the sense that not all problems had been successfully handled. Illiteracy and poverty were still worldwide problems. Without wanting to meddle in Brazil's internal affairs, he could not avoid saying that the local black population was not fully integrated into the economic structures of the country. His message to the anti-racist movement was: "We salute you and support all communities fighting for racial equality in all spheres." He called for an end to racism and the building of a more just society. He reminded his audience that the struggle was a long one because racism did not simply roll over and die, nor could it easily be cast under a rug or subjected to plastic surgery to remove some of its ugly features. It degraded both victims and perpetrators. His aim was to see a non-racist society which was democratic and in which all people can live in mutual solidarity.[5]

Governor Antônio Carlos Magalhães declared that there were only exceptional cases of racial prejudice in Brazil. "It does not and will not exist in Bahia" ("Governador nega discriminação"). Dom Lucas Mendes, Cardinal Archbishop and Primate of Brazil, saw similarities between Mandela's objectives to unify all peoples and to fight against discrimination and the position of the Catholic Church on these issues. But what was the actual state of race relations in Salvador, Bahia, when Mandela came?

Mayor Fernando José had said that there was integration, not discrimination, in Salvador. Having lived in this city from birth, he could calmly attest to the absence of racial discrimination. There was no other

Brazilian city that had so many reasons for celebrating Mandela's visit as Salvador, the city with the largest black population in Brazil.

> In Salvador today all African origins in culture, in the arts, and in music have been conserved. In Salvador, blacks, whites, mulattos, and mestizos live in perfect harmony: this is what Mandela preaches and we are saying. He is at home. We want the whole world to live this way, especially those in South Africa. ("Prefeito diz . . .")

The mayor's vision of a perfectly integrated city was not shared by Antônio Carlos Vovô, president of Ilê Aiyê, who commented that it was only during carnival that blacks and whites really intermingled. Day-to-day interactions always resulted in prejudice toward the blacks, he concluded. Clearly, this was far away from the roseate visions enunciated by the governor and the mayor (*Tribuna da Bahia* [Especial], August 4, 1991, p. 2).[6]

The Black Movement spelled out the difficulties affecting black Brazilian lives in an open letter to Mandela. What kind of democracy is this in which there has never been a black president, under which a black worker earns 40 percent of a white worker's salary? It was a pity, the letter continued, that it had not been possible for Mandela's party to visit schools and hospitals in states of disrepair or complete destruction, or to see slum settlements, to appreciate the kinds of policies which reduced blacks to living in the equivalent of the Bantustans in South Africa. More than twelve black groups participated in activities surrounding Mandela's visit.[7] Mandela's presence was a source of inspiration for their own struggles just as they continued to manifest their solidarity in the struggle against apartheid.

João Jorge Rodrigues of Olodum emphasized the *solidarity* extant in the mutual struggle against "the sickness of racism" ("O racismo cínico"). Afro-Brazilian groups denounced what they characterized as a form of apartheid existing both in Bahia and in Brazil, although it was camouflaged by socioeconomic inequalities. They quoted from the data of the Brazilian Institute of Geography and Statistics (IBGE) with reference to differential living standards, access to education, and jobs, which were all racially coded. They asked, "Who are the majority of the poor?" (Lopes 1991a). In the same article, Júlio Braga, the director of the Centro de Estudos Afro-Orientais (CEAO), observed that the high cost of living makes life hard in Bahia, especially for blacks. In Bahian politics black representation is almost insignificant, and some blacks who make it in politics get there with virtually no commitment to the cause of the black population. And there were some who were black but did not know it—"outros são negros e nem sabem."

Jônatas Conceição of the Unified Black Movement (MNU) argued that blacks did not have to accept pittance from whites in the struggle for (racial and social) justice. Fighting on different fronts was not mutually exclusive with fighting for society at large. There were no miracles in the offing. Those who think the situation of the Black Movement today is bad should think back to only 1978. There is an incontrovertible reality: the absorption by black folk of society's anti-black images, that is, the internalizing of hegemonic ideas by the "people" (Lopes 1991a).

Official Brazil might not deviate from its appointed task of promoting its objectives in relations with African countries, part of whose articulation is the extolling of the virtues of Brazilian race relations and the honoring of African historical and cultural traditions in the country with the "second largest black population in the world." But it is not difficult to puncture this image and rhetoric because of the conspicuous lack of evidence attesting to how present-day Afro-Brazilians feature in this scenario. To the extent that a gap persists between proclamations and actual behavior, there is no way out for Brazil, officially and unofficially, but to address the issue of the predicament of Afro-Brazilians if only because, in international relations, attention is readily drawn to the issue. Afro-Brazilians, especially Afro-Brazilian political activists who see beyond historical and cultural manifestations of Africana and Afro-Braziliana, consistently raise questions about the one-sidedness of the situation, equating it to being on a constantly frustrating treadmill. On the one hand, they expect a certain amount of understanding and solidarity from African officialdom in Brazil; on the other hand, such African action is not usually forthcoming because of a fundamental problem: the absence of a clearly articulated position vis-à-vis Afro-Braziliana.

In practical terms, therefore, official Africa ends up espousing the same historical-cultural platitudes as if they had no bearing on the present-day Afro-Brazilian predicament, save for the occasional public voicing of frustration which is quickly characterized by official Brazil as "non-diplomatic." The way out of this conundrum might well lie in creatively challenging the historical-cultural evocations and linking them to present-day society and realities.

If African-Brazilian relations are different from, say, African-German relations because of history and culture, then these have to be examined at some length. Otherwise, it might be more meaningful to treat these relations as any other bilateral relations freed from mystification and hyperbole at both official and unofficial levels. The challenge at the unofficial level is something else. Neither slavery, abolition, nor the return of Afro-Brazilians to settle in West Africa, important as they are, have any direct bearing on present-day African-Brazilian relations unless and until Afro-Brazilians themselves make a real issue of it and succeed in inserting their perspective into internal Brazilian political discourse, especially in their race relations manifestations. It will take much more than demographic data, shifts in earning power and income, and differences in color classifications to get there. Herein, precisely, lies the interconnectedness of official, unofficial, cultural, economic, and political activities and the exigency of transcending the boring, repetitive shibboleths such as "Brazil as the country with the second largest black population in the world," which sounds impressive but which, until now, has been of no real consequence for either Afro-Brazilians or continental Africans.

At least from the Brazilian end, we have some evidence of twists and turns in intermittent efforts to deal with post-colonial Africa. The gaping hole remains on the African side. Perhaps at some future date (near rather than remote future) it might be possible to write about Africa's views of Brazil's shifting initiatives. A starting point on this journey would be coming to terms with the reality of Afro-Brazil within Brazil today. It is possible. There is always something new coming out of Africa.

NOTES

1. Blake writes the following: "C. Eric Lincoln had noted three decades ago that in the American Negro groups of highest and lowest status, hardly anyone wants to be a 'Negro'. Upper class Negroes seek to identify themselves with the white society, lower class Negroes prefer to identify themselves with any group except the whites in order to escape the danger and humiliation that all Negroes incur."

2. Olinto served as Brazilian cultural attaché in Lagos, Nigeria, in the 1960s and occupied the same position in London. He is the author of *A Casa d'Água* (The Water House) which discusses transformations in the life of returning Afro-Brazilians to West Africa and their West African progeny.

3. For historical-cultural links see (also) Pierre Verger's comments in *Jornal da Exposição*, where he discusses his discoveries and offers reflections on mutual reciprocities.

4. A famous church under the protection of the patron saint of blacks, Rosário dos Pretos is located in the historic Pelourinho district of Salvador, Bahia.

5. See Lopes 1991b. Mandela did not address Brazilian race relations directly but he referred to "preconceito velado" (veiled prejudice). See also "Elogio à constituição," *A Tarde*, August 4, 1991, p. 3.

6. In a June 1993 *Veja* interview, João Jorge Rodrigues, the president of Olodum, said, "There is an invisible wall separating blacks and whites in Brazil. It is an apartheid not based on written law" ("O racismo cínico").

7. Among these groups were União dos Negros Pela Igualdade, Grupo Niker Okan, Grupo de Estudos de Capoeira Angola João Pequeno, Afoxé Obá Dudú, and Ilê Aiyê.

REFERENCES

Abranches, Carlos A. Dushee de. 1971. "Perdão embaixador." *Jornal do Brasil* (October 16).

Amado, Jorge. *Tent of Miracles*. 1978. Tr. Barbara Shelby. New York: Avon Bard. Originally published in Portuguese in 1969.

Barros, Alexandre de S. C. 1984. "The Formulation and Implementation of Brazilian Foreign Policy: Itamaraty and the New Actors." In Heraldo Muñoz and Joseph S. Tulchin, eds., *Latin American Nations in World Politics*, pp. 30–44. Boulder and London: Westview Press.

Bernardes, Bettina. 1990. "Entrevista: Januário Garcia." *Perspectiva Universitária* 254 (November):6–7.

Cabral, Amílcar. 1973. *Return to the Source: Selected Speeches*. New York: African Information Service; Conaky, Guinea: P.A.I.G.C.

Camargo, Adalberto. 1980. *12° Aniversário e lançamento do Primeiro Simpósio Brasil-Africa*. São Paulo, November 12–13.

Cunha, Manuela Carneiro da. 1980. *Negros estrangeiros: os escravos libertos e sua volta à Africa*. São Paulo: Editora Brasiliense.

Diário do Congresso Nacional. 1993. República Federativa do Brasil, vol. 47, no. 39 (March 12).

Drake, St. Clair. 1975. "The Black Diaspora in Pan-African Perspective." *The Black Scholar* (Journal of Black Studies and Research) 7(1):2–13.

Dunn, Christopher. 1992. "Afro-Bahian Carnaval: A Stage for Protest." *Afro-Hispanic Review* 11(1–3):11–20.

Duran, Christina. 1993. "Portugal quer ser ponte com CE, mas a atenção comunitária está voltada para outros problemas." *O Estado de São Paulo* (February 14), p. 5.

Felicidade, Vera. 1986. "Paixão, glória e cruxificação de Menininha de Gantois." *A Tarde* (August 21).

Ferris, Elizabeth B., and Jennie K. Lincoln, eds. 1981. *Latin American Foreign Policies: Global and Regional Dimensions.* Boulder and London: Westview Press.

Gryzinski, Vilma. 1993. "Não somos mascates" (Interview with Italo Zappa). *Veja* 26 (March 3):7–9.

Hirst, Monica. 1984. "Democratic Transition and Foreign Policy: The Experience of Brazil." In Heraldo Muñoz and Joseph S. Tulchin, eds., *Latin American Nations in World Politics,* pp. 216–229. Boulder and London: Westview Press.

Ince, Basil. 1977. "The Racial Factor in the International Relations of Trinidad and Tobago." *Caribbean Studies* 16(3–4; October 1976/January 1977):5–28.

Irele, Abiola. 1965. "Negritude or Black Cultural Nationalism." *Journal of Modern African Studies* 3(3):321–348.

Jackson, Richard. 1975. "Mestizaje vs. Black Identity: The Color Crisis in Latin America." *Blackworld* 24(2):4–21.

Jornal da Exposição. 1988. Pinacoteca do Estado, Governo do Estado de São Paulo.

Lampreia, Luiz Felipe. 1993. "Em defesa do Itamaraty." *The Brasilians* (June):18.

Lopes, Ana Lívia. 1991a. "Racismo diminui a distancia entre a Bahia e a África do Sul." *Tribuna da Bahia* (Especial 2), August 4. (Includes comments by Júlio Braga, Antônio Carlos Vovô, Jônatas Conceição, Paulo Sérgio Pinheiro, and Décio Freitas.)

_____. 1991b. "Racismo tem que ser combatido com firmeza." *Tribuna da Bahia* (August 4).

Magubane, Bernard M. 1989. *The Ties That Bind: African-American Consciousness of Africa.* Trenton, N.J.: Africa World Press, Inc.

Maia, Gabriela Rossi. 1991. "Mandela em Salvador." *Tribuna da Bahia* (Especial), August 4.

Montilus, Guerin. 1979. "Africa, the Motherland, in the Haitian Collective Memory: A Study of African Religions Continuity Among the Haitians." Paper presented at the conference "The African Diaspora: Caribbean Expressions," New York.

Muñoz, Heraldo, and Joseph S. Tulchin, eds. 1984. *Latin American Nations in World Politics.* Boulder and London: Westview Press.

Nazário, Olga. 1983. "Pragmatism in Brazilian Foreign Policy: The Geisel Years, 1974–1979." Ph.D. dissertation, University of Miami.

Olinto, Antônio. 1993. "Africa é a outra face do Brasil." *O Estado de São Paulo* (March 7).

Prieswerk, Roy. 1970. "Race and Colour in International Relations." *The Yearbook of World Affairs*, pp. 54–87.

Rabinovici, Moisés. 1993. "Itamaraty aposta no futuro do continente." *O Estado de São Paulo* ("Africa Especial"), March 7.

Rodrigues, Danúbio. 1991a. "Câmara quer intensificar comércio afrobrasileiro." *Correio Brasiliense* (May 6).

_____. 1991b. "Africanos querem estreitar relações." *Correio Brasiliense* (May).

_____. 1991c. "Brasileiro ensina como fazer negócios com os africanos."- *Correio Brasiliense* (May).

_____. 1991d. "Embaixador lamenta que Brasil depreze Africa." *Correio Braziliense* (March 6).

Selcher, Wayne. 1981. "Brazil's Foreign Policy: More Actors and Expanding Agendas." In Elizabeth G. Ferris and Jennie K. Lincoln, eds., *Latin American Foreign Policies: Global and Regional Dimensions.* Boulder and London: Westview Press.

Wafer, Jim, and Hédimo Rodrigues Santana. 1990. "Africa in Brazil: Cultural Politics and the Candomblé Religion." *Folklore Forum* 23(1/2):98–114.

Periodicals

"Brasil-Senegal." *Correio da Manhã* (Editorial), September 20, 1946.

"Embaixador nigeriano conclama negros a luta por mais espaço." *A Tarde*, July 29, 1991.

"Governador nega discriminação." *A Tarde*, August 4, 1991.

"Henri Senghor's despedida."*Jornal do Brasil,* October 16, 1971.

"Mandela em Salvador." *Tribuna da Bahia* (Especial), August 4, 1991.

"Médici fala hoje à noite: política." *O Estado de São Paulo*, August 12, 1971.

"Missão política." *Jornal do Brasil* (Editorial), March 3, 1993.

"Prefeito diz que em Salvador há integração." *A Tarde*, August 4, 1991.

"O racismo cínico" (Interview with João Jorge Santos Rodrigues). *Veja*, June 9, 1993.

"Rio Branco matricula dois africanos." *Jornal do Brasil*, April 3, 1976.

"Senghor parte de Brasília para São Paulo." *Correio da Manha,* September 25, 1964.

"Senghor sugere a criação de comunidade Afro-Luso-Brasileira." *O Estado de São Paulo*, September 24, 1964.

9

Art History, Agency, and Identity:
Yorùbá Transcultural Currents in the
Making of Black Brazil

HENRY JOHN DREWAL

One of the objectives of the conference "Black Brazil: Culture, Identity, and Social Mobilization" was to "integrate scholarly discussions of modes of cultural practice and cultural performances," putting them "center stage . . . rather than marginalizing them . . . as epiphenomena reducible to social, economic and class structures" (conference prospectus). I certainly agree, yet I would extend and enlarge such a perspective even further. Since social life and culture *are performed, practiced*, they can never be "epiphenomena"—they *are* the phenomena, the "practice of everyday life" (de Certeau 1984). In my view, informed and formed by many years of living among Yorùbá-speaking people in West Africa, and shorter stays in the Afro-Brazilian world of Bahia, cultural practice can never *not* be fundamental to social formations. This "scholarly" discussion is cultural performance—I am performing the role, assuming the identity of "scholar." Additionally I do it as a *multidimensional* and *transcultural* person. Multidimensional in the sense that I negotiate multiple, slippery, sometimes resonant, sometimes dissonant, always evolving personas—those I attempt to actively shape for myself, in a field where others often try to formulate labels for me. We (individually and/or collectively) do this every moment of our lives, whether consciously or not. Transcultural in the sense that life, as James Clifford (1988) discusses in *The Predicament of Culture*, occurs in the permeable space of many "cultures"—we are shaped by and *shape* all of these for our specific social, economic, religious, political, historical purposes—just as I am doing here, and Yorùbás do wherever they are.

And just as Afro-Brazilians did in nineteenth-century Catholic lay organizations, the *irmandades*. Whether they were Muslim, Christian, or followers of the *òrìṣà*, they managed to operate effectively within such Church groups, using them to their own advantage, for their own purposes (Poole 1992). Rather than thinking of this as a matter of religious "syncretism" which tends to convey a sort of "blending, homogenizing process," I would suggest we recognize the distinctiveness of each faith, the simultaneous interplay, a kind of "suspension of belief or disbelief" of multiple, sometimes mutually supportive, sometimes conflicting, always competing beliefs and practices for persons whose histories demanded a refined, subtle, and effective facility for *multiple consciousness*. What was required was openness, adaptability, flexibility, a strategic pragmatism to multiple realities in order to be adept at survival. Pierre Verger (1968:526) cites the nineteenth-century English visitor to Bahia, James Wetherell (1860:54), who remarked on how Afro-Brazilians greeted people in the streets of Salvador. One greeting (Muslim) was in Arabic; another was in Portuguese; and a third was in Yorùbá— *occuginio (o kú jí ni o)* "hope you got up well!" or possibly *okúùjíònío*, "it's good you woke to enjoy another day." Such persons moved easily among various linguistic/cultural worlds—operating in multiple social spheres with ease, negotiating and bridging multiple identities and realities.

In this essay, of the countless African peoples (among them Fanti, Ewe, Fon, Mahin, Aja, Gun, Mina, Mande, Edo, Kongo, etc.) that have indelibly marked Brazil's historical and cultural landscape, I examine only Yorùbá-speaking peoples from West Africa, often known as Nagô in Brazil. The Brazil/Africa connections I analyze are derived from my own personal, lived experiences. I make no claim of "objectivity" (in any case, an impossibility) and hold no positivist view of some concretely measurable "reality" outside of my own construction of it—only the subjective arguments of this subject/writer as I attempt to inform and persuade you about the importance of such topics as art, history, agency, and identity in Yorùbá transatlantic transculturalism, and the roles I believe they have played in the making of black Brazil. In addition, I hope to suggest the ways in which Afro-Brazilians have used artistic/cultural expressions (forms and performances) to construct identities and how these have been and continue to be socially mobilized to confront, divert, and resist hegemonic forces in racist Brazilian society.

Such questions revolve around theories of agency and practice—both for those situated in particular socio-historical situations and for those writing about and interpreting them, historians or art historians. I both *write about* and am *imbedded in* the politics of representations.

I begin first with a Yorùbá metaphor that helps us understand their views on the dynamics of cultural practice over time and space. Next, I consider several Yorùbá philosophical concepts which since the late eighteenth century have shaped cultural practices on both sides of Atlantic—in Africa and Brazil—and are evident in various arts. Finally, I examine the continuing and expanding vitality and pervasiveness of Yorùbá currents in nineteenth- and twentieth-century Brazilian arts and culture—from architecture and Candomblé, to the works of several late-twentieth-century artists, to the popular arts of carnival in 1993.

A Yorùbá River of Culture

Yorùbás speak of their culture as a "river that never rests." Such a metaphor conjures up a sense of continual flow, endless change, fluidity, and flexibility. Yorùbás also recognize that some parts of rivers move slowly and run deep, while other, more shallow parts may change rapidly and dramatically. Too, the countless tributaries, eddies, ebbs and flows, swirls, backwashes, and cross-currents over time (distinctive city-state histories, for example) or space (western Yorùbá realms such as Kétu versus southeastern ones like Ìjèbú) can help us appreciate the remarkable diversities and unities in Yorùbá-speaking worlds. Dynamic qualities are both transformative and transforming. Extending this metaphoric image, I would regard the Atlantic as just another Yorùbá river (conveyed remarkably, although unintentionally by early European map-makers), one that carried people (although against their will) and their beliefs, cultural and artistic sensibilities, and practices to new lands, and under new conditions.

Ọrọ̀ ìjìnlè, or "deep discourse," treats ideas and concepts that are important for an understanding of a Yorùbá world, whether in Africa or in the African diaspora. Such deep discourse articulates àṣà ìbílè, "indigenous custom, cultural practice," or ìpilèsè, "foundations" that are pervasive and persuasive. There are many such "practices" and "foundations," but here I focus only on those that continue to be *named* and to exert strong influence on *both* banks of the Atlantic—that is, the *Yorùbá* river of cultural transmission, transition, and transformation.

Cosmos and Concepts

Many Yorùbá share a view of the cosmos as consisting of two distinct yet interactive, inseparable realms—the visible, tangible world (*ayé*) of the living and the invisible, spiritual otherworld (*òrun*) of the ancestors (*eégún/ará òrun*), gods (*òrìṣà*), and spirits (*òrò/iwin*). In Africa, such a cosmos is sometimes visualized as either a spherical gourd whose upper and lower hemispheres fit tightly together, or as a divination tray with a raised figurated border enclosing a flat central surface. The images clustered around the perimeter of the tray refer to mythic events and persons as well as everyday concerns. They present a universe populated by countless competing forces. The intersecting lines inscribed on the surface by a diviner at the outset of divination symbolize the metaphoric crossroads (*oríta méta*), the point of intersection, between cosmic realms (M. T. Drewal 1977). Drawing such lines "opens" channels of communication between *ayé* and *òrun* mediated by the diviner who works to reveal forces at work and to interpret their significance for a particular individual, family, group, or community. The Yorùbá *imago mundi* is thus a circle with intersecting lines.

Yorùbás also dance this image of the cosmos. Worship is a celebration, "serious play" (*eré, ṣiré*) for spiritual forces that includes various arts—music (percussion, song), dance, and costume—and it almost always takes the form of a leftward-turning (counter-clockwise) circular dance around or near a sacred site. Dancing leftward keeps the sacred or left side of the body turned inward to the center. This moving circle of the devout enacts the cosmos with its metaphoric crossroads at the center and activates its forces. The same practices live in Brazil, where *oríta méta*, the crossroads, may be even more visibly rendered as the central post of a *terreiro* around which the *filhos de santo* dance and the elders sit while songs, rhythms, and gestures call the gods to come from *òrun* to *ayé* in order to join the party in their honor.[1]

Òrun, the otherworldly abode of the sacred, is populated by countless forces who are frequently involved in human affairs. The gods (*òrìṣà*) are deified ancestors associated with specific natural forces or sites. They are grouped broadly into two categories depending upon their personalities and modes of action—the "cool, calm, composed, temperate, symbolically white gods" (*òrìṣà funfun*) and the "hot/temperamental gods" (*òrìṣà gbígbóná*). The former tend to be gentle, soothing, slow to anger, and reflective and include Ọbàtálá/Òrìṣànlá/Oxala—divine sculptor; Ọsanyìn—lord of leaves/medicines; Odùduwà—first monarch at Ilé-Ifè; Yemoja, Ọsun, Yewa, Ọbà—queens of their respective rivers; Ọlóṣà—ruler of the lagoon; and Olókun—goddess of the sea. The latter tend to be harsh, demanding, aggressive, and quick-tempered. Many of the "hot gods" are male though some are female: Ògún—god of Iron; Ṣàngó—former king of Ọyọ́ and lord of thunder; Ọbalúayé—lord of pestilence; and Oya—Ṣàngó's wife and queen of the whirlwind are counted in this group.

This characterization of *òrìṣà* has nothing to do with issues of good and evil. All gods, like humans, possess both positive and negative valences, strengths as well as foibles—as Yorùbá say, *tibi tire*, "good and bad always come together." Only their modes of action differ, which is activated by their distinctive life force (*àṣẹ*) and expressed as their natures or personalities (*ìwà*). Furthermore, the gods are not ranked in any hierarchy. The order in which they are invoked during ceremonies has to do with their roles in rituals and their relationships to each other and their followers. Their relative importance, based on numbers of adherents, reflects their popularity, reputation, influence, and effectiveness in different parts of the Yorùbá-speaking world both in Africa and the diaspora as we shall consider below.

On both sides of the Atlantic river the gods regularly enter the world through their mediums—worshipers who have been trained and prepared to receive the spirit of their divinities in possession trances during religious ceremonies. When the gods are made manifest in this way, they move and speak through their devotees, blessing, scolding, praying, and giving guidance.

Òrìṣà, literally "specially-selected-heads," are those remarkable, memorable ancestors elevated to deified status because of the mark they left in *ayé*. They serve as guides, as models for our reflections, interpretations, and actions in life. Because they help shape the ways people operate in the world in specific situations and historical moments, that is, their practice of everyday life, it is important to consider how and why *certain òrìṣà* have flourished in Brazil and not others. Artur Ramos (1939:94) indicates the following ones as widely worshiped: Èsù, Ògún, Ọbàtálá/Oxala, Ṣàngó, Ọ̀ṣòosì, and the female *òrìṣà*—Yemonja (Yorùbá)/

Yemanja (Brazil), Ọsun, Yansan/Ọya, and Ọbà. Different factors may
have contributed to this. For one, the sites and eras of captive-collection
on the West African coast seem to have determined which persons were
taken from which city-states, such as Ọyọ́, Kétu, Ìjẹ̀sà, or Ìjẹ̀bú, where
some òrìṣà were widely worshiped, and others not at all. Another demographic element might have been the age and gender of captives. For
example, elders and women, involved in honoring certain deities, were
not preferred by slavers in the earlier years, when strong, young men
were. This might explain the rarity of Ìyá Màpó, female deity and
patron of elderly female potters, in contrast to the widespread and vigorous worship of Ògún, Ọsọ̀ọ̀sì, and Ṣàngó—all warrior-hunter gods
who would have counted many adherents among the young male war
captives.

Too, the survival needs of newly arrived Africans undoubtedly
shaped religious practices. Divine inspiration in the face of the new and
harsh realities of Brazilian slavery would have brought to the fore such a
presence as Èṣù-Ẹlẹ́gba, divine mediator and principle of uncertainty.
I would suggest that the great importance of the padê ceremony and
despachos for Èṣù-Ẹlẹ́gba, the cleansing of sacred spaces and persons to
remove dangerous, destructive, disruptive forces, may in part be due to
the ever-present need to neutralize the police and other authorities who
were constantly attempting to disrupt and destroy Afro-Brazilian religious practices.

The popularity of Ògún, Ọsọ̀ọ̀sì, Ṣàngó, and other warrior òrìṣà
may have been because so many captives were in fact warriors. Being
devotees of Ògún and Ṣàngó (or the warrior-prophet Mohammed), they
would have used their divine patrons as models for behavior, for courage,
and for certain strategies and tactics that eventually produced a series of
major revolutions, revolts, and uprisings throughout the nineteenth century in Bahia and other places in Brazil.[2] And what of the wise elder òrìṣà
such as Ọbàtálá/Oxala (fig. 1) whose composure (ìtutù) and patience
(sùúrù) would have inspired some to endure and survive rather than
revolt, flee, or commit suicide, as many did?[3]

Female òrìṣà are equally prominent in Brazil, all associated with
water forces. Perhaps this developed out of remembrances of the Middle
Passage and widespread beliefs about the voyage home to òrun and the
ancestors as a journey across the waters? Or because women's leadership
roles as revolutionaries (e.g., Luiza Mahin, Zeferina, and countless others), as traders, and as mãe de santo enlarged the roles and impact of

Figure 1. The famous metal artist Mimito displays regalia for the wise elder *òrìṣà* Ọbàtálá/Oxala. Photograph by Henry Drewal.

female *òrìṣà*, even beyond their already substantial presence in West Africa? My point is this: Beliefs and practices are *grounded*, shaped by specific social, economic, political, ideological, aesthetic, and historical circumstances. Considering these factors, we can better understand how Yorùbás and their descendants (and Afro-Brazilians generally) fashion themselves and their gods continually, making and re-making, envisioning and re-visioning them in meeting new challenges in new situations.

The ancestors (*òkú òrun, oṣi, bàbànlá, ìyánlá*) constitute another category of beings in *òrun*. They are departed, not deceased, for they can be contacted by their descendants for support and guidance, and they can return to the world either as part of new persons in their lineages who are partially their reincarnation[4] or for short stays in the form of maskers called *eégún* or Egúngún or Bàbá Egún in Brazil (fig. 2). One of the central tenets of ancestral masking is the concept of *paradà*, "transformation." Masking is a means of transforming outer image while retaining inner essence. The departed exist in another form, another cosmic plane (*òrun*), yet they can periodically visit their descendants in *ayé*. It may be that the importance of masking traditions among Yorùbás, and among many other African peoples who came to Brazil, facilitated comparable artistic performances, like those associated with so-called Brazilian folk performances such as the *congadas* or Bumba meu Boi (see Kazadi wa Mukuna, Chapter 16 in this volume), and of course carnival.

A Yorùbá saying evokes other ideas about *ayé/òrun* and life: "The world is a marketplace (we visit), the otherworld is home" (*ayé l'ojà, Òrun n'ilé*). Existence in *ayé* is brief, transitory, and unstable, for what happens to us is not only due to things or persons, but also to invisible otherworldly forces (ancestors, gods, spirits) that visit frequently and exert strong influence in human affairs. A variant of this saying, "the world (life) is a journey, the otherworld (afterlife) is home" (*ayé l'àjò, òrun n'ilé*) connotes the ever-changing dynamics, the unpredictability of life as contrasted with the haven of the afterworld that promises immortality, spiritual existence for eternity.

The notion of *ayé* as a terrain of dynamic change and continual contestation has always been clearly understood in Brazil. One of the first systematic studies of African influences in Brazilian Portuguese (Mendonça 1935:170) defined *ayé* (*aie*) as a "festa que celebrava entre os nagôs o ano novo. Termo iorubano" (a festival celebrated by the Nagô at the new year. A Yorùbá term). Mendonça captured the ideas of annual renewal and purification in a world of powerful competing forces. More

Figure 2. Masker honoring and embodying ancestors, often called Bàbá Egún in Brazil. Courtesy of the UCLA Fowler Museum of Cultural History.

recently, one of the most popular blocos afro (carnival groups presenting pan-African or Afro-Brazilian themes) has taken as its name—Ilê Aiyê. The name couldn't have been more appropriate. Literally "House of World," it connotes for Yorùbás and their actual and/or ideological descendants in Brazil all the forces (supportive or detractive, worldly or spiritual) that one must confront in order to survive and thrive. Moreover, the term *ayé* or *ọmọ aráyé* also has a more specific and threatening connotation of all those dangerous, troublesome persons in the world, those detractors who wish us not well, but ill. Certainly the police and other government officials who tried systematically to wipe out Afro-Brazilian religion would be considered *ọmọ aráyé*. Given both past and present oppressions endured by Afro-Brazilians, the name Ilê Aiyê demonstrates an awareness of the powerful forces to be dealt with and asserts that the world is *our house*—a call to sustained, self-determined action—for as some "words of wisdom" from Ifá divination remind us, "life is the bailing of waters with a sieve" (Mason 1988:16).

Àṣẹ is another foundational concept in Yorùbá and Afro-Brazilian thought. Àṣẹ may be understood as the innate generative force possessed by everything—gods, ancestors, spirits, humans, animals, plants, rocks, rivers, and voiced words such as songs, prayers, praises, curses, or even everyday conversation. Àṣẹ is performative power, the power to make things happen, to bring something into existence, to get something done. It is a Yorùbá theory of agency par excellence for it concerns the knowledge and power to deal with hegemonic forces. It is about instrumentality, the means by which something is accomplished. The wise use of *àṣẹ* demands reflection, careful interpretation, and considered action.

Àṣẹ, *axé* in Brazil, has deep resonances both past and present. In Candomblé, it has been referenced in the *axexê* ceremony—a rite that sends the soul of a departed person to *òrun*. In contemporary Brazilian culture, the concept of *axé* has been widely popularized, commodified, and commercialized, all with uncertain results. For example, *axé* music has become the rage, named presumably for its power to energize, to move people. Thus millions of Brazilians sing the praises of *axé*, yet how many of them are aware of its Afro/Nagô origins, or its deeper meanings in Yorùbá philosophical thought? Billboards lining the streets of Salvador and Bahia welcome people to carnival with greetings and blessing of AXÉ!, using the Yorùbá word *àṣẹ* which conveys the message "may it come to pass." The African-American jazz musician Ernie Watts teamed up with Gilberto Gil to produce the popular CD titled *Afoxé*, which in Yorùbá means "powerful incantations." And even a major cosmetics corporation has produced a popular cologne called AXÉ!, again presumably to suggest the "power to attract," packaged in a *black* container with yellow concentric circles as its logo. I am not trivializing the importance of the concept of *àṣẹ/axé*. On the contrary, I am suggesting that the very pervasiveness and adaptability of the idea of *àṣẹ/axé* may indicate its capacity to shape beliefs and *practices*, to mold Brazilian society in *African* ways, no matter how obliquely, unconsciously, or subversively.

Another important Yorùbá concept, fundamental to any under-standing of cultural practice/performance, is the idea of what might be termed "serious play," and improvisation, *ṣeré*.[5] *Serious* play recognizes the inventiveness and dynamics of play *at work*. Worship is serious play, as is life in general. A Yorùbá name for religious ceremony is *ṣiré*, the same term that continues to be used in Brazil (*xire*) (and among the Yorùbá-Nagô-influenced African diaspora in the Americas generally), a "party" for the gods, sacred celebrations that activate forces for our benefit.

There is another dimension to this as well. After the gods have joined the *ṣiré* and the public ceremony has ended, the initiates who embodied the gods during possession trance enter into a transitional state termed *eré*. *Eré*, a word linked etymologically with *ṣiré/ṣe-eré*, denotes "a playful, childlike state of being" which is regarded as a period of great clairvoyance and insight about persons and portended events. A mental attitude of playful looseness, an openness to intuitive wisdom, are subsumed in the notion of "serious play," *ṣiré*.

Serious playfulness is especially expected of artists (*oníṣònà*), those who skillfully manipulate media in creating images and ideas that enliven, uplift, enlighten, and *surprise*—evocative forms that have the quality of *àrà*, inventive playfulness, the capacity to open up thought and to encourage insights (*ojú-inú*) as they comment on self, society, past, present, and future. For example, an altar centerpiece for the *òrìṣà* Ṣàngó, the Thundergod, offers one scene as we view it from the front—a kneel-ing female devotee carrying a large vessel on her head and flanked by supporters. But as we approach it and see more of the carved lid of the vessel, as we would upon entering the shrine room, we discover another devotional scene—a male worshiper holding offerings and dance wands (*oṣé* Ṣàngó) and lying prostrate in the customary form of respectful greeting known as *dòbálẹ̀*. That same kind of artistic license and playful juxtaposition appears in Afro-Brazilian religious art as well. A Ṣàngó altarpiece shows a standing male supporting a broad tray, recalling the same theme as in the African one, except here he wears a new status sym-bol—a top hat.

Given such Yorùbá concepts of the cosmos, the forces inhabiting it, and the ways one operates within it, let us turn to specific examples of Yorùbá currents in the history of Brazilian arts and culture.

Presencing Absence: Africanizing Brazilian Art in the Eighteenth and Nineteenth Centuries

Examples of African and more specifically Yorùbá-inspired art and architecture in eighteenth- and nineteenth-century Brazil reveal some of the ways Afro-Brazilians fashioned their survival in such a hostile environment, how they formulated and asserted a sense of themselves in the face of hegemonic forces in the dominant society for, I would suggest, while dominant forces may have controlled the (written) historical record, the voids in that record speak volumes, and the fashioning of forms became silent documents of resistance that can help us re-vision that past.

Despite seemingly impossible circumstances, Africanisms became an integral part of the fabric of Brazilian culture from the very beginning. The art in Brazil's early churches included non-Portuguese cultural (and religious) presences, for those who did the *actual* creative work were Africans or Afro-Brazilians who introduced their own images and aesthetic preferences. For example, grapes (symbolizing the Eucharistic wine and blood of Christ for Catholics) became pineapples. And lily-white Virgins and cupids turned the color of their creators—dusky brown to shiny black!

Such artistic ingenuity (and playfulness) flowered most fully during the eighteenth-century Brazilian baroque. This unique style was epitomized in the work of Aleijadinho, often described as Brazil's greatest artist and architect. Aleijadinho, a man of color, created an exuberant and sensual expressionism that was unmatched. He, together with a large group of craftsmen, either Africans or of African descent, transformed the Catholic architectural landscape of Minas Gerais. A different African presence can be seen in the Church of Lapinha, in the district of Liberdade, Salvador, which may have been designed and built by Mestre Manoel Friandes (b. December 25, 1823–d. August 4, 1904).[6] Friandes was African, more particularly an Afro-Muslim or *ìmàle*, the Yorùbá word for Muslim. He may have been a Yorùbá, for many African Muslims were either Yorùbá, Nupe, or Hausa, but we are uncertain. We know that he was a well-known and successful architect and builder who was commissioned to do a large number of commercial and ecclesiastic buildings including the Ordem Terceira de São Francisco in Salvador (Querino 1909:206). The Church of Lapinha stands as a monument to nineteenth-century Afro-Brazilian religious and cultural resistance in architectural form, of self-expression in the face of hegemonic forces. The exterior of the church is very simple, staid, stark, and unelaborated compared to many Brazilian baroque structures. Commissioned by the Church which must have known he was Muslim, Friandes created a subdued, quiet, Christian exterior. But within, he designed a forcefully exuberant Islamic interior—Moorish arches, decorative tiles, and, most striking of all, Arabic script etched into the walls over the arches and surrounding the nave that contained excerpts from The Creation (Genesis) of the scriptures. How was such a building commissioned, conceived, financed, and constructed? How and why did Friandes obtain the patronage to design and construct this church? How did he negotiate the obviously Muslim interior design and combine it with the equally obvious Christian paintings, sculptures, etc.? What were the responses of the Church hierarchy and parishioners, especially since the church was built while the memory of the *ìmàle* revolutions of the first half of the nineteenth century (the last major one in 1835, and many smaller ones after that) would have been still fresh? What did Friandes think and say about what he was doing, and how did it fit in with his other architectural projects? Is this an example of subversive expression—an assertion of self-identity as a Muslim, as an African, as a cultured, sophisticated professional man? Or all, or some (or none?), of the above? We will probably never have precise answers to such questions, but the Church of Lapinha certainly stands as a monument to the enormously complex, seemingly incongruous, and fascinating juxtapositions of contesting religious ideologies, racial and class hierarchies, political possibilities, and economic forces which Afro-Brazilians had to negotiate in order to survive and, despite the enormous odds, to thrive. This is a hidden history, like so many others about Afro-Brazilians, that needs to be researched, analyzed, and told.[7]

There are also other nineteenth-century Afro-Brazilian forms, religious images that managed to negotiate the difficult terrain between an officially imposed state religion (Catholicism) and remembered, re-constituted, and/or re-invented African ones, like the *òrìṣà* faith of Yorùbás.

Figure 3. Nineteenth-century Brazilian examples of memorial statues for departed twins or *ìbejì*. Photo by Henry Drewal.

Afro-Brazilian Sacred Art

The untold story throughout Brazil's art history is that of its "unofficial," "underground," and un-Catholic religious art linked with African faiths that were practiced secretly. These have continued unbroken since the first days of colonization. As one Brazilian writer put it, African culture "expelled through the front door, returned by the back door in its food and seasonings, in the music of the slave quarters and in the belief in . . . the African gods who surreptitiously started penetrating the manor house" (*Brazilian Art* 1976:4).

The earliest examples of that art are probably now lost, but at the end of the eighteenth and early nineteenth centuries these sacred art traditions strengthened with the massive influx of primarily Yorùbá-speaking peoples to Bahia. From that period, they Yorùbánized and enlarged the corpus of African images and ideas that have had a profound impact on Brazilian art history and culture up to the present.

The performing arts—music, song, dance—made the strongest impact since they could be brought in the minds of persons raised in oral and performed traditions. The culinary arts survived as well. They were viewed as secular activity and essentially non-threatening to those in power, who were unaware that they were in fact an important part of African religious practices. The visual arts—dress, body arts, sculpture, shrine painting, masks, and so on—were harder to sustain. These had to be re-created in secret, or re-worked in various ways, in order to survive since they were linked with cultural and religious traditions banned and actively suppressed in Brazil.

And survive they did, like memorial statues for departed twins or *ìbejì* (fig. 3). The Yorùbá, who have one of the highest instances of twin births in the world, regard twins as spirit children who can bring either double fortune or double trouble to a family. Should one or both depart, the parents may be required to commission an artist to carve a memorial figure which then is cared for by subsequent generations. Such figures were widely distributed across Yorùbáland in the early nineteenth century. The pair shown here is by an Afro-Brazilian sculptor perhaps in the latter half of the nineteenth century. The artist has combined the Western doll tradition of moveable-jointed limbs and naturalistic proportion with Yorùbá traditions of body arts—scarifications on cheeks (here painted) and beads about the neck and waist. They are specifically modeled on plaster statues for two Italian Catholic saints, Cosmos and

Damien, who were associated with twins and served as a "cover" for their sacred images.

Certain masking traditions also survived the trials of the Middle Passage and Brazilian oppression. One was the Egúngún masking for ancestors (fig. 2). Cloth, the primary medium for such ensembles, envelopes and transforms the human shape into something otherworldy. Beads evoke the glorious nobility of the past. Despite the differences of detail, a shared vision of ancestral presence continues to resonate on both sides of the Atlantic.

Such sacred images help to focus and intensify worship. They are *not* objects *of* worship. As the Yorùbá divination priest Kólawolé Òsítólá once explained to me, "the gods do not come because of the images, the images come because of the gods." In Brazil, each òrìsà was linked with a specific Catholic saint on the basis of character or attributes and the interpretation of her/his iconography. Since Yorùbás used art much as Catholics use saints' statues, Yoru-Brazilians easily adapted them for their own purposes. They saw no conflict in this, since both faiths recognized similar spiritual entities, but under different names and histories.

But they had another reason as well—to camouflage their sacred art and worship. They had to disguise their personal beliefs and practices in order to sustain them. So they adopted a pragmatic and effective strategy in a very difficult situation. The use of Catholic imagery in a Candomblé context does not connote capitulation or conversion, rather it represents a tactic of *masking inner essence with outer appearance*. Catholic saints' statues and paraphernalia were prominently displayed on domestic altars in parlors, while the sacred stones and other witnessing objects of the òrìsà were hidden from view in containers or under tables and in armoires.

The oppressive Brazilian context demanded creative strategies since African faiths were seen as subversive by the authorities. They were the target of police harassment over the centuries, which is why the largest collections of Afro-Brazilian sacred art are found not in art museums, but in Brazil's police museums. Practiced in secret, they had to conceal or camouflage their icons in order to protect and sustain their àse. Threads of these Yorùbá concepts can be seen in works by many contemporary Afro-Brazilian artists and in carnival performance.

A Luta Continua: Yorùbá Echoes in Twentieth-Century Afro-Brazilian Art

Artists' strategies for survival and success are frequently embedded, rather than explicit, in their art.[8] Some involve the transformation of certain visual aspects in order to mask or camouflage other dimensions. Others widen their concerns toward global, human issues, or focus inwardly on psychological states of mind. As idealists, artists expect their work to be judged by its efficacy, its capacity to move its viewers, without the interference of other factors. As pragmatists, they know it must be able to touch new, wider, and different audiences if it is to succeed. They also know those viewers are creations of cultures in which racism is endemic. Since such racism cannot be ignored, various means must be employed to overcome, conquer, or neutralize it.

Emanoel Araújo and Rubem Valentim mask in different ways. Emanoel Araújo says, "Perhaps my art is Afro-Minimalist or Neo-Ancestral" (Preston 1987:15). He builds opaque colored crystals in the sky—angular forms that thrust upward and outward as they merge with and emerge out of each other, enclosing interior negative spaces and transforming exterior ones. His colors heighten the strength of his volumes. The reds and blacks that dominate his work are deep and rich, powerful and aggressive. Their placement on segmented, angular forms defines the movement in the piece—whether of continuity and flow or breaks and stops.

His work may appear to be solely non-representational—plays of hard-edged form and color—but appearances can deceive. His works are not only about significant form, they are forms with significance. Specific sacred entities are present, Yorùbá gods who survive and thrive in contemporary Brazil. Araújo captures their essence. His visual abstractions match the abstractness of the Yorùbá concept of *àṣẹ*.

For example, Ògún, Yorùbá god of iron and war, embodies strength, force, quickness, and directness. Like his metal, Ògún is hard and sharp. He builds civilizations, or he destroys them. All of these Ògún attributes reverberate in sculptures dedicated to his powers and presence. In one work called "Totem Ògún," Araújo builds blade-like forms on top of a pyramid, symbol of Egypt, Africa's most famous civilization. Then these thrust upward, first one way, then sharply angled to thrust in another way like a pivoting cannon, or active phallus—both images supremely evocative of Ògún. Ògún's colors (dark blue and black) cover the work making it appear heavy and dense like his metal.

Emanoel Araújo captures the essence of Yorùbá gods in colors, forms, movements, and rhythms—not in realistic representations. A Yorùbá proverb says, "only half a speech is necessary for the wise, in their minds it becomes whole." Emanoel Araújo demonstrates such wisdom.

The late Rubem Valentim created a visual metaphysics that transformed a Yorùbá iconic language into a global one. Like the man himself, the art of Rubem Valentim is precise, meticulous, strong, and straightforward. He "works with geometry," with paintings, relief, and three-dimensional sculptures filled with an endless recombination of geometric, hard-edged shapes—triangles, spheres, arcs, stars, parallelograms, arrows. Most are strictly symmetrical arrangements, *all* are supremely balanced. They are rendered with extreme care, giving the sense of having been mathematically, scientifically created. His colors reinforce this impression. They are bold and flat, essentially primary and secondary hues juxtaposed with their complements to produce dramatic optical effects—again science at work.

Yet despite the impression of seemingly remote, mechanical, and coldly objective forms presented solely for their optical effects, Valentim worked to express spiritual matters: He said (personal communication, March 1987), "Today physics approaches both religion and aesthetics ... I am creating a new METAPHYSICS." Valentim has achieved a true synthesis of the physical and the spiritual, for all these seemingly "meaningless" forms are in fact signs and symbols of spiritual forces at the heart of Candomblé Nagô that was part of his childhood in Bahia which he described as "very strong in mysticism, religiosity" (Valentim, personal communication, March 1987).

Even his working process is a synthesis of science and spirit. Every day, he begins by making a large series of small studies or models in a very systematic and disciplined way which he describes as both "laboratory experiments" and "devotions"—daily efforts to evoke and invoke spiritual forces that inhabit his thoughts, his world, and his work.

When one is aware of this metaphysical synthesis in Valentim's work, it takes on many unsuspected aspects. Forms become meaningful. The persistence of threes is not simply a matter of composition, it is a sacred number that invokes sacred forces (fig. 4). The blood-red,

Figure 4. This Ruben Valentim work creates a metaphysical synthesis where forms become meaningful. Courtesy of the artist. Photo by Henry Drewal.

hard-edged form signals the axe of Ṣàngó, Yorùbá god of thunder and lightning who came to Brazil at the end of the eighteenth century and who lives in the spiritual consciousness of many Brazilians today.

These sharp-edged axes refer to thundercelts (*ẹdun àrá*) that are the primary symbol of Ṣàngó's power and presence in the world. They represent the god's essence, his mystical life force or *àṣẹ*. Their boldness *strikes* the viewer. Valentim creates lines of sharp action and move-ment—thrusts upward, outward, and downward—all evocative of the qualities of movement of Ṣàngó devotees who carry his axe during trance dances in his honor.

Other geometric motifs and colors reveal other Yorùbá or African spiritual presences. Staff-like forms bathed in whiteness signal the pres-ence of Oxala (Ọbàtálá/Òrìṣànla), lord of creation, and draw inspira-tion from Oxala's ritual staff, *ọpá ọṣóòró*. Oxala is a most appropriate subject for he is the divine artist who shapes all existence. Strong, stable forms and a cool color capture visibly and symbolically the essence of Oxala.

While deeply rooted in African sacred signs and cosmological con-cepts, elements of Valentim's compositions visualize cosmic shapes and forces that come from other, universalizing intentions. He explains that he wants to "popularize," that is, reach beyond, specific symbolic, meaning-full systems to "signs" that are "pure" forms expressing "feelings and rhythms" universally. His work is often described as being full of Jungian archetypes, things stored in the human subconscience. Thus he is an artist who combines many seemingly contradictory attributes to create powerful images: science, religion, aesthetics to create a new meta-physics; a semiotic system based on language to create a visual language; and signs and symbols rooted in Africa and his early life as a Brazilian of color in order to create a universal imagery that can touch people every-where. Araújo and Valentim have succeeded by working an aesthetic alchemy, turning potent roots into hybrid flowers.

Others have chosen a different path. Terciliano Jr. asserts his Afro-Brazilian heritage in large paintings devoted to the ritual arts of Can-domblé. His abstractions relate to the ineffable qualities of the gods and of *àṣẹ*. But a pragmatism emerges when he explains (personal communi-cation, March 1987), "I try to do work that is truly representative of the black people, not caricatures of black culture."

Terciliano grew up in a large, and poor, family. Over the years, he had many jobs in order to survive—blacksmith's apprentice, fabric sales-man, receptionist, soap opera actor, and poet—before deciding to live by his art. His devout family has always been deeply involved in Afro-Brazilian religion, specifically the Angolan Candomblé called Bate-Folha which combines several African faiths. It has always been a source of spiritual as well as artistic inspiration. Terciliano says, "As an artist, I see African religion in a different way from my family, not without the same

Figure 5. This painting (1993) by Terciliano captures the rhythm and movement of a Candomblé ceremony. Courtesy of the artist. Photo by Henry Drewal.

respect, but also as a cultural source from where I can find elements for research and expression. . . . It is a strong form of resistance that survived slavery, racism and still today struggles to maintain its identity" (personal communication, March 1987).

His art has gone through major style changes over the years. His early work centered on genre scenes from Bahia—street and market scenes, the dress, movement, and color of Salvador. Now he has turned bold, transforming his partial figures into strongly colored solid ones, moving toward abstraction and overall pattern, and working on a large scale (fig. 5). Strong oblique lines of force work with and against each other. He has recently focused on Candomblé. His increasing abstraction has reasons. For one, he explains that he is exploring new ways to express this reality, "to situate it in a wider space, in a subtle and lyric way, blending my art and life experience." Too, he is dealing with intangible ideas of the sacred—*àṣẹ*, the *òrìṣà*, ceremonies (*ṣiré*), and sacrifice (*ẹbọ*).

In these works on Candomblé, Terciliano celebrates his family, ancestors, and the generations of Afro-Brazilians who have kept the gods of Africa alive and well in the hearts and minds of Brazilians today.

He believes that Brazilian society has tried to suppress black culture. He explains, "I suffer the oppression of the dominant group . . . which tries to fight not only me but all black artists who refuse to play the characters it chooses for us. I try to express and assure the reality of this [black] culture . . . not only to survive but to become predominant in most levels of our community."

The works of these three Yoru-centric Brazilian artists present us with a vast array of styles, media, and imagery. Diversity is, by its very nature, an expression of artistic and personal freedom, the freedom to determine one's direction and identity and express it in whatever manner one chooses. Such diverse work is the creation of independent, *un-colonized* minds, of free persons who are actively *defining* and proclaiming their identities through their works, and thus celebrating the freedom of the human spirit.

Yorùbá Themes in Contemporary Brazilian Carnival

Carnival in Brazil exposes much more than bodies. As a supreme moment of briefly sanctioned cultural catharsis, carnival reveals many hotly contested battles for social, political, and economic power, while projecting a thin veneer of wild, mindless abandon. The masses of dancing, singing people are known as *folias*, "Carnival madness followers" (João Reis, personal communication, February 1993), yet much of that "folly," mirth, or "madness" is also *serious play*, or *ṣiré*, that engages in pointed cultural critique as much as celebration. Like "signifyin'," the northern African-American tradition of subtle (and not so subtle) commentary, satire, and cultural critique (Gates 1988), the *ṣiré* of Afro-Brazilian carnival performances uses the transformations, the *paradà* of *masking*, as a primary mode of expression—masking that disguises as it discloses, hides as it reveals, formulates as it transforms. Carnival masking offers an annual opportunity for parading some of the multiple personas we negotiate, yet rarely express so openly and extravagantly. Identities change as positions, strategies, and discourses shift in relation to issues being raised and forces being confronted.

African themes have surfaced in Bahia's carnival only in the last twenty years although a powerful black political movement had developed in the 1930s called the Black Brazilian Front (Bairros 1989:23–25). Under dictatorial rule, it survived only a short time but resurfaced in the 1970s in various cultural and artistic forms, most notably in the *afoxés* and blocos afros (Risério 1981; Crook 1993; João Jorge Santos Rodrigues [Chapter 4, herein]; Omari 1984; Crowley 1984). This resurgence was inspired by the conjunction of several factors: the civil rights struggles in the United States; liberation movements in Africa (FRELIMO in Mozambique, MPLA in Angola, Mandela and the anti-apartheid movement in South Africa); and pan-Africanist forces in the Caribbean, especially the Rastafari in Jamaica who inspired the samba-reggae sounds that rock Bahia today. Taking advantage of a liberalizing policy (*abertura*) or "opening" in Brazil, black organizations quickly and publicly challenged Brazil's supposed "racial democracy" and asserted black pride, identity, and consciousness through various community self-help projects and carnival performances based on African themes. Their efforts to shape Brazilian consciousness is an ongoing struggle for cultural space, recognition, and power, as certain events and controversies during Bahian carnival 1993 revealed.

One could be seen in bloco afro Ilê Aiyê's 1993 theme, "América Negra, Sonho Africano, uma reflexão sobre os 500 anos da chegada dos Europeus do ponto da vista da cultura negra" (Black America, African Dream, reflection on the 500 years since the arrival of the Europeans from the point of view of black culture). As Ilê Aiyê defined and performed its theme during carnival, it celebrated pan-African leaders such as Marcus Garvey, and those of the civil rights and black nationalist movements of the 1960s and 1970s—Martin Luther King, Malcolm X, the Black Panthers, and others—as concrete examples of efforts to raise black consciousness and to fight for liberation and power. The "African Dream" evoked a more distant and glorious past—of civilizations, empires and kingdoms, kings and queens—inspiration of another sort that stressed ancient roots and cultural continuities, asserting the need to remember and proclaim the achievements of the past in order to claim rights and place in the present.

If culture may be taken as an aesthetic system writ large, then the definition and celebration of "beauty" according to African tenets/criteria is an important part of consciousness-raising efforts by Afro-Brazilians. One of the major events leading up to Ilê Aiyê's carnival outing was "A Noite de Beleza Negra" (The Night of Black Beauty). Held at the Athletic Club in the Barra district of Salvador (February 6, 1993), it featured performances by various groups and individuals both within and outside the Ilê Aiyê membership. Some were children's sections of Ilê Aiyê, others were "stars"—singers, musicians, entertainers (and politicians) associated either closely or distantly with the black consciousness movement in Brazil—who made guest appearances. Besides raising funds for the bloco, the main purpose of the evening was to select the Ilê Aiyê Queen of Carnival 1993. All the contestants performed various interpretations of African choreography and fashion, some re-creations and other creative transformations of dance, dress, and coiffure. As one might expect, different views of African beauty and "authenticity" were contested. According to one Brazilian colleague (João Reis, personal communication, February 1993), the band Ara Ketu had been criticized in previous years for introducing guitars and electric instruments because these were not viewed as "Afro-instruments." Yet in 1993, they performed at "A Noite de Beleza Negra" for Ilê Aiyê, regarded as one of the most "authentically Afro" of the blocos.

All of this was set in what appeared to be the framework of a "Western-style" beauty pageant, yet at the same time it recalled Afro-Brazilian antecedents of *congadas*, those festivals, possibly based on Portuguese *autos* (Ramos 1939:105–106), in which Brazilian authorities permitted "kings and queens" of specific African communities to be "crowned" and feted annually (see Brandão 1976). These may have been "invented" by colonial officials to encourage interethnic distinctions and thus rivalries in order to divide and more easily rule Africans.

Yet, at the same time, Africans may have used it as a model and mechanism for self-government which helped shape the formation of sociopolitical institutions and processes. These *congadas*, dramatizations of the coronations of African kings and queens, date in Bahia to the beginning of the seventeenth century. The earliest published reference occurred in 1706 in Iguarassu, Pernambuco (Ramos 1939:106). According to Ramos (1944:159–171), these re-created the idea of *nation* and probably contributed to the creation of independent African states or *quilombos* in seventeenth-century Brazil, especially in the state of Alagoas where the *quilombo* of Palmares survived throughout much of the seventeenth century, and the memory of which remains strong today.

All these various strands in histories of domination and resistance, of suppression, appropriation, re-appropriation, and assertion need consideration as we attempt to weigh and comprehend the multitude of complex factors and processes involved in constructions of identities—continuities/dis-continuities, traditions/inventions, syncretism, creolization, camouflaging, signifyin', satirizin'.

The dynamism and elasticity of serious play was again evident on the night Ilê Aiyê was preparing to go out during carnival. An African-inspired public ritual of blessing and opening, developed over the last few years, took place in the Curuzu neighborhood of Salvador near the home of Vovô, the current head of Ilê Aiyê. Vovô's mother, who is a *mãe de santo*, was joined by several of her sisters in the faith, blessed the large assembled crowd with words and gestures, and then moved through the crowd spraying popcorn on the heads of people as an offering to Ọmọlú, Yorùbá deity of disease, to give all good health and prosperity. Afterward, she again prayed and, joined by others, released a flock of white doves into the air as a flurry of fireworks exploded overhead. The *mãe de santo* followed this with the marking of bodies—forehead, pectorals, shoulder blades, feet—with *pemba*, the Bantu word for "white chalk/kaolin." While the name reveals ancient Bantu/Kikongo and Angolan roots in Afro-Brazilian culture, chalk is used very widely in West and Central African rituals to signify sacredness, ancestral presence, purity, protection, and blessing. The priestesses marked people with a "+" sign—which in this context could be read as a reference to the Yorùbá cosmic sign of the crossroads (see above); the Kongo "four moments of the sun" (Thompson and Cornet 1981); the Christian cross; Masonic emblem; and so forth. This combination of celebratory elements was both transnational and transcultural: the popcorn from Candomblé traditions; the doves from Olympic ones; the fireworks from patriotic/nationalist ones; the body-marking from multiple, nearly pan-African rites of purification.

The black consciousness movement in Brazil continues to struggle to survive and spread its message to wider audiences as revealed in a battle to control representation: the public controversy about 1993 carnival decorations in the streets of Salvador.[9] It began when city officials announced their decision to "celebrate" Salvador as the "city of the *òrìsàs*" without consulting those most concerned—*òrìsà* devotees—the Candomblé community as officially represented by the Federação Baiana do Culto Afro-Brasileiro (FBCAB; Bahian Federation of Afro-Brazilian Cults). This decision led to a protest and the appearance of a series of articles and editorials in the local newspapers and on TV. Eventually the city negotiated a compromise. It agreed to reduce the number of decorations and avoid direct reference to specific *òrìsà* icons and symbols, replacing them with generalized "folkloric" images. The compromise also eliminated the plan to create elaborate "decorations in *pemba*," which had been billed as the "symbol of Salvador." There are many issues and questions to be considered in order to unravel the forces operating in this debate. For one, the generally independent, decentralized, politically and economically powerless Afro-Brazilian religious organizations were confronting powerful political and economic factions aligned with the government, tourist businesses, and the centralized and ubiquitous Catholic Church. This was a hard battle to win, for if, as they say in Brazil, "money whitens," then the Church is pristine! Money not only whitens, it "talks." The FBCAB was resisting the long-term Brazilian tradition of "folklorizing" African cultural and religious practices, here being used for explicitly profit-making purposes as was evident in the enormous media battle between Salvador and Rio to attract tourist dollars to the most "authentic," that is, "exotic," carnival in Brazil. Many questions remain to be considered. What would have happened if the FBCAB had been consulted in advance? Would the members have agreed to go along with the plan? Would they have opposed it? If they had demanded that the city, "Bahia de Todos os Santos," the "Bay of *All* Saints," include Catholic saints with African *òrìṣà*? Or if the officials suggested adding saints, would the FBCAB have agreed? Would the Catholic Church have agreed, or would it have opposed this juxtaposition with *òrìṣàs/cultos* that equated Christian saints with African deities? Perhaps a systematic survey of the "players" involved in this contest might suggest *how* specific interests were turned into practices (or not) and *why*—central issues in any adequate theory of social history.

The Creation of the World (and Brazil) According to Yorùbá Myth?

In the midst of all the erotic dancing images of barely-clad *mulata* bodies of the 1993 Rio carnival as broadcast on Brazilian Globo TV (see essays by Antônio Pitanga, Chapter 3; Denise Ferreira da Silva, Chapter 18; and Michael Leslie, Chapter 19, herein), came myths, images, and a samba by Martinho da Vila that presented an African Genesis to a wider world—the creation of the world according to Yorùbá legend. Not only did key figures in the myth appear, such as the supreme creator Ọlọ́run and divine sculptor of life Oxala, but also several key Yorùbá philosophical concepts. One, which served as the keynote for the entire extravagant display, was *gbàlà*, the Yorùbá word for *save, rescue, re-claim* which was translated as *resgatar, salvar*.[10] One float presented images of living forms emerging from clay (the medium from which Oxala shaped life) and surrounding a "tree of life." As the Samba School passed in review, the following lyrics flashed on the TV screen for viewers to read (and learn?):

Gbàlà é resgatar, salvar	*Gbàlà* is to rescue, to save
e a criança	And the children
esperança de Oxalá	The hope of Oxala
Gbàlà, resgatar, salvar	*Gbàlà* rescuing, saving
vamos sonhar	Let us dream
meu Deus	My God
O grande criador adoraçeu	The great adored/worshiped creator
Porque	Because
a sua geração já se perdeu	His generation had already been lost
quando acaba a criação	When creation was finished
desaparece o Criador	the Creator disappeared
pra salvar a geração	To save the generation [human family]
só esperança e muito amor	With hope and much love
então	Then
foram abertos os caminhos	were opened the paths
e a inocência entrou	And innocence entered
no templo do criação	Into the temple of creation
lá os guias petores do planeta	There the protective guides of the planet
colocaram o futuro em suas mãos	Put the future in his hands
e através dos *orixás* se encontraram	And through the *orixás* we met
com deus dos deuses, Olorum	with god of gods, Ọlọ́run
e viram	and they saw
viram como foi criado o mundo	they saw how the world was created
se encantaram	they became enchanted
com a Mãe Natureza	with Mother Nature
Descobrindo o próprio corpo	Discovering their own body
compreenderam	They understood
que a função do homen	That the purpose of Man
é evoluir	Is to evolve
conheceram os valores	They learned the values
do trabalho e do amor	Of work and of love
e a importância da justiça	And the importance of justice
sete águas revelaram	Seven waters revealed
em sete cores	In seven colors
que a beleza	That beauty
é a missão de todo artista	Is the mission of every artist
Gbàlà é resgatar, salvar	*Gbàlà* is to rescue, to save

It was a fantastic spectacle of life animated by *axé*, but how are we to understand its significance? What were the intentions of its creators, and how and by whom were they formulated? What was its reception—its impact upon those privileged few who witnessed it live in Rio, or the millions of Brazilians who watched it on TV? Was this the same kind of appropriation by dominant society (via the Hege[monic!] Globo network) that the Bahian Federation of Afro-Brazilian Cults protested and opposed? By incorporating elements of Yorùbá culture (Ọlọ́run, Oxala, *gbàlà*, and *orixás*) into the monied spectacle of the Samba Schools of Rio's carnival, was Brazilian carnival giving space, legitimacy, and importance to African elements in the formation of Brazilian identity? Or was it primarily a co-optation of an exotic, marginal mythology with no real connections to Brazilian society or the current religious, social, political, or cultural beliefs and practices of any significant segment of the population? The Creation story stressed a supreme being, Ọlọ́run, although Oxala and the *orixá* are mentioned. And the Yorùbá word *gbàlà* was heard and seen repeatedly. Yet how did Brazilians understand these references? If these are some of the important questions surrounding issues of hegemony and resistance, agency and effect, then how are we to judge the nature of this artistic/cultural expression and its impact in formulating identities/consciousness, its role in fostering social movements, and, ultimately, in shaping Brazilian society? I do not yet know the answers to such questions, but I think the questions are important for any considerations of black Brazil and the ideas of culture, identity, and social mobilization.

Envoi

According to Ọlábìyí Yáì, Yorùbá-speaking peoples have always thought of themselves as a diaspora and their artists as *arè*, "itinerant persons," always strangers who engage in "constant departures" of creative invention (Yáì 1994). A Yorùbá saying he cites expresses it well: "Outside the walls of your home you have the right to choose the name that pleases you" (*orúko tó wu ni làá jé léhìn odi*). For centuries in West Africa, during the horrors of the Middle Passage and the enormous challenges of more than five hundred years of slavery and oppression in the Americas, Yorùbás and their descendants, as well as other people of color, have *named*, that is, identified, and defined themselves, in the face of seemingly overwhelming odds. I have no doubt they will continue to do so as they reflect on the past and present, interpret their situations pragmatically, and then take action using their *òrìṣà*-given *àṣẹ/axé*. . . *AXÉ!*.

NOTES

Author's Note: I acknowledge with gratitude Cleveland State University for a Faculty Research Grant for work in Brazil in summer 1974; the California Afro-American Museum, Los Angeles, for funds to interview Brazilian artists in 1987 and 1988; and especially the Newberry Library/National Endowment for the Humanities for a Fellowship in 1992–1993 that permitted me to complete archival research and to write this paper. I also thank my colleagues from whom I have learned so much about Yorùbá ways in Africa and the Americas: Rowland Abíódún, Samuel Akínfénwá, Làmídí Fákéye, Folúṣọ́ Lóngé, Moyò Òkédìjí, Kọ́láwọlé Ọṣítọ́lá, Ràímì Akaki Táíwò, and Ọlábìyí Yáì; C. Daniel Dawson, Margaret Thompson Drewal, John and Valerie Mason, Mimito, José Adario dos Santos, Sauda and Joseph Smith, João Reis, and the artists discussed in this essay; and friends whose support has sustained me: Eneida Sanches, Giba Conceição, and Rowney and Tania Scott. I also wish to express my gratitude to Akin Adeṣokan, a visiting scholar in the James S. Coleman African Studies Center at UCLA, and Bọ́lájí Campbell, a graduate student at the University of Wisconsin–Madison, for assistance with Yorùbá diacritics. Any shortcomings in this essay are, of course, my own.

1. This centrally placed "passage" is visibly rendered in the *poteau mitan* or "central post" of Haitian *vodun* temples, and reinforced in the array of sacred signatures or *veve* for the *loa* (deities) that are drawn in flour on the floor around the *poteau mitan* to attract them.

2. See the works of Nina Rodrigues (1935), Artur Ramos (1939; 1944), and especially João Reis (1987) on Afro-Muslim (*ìmàle*) revolts in nineteenth-century Bahia.

3. Debret (1954:pl. 87), in a narrative that accompanies one of his watercolors of an African wearing an iron mask, states that, "Nègre au masque—masque de fer blanc que l'on fait porter aux nègres qui ont la passion de manger de la terre" but neglects to explain that "eating earth" was a way to commit suicide.

4. For example, a young female child revealed to be the incarnation of her grandmother will be named Yétúndé, "Mother-has-returned." The grandmother continues to exist in *òrun*, but part of her spirit or breath (*èmí*) is a constituent element of the new child.

5. See Margaret Thompson Drewal (1992) for a detailed examination of the notion of "play" in Yorùbá ritual and its implications for theoretical understandings of performance generally.

6. I want to thank Mr. Cide Teixeira for the suggestion to research this structure and Pierre Fatumbi Verger for showing me brief biographical information on Manoel Friandes in his copy of Querino's 1909 book. Research in Brazil since the writing of this chapter complicates and questions Friandes's connection with the Lapinha church. Yet other aspects of his life, work, and faith substantiate the agency of Afro-Brazilian Muslims in the nineteenth century.

7. For a brief overview of Afro-Brazilian art history see Drewal and Driskell (1989:31–34). A more thorough treatment can be found in Araújo (1988).

8. Parts of the following section are excerpted from my essay in Drewal and Driskell (1989:31–50).

9. I was not able to study this contest in detail, but it would certainly merit a systematic analysis as one example of how battles for recognition and for control in "politics of representation" are being waged. The following discussion was based on comments made by various Brazilian friends as well as strangers, discourse in the streets, and a brief review of several newspaper articles in 1993. It was an impressionistic and "unsystematic" reflection, yet I believe it suggests the contests constantly waged by Afro-Brazilians, whether past or present; personal, communal, or national; subversive or openly confrontational. Research in 1997–1998 confirms these initial impressions, which will be published in a forthcoming work.

10. Ọlábìyí Yáì has pointed out to me that the Yorùbá term gbàlà was probably a nineteenth-century missionary invention to convey the notion of "redemption," a concept alien to Yorùbá thought since it is predicated on the idea of "original sin." Thus the carnival spectacle of Villa Isabelle brought together a remarkable juxtaposition of ancient as well as more recent Christianized-Yorùbá and Brazilian Catholic references, together with a generalized "environmentalist" sensibility to energize its diverse audience.

REFERENCES

Araújo, Emanoel, ed. 1988. *A mão afro-brasileira: significado da contribuição artística e histórica.* São Paulo: Tenenge.

Bairros, L. 1989. "Brazil: Birthplace of Racial Democracy?" In Henry John Drewal and D. Driskell, eds., *Introspectives: Contemporary Art by Americans and Brazilians of African Descent,* pp. 23–25. Los Angeles: California Afro-American Museum.

Brandão, Carlos Rodrigues. 1976. "Congos, congadas e reinados: rituais de negros católicos." *Cultura* (Brasília) 6(23):78–93.

Brazilian Art. 1976. São Paulo: Ministry of External Affairs.

Clifford, James. 1988. *The Predicament of Culture.* Cambridge: Harvard University Press.

Crook, Larry. 1993. "Samba-reggae: Black Consciousness and the Reafricanization of Bahian Carnival Music in Brazil." *The World of Music* 35(2):90–108.

Crowley, Daniel J. 1984. *African Myth and Black Reality in Bahian Carnaval.* Los Angeles: UCLA Museum of Cultural History.

Cultura. 1977 [article on *congadas*].

de Certeau, M. 1984. *The Practice of Everyday Life.* Berkeley: University of California Press.

Debret, J. B. 1834. *Viagem pittoresca e histórica ao Brasil: aquarelas e desenhos que não foram reproduzidos na edição de Firmin Didot - 1834.* R. de Castro Maya, ed. Paris, 1954. [Debret original volumes published as *Voyage Historique et Pittoresque au Brésil, ou séjour d'un artiste français au Brésil.* Paris: Didot Freres, 1834, 35, 39.]

Drewal, Henry John, and D. Driskell, eds. 1989. *Introspectives: Contemporary Art by Americans and Brazilians of African Descent.* Los Angeles: California Afro-American Museum.

Drewal, Margaret Thompson. 1977. "Projections from the Top in Yoruba Art." *African Arts* 11(1):43–49, 91–92.

———. 1992. *Yoruba Ritual: Performers, Play, Agency.* Bloomington: Indiana University Press.

Gates, H. L. 1988. *The Signifying Monkey.* New York: Oxford University Press.

Mason, J. 1988. "Old Africa, Anew." In *Another Face of the Diamond: Pathways through the Black Atlantic South*, pp.14–21. New York: INTAR Latin American Gallery.

Mendonça, R. 1935. *A influência africana no português do Brasil.* 2d ed. [illustrated with maps and engravings]. São Paulo: Companhia Editora Nacional.

Nina Rodrigues, Raimundo. 1935. *Os africanos no Brasil.* 2d ed. São Paulo: Companhia Editora Nacional.

Omari, Mikelle Smith. 1984. *From the Inside to the Outside: The Art and Ritual of Bahian Candomblé*. Los Angeles: UCLA Museum of Cultural History.

Poole, D. 1992. "The Struggle for Self-Affirmation and Self-Determination: Africans and People of African Descent in Salvador, Bahia, 1800–1850." Ph.D. dissertation, Indiana University.

Preston, George. 1987. *Emanoel Araújo: Brazilian Afrominimalist*. São Paulo: MASP.

Querino, M. R. 1909. *Artistas bahianos*. Rio: Imprensa Nacional.

Ramos, Artur. 1939. *The Negro in Brazil*. Translated from the Portuguese by Richard Pattee. Washington, D.C.: The Associated Publishers, Inc.

――――. 1944. *Las poblaciones del Brasil*. Tr. T. M. Molina. México, D.F.: Fondo de Cultura Económica.

Reis, João. 1987 [1986]. *Rebelião escrava no Brasil: a história do levante dos malês (1835)*. 2d ed. São Paulo: Editora Brasiliense.

Risério, Antônio. 1981. *Carnaval Ijexá: notas sobre afoxés e blocos do novo carnaval afrobaiano*. Salvador: Corrupio.

Thompson, R. F., and J. Cornet. 1981. *The Four Moments of the Sun*. Washington, D.C.: The National Gallery of Art.

Verger, P. 1968. *Flux et reflux de la traite des nègres entre le golfe de Benin et Bahia de Todos os Santos du XVII au XIX siècle*. Paris: Mouton.

Yáì, ỌláBìyí B. 1994. "In Praise of Metonomy: The Concepts of 'Tradition' and 'Creativity' in the Transmission of Yoruba Artistry over Time and Space." In Rowland Abiodun, Henry John Drewal, and John Pemberton, eds., *The Yoruba Artist: New Theoretical Perspectives on African Arts*. Washington, D.C.: Smithsonian Institution Press.

Wetherell, James. 1860. *Stray Notes from Bahia: being extracts from letters, etc., during a residence of fifteen years*. Ed. W. Hadfield. Liverpool: Webb and Hunt.

10 Black Brazil: African Notes on a New Negritude

FEMI OJO-ADE

> In a country where the people are conditioned
> by the concern with being white, the ability for
> each person included in the census to declare
> his or her own color or race means that a great
> number of blacks, as well as mulattos, may have
> declared themselves white.
>
> —Abias do Nascimento, *O genocídio do
> negro brasileiro*

Negritude, Dead or Alive?

As an African interested for many years in the problematics of being black in the world, I have continued to read and write about *negritude* (Ojo-Ade 1989, 1993). I have witnessed many symbolic burial ceremonies of the controversial ideology, performed by "progressive" intellectuals peeved by its contradictions, its collusion and collaboration with our conquering masters from the West, and its attachment to what has been called a dead past. Yet, at each and every solemn ceremony, I have also seen a certain desperation, an endless search for self and for solution, a need to fill a void, a continuous questioning of our situation and condition in the world. In other words, those burying their dead parents, as it were, remain pitiable orphans left to twist in the maelstrom unleashed from afar by those determined to destroy our culture while at the same time denying that they actually stole from us to build their supposedly superior civilization. And, as we file out of the conference centers, we carry with us the burden of blackness and the coffin and, most significantly, the spirit of our dead who, fortunately for us, remain alive (even if we may have forgotten the linkage), inspiring us to struggle to survive, to triumph over tyrants, to rehabilitate our heritage, to maintain black as human.

To be sure, negritude must not be construed in absolute terms as an ideology, doctrine, or philosophy. It cannot be monolithic or monopolitic, as Senegal's Leopold Sedar Senghor wanted it to be (see Ojo-Ade 1978). However, that does not mean that negritude is dead and buried. Even if, out of shame, despair, a desire to be *civilized* (read: in Western terms) and to rise gloriously to the paradise of Eurocentric universalism, we wanted to bury it in our psyche, the realities of our lives will not allow us that privilege. Brazil's Abdias do Nascimento alludes to Aimé Césaire's "three elements of negritude: identity, fidelity and solidarity" (Nascimento and Nascimento 1992:104). In my opinion, it is a question of realities, relevance, and responsibilities: the realities of racism; the relevance of struggle and revolution; the responsibilities of everyone claiming to represent the black race. Of course, it all begins with the acceptance of one's blackness. Many would rather hide behind a white mask (cf. Frantz Fanon's *Black Skin, White Masks*) or blend into a snowy sea of universalism. The Brazilian example gives ample proof of the need for some form of negritude. "Racial democracy," "whitening," "deracialization," "blackening," whatever terminology one may use, perspicacious observers recognize the process and practice of racism and white supremacism. Nascimento's classic *O genocídio do negro brasileiro* (1978) is essential reading, but whoever really wishes to know the whole truth should visit Brazil.

Contrary to the sugar-coated tales told by Gilberto Freyre and other apologists for the humaneness of slave-masters in the notorious *casa grande*, there are many examples of their mind-boggling beastliness. One kind-hearted master commented on his female house-slave's big, beautiful eyes (note that everything relating to Africa must be big, raw, in its most elemental form, indeed, wild and savage) and he went out. When he returned home for lunch, his dear wife served the slave's eyes for sumptuous dessert. When abolition was finally declared in Brazil in 1888, some slave-owners in the Recôncavo put all their slaves in a big cauldron and set them on fire. In the late twentieth century, things have naturally become more civilized.

In 1990, Aline França, a black writer from Salvador, appears before a book festival audience in Brussels as a representative Brazilian writer. The audience is shocked and wonders aloud why Jorge Amado was not brought instead. In 1993, a store attendant in the ultramodern

Salvadoran shopping plaza called "Iguatemi," trying to attract customers, calls out to a very dark-skinned man (actually an African), "Venha, branco!" (Come here, whiteman!). The attendant himself is as black as his "whiteman." Also in 1993, it is carnival time, three days of splendor in the tropical sun of Salvador (the name means "savior"), Brazil's first capital and landing point of African slaves. Besides the fantastic celebration and the flush of colors, the visible signs of happiness and harmony, and the picture of perfection and prosperity in that earthly paradise, a discerning observer is struck by one fact: the parading *blocos* are separated according to skin color. Still in 1993, arriving at the Rio de Janeiro international airport, one is almost immediately faced with the reality of racism: color as determinant of human condition, with the fairest perched at the top looking down on the darkest, who are armed with brooms and trolleys, sweeping floors and carrying passengers' luggage. As a dark-skinned visitor, you try to shrug it off as mere coincidence, but then you realize that it is a sight you have seen before where whites are in control. So you, a black man decked out in your African "costume," rich enough to buy a plane ticket, might be considered a tiger out of the jungle, a stranger in civilization. You smile cynically, satisfied that you are only there for a while. You sip your beer under the confused gaze of the *moreno* whom you would normally call black, but who would simply die if you ever whispered the word to him; you read the message of love of *morenas* and *loiras* on the colorful beer coaster covered with sketches of long-haired women; and you recall the interesting story related by your African diplomat friend who had a very hard time convincing his daughter's school mistress in Brasília that the little girl was, in his own opinion, a *negra* and not at all a *morena*.

Abdias do Nascimento and Adão Ventura: Two Examples of Brazilian Negritude

When the organizers of the University of Florida conference chose the title "Black Brazil," they may have been unaware of the significant statement being made by the word "black"; for, despite all evidence to the contrary, the powers that be have incessantly propagated a policy of de-negrification and de-Africanization. That Afro-Brazilians like Abdias do Nascimento and Adão Ventura are involved in the struggle for black liberation, using the symbolic word "negritude" should not be surprising, given the lived realities of their country. The more I think about the choice of that word, that some of us would rather wish away, the more I become convinced of its relevance and adequacy. Anglophone Africans, including myself, are too eager to condemn its use and usefulness, as we sneer at the Francophones and Lusophones. We forget that through subtle paternalism or blatant perniciousness, in certain situations the enslaver and colonizer succeeded in creating acculturated blacks who must make desperate efforts to free themselves, particularly their minds. If the tiger does not have to proclaim its tigritude (the famous comment on negritude by Nigerian Nobel Laureate Wole Soyinka), it is because there is no hunter determined to deal it a death blow with his civilized weapon. Moreover, the tiger, we dare say, is not a human being; blacks, depersonalized and treated like possessions in a category comparable to that of horses and housewares, cannot but proclaim their humanity.

Abdias do Nascimento, in the spirit of the negritude pioneers (especially Aimé Césaire), has worked from a basic commitment to his color and culture, striking an often precarious balance between the responsibilities and realities of the private and public person; the poet, painter, and politician, combining the word and the work, symbol and substance, mixing creativity and constructivity. His definition of negritude is decidedly all-inclusive and non-intellectual. This point is of great importance because our tormenting teacher never ceases to tease us with accusations of "lack of objectivity," "emotionalism," and "sentimentality," and to remind us of the necessity for "logical, scientifically correct reasoning." Indeed, as one travels through the world and witnesses the progress of racism, one better understands why the modern masters encourage "rational thinking." Nascimento objects, calling upon us Africans

> not to engage in detailed academic discussion, but rather to reflect on questions of historical and immediate importance to the destiny of the African world. . . . African scholars and thinkers [must] remove themselves from the minutia of current research engagements in order to discuss the broader concerns which . . . we have a responsibility to consider in the interests of our people. (1992:83)

Nascimento uses the notion of negritude as a springboard for Afro-Brazilian liberation struggle. From the firm premise that "Brazil is demographically and culturally an African country" (1992:88), he has proceeded to act on behalf of his people. In public life, he has worked as politician in both Brasília and Rio de Janeiro. Senator Nascimento proposed many bills, supported every piece of legislation pushing for the betterment of the black population. He does not work alone. As a prominent member of the Unified Black Movement (Movimento Negro Unificado), he cooperated with comrades from across the country to draft proposals for presentation in political forums. Unfortunately, not much has changed. Most of the proposals have not been adopted. One problem is that the few other blacks with positions on the national political scene have mostly preferred the reactionary stance of being "Brazilian," not black. "While other African-Brazilian legislators have existed, they do not identify themselves as black, much less carry the banner of the Afro-Brazilian cause" (Nascimento and Nascimento 1992:100). Nascimento the politician stated his objectives: "Our goal is to consolidate the autonomy of the Afro-Brazilian movement, rejecting its cooptation by any political party" (1992:101). Now, achieving that goal is a tall order. Nascimento himself has mentioned the daunting diversity of the black movement. In a country as vast as Brazil, it is difficult to galvanize efforts into a united whole, especially given what the professor-politician himself calls the collective psychology of Brazilians in regard to racism. "In Brazil, law is not necessary: it is codified in all culture and speech of the dominated and ruled classes."[1] Nascimento's valiant work does not seem to have succeeded in realizing the lofty goals of equality and emancipation. Apart from publication of the black movement's journals and manifestations at symbolic ceremonies, officialism has managed to limit its progress within the community. One needs to read Nascimento's words to feel the depth of the "pressure from birth—from one humiliation to another, despised, victim of violence—physical and moral" (Rio interview). In the Senate, he has single-handedly waged an Afro-Brazilian war, as "a survivor of the greatest holocaust ever experienced by a people in the history of humanity"…"out of love for [his] people and for Brazil" (Nascimento 1991:7, 8). Nascimento calls himself "a black stain" in the Brazilian Senate, and he condemns "Brazilian apartheid" and "this pathological compulsion to be white and European. . . . Geographically etched into the political elite of our country" (1991:11). And I remember the man bursting into tears in Ile-Ife in 1977, during a speech marked by the vigor and violence of a victim defying the implacable enemy. The little impact of that eloquently stated defiance and call to action, culminating in the seminal text *O genocídio do negro brasileiro*, shows how far the Brazilian struggle still has to go. Nascimento comments again:

> I left the army in 1936 as a result of racial discrimination, but the ostensible reason given is that I was accused of unruliness at the door

of a bar. . . . Blacks are never given the chance to lead, maybe in football and samba shows. In the judiciary, there are no blacks—the
blacks are the judged, condemned by white judges. (Rio interview)

With regard to his work in theater, Nascimento mentions the same lack of
progress. The Teatro Experimental do Negro (Nascimento 1978:129–135)
prospered until he went into exile in 1968, but, "as now, the situation of
blacks in theater is precarious as they have no money" (Rio interview).

Along these lines, the figure of Mário Gusmão comes to mind.
A veteran actor who has spent most of his 65 years on stage and on both
the small and big screens, he has suffered from the sin of his skin color.
After a bohemian life from south to north and all over the country trying to make ends meet, Gusmão was back in his native Bahia in spring
1993 for a belated honor at the Centro Gregório de Mattos. Sitting there
before a small crowd of admirers, he tried very much to hide his pain.
However, the face gave it all away: deep lines etched into the dark skin,
meandering across the face like a river of mysteries and miseries; eyes
dark and dreamy, as if in search of a solution awaited for too long, and
accusing, for knowing but pretending not to know. Someone asked Gusmão whether or not he was bitter for all the anguish, neglect, dehuman-
ization, when, considering his immense talent, he should have had it
made forever. He smiled and told the story of another honor once offered
him by the state authorities but which he could not accept because he
had no means of going to the ceremony. Without the help of family and
friends and payment from odd performances, he would hardly be able to
eat three meals a day.[2] Surprisingly enough, the man has not let the pain
conquer him. He vows to continue to struggle to the very end and urges
the younger generation to take up the mantle.

From all indications, the young generation, more militant than the
older one, stands to succeed where there once has been failure. The feeling here is that Abdias do Nascimento and other leaders of Brazilian
negritude have to educate youth more, to raise their consciousness and
give them faith and direction. The demise of the Teatro Experimental
and Nascimento's own career may discourage the weak, but history provides us with reason to hope. Zumbi in Palmares, Toussaint L'Overture in
Haiti, Nelson Mandela in South Africa, as well as other heroes, symbolize the inevitable success of the irrepressible struggle. But success, as
Léon Damas once said, comes only through hard work.

When Nascimento declares the resolve of the black movement to reject being co-opted by any political party, he actually underlines a delicate aspect of the struggle. To date, the Brazilian movement has revealed a certain ambiguity in its program. The few individuals having some political success (for example, Nascimento and the Rio de Janeiro politician Benedita da Silva) have worked from within political parties. Nascimento himself makes mention of the new sensitivity of such affiliations. For example, the Communist Party of Brazil and its several splinter groups "are sympathetic and actively seek to recruit and develop Afro-Brazilian militants within their ranks" (Nascimento and Nascimento 1992:101). That, nonetheless, does not mean that the cooperation (or is it co-optation?) automatically bodes well for blacks. Events in other countries lead one to be wary of Communist-Marxist alliances. The proletarian paradise preached and promised by the famous manifesto hardly ever materializes, and blacks have often ended up being frustrated to the point of quitting the Party.[3]

One action might be the creation of an African-Brazilian political party that would, from its independent position, cultivate linkages with other progressive parties. Such action would appear to be idealistic for now: first and foremost, black consciousness has to become real—not *moreno*, but *negro*. When commitment is at issue, time becomes a factor. Abdias do Nascimento is almost 80 years old. There is thus some concern about the continuity of the black cause. As usual, the question mark is followed by an exclamation, which is one more element shared by blacks the world over. One thinks of the United States: after the passing of Martin Luther King Jr., there has been a void in leadership. One thinks also of South Africa: Mandela may die tomorrow and no one is ready to pick up the baton and continue the race. In Brazil, the problem is particularly aggravating because a capitalistic current of self-preservation and individualistic progression is obviating collective action. The already addressed white supremacism stands to maintain its position in a situation of economic depression.

One criticism made of Abdias do Nascimento is that he is married to a white woman. An ex-student of mine who has studied and lived in Brazil recently dismissed the man as "another sell-out." It is another sign of the burden that blackness brings in a world where, for ages, white men used to rape black women with impunity and have had the freedom to fornicate and frolic with whomever they wish, while a black man was

lynched for merely looking at a white woman; today he is closely watched
every step of the way. Under the circumstances in which we have lived,
with the disease of racism eating away at the very core of our existence,
would it be a sign of reaction for a black man to marry a white woman,
or would it be a matter of revolt? Should you preach the beauty of blackness and choose whiteness in the most intimate aspect of your life? Can
you claim to be truly committed if you do? Is it not possible for you to
raise the consciousness of your spouse so that she may participate in
your struggle? Years ago, a similar criticism was made of Senghor. The
matter was so important that Claude McKay, a Jamaican-American
writer of the Harlem Renaissance period, included it in his novel *Banjo*
(1929). Ray, a West Indian writer just arrived in Marseilles, the French
port-city where many black people of all shades and backgrounds con-
gregate, expresses his disgust at

> an intelligent race-conscious man marrying a white woman. Espe-
> cially a man who is bellyaching about race rights. He is the one who
> should exercise a certain control and self-denial of his desires. Take
> Senghor and his comrades in propaganda for example. They are the
> bitterest and most humorless of propagandists and they are all mar-
> ried to white women. It is as if the experience has over-soured them.
> As if they thought it would bring them closer to the white race, only to
> realize too late that it couldn't. (McKay 1929:207)

McKay's novel is far too complex to discuss in this essay. Suffice it to say
that neither Ray nor any other of the caste-oriented blacks is in a position to criticize another since they all are confused. We should note, however, that Senghor's mixed marriage blends well into his vaunted
"civilization de l'universal" and "métissage culturel." Senghorian negritude thus avows the essential mixture of all races and cultures with the
proviso that black culture be given a chance to reclaim its deserved place
in that universal culture.

Abdias do Nascimento's negritude and his marital status would fall
into another category, nonetheless. His American wife, Elisa, is engaged
in Afro-Brazilian struggle and is author and co-author (with him) of several useful works. One appreciates Nascimento's activism better when
one compares him to another black man with whom he shares a sur-
name, Edson Arantes do Nascimento, universally known as Pelé. "O rei
do futebol" ("the king of soccer") is reactionary to the bone. He is Brazil's
ambassador of "whitening," always by the side of blond, blue-eyed bomb-
shells (e.g., Xuxa), forever denying any sign of racism in his beloved

nation. Ironically, while millions of Africans revere "the king," few recognize Abdias do Nascimento.

During a visit to Brasília in 1992, I met Adão Ventura, then president of the Fundação Cultural Palmares (Palmares Cultural Foundation), a governmental organ resulting from the efforts of the black movement to bring Afro-Brazilian culture to the fore (Nascimento and Nascimento 1992:102). The foundation, created in 1988 as part of commemorations of the centennial of abolition, as yet has no program or policy for cooperating with progressive elements within the black community. My African-Brazilian acquaintances are not impressed by its record because it is a governmental creation. Is it therefore an instrument of control, a camouflage?

My interview with Adão Ventura convinced me of his personal awareness, and his poetry marvelously proves that point. The very titles of his latest two collections, *A cor da pele* (Skin Color, 1980) and *textura-afro* (afro-texture, 1992), emphasize the poet's Afrocentricity. Brazil's Eurocentric critics note his talent, as well as his evolution into race-consciousness. A few examples:

> Henrique Alves: [Adão] "reaffirms a concept of Senghor's when he focuses on negritude and says that the poet needs to have 'the emotional warmth that brings words to life.'"

> Duílio Gomes: "His concern with form and his black roots are his greatest victory.... [His poetry constitutes a] clean, politically correct and expressive work that has already caught the attention of the nation's critics and that makes him shine alone and unbeatable."

> Silviano Santiago: "Adão Ventura is affiliated with what could be called—insisting to the maximum on the paradox—the Western tradition of black poetry, a tradition raised to a sovereign condition by a Cruz e Souza[4] in the symbolist movement. This means that Cruz e Souza and Adão *write legitimate poetry at the same time as they make excellent black poetry* (emphasis added).[5]

Overall, these comments add to the widespread racist attitude noticed in other spheres of Brazilian life. Creative works are judged according to the Western canon. Black poetry is not considered real poetry. When Adão's work did not address the theme of blackness, he was praised as one of Brazil's best poets. Now that he has fixed his gaze on his existential dilemma and cultural matrix, critics are complaining, albeit with civilized subtlety.

Adão's new negritude poems vividly describe Afro-Brazilian history, from slavery ("o negro escravo") to the present condition in which blacks are encouraged to sell their soul in order to survive ("preto de alma branca"), with a clearly stated necessity for revolution ("flashback") through interaction and cooperation with Africa ("Papai-Moçambique") and constant questioning of racist, sacrosanct lies ("Por que Jesus Cristo é sempre branco?"). Adão declares his Africanity and assumes his activist role as a poet (from *texturaafro*):

ORIGIN

to wear the shirt
of a black poet
—to pierce your heart
with the sharp
point of a knife
—one of those old ones,
the *Curvelo* brand,
in steel without incision,
made for death

—And to accommodate
in the scant space
of a sheath
your slave-quarter grief.

The poet, revolutionary, is ready to kill symbolically any reactionary elements in the community. His brand of violence, however, is not gratuitous or absolute. Well aware of the depth of black grief, he is also ready to rehabilitate, to offer hope, to encourage change for the better. The identity of the audience could actually be double, both black and white: the man in the big house, *casa grande*, racist and inhuman, would thus reap the fruit of the seeds of destruction sown in his plantation, while he of the *senzala* of Adão's poetry would be comforted by the poet. The poignant message of Adão's poetry is the urgent need for change in the black condition, not tomorrow but today.

NOW

It is time
to get out of the ghetto/fields

the slave-quarter
and to come into the room
— Our place is in the Sun.

The poet's words are not always transformable into action. To move into the room (house), the slave has to dislodge its occupant, who has no intention of leaving. The last two lines of the above poem also subtly imply the dilemma of the enslaved. To occupy the house, you have to leave the sun. The double symbolism of the sun is not lost on the reader. Strong and sharp, the rays can sap your strength; soft, they can be soothing and satisfying. The suffocating sun suffered by the slave toiling on the plantation would contrast with the warm rays enjoyed by lazy, relaxing throngs on the beach. And, finally, the sun remains the symbol of light, of happiness. In a quotation prefacing *texturaafro*, Adão reveals the depth of the dilemma being discussed: "We are," he quotes from Manuel Bandeira, "doubly prisoners: of ourselves and of the times in which we live." The objective has to be to free ourselves. Negritude's relevance is in helping us to begin to think about that goal and how to achieve it. Compared with Abdias do Nascimento, Adão Ventura would seem to have more difficulty harmonizing the state of the artist (working in absolute terms) and the public figure (working within reality and therefore risking and being forced to compromise).

Blacks in Bahia: Still Waiting for the Savior?

Bahia, a state where blacks represent a vast majority, is an excellent example of the potential and pitfalls of negritude. As far as oppression and suppression go, "Bahia is a portrait in miniature of Brazil's overall society," affirms Abdias do Nascimento. The most annoying aspect of Bahian reality is that, with consciousness and commitment, with determination and direction, blacks could change their condition immensely and take their "place in the sun." As of now, they have to contend with the enemy within (themselves and their inferiority complex) and the one without (the ruling, wanna-be-white aristocracy preaching the civilized sermon of racial democracy, and their superiority complex).

Popular wisdom says there is no one in Bahia, even among the aristocrats, who does not have at least a distant drop of African blood. Indeed, in their efforts to present Bahia (and themselves) as a world example of anti-racism, such aristocrats are sometimes the first to

stress this fact. They also cite the prevalence of African culture, from
the culinary to the religious. Yet the African cultural matrix is still seen
as exotic and classed as folklore, while European norms and values
prevail in Bahian society. Power relations are divided not so subtly.
There are no African congressmen from the state. (Nascimento and
Nascimento 1992:146)

Walking on Salvador's downtown streets, one has a strong sense of
African presence, with smiling, beautiful, black women frying and selling *acarajé* (the Yoruba word, *akara*, a cake-like delicacy, very much like
the ones made in Lagos and in all Yoruba-land); beaming black faces welcoming one like a long lost sibling; and, in the Candomblé shrines, the
engaging, aged *iyalorixá* still speaking Yoruba amidst religious devotees
dancing to the scintillating rhythm of the drums in praise of African
deities providing hope and affirming credibility. Indeed, Brazilian negritude is most visibly and viably represented in religion and culture. And
therein lies the contradiction.

First, the pitfalls. Both upper and under classes adhere to African
religion and many Bahians would probably claim to be Candomblé worshipers even when they are Catholics. Unfortunately, that association and
belief are not translated into political (in the sense of real, pragmatic)
action for the good of both individual and community. Vaunting one's
Candomblé connection seems to be a fad, a fancy, like showing off one's
African "costumes"; it is a symbol of exoticism, of having experienced
something unserious, to be dealt with outside the scope of important
matters. Presidential candidates travel to Bahia to pay homage to African
religious elders. The pilgrimage is publicized in the media. The propa-
ganda is built up into a policy statement. When the elections are over,
blacks remain as far away from the presidential palace as they were
before. And they continue to pray to the *orixás* (deities) on behalf of
Mr. President and other politicians making false promises.

Examples in many countries tell us that religion is not only a question of politics but also economics. Our experiences of slavery and colonialism are the best proof. I once thought that Bahia's African-religious
groups were not economically aware. Now I know that they are. Witness
the competition among shrine-owners to prove superiority through
a show of material ostentation. Witness the commercialization of the
cult by superficially trained experts declaring their competence after a
quick trip to Nigeria. Witness the cutthroat jostling for personal space
where, traditionally, the community is more important than individual

aspiration. The economics of Candomblé is controlled to a large extent by *morenos* and whites; black skin is once again stigmatized.

I mentioned the welcoming smile on the faces met on Salvadoran streets and the warmth of the hosts at shrines. Again, beyond the smile and warmth lies a conflictual attitude toward the African, not always overt, but subtle, ferreted out only by the inquisitive mind. Candomblé has not helped blacks become more aware of their blackness and Africanity in the revolutionary sense underlined by Abdias do Nascimento. The mis-education masterminded by the ruling class is deep and difficult to eradicate. Those Bahians traveling to Africa—the mythical return to roots—do so for personal gain; they are not interested in any pioneering effort at consciousness-raising. As for Africans visiting Bahia, we are either too ignorant to understand or too immersed in the "civilizing mission" to want to undertake the task of approximating our two peoples. The religious worshiper is usually nonplussed to note that his African visitor, for him a symbol of the ancestral family, finally reviving the lost link, is totally shocked out of his Western shoes at the "pagan practices of people who should know better!" The dancing and wining and dining continue, we embrace and exchange addresses and amble off to the next dance, and we continue to live by lies without ever wishing to tell the truth for fear that it might destroy our shaky solidarity.

The potentials for negritude's success are many but, to begin with, we must tell the truth about our heritage and experiences; we must re-define our solidarity. The International Congress of Orixá Tradition, an umbrella organization of Africans on the continent and in the diaspora formed over a decade ago, is one of the forums for possible action. Every believer in African deities is welcome and, until recently, conferences were held every other year. Among the Congress's goals is the promotion of African religion as a sociopolitical and economic force. The branches in Salvador and São Paulo (already host of the organization's meetings) are quite strong, although one cannot but regret the internal wranglings that militate against real progress. Moreover, the reality of the religion's weakness in Africa does nothing to aid its destiny in the diaspora; nor does the existence of rival groups in the United States where entrepreneurial aspirations have their roots.

The ground gained in the past by the invading forces of Christianity and Islam continues to be reinforced in Africa while diasporan Africans cling to an Afrocentric religiosity as a viable reaction against those who brought them into bondage. We Africans may be too far gone in our sleepwalking into civilization to recognize the importance of a return to our religion. For Bahians and others, there may still be a chance to tap from its strength as did Zumbi and his comrades in Palmares.

Olodum, the Bahian cultural group, is a rare example of a well organized, sociopolitically conscious force. João Jorge Santos Rodrigues, its president, explains that the diverse activities—training of youths, musical and commercial activities (with the now very famous band touring abroad and selling millions of records and tapes)—are geared toward black liberation and rehabilitation of the African heritage as part and parcel of Brazilian civilization and culture. Olodum is without doubt a very important organization for the future of the community. It promotes black culture; it offers an opportunity for young men and women to live a meaningful life in a society where they normally exist in abject poverty and obscurity. It gives them pride and purpose. Finally, it stands up to the reactionary establishment. Olodum's publications include poems and pamphlets in which those progressive ideas are loudly expressed, and João Jorge and his comrades do not shy away from controversy. When, for instance, the band was honored with the Sharp Prize in May 1993, they rejected the award because it was given under the category of regional music (see interview in *Correio Brasiliense*, May 22, 1993, p. 3). João Jorge said:

> There was discrimination on the part of the organizers, those picking winners of the Sharp Prize, in regard to Olodum. We reject our classification as a regional group. Today, Olodum's work is recognized in Brazil and the world. . . . That is not even right, for Brazil is seeking universalization of its music.

Olodum's point is well taken. One could go further to remark that Brazil's mainstream has also deliberately downplayed the African components of Brazilian music. Samba-reggae, lambada, and other forms of music and dance are rooted in African religious and secular rhythms. Olodum itself (originally a carnival *bloco*) is in a position to do more to accentuate that African connection.[6] The group has toured North America, Europe, and Japan; we have not heard of any plans to go to Africa. The accent placed on the band and its music adds to the misconception that it is simply another money-making enterprise by exploiters of a sad situation and that, as in past years, it is one more form of entertainment for our capitalist masters.

The diffuse nature of negritudinal groupings in Bahia is also noticeable in intellectual circles (and one must bear in mind the very small percentage of educated blacks). The fact that there is no black congressman or congresswoman from Bahia can be blamed not only on white supremacists but also on the lack of organization within the black collectivity. In the last state elections, the prominent lawyer and professor Edvaldo Brito[7] ran for office. His family background is entrenched in the African religious community. But he could not build a political base among his people who, in general, did not appear to understand that they should support him as *their* candidate. Brito lost as a result of their ignorance of his own (ironical) political sophistication. Since those elections, Brito has remained in the shadow.

Other individuals project ideas of negritude from time to time, most visibly at conferences and other gatherings. Among them are writers. A collection of poems, *Poetas baianos da negritude*, published by the Centro de Estudos Afro-Orientais in Salvador (Vieira 1982) is the outcome of the celebration of Black Consciousness Day in November 1981. A close look at the work makes for a greater understanding of the concept of negritude and the writers' relationship to Africa. First, the editor's (Hamilton de Jesus Vieira) introductory remarks on each poet strike me as rather ambiguous, when not Afrophobic. On Durval Rosário de Azevedo, a student-poet, he writes: "Durval presented 'Trajetória,' which speaks of the coming of the *negro* to our country and of the need for all, blacks, whites and Indians, to fight for true freedom" (1982:15). On Arnaldo do Rosário Lima, once a Portuguese instructor at Obafemi Awolowo University, Ile-Ife, Nigeria: "Arnaldo returned to Africa, not to search for his lineage but to show Africans the legacy of the culture that their ancestors left here in Brazil, forming the richness of Brazilian culture" (1982:19). And, about Maria Dionísia de Santana Tosta: "In her poem, 'Mãe Menininha do Gantois,' she pays homage to that famous priestess, perhaps because she reminded her of the old figures of the nannies" (1982:27).

Durval's "Trajetória" (Trajectory) forcefully states the problematic nature of African-Brazilian heritage: the ancestors are accused of having abandoned their children in the hands of the white enslaver. Durval's poem thus raises a matter that many of us are hesitant to discuss, out of hypocrisy or fear. Contrary to the editor Vieira's comments, however, the poem does not categorically propagate an all-color-culture-nationalistic struggle for freedom. The unity being sought is first among blacks, the enslaved, the disenfranchised. The ultimate goal is integration, which is the point where all the races will live together without discrimination. To downplay the stage of struggle—a concerted effort by blacks them-selves—is to confuse issues, just as Brazil's mainstream aristocracy has done all along. When Vieira adds the Indians to the joint effort, he reveals not genuine progressiveness and nationalism, but a spurious liberalism that fails only to make us wonder what has happened to the original owners of the land.

The case of Arnaldo Lima is of particular interest to me since we were departmental colleagues at Ile-Ife before he suddenly departed for Guinea-Bissau. His poem "Lembranças Históricas" (Historical Memo-ries) starts with the cries of agony of slaves, the moanings of ancient war-riors who are "proclaimers of justice and freedom." Pity that the proclamation has not meant much; for, until now, "We are agonizing over the sad heritage." But then the poet jumps into an optimistic mood and ends his poem with:

> Living in the present time,
> constructing a new roof,
> confirms us as true agents of History.

Vieira's statement has to be extra-textual: this poem in no way shows the legacy of African-Brazilian culture. In order to have strength and authenticity, the "new roof" has to be built upon a firm foundation. In Africa, Arnaldo Lima has actually been engaged in finding his African-ity. The presence on the continent of people of his caliber can help create and cultivate the sort of pan-African–Brazilian body from which both sides would derive great dividends, provided that neither side gets car-ried away by egomania. The teacher of Portuguese can, and must, be a student of African culture if he is interested in authenticating his her-itage. The desire to learn should do nothing to diminish his status; rather, it can only enhance it.

Hamilton Vieira's ideas tally with those of the aristocracy looking down on the Afro-Brazilian lower class. That is the only possible expla-nation for his statement on Dionísia's homage to the much revered Mãe Menininha, whom the poet asks to intercede with the orixá on her behalf. Even if most of the priestesses are "uneducated" according to dominant Western definitions, they are most knowledgeable of what matters most, that is, their culture and civilization, sources of strength and survival of their people and invaluable springboard for progress in a racist society.

That estimation of the quality of the priestesses and priest and the African ancestry is found in the work of Aline França, herself a lower-class employee of the Federal University of Bahia. Her poem "Mensagem dos Nossos Ancestrais" (Message from Our Ancestors) is at once a declaration of the continuum of culture as a dynamic process of existence and struggle and a call to pan-African revolutionary action. França's prose and poetry are steeped in the traditional belief in the cultural existential cycle in which the past, present, and future are intertwined and the ancestors continue to influence the lives of the living. The poet echoes lines written by past generations when she has the ancestors call out to us all:

> Awake, blacks all over the world
> Go on struggling for better days
> Together Brazil and Africa!
> We shall go on inspiring your hearts
> and shall provide the strength
> to support a glorious battle.
> Zumbi dos Palmares will always be
> with each one of you.

The poem ends:

> We were not sad. Their message remained.
> They will return whenever they want . . . [8]

The danger is that, instead of struggling, blacks might be waiting for their ancestors to return and save them. We have seen that attitude in religion, in politics, in fact, in all facets of Bahian life. Most people lack the resolve of the likes of Aline França. They would rather blend into the utopic Brazil planted into their psyche by the ruling class. In such a mindset, their struggle is but a farce, an attempt to further alienate themselves from their Self in order to be re-born in the Other. Some believe the kind of white lie embedded in the "scientific analysis" of individuals such as Clarival do Prado Valladares, a member of the Federal Council of Culture who has stated that "whites did not hunt blacks in Africa, but bought them peacefully from black tyrants" (quoted in Nascimento and Nascimento 1992:114). For those "scientifically minded" people, Africa would be a jungle to be rejected. Other Brazilians know only of South Africa, having been taught that apartheid is the worst inhumanism on earth and that their beloved Brazil is committed to tearing down that African monster. Because of their misery, they have never had an opportunity to travel as far as the magnificent international airport of Rio de Janeiro where South African jets basked in the Carioca sun even during the worst days of apartheid. Charmed by the national brainwashing-whitewashing, they are blind to the analogy between their status and that of the black victims in South Africa.

If negritude is to have any meaning in the Brazilian setting, Bahia simply has to be the starting point, or the center of activism. Sad to say, it is not and may not be for a long time. In spite of programs of such groups as Olodum, the Afrocentricity of Candomblé, the sporadic militant manifestations by poets and artists, and some linkages with Africa, there remains a lack of strong, dedicated, and focused leadership able to offer the people a sense of purpose and the strength to take charge of the state that they built ... for the white man.

Conclusion: Black Brazil and Africa

When we complain of diasporan Africans' ignorance about Africa, we must remember that Africans encourage the degradation and disrespect. As the saying goes, Africans are quite adept at out-whiting the white man. Of course, wit serves a useful purpose, but not when it leads to a death wish of whitening one's self and society. Think of religion, culture, education, technology, the whole notion of *civilization*: those shipped abroad are desperately trying to revive the lost self and those of us fortunate to keep the space at home are dead-set on losing ourselves abroad.

The process of self-reawakening must begin at the top; for, in a vein similar to the original negritude, the loss of self occurred among the chosen few who, sent to learn about the white man's way and to interpret it to the community and help it survive the European onslaught, returned with a new, borrowed self and as slaves or allies of the invader. Negritude has been the necessary step toward finding that lost self. For Senghor's generation, the loss was almost absolute. The consolation is that they left a legacy of struggle and of the importance of insisting upon the quality of life of African culture. African leadership has not learned that lesson, however. The man who claimed that blacks were not hunted down in

Africa for enslavement was placed on the jury of the First World Festival of Black Art (Dakar, 1966). At the 1977 Festival in Lagos (FESTAC), Abdias do Nascimento and other genuine voices of African-Brazilians were prevented from participating. No African government to my knowledge has ever stood up to condemn Brazilian racism. (Nigerian ambassador to Brazil) Jaiyeola Lewu's call for Bahian blacks to stand up and "contribute significantly to [their] country's development" is dramatic but inconsequential. The Nigerian government has done absolutely nothing to encourage black consciousness or promotion of Nigerian-Brazilian cultural linkage. The two countries have many economic ties, but nothing to show that we have a common heritage. Pelé and other soccer maestros have been known to Nigerians for many years; yet the average Nigerian is not aware that Brazil is the second largest black country in the world, after Nigeria. Part of the reason is that Yoruba, the mother-culture of the black presence in Brazil, is peripheral in the Nigerian power structure, where the Moslem hegemony is resentful of any other heritage. Where linkages have been established—the Ife University, for instance, has had academic and exchange agreements with universities in Bahia, Brasília, and São Paulo for some fifteen years—Nigerian officialdom has failed to follow up possibilities of cementing interaction. Surprisingly, Brazilians still express faith and pride in Nigeria and Africa. Abdias do Nascimento:

> Africa is my fatherland, my native land. My one year in Nigeria was extremely invigorating and it reinforced all my visions and expectations. I was not romanticizing Africa; I expected a continent suffering, coerced, vandalized for centuries. However, Nigeria had practically recovered, completely free.... Since all documents on our African origin have been destroyed by the Portuguese, African-Brazilians claim the whole of Africa for our motherland.... The link is deep, we are the same people.[9]

Aimé Césaire made similar remarks before (see Kesteloot and Kotchy 1973:233). Now, at the end of the twentieth century, African-diasporan cooperation and complimentarity are still being made in spurts, according to the caprices of men ignorant of history and overtly interested in lining their pockets and constructing castles in Europe.

   If changes must begin at the top, and since the top is heavy with alienated, satanic saviors, the onus falls on the knowledgeable intellectuals and culture-conscious, intelligent individuals to prod the top into action as they themselves arouse in the majority the latent will to stand up. Western critics are too quick to accuse Africans of communism. African culture, rooted in communalism, has always placed people, human beings, at the center. Communism made that claim even though it soon betrayed its stated position. We have noted Nascimento's assessment of Brazilian communism. Marx was right in positing the idea of empowering the producers of the food grabbed by the smart, greedy parasites. But he failed to proffer solutions to the sickness of racism and the common malady of greed and graft which have drifted down into the ranks of "the wretched of the earth"; the big, fat ego of so-called popular leaders is incessantly fed in African states. Capitalism probably knew of all these pitfalls long ago and smiled and stoked the fire that consumed communism in a blaze of Western glory. So what is the "Third World" supposed to do? Whether socialist or capitalist or *existist*, they are caught in the hell of misery aided by mismanagement by self-anointed messiahs. Brazilian blacks are as victimized as Africans; indeed, more.

We say that both peoples cannot but come together. Not just in Candomblé shrines. Not just on the streets on days of respite from the hell named carnival. Not just at conferences that, by their very nature, constitute a stage for the privileged to shine and show off their research on intangibles having nothing to do with the people whose existence and experience they are exploiting to build their reputation. When Abdias do Nascimento mentioned his shock and aversion for the original negritudinists' passion for the French language (1992:106), he was actually pinpointing the essential alienation of that movement and the necessity for today's generation to truly return to African roots by all means and, as Frantz Fanon said, language is the essence of culture. In Brazil, the Yoruba language is still alive, although barely. Part of the negritude efforts should be the teaching and learning of that language. In the mid-1970s the University of Ife began a program at the Federal University in Bahia (Olábìyí Yáì, now at the University of Florida, was the first professor sent to teach in the program) whereby Yoruba lessons were given to Bahians from all walks of life. It was deliberately not an intellectual exercise. It succeeded in awakening a sense of pride and belonging in all quarters of the community. But, as usual, there was no continuity. Through a combination of factors (malaise and lack of genuine interest in both Ife and Salvador, but mostly in the latter), the Yoruba program was soon reduced to a sham exercise in ego-inflation and hypocrisy. The intellectuals took over and destroyed all elements of authenticity.[10] And that brings us back to the theme of the Florida conference. Abdias do

Nascimento insists on the de-intellectualization of discussions about the destiny of black Brazil. The conference organizers, by the title chosen, already made a statement that they were moving away from that Eurocentric standpoint parading scientific explications of Brazil's "de-racialized, democratic society." They have thus contributed to the process of focusing the problem of racism, which, if not resolved, will leave our people in their current state as "the wretched of the earth." We cannot and must not forget that

> The history
> of the black man
> is a trace
> in a clasp
> of iron and fire. (Adão Ventura, *texturaafro*)

NOTES

1. From an interview with Nascimento that took place in Rio de Janeiro on March 3, 1993. The interview is part of a book-in-progress on black Brazilian writers. Subsequent references to that interview will be made as "Rio interview."

2. Mário Gusmão is but one example of many brilliant black actors condemned to a state of absence in Brazil. Gusmão's latest work is in the video of a promising young artist, Sérgio Machado, called *Troca de Cabeça*. Gusmão and another experienced black actor, Grande Otelo, recently reminisced about their careers. See "Aquele abraço!" in *A Tarde* (Salvador), May 25, 1993, Caderno 2, p. 1.

In Brazil, blacks are hardly seen on television; when they appear, they invariably play roles of servants. Of course, they are to be seen in large numbers in Candomblé, on the soccer field, or as entertainers. Concerning soccer, any fan of Brazilian football must have noticed a sharp decline in recent years in the quality of the national team. Could that be due to the visible "cleansing" of players wearing the national colors? A comparison between the black condition in the United States and Brazil would show how far Brazil still has to go in improving the lot of the race that built the nation. In both Brazil and the United States, it is a choice between the subtle and the salient. Covert or overt, both societies stigmatize the color black, although it would have been best to never have to choose, just to be able to live life in either society as a normal, total human being.

3. Cf. Césaire (1956) on the Martinican's resignation from the French Communist Party. In the United States, there are also the many cases of blacks (such as Richard Wright) who, in the 1930s, joined the Party only to later

distance themselves when they realized that racism also existed among the partisans of international brotherhood of workers.

4. João da Cruz e Souza (1861–1898) is recognized as one of the greatest symbolist poets in Brazil. He is so much of a mainstream artist (the French critic, Roger Bastide, calls him a writer of "white poetry") that it is forgotten that he was actually black. The Souza case is somewhat of an eye-opener when one examines the black condition. By eschewing the notion of race in his poetry, Cruz e Souza might have shown signs of an inferiority complex, but it earned him public acclaim. Critics were all too happy to keep him "clean," considering the high quality of his art, his sensitivity, his grasp of signs and symbols which, according to critics, could only be found in a white writer. Now, it is also true that, in prose, Cruz e Souza did address the issue of racism; only nobody wanted to deal with that.

5. Section, "fala crítica," in Ventura's *texturaafro* (n. p.). This translation and others, except where otherwise stated, are my own.

6. The name Olodum was adopted from the Yoruba, Olodumare, God. However, that abbreviated form could connote "celebrant," "merry-maker," "entertainer." In other words, ironically, the thrust and serious nature of the organization are downgraded by the name adopted.

7. Edvaldo Brito was in the official delegation of the Federal University of Bahia (UFBA) that visited the University of Ife, Nigeria, in 1980, to initiate what, it was hoped, would be a comprehensive, meaningful linkage between the two institutions. Events have since led one to believe that the symbolic gesture would lead nowhere. Ife students of Portuguese continue to trickle over to Salvador for a one-semester sojourn. Nothing beyond that.

8. Vieira (1982:9). See Césaire (1947); *Présence Africaine* (1971:139). See also Roumain (1972:247).

9. Rio Interview. I express my sincere gratitude to my former student and now Nigerian diplomat Lawrence Obisakin for his patience in recording and translating the Nascimento interview into English.

10. I personally was responsible for the Ife-Brazil linkage through which the university signed exchange agreements with the universities of Brasília, São Paulo, and Bahia. Between 1978 and 1987, when I left Ife, serious efforts were made, with the encouragement of Wande Abimbola who, for seven years, was the university's vice-chancellor, to build cultural and academic bridges between both communities. The initial basis was the Ife Portuguese program that required students to spend a year abroad at a Brazilian university. That was supposed to be the springboard for many other exchange programs. Contrary to our expectations, however, the whole effort never went beyond that. Brazilian universities would rather send their students to the United States since they were not interested in linkage with Africa. For their part, the Ife authorities and faculty embarked upon a few projects, but largely on a short-term, individual basis.

As part of the long-term projection, we succeeded in purchasing a house in Salvador that was and is still used to accommodate Ife Portuguese students. I made a proposal to have the property (strategically located in Salvador) upgraded by the Nigerian government and used as the Nigerian consulate while still housing students. My intention was to move up from the particular and microcosmic (Ife University) to the public macrocosmic (nations), in order to cement our common cultural heritage with Brazil. That proposal probably ended up in the garbage can.

REFERENCES

Césaire, Aimé. 1947. *Cahier d'un retour au pays natal.* Paris: Bordas.

———. 1956. *Lèttre a Maurice Thorez.* [N.p.: n.p.]

Fanon, Frantz. 1968. *Black Skin, White Masks.* Tr. Charles Lam. New York: Grove Press.

Kesteloot, L., and B. Kotchy. 1973. *Aimé Césaire, l'homme et l'oeuvre.* Paris: Présence Africaine.

McKay, Claude. 1929. *Banjo.* New York: Harcourt Brace Jovanovich.

Nascimento, Abdias do. 1978. *O genocídio do negro brasileiro.* Rio de Janeiro: Editora Paz e Terra.

———. 1991. *A luta afro-brasileira no senado.* Brasília: Senado Federal.

Nascimento, Abdias do, and Elisa L. Nascimento. 1992. *Africans in Brazil.* Trenton: Africa World Press.

Ojo-Ade, Femi. 1978. "Diverses faces de la négritude ou l'expression par excellence de l'ambiguïté et de la mystification nègres." *Présence Francophone* (Spring), no. 16:47–67.

———. 1989. *On Black Culture.* Ile-Ife: Obafemi Awolowo University Press.

———. 1993. *Léon Damas: The Spirit of Resistance.* London: Karnak House.

Racine, Daniel, ed. 1979. *Léon-Gontran Damas, 1912–1978.* Washington, D.C.: University Press of America.

Roumain, Jacques. 1972. *La montagne ensorcelée.* Paris: Eds. Français Réunis.

Ventura, Adão. 1980. *A cor da pele.* Belo Horizonte: Edição do Autor.

———. 1992. *texturaafro.* Belo Horizonte: Editora Lê.

Vieira, Hamilton de Jesus, org. 1982. *Poetas baianos da negritude.* Salvador: Centro de Estudos Afro-Orientais.

| Part | RELIGIONS, CULTURE, |
| Four | AND RESISTANCE |

This section, comprising three essays by anthropologists, explores the importance of religion—in this
case Candomblé, Umbanda, and Pentecostalism—as sites of black identity, resistance, or accommodation.

In his essay, Júlio Braga, who, at the time of the Black Brazil conference, was director of the Centro de Estudos Afro-Orientais in Salvador,
Bahia, traces the role of Candomblé as a mechanism of resistance and
identity for Salvador's black community. Focusing primarily on resistance against police repression of Candomblé *terreiros*, he rejects the
portrayal of blacks as victims, which leads, in his view, only to the perpetuation of racial discrimination, and asserts, instead, that the Afro-
Bahian community often found ways to negotiate in unfavorable social
situations and preserve the values that constitute the foundations of cultural identity. Braga argues that the history of Bahian Candomblés is in
fact the history of black resistance to oppression and to attempts to limit
religious freedom.

Diana Brown situates her essay on the Umbanda religion in the
broader contexts of the "whitening" process that has supposedly characterized Brazilian society at least since the nineteenth century and the
more recent emergence of the black consciousness movement. Working with Hobsbawm and Ranger's concept of "invention of tradition,"
she argues that despite the historical trajectory of Umbanda from a
deAfricanized (whitened) to a reAfricanized (blackened) tradition,
Umbanda continues to be a potent symbol of Brazilian national identity
tied to the ideology of racial democracy.

Basing his analysis on a dramatic incident witnessed in an Assembly of God church in the outskirts of Rio de Janeiro, John Burdick writes of the important, yet often neglected and typically mistrusted, black presence in Brazil's Pentecostal churches, the fastest growing religious movement in the country. Through a critical dissection of this incident, he outlines some of the multiple contradictions of substantial black participation in evangelical Protestantism and the dilemmas it represents for Brazil's black consciousness movement.

11 | Candomblé in Bahia: Repression and Resistance

JÚLIO BRAGA

> For my interest in reading the police reports of Rome they censured me. In these I always discover cause for surprise—friends or suspects, strangers or relatives, all these people trouble me and their insanity serves as an excuse for my own.
>
> —Marguerite Yourcenar, *Memórias de Adriano*

More than in any other region of Brazil, in Bahia, especially in the city of Salvador and in the Recôncavo,[1] which have been characterized by the strong concentration of African slaves particularly starting from the nineteenth century, the black population has been able to impose the expressive effects of Afro-Brazilian civilizing values.[2] For centuries, through sacrifice and arduous struggle, blacks have constructed a solid foundation which even today sustains and promotes the continuity of cultural values permeating different forms of the struggle and assists the effort to incorporate those values into the larger society. All of this, evidently, was done without losing sight of black identity and cultural specificity. At the beginning of this century, dominant social segments reacted strongly to attempts by blacks to play an active role in the formation of the values that characterize and define Bahia's society and culture. Blacks were forced to develop strategies permitting them to gain the space necessary for their psychosocial affirmation. During the first decades of the century, several organized movements emerged which tended to confront, albeit not necessarily openly, the different forms of social discrimination to which the black Bahian population was subjected.

It is profoundly incorrect—and perhaps even prejudiced—to suggest that blacks were merely victims of the social system and the dominant class which controlled it. In fact, they knew how to create and take advantage of social and cultural situations which allowed them to achieve practical results necessary for consolidating some of their fundamental interests. The portrayal of blacks as victims has been frequently offered in reflections and studies replete with *ufanismo*.[3] This inaccurate portrayal has only served to hide or mask many actions of blacks against a society which insisted, and not always successfully, on pushing them permanently into a socially inferior position. This distorted vision of the black struggle for basic rights long nourished what we might call the abject and harmful ideology of "the poor little thing," which only helped maintain prejudice and racial discrimination, and it did not further understanding or advance the struggle. In fact, the perspective seems to have functioned as an obstacle in the difficult process of integrating blacks into a class society.

In truth, whenever it helped them attain their social demands, blacks were highly capable of taking advantage of their social situation and skillfully negotiating social ascension. They knew how to negotiate and to take advantage of favorable (if infrequent) opportunities in order to build the solid bases that still serve as the foundation of various fronts of today's political struggles and challenges. The manner in which blacks reacted to police repression is a compelling example of their capacity to negotiate in adversity and to make important advances toward preserving the fundamental values of their cultural identity.

During the first half of this century, police repression of Candomblé *terreiros*[4] occurred almost systematically in Bahia. Although various authors have made frequent references to these police raids, occasionally citing a newspaper article, practically nothing has been written about such police repression. At the same time, people from Candomblés themselves do not show much interest in discussing the subject. In fact, there seems to be a sort of mental restriction about one of the most serious problems confronting the Afro-Bahian religious community in recent years. The impression is that there exists, in the collective memory, a veiled interest in forgetting the police actions which violated sacred temples and brutally attacked religious leaders as well as those who were present during the notorious assaults, thus harming the dignity of the religious community (*povo-de-santo*).

But, the history of Bahian Candomblés is the history of black resistance to oppression and restrictions on religious freedom. Police brutality was never able to desecrate the most sacred essence of Afro-Brazilian religion, and even less the profound commitment between religious adherents and their deities. Renato Ortiz has pointed out the difficulties encountered and overcome by the Umbanda religion in the process of social legitimation and recognition. Police repression, part of society's resistance to cultural values different from the ideal Western model, was certainly one of the most difficult obstacles for the religious black community to overcome, requiring a variety of strategies ranging from pure and simple confrontation to different forms of negotiations or accommodation.

Ortiz comments further that the history of police repression of the terreiros has not yet been written and that "it is buried in police dossiers, waiting to be deciphered" (Ortiz 1978:178). In Bahia, researchers have experienced difficulties gaining access to documentation dealing with police raids which, without doubt, should exist. For example, criminal proceedings in the Bahian archives, principally those covering this century's most intense period of police repression (1920–1930), are still in a preliminary phase of being systematized and cataloged. Until now, the search for these proceedings has been in vain, but they should provide valuable information about blacks' response to the police aggression which the religious community experienced during the first half of the twentieth century.

Whether for lack of data or some other reason, few authors have analyzed, in-depth, police repression and its consequences for the survival of these religious manifestations. Nina Rodrigues was the first to consider the subject more carefully, devoting several pages of his classic book *Os africanos no Brasil* to the topic. In an explanatory note he asserts that in Africa these religions were truly state religions and therefore their practice was guaranteed by government and by custom. He continues:

> In Brazil, in Bahia, to the contrary, they are considered practices of witchcraft, and they exist without the protection of the law, condemned by the dominant religion and by the often concealed disdain of the dominant classes who, despite everything, fear them. During the period of slavery, not yet twenty years past, these religions suffered violence on the part of slave masters, who were all tyrants and who delivered blacks from farms and plantations to the jurisdiction and

the almost unlimited arbitrary rule of administrators and overseers
who were as brutal and cruel as they were ignorant. (1935:353)[5]

Africa, especially West Africa, experienced major transformations as a
result of colonization, especially during the second half of the nineteenth
century. The colonizers used all means of persuasion to convert Africans
to their religions. Consequently, since the last century, indigenous religions were in continuous contact with foreign religions and suffered the
impact of cultural frictions. They were almost always in a position of
inequality, especially when political life was restructured along European
models. Traditional African religions lost much of their force and ability
to intervene directly in the political affairs of African society, even
though their presence was part of daily life for many Africans, especially
for those who lived farther away from large urban centers.

In the same sense, in Bahia these traditional religious practices were
rejected under the allegation that they involved witchcraft. It was
believed, therefore, that they should be removed from a social environment which derived from and should carry forth Western civilization.
Even in this century, this argument has been used to justify violence
against Afro-Bahian religious centers throughout the city of Salvador.

Nina Rodrigues, a privileged observer for having lived in Bahia at
the turn of the century, synthesized the denigration of these religious
practices:

> Today, with the end of slavery, the religions have fallen to the prepo-
> tency and arbitrary rule of police who are no more enlightened than
> the former master, and to public opinion protests which pretend to be
> free-spirited and cultivated, but which always reveal the most extreme
> ignorance of sociological phenomena. (1935:353)

Nina Rodrigues also notes the manner in which the press delighted in
reporting, without impartiality, the frequent police incursions in different Candomblé terreiros. As a matter of fact, an ironic, almost mischie-
vous tone is almost always present in news reports about police
repression. The hostile discourse was quieted only with the appearance
(starting in 1936) of a series of reports on the Bahian Candomblés organized by Edison Carneiro and published in the newspaper O Estado da
Bahia. These reports seem to have marked a new posture of newspapers
and journalists toward Afro-Bahian culture. This shift, at least in terms of
less aggressive language, however, did not induce profound changes in
social relations, which remained unfavorable to Bahia's black population.

Further commenting on the insidious manner in which the press reported on police raids of Candomblés, and still revealing the same sense of intransigence, Nina Rodrigues writes:

> We should lament no less the fact that the local press reveals the same disorientation in its treatment of the subject, preaching and proclaiming the belief that the sword of the ignorant police officer and the senseless violence of equally ignorant police commissioners have a greater dose of catechistic virtue, and greater effectiveness as an instrument of religious conversion, than did the overseer's whip. (1935:354)

Nina Rodrigues failed to say that the "police raids" reflected not only the dominant society's power but also its fear on seeing that these forms of popular religion, derisively called "primitive cults" or "witchcraft," were gaining ground and multiplying rapidly, and that they constituted a serious obstacle to achieving the dominant society's ideal civilization based on European patterns. Above all, the Afro-Bahian religions presented serious problems for the hegemony of the Catholic Church, which represented, in religious matters, the interests of the powerful and of the state. It is thus not surprising that repression of different religious cultures would emerge. Moreover, these Afro-Bahian religions displayed an ability to grow among the popular classes, especially among blacks and mestizos, who were the majority of Bahia's population. But the hostilities against these religions would provoke a strong feeling of resistance molded on the basic idea that they represented deep values rooted in the Bahian black's very notion of being. Perhaps this explains what Nina Rodrigues called the "extraordinary resistance and vitality of the beliefs held by the black race. The old and prolonged repression, always violent and sometimes inhuman, by slave masters and overseers, no less violent than the police, has been futile" (1935:362).[6]

Police raids, like other responses of the dominant class toward Afro-Bahian cultural values, became less frequent beginning in the 1950s, owing to a new attitude within the black community which began to organize to defend its own interests and cultural well-being more effectively. During this period, as industrialization progressed, a triumphant ideology spread throughout the country, imprinting a new awareness about the country's destiny. The new ideology deflected attention away from these other concerns and instead focused on the construction of a society which would be industrially better equipped and, hence, able to stimulate profound reforms in the Brazilian social structure. With this new orientation, religious forms considered peculiar and bizarre ceased being a matter of major interest and remained within the limits of more localized concerns.

In truth, this meant the adoption of a new attitude by the dominant society, which could be initiated by other mechanisms capable of controlling the constant advance and consolidation of Afro-Brazilian religion in Bahia. At this time a type of special oppression became institutionalized—that of police control of the Candomblé terreiros, which were now required to register with the Delegacia de Jogos e Costumes (Office of Games and Customs) of the Secretary of Public Safety.[7] Beginning in the 1950s, a license to *bater*[8] was required in order for the terreiros to perform their religious ceremonies, which generally followed an internally established liturgical calendar.[9] Priests who did not make advance arrangements to obtain a license for public celebrations committed crimes and risked having their sacred places closed down or invaded as aggressively as they were during the first decades of the twentieth century.

Nevertheless, many of Bahia's powerful and influential Candomblés did not register with the police and boasted of never having experienced the humiliation and disgrace of being forced to obtain a license to hold their religious celebrations. In fact, many of these Candomblés already enjoyed the considerable prestige associated with their power. Their good standing among people of higher classes and their alliances with police authorities exempted them from this obligation. This situation was ideologically manipulated and utilized by these Candomblés as a symbol of their social prestige and power, not only within the terreiro community, but also in Bahian society at large.

However, if the various forms of aggression did not achieve the desired results—one of which was making these so-called primitive cults disappear—it was hoped that the new social and economic order which was gradually being implanted in Bahia in the 1950s would be able to transform these religions from something "despicable" into something which, under the best of terms, could be accommodated submissively in the dominant social system along with other folklorized and inoffensive elements. Given the enormous power of Afro-Brazilian religion today, however, the dominant class demonstrated its inability to impede the rapid advance of these religions into the lives and minds of the Bahian people.

Police repression, an index of society's intolerance of different forms of religious expression, reveals and lays bare the mechanisms and the underlying ideology which rejected black-mestizo values. These values were shaped and crystallized into an effective substratum of the emerging cultural order shaping Bahian society. In the black community, police repression reinforced the already strong feeling of social exclusion derived from the social and racial relations that had characterized slave society. From the beginning, however, blacks created and frequently employed highly effective strategies of resistance which were intelligently adjusted to each specific case in accordance with the greater interests to be protected. In the neighboring state of Alagoas, the persecution was so cruel that the povo-de-santo practically had to restructure the cult, eliminating the use of percussion instruments such as the *atabaques* and singing the songs in a low voice to avoid police admonishments. Reginaldo Prandi reminds us that "the *povo-de-santo* of Alagoas had to 'invent' a new religion, the 'Xangô prayed softly' as Gonçalves Fernandes called it, without percussion instruments and with voices singing *pianissimo*. To 'scrape one's head and open cures' [ritual incisions in the skin] was exactly [the same] as turning one's self over to the police, the powerful enemy of that religion" (Prandi 1991:221).

In Bahia, the tradition of negotiation dates from the period of slavery. João Reis, who has analyzed nineteenth-century slave revolts and liberation movements in the region, noted that blacks resorted to the strategy of negotiation with their masters and the authorities whenever they felt it would be more effective than direct confrontation. "The slaves did not confront their masters only though individual or collective force. The revolts, the formation and the defense of *quilombos*, and personal violence coexisted with peaceful means of resistance. Slaves disrupted daily domination through small acts of disobedience, personal manipulation, and cultural autonomy" (Reis and Silva 1989).[10] In terms of the Afro-Brazilian community's response to continuous police invasions of their sacred places, passive forms of resistance were frequently employed during the first half of the twentieth century, and they were extremely successful in preserving Afro-Brazilian characteristics in Bahia. One of the most direct consequences of these strategies was the gradual dislocation of these religious groups to the city's periphery. "Confronted with police violence," asserts Nina Rodrigues, "black practices will be hidden from public view; they will seek refuge in forests, in the corners of shanties and slums; they will withdraw to the late hours of the night; they will use the protection of powerful people who seek orgies and debauchery which will be provided to them; finally, they will take on the superficialities of Catholicism and the surrounding superstition" (1935:246).[11]

Nina Rodrigues is not felicitous in his diagnosis when he asserts that these religions were available to whomever wished to use them for all types of entertainment, including orgiastic practices and debauchery. Candomblé is not free to be used improperly for questionable ends. Becoming gradually more organized and more like a religious institution, Candomblé sought to eliminate unscrupulous people who used it for other purposes or personal gain. In fact, this has been a continuous struggle of considerable importance to Candomblé leaders who find themselves fighting for the religion's moralization and discipline. Whether this "moralization" has had positive results and has been able to eliminate definitively the use of Candomblé for non-religious purposes does not fall within the scope of the discussion here.

It was inevitable that these Candomblés would distance themselves from the urban center and become established in outlying zones. The wealthier parts of society had turned the center into an elite area, and they interfered with the religious groups and their cultural practices. At the same time, the urban structure was redefined so that poorer segments of society were pushed into the less desirable areas of the city.

Donald Pierson, who conducted research in Bahia in the 1930s, mentions that Candomblés during that era were located in outlying areas where the majority of the population was black. He writes:

> The sects are located in areas where the population is almost entirely black or dark mulatto, or in the outskirts of the city. They numbered between seventy to one hundred when I was in Bahia in 1935 to 1937. Some say there existed two or three hundred, but that number seems exaggerated. Around the *Lago Sagrado* [sacred lake] or *Dique*, and in the area between the upper and lower *Rio Vermelho* streetcar lines, there were more than twenty. A black who regularly frequented the sect known as *Engenho Velho* personally knew of eighteen, could find them, indicate their African lineages, and name their leaders. According to him, eleven of the eighteen sects were *nagô*, six *angola*, and one *gêge*. All of them were located on the outskirts of the city in areas inhabited primarily by the darkest portion of the population, or in remote areas. (Pierson 1945:341)

However, because of Salvador's growth, they were rapidly reintegrated into the urban landscape. The leaders of many of the first religious groups about which we have information, who had previously lived in or near the urban centers, moved to the valleys or hillsides. During the last few decades, the construction of the highway system turned the big valleys and less desirable areas into wide avenues as the city enveloped them.

In more isolated areas, the terreiros could carry out their activities with more security. During those times, when a priest wanted to establish a new terreiro, he searched for areas farther from the city's center, where tranquil conditions were more conducive to different rituals. For example, an expression used by Candomblé people states that the Gêge really like the forest, a clear allusion to the cult's need to locate in areas of abundant vegetation, where the symbolic elements and the representatives of certain deities of the Afro-Brazilian pantheon are "seated."

In order to complete this picture I should mention the difficulty this population had in purchasing land close to the wealthy centers—where vacant space was quite scarce—owing to their lack of power and necessary resources. Land farther from the center of the city could be purchased at a better price, and there was an opportunity to choose an area close to a lake or a stream, or in the vicinity of a forest where the roots, leaves, and fruits required for Candomblé rituals can be collected. The movement to the city's periphery might be considered a retreat from continual police incursions and raids. In truth, in the medium and long term, the positive consequences of relocation suggest it to be a victory of sorts. For instance, settlement patterns allowed different groups to establish themselves in areas more suitable for the worship of Afro-Brazilian deities, and allowed better and more definitive structuring of terreiros. In fact, this forced migration may have played an essential role in the preservation of ceremonies which could now be practiced more freely because they were removed from the undesirable and impertinent interruptions of outsiders.

The truth is that these religious groups avoided confrontation with the police because of their absolute inability to stand up to them with any hope of success. It was difficult for a Candomblé terreiro to confront an extremely aggressive and well-armed police force. Occasionally, a particular group would respond in a confrontational manner, but it was an unequal battle, and the police always had the advantage. In this way, we can say that black resistance was almost always limited to subtler forms of tempered aggression, without blacks ever losing a strong sense of resistance. Such forms of resistance could be disguised as subordination. Before the eyes of the aggressors, these religions would be easily abandoned or otherwise substituted by more "sophisticated" forms of religious practice, compatible with the interests of the dominant class.

To conclude, I want to emphasize that the attacks by the Church and the dominant classes were unable to diminish the desire of Bahia's black community for religious freedom. To the contrary, such repression strengthened a profound religious feeling among the povo-de-santo capable of overcoming the adversity and intolerance of segments of the society who even today are unwilling to accept black cultural identity in Brazil.

NOTES

Author's Note: An earlier version of this essay, "Candomblé de Bahia: Repressão e Resistencia," was published in *Revista USP* 18 (June/July/August 1993):52–59. The present text is a preliminary version of the introduction to a study in preparation titled "Police Repression and Forms of Resistance of Candomblés of Bahia." All the documentation in regard to police repression will be cited and analyzed in the final document. The research for the present study, undertaken in the Centro de Estudos Afro-Orientais of the Federal University of Bahia, was made possible with support from The Ford Foundation and Conselho Nacional de Pesquisa (CNPq). I thank Professor João Reis for the careful reading of the original text. Many of his suggestions have been incorporated into the final version.

1. The Recôncavo is the geographic/cultural area surrounding the Bahia de Todos os Santos (Bay of All Saints). Salvador is the port city located at the entrance to the bay.—Ed.

2. For general information on the origin of Africans and their presence in Bahia, see, among others, Viana Filho (1964), Rodrigues (1935), and Verger (1987).

3. *Ufanismo* expresses a patriotic Brazilian optimism based on the country's rich natural and human resources.—Ed.

4. *Terreiro* is the physical location (the actual place) of a Candomblé house.—Ed.

5. For this essay, I will utilize the texts which Nina Rodrigues gathered from the newspapers of the day, which complement my own search of large-circulation newspapers.

6. In view of the significance of these observations in showing the capacity of the Afro-Brazilian cults to resist the intense and relentless attack of the police to which they were subjected during Nina's time, the complete passage from which this quote is drawn is provided: "The eloquence of these documents does not allow for misinterpretation.... What distinctly stands out in them is the extraordinary resistance and vitality of those beliefs of the black race. Everything that was done to extinguish them was futile: the old and prolonged repression, always violent and sometimes inhuman, by slave masters and overseers, no less violent than the police; the incessant complaints of the press, like the incitement of the other classes, in order to eradicate the evil. The Gêge-Nagô cult and terreiros such as Candomblés *(sic)* continue to function normally and increasingly establish themselves in the principal cities of the state" (Nina Rodrigues 1935:362).

7. A discussion of the requirement forcing the cults to apply to the Secretary of Public Safety for a license in order to celebrate publicly will be the subject of a more extensive study by the author about police repression against the Candomblés.

8. The use of the Portuguese verb *bater* (to beat) in this case implies the fundamental importance of religious drumming to Candomblé and its ceremonies.—Ed.

9. The most highly structured Candomblé terreiros followed a yearly liturgical calendar of feasts. These calendars are organized according to various functional circumstances of the terreiro that attempt to observe significant aspects of history, such as the date of founding, the deity for whom it was founded or the leader of the group, or some other connection to the religious leader who helped guide the direction of the terreiro. At times, these calendars equally respect the liturgical calendar of the Catholic Church, performing no rituals during the most sacred periods of Catholicism, such as Holy Week and the entire Easter period when almost all of the Candomblés are closed, only resuming their normal activities after Resurrection Sunday.

10. See also Reis and Silva (1986).

11. Nina Rodrigues concludes his observations in the following manner: "In such cases, through the motives which they obey as from the form from which they proceed, the action of our police only serves to reproduce the passionate, violent, and blind power of the small rulers and little kings of Africa."

REFERENCES

Nina Rodrigues, Raimundo. 1935. *Os africanos no Brasil*. 2d ed., revised and enlarged. São Paulo: Companhia Editora Nacional.

Ortiz, Renato. 1978. *A morte branca do feiticeiro negro*. Petrópolis: Editora Vozes.

Pierson, Donald. 1945. *Brancos e pretos na Bahia: estudo de contato racial*. São Paulo: Editora Nacional.

Prandi, Reginaldo. 1991. *Os Candomblés de São Paulo*. São Paulo: HUCITEC-EDUSP.

Reis, João José, and Eduardo Silva. 1989. *Negociação e conflito: a resistência negra no Brasil escravista*. São Paulo: Companhia das Letras.

Reis, João José, and Renato Silva. 1986. "Violência repressiva e engenho político na Bahia do tempo dos escravos." *Comunicações do ISER* 5(21):61–66.

Verger, Pierre. 1987. *Fluxo e refluxo do tráfico de escravos entre o Golfo de Benin e a Bahia de Todos os Santos. Dos séculos XVII a XIX*. São Paulo: Corrupio.

Viana Filho, Luis. 1964. *O negro na Bahia*. Rio de Janeiro: Livraria José Olympio, Editora.

12 | Power, Invention, and the Politics of Race: Umbanda Past and Future

DIANA DeG. BROWN

In recent years, observers have noted a growing trend toward "reAfrican-ization" or "blackening" in Afro-Brazilian culture, with African themes, identities, and rituals increasingly displacing non-African cultural references. This development appears to be especially pronounced in Bahian carnival (Dunn 1992; Risério 1981) but is occurring as well in other areas of Afro-Brazilian religious and artistic culture such as Candomblé (Birman 1984; Dos Santos 1989; Prandi and Gonçalves 1989) and *capoeira* (Dossar 1992). It suggests that a shift is under way in the direction of Afro-Brazilian cultural change which throughout this century had been moving in an opposite direction, toward the progressive loss of African cultural forms and the "whitening" of Afro-Brazilian culture through progressive admixture, or "syncretism," with other traditions.

Many researchers have assumed the gradual dilution of Afro-Brazilian culture to be an irreversible process, and many members of the Brazilian upper classes have devoutly hoped that it would be. In the aftermath of abolition, elites pinned their hopes for the development of a modern Brazil on the progressive "whitening" of the Brazilian population and culture through miscegenation and European immigration (Skidmore 1974). These ideas, which were based on notions of biological determinism embedded in nineteenth-century scientific racism, went officially out of favor during the 1920s, but persist and continue to form an undercurrent in contemporary Brazilian attitudes. Subsequent cultural and sociological theories have rejected biological determinism and reversed the causal relationship among Afro-Brazilians,[1] their cultures, and the process of Brazilian modernization, making modernization the agent rather than the end product of whitening. But they have continued

213

to assume a direct link between Brazil's development and the progressive loss of its African cultural traditions. Advocates of acculturation theory, even as they extolled the richness of Afro-Brazilian cultures, implied their inevitable dilution within a modernizing nation by their association of more assimilated Afro-Brazilians with more syncretic Afro-Brazilian cultural forms (Costa Eduardo 1948; Herskovits 1966; Landes 1947). Various models of the modernization process have reaffirmed these expectations by treating Afro-Brazilian cultures as archaic survivals of an agrarian past, associated with the least modernized sectors of society, and thus bound to disappear under the pressures of modern development (Costa Pinto 1952; Fernandes 1978; Hutchinson 1952; Willems 1966). Even recent class-based models of Brazilian culture that portray a "blackening" of the dominant sectors of Brazilian culture depict a reciprocal whitening within its lower sectors, where the great majority of Afro-Brazilians and their cultures are found (Matta 1991; Ortiz 1978).

However these models of progressive whitening may have seemed to be confirmed by the cultural developments of previous years, they have not and could not have anticipated the current trend toward reAfricanization because they have ignored the continued salience of race. They assumed a Brazilian racial democracy in which Afro-Brazilians and their cultures would willingly assimilate within a society that would accept that assimilation. They failed to consider Afro-Brazilians' own interests in asserting their African cultural identity, the cultural context of continuing racial discrimination in Brazilian society within which this has taken place, and the increasingly transitional arena of African diaspora politics, exactly the factors that underlie the current Africanization of Afro-Brazilian culture. Researchers have related its various current manifestations to new attitudes and activism among Afro-Brazilians combating continuing racism at home, to new articulations of racial consciousness and African pride, and an increased valorization of their African heritage and identity. These new expressions draw inspiration and imagery from Afro-Brazilians' diasporic ties to Africa, the Caribbean, and the United States.

These new developments have inspired me to reexamine Umbanda. My previous work on this Afro-Brazilian religion has dealt with the racial politics of an earlier period, and its influence on deAfricanizing and whitening this religion until, by the 1970s, Umbanda offered a prime example of the whitening process in Afro-Brazilian culture change and had become an agent of its expansion.[2] I want now to explore the implications for this religion of the current reAfricanization process. My concern will not only be with the potential for changes in Umbanda's rituals and identity, as implied in the term "reAfricanization," but also with the social and political changes implied in the new attitudes and activities to which the Africanization process is connected, and which potentially threaten its structural and ideological underpinnings.

I should say at once that my analysis will be speculative, based on my own and others' previous research on Umbanda, on new analyses of race and its significance within the Brazilian political economy and culture, and on studies of reAfricanization. Since Umbanda itself is the creation of a previous era of racial politics, I will first review the development of this religion from the 1920s through the 1970s, the period of its "whitening," highlighting issues of racial politics. I have dealt previously with much of this material (see Brown 1977, 1979, 1986; Brown and Bick 1987) and will make only schematic references to it here. I will employ Hobsbawm and Ranger's (1983) concept of the invention of tradition in analyzing the development of its racial politics in relation to the expansion of state power. I will then turn to the contemporary picture and after a brief discussion of recent changes in racial politics will examine their relationship to the process of reAfricanization in two areas of Afro-Brazilian culture, carnival and Candomblé. Finally, I will consider the implications of this material for Umbanda, both for its ritual orientation and identity, and for the structures and ideologies upon which these have rested.

DeAfricanizing ("Whitening") Umbanda, 1920s to 1970s

Hobsbawm and Ranger (1983) have employed the phrase "the invention of tradition" to refer to situations in which states, and the groups within civil society that support them, make "largely factitious" claims of ancient origins for certain public rituals in an attempt to give increased legitimacy to the events or the powers that they celebrate. The rituals themselves may be of recent origin, or they may be "customary traditional practices" "modified, ritualized, and institutionalized for new national purposes" (1983:6–8). This latter case, the modification of ongoing cultural traditions for new national purposes, is a useful concept for exploring the politics of race in the development of Umbanda, in which ongoing Afro-Brazilian traditions were transformed by members of the white middle sectors. As I have demonstrated elsewhere, this has occurred during the process of state building and represents an effort to integrate Afro-Brazilians and their cultures into the modern state both through the creation of political alliances and through the dissemination and promotion of national political ideologies or race. The development of Umbanda also involved the appropriation and transformation by the dominant classes of ongoing Afro-Brazilian practices of the sort referred to by Hobsbawm and Ranger as representing "historic continuity and tradition," or as "genuine" rather than "invented" traditions (1983:7).[3]

The moment of "invention" in Umbanda occurred in Rio in the mid-1920s when a group of middle-class whites, some of them aspiring politicians, established a religion they called "Umbanda." Its name and many of its rituals were appropriated from existing religious practices among poor, and mainly Afro-Brazilian, populations, but its "inventors" sought to transform them in accordance with their own vision of this new religion, and to impose them upon the groups from which they had been drawn.

Their vision, and what they conceived of as their central mission, was to restore Umbanda's ancient rituals, morality, and dignity by stripping away certain more recent harmful influences upon it. The restoration involved an emphasis on Spiritist practices and philosophy, and on Christian (Catholic) moralism and charity, traditions drawn from European culture. The harmful influences declared to be evil and immoral, and which they wished to remove, were those identified as African: certain African deities; such "barbaric" rituals as animal sacrifices and the ritual use of blood; and above all, the many evils associated with witchcraft, known as "black magic," which were likewise identified as African.[4] The form of Umbanda established at this time quickly came to be referred to as "pure" or "white" Umbanda.

Its founders' rationale for conducting these moral and ritual renovations was their claim that they were restoring an ancient tradition whose origins lay not in Africa, but in the far older high civilizations of the ancient world, in Egypt, or India, and whose very name, "Umbanda," derived from Sanskrit. The mistaken notion that Umbanda was African, they explained, was the result of damaging accretions that it had acquired on its diffusionary travels through Africa, which had caused alterations in its rituals and beliefs, corrupted it, and caused it to degenerate into "fetishism." What was required, they asserted, was to restore this ancient religion to its original (non-African) purity.

Through the invention of a fictitious history linking Umbanda to the high civilizations and religious traditions of the ancient world, these early Umbanda leaders asserted the legitimacy of their own practices and explicitly denied legitimacy to both ongoing, "genuine" Afro-Brazilian religions and to their African parent traditions. Though they drew openly upon these ongoing traditions, they sought to deAfricanize and "whiten" them, in the process denigrating African religious culture in terms that left little doubt about their attitudes toward the bearers of that culture.

Their ideas were influenced by the concept of "whitening," a racist doctrine of white (European) physical and mental superiority that linked cultural development to the putative mental capacity of the various races (Skidmore 1974) and often used religion as the cultural benchmark of mental capacity. Notions that the "lower" races, which included African, were destined to have "inferior" forms of religion, often referred to as "fetishism," or "barbarism," in comparison with the "superior" religions of the late nineteenth century, were routinely cited in early analyses of Afro-Brazilian religious forms (Nina Rodrigues 1935, 1945; Ramos 1934; see also Skidmore 1974) and were quoted in early Umbanda writings. This thinking reflected as well a cultural reformulation of nineteenth-century European racial degeneration theories influential in Brazilian thinking through the 1930s (Borges 1993) in which through mixture with inferior races, conquering races were believed to lose their special qualities and energy. In Umbanda, the presence of African influences and practices was taken as the sign or "stigma" of Umbanda's cultural degeneration. But Umbanda drew as well upon stirrings of nationalism articulated in the Modernist movement of the 1920s, which urged Brazilians to turn from their preoccupation with Europe and to explore the traditions within their own national boundaries. These two currents, one of which rejected African culture, the other of which valued it, came together in Umbanda to express a contradiction that has remained central in the attitudes of Brazil's dominant classes toward Afro-Brazilian culture: a fascination strongly qualified by contempt.

The founders of Umbanda established *centros* or churches, where they practiced their "whitened" Umbanda rituals, and Umbanda federations, through which they publicized their new vision of its doctrine and practices. They sought to affiliate Afro-Brazilian groups and to influence their religious content, that is, to deAfricanize, or whiten, their practices. Their activities, which carried into the early 1940s, coincided with a formative moment in Brazilian history. The locus of economic growth and political power was shifting from the agrarian Northeast to the urban South of the country, and the Brazilian state was emerging as a strong centralized power over formerly dispersed, strongly regional centers of power. Rio, the national capital, was at the center of this urban growth. It was a major city with expanding middle sectors and impoverished urban "masses" feared as repositories of crime, violence, and radicalism. The project of the Brazilian state, under the dictatorship of Getúlio Vargas, was to bring these new urban sectors under control, which was done through co-optation and through the creation of widespread patronage networks that bound these various sectors to the state. Patronage became the social, political, and economic idiom through which upper sectors sought their own bases of power in clienteles, and the lower sectors sought favors and patrons.

State leaders also held contradictory attitudes toward Afro-Brazilians: on the one hand, they were considered inferior and viewed as obstacles to progress; on the other, they constituted a significant population among the urban poor, requiring control but also susceptible to political mobilization. The ideology of whitening, while tempered increasingly by nationalist sentiments, also found reinforcement during the Second World War from European racist currents. The Estado Novo was modeled on the Italian Fascist state, and Brazil had its own right-wing pro-Nazi party, the Integralistas. Early Umbanda leaders shared the interest of state builders, whom they served as local politicians and military officers, and there were even some Integralistas among them (Brown 1986; Concone 1981). Their activities during this period constituted an effort from within sectors of civil society linked through various social and ideological ties to the Brazilian state to impose their own contradictory attitudes and interests, which were shared by the state, upon Afro-Brazilian populations through the vehicle of their own religious traditions.

The linking of Afro-Brazilian churches within middle sector Umbanda federations resulted in vertical, patronage alliances between middle and lower sectors of the population. These alliances created avenues of political control and support and carried the ideology of whitening, with its message of African racial and cultural inferiority and the benefits of assimilation, deeply into the Afro-Brazilian community. Many Afro-Brazilian religious groups, carriers of "genuine" traditions, were drawn into the orbit of Umbanda by the protection offered by federation leaders' military connections against the widespread harassment and persecution of social groups and organizations carried out by the Estado Novo. Thus, the invention of Umbanda created the structures and ideology for the white middle class to appropriate and modify the existing cultural practices of a subordinate group, and to mold its traditions and its adherents to the interests of the Brazilian state.

In the early 1940s, Umbanda ideology was significantly modified and took as its new and lasting theme the celebration of Brazilian nationalism. A major influence on this new direction was the publication in 1933 of Gilberto Freyre's enormously influential book *The Masters and the Slaves* (see Freyre 1946), which was to furnish the major ideological underpinning for both the cultural nationalism of the post–World War II period and for Brazilian racial hegemony, that is, the premise that Brazil was a racial democracy. Both rested upon Freyre's argument that Brazil's greatest resource, the key to its future greatness and its identity as a nation, lay in its multiracialism and multiculturalism, its unique blend of three races—the Portuguese, the African, the Indian—and their combined cultural contributions to the formation of Brazil. Freyre's ideas accommodated the growing recognition that Brazil remained a multiracial society, celebrated multiracialism and multiculturalism, and provided the basis of "the myth of racial democracy," the claim by successive governments and by the dominant classes that in Brazil there is no racism. While these ideas constituted "a move away from racist assumptions that dismissed the African as a barbarian of inferior stock," they were only a variation on the model of whitening, since Freyre's argument still reinforced the whitening ideal by its emphasis on the cultural gains to a (primarily white) elite from its intimate contact with the African and the Indian (Skidmore 1974:192).

Umbanda leaders embraced Freyre's ideas and incorporated them into their own ideology. Umbanda literature of this postwar period, of which there was a great deal, abandoned earlier claims to Umbanda's Eastern origins. Leaders now acknowledged its African influences and claimed that Umbanda was a representation in religious form of the unique Brazilian heritage and the religious exemplar of racial democracy. They argued that Umbanda's combined traditions of Portuguese Catholicism, Amerindian "totemism," and African "fetishism" found their most perfect symbolic expression in the Umbanda pantheon of Catholic saints, Brazilian Indian Caboclo spirits, and Preto Velho ("Old Black") African spirits. The latter constitute a major category of spirit helpers in Umbanda rituals. Elderly, humble slaves from Bahia, they convey the image of the acculturated, Brazilianized, pacified African and contrast with the African *orixás*, powerful, proud, and distant dignitaries from the Afro-Brazilian tradition, whom they displaced in importance.[5]

Freyre's ideas flourished at the end of the Vargas dictatorship in 1945. They converged with the return to electoral politics and the loosening of repression, and with the postwar economic growth. It was an era of heightened nationalism and the flowering of populist politics, of political clienteles, and of patronage on a national scale, emanating from the Brazilian state. Umbanda, which had been conceived on the basis of patronage networks that reached deeply into the lower sectors, and which actively promoted a nationalist image, was ideally situated for a period of religious takeoff. Umbanda public rituals and activities now gained increasing state support and publicity, which in turn created increasing numbers of Afro-Brazilian *terreiros*, "whitening," de-Africanizing their practices, and drawing growing numbers of adherents, among them many Afro-Brazilians, into its orbit of influence.

It was during this period that what might be called the "classic" form of Umbanda centros (churches) developed. Multiclass and multiracial, they were constructed around the ideal of providing spiritual and material forms of charity. Their members insistently proclaimed the democratic, egalitarian spirit of their centros, their racial and class equality ("Aqui não tem nem raça nem classe"; see also Willems 1966). These centros did convey a certain image of equality, through instances in which ritual statuses provided reversals of secular racial, gender, and class status, and poor blacks, often women, wielded considerable authority. Like Freyre's powerful image of white plantation children at their black (slave) wet nurse's breast, Umbanda promoted the image of white clients gaining help, comfort, and spiritual sustenance from Afro-Brazilian spirit helpers at the font of African religious power. These instances did occur, but as with Freyre's image of the wet nurse, framed within the social and racial hierarchy of the plantation, these instances in Umbanda were also framed within the secular structures of the centros within which rituals were housed, and in the secular forms of charity that were so closely intertwined with its ritual forms. These secular structures reproduced class and racial hierarchies and contradicted assertions of equality. In the Umbanda federations and large multiclass terreiros, the great majority of the leaders were middle class and white. Racial prejudice and racial discrimination continued to permeate the many secular activities of daily life in these organizations. My field notes from the period provide a typical example: one day a young black woman came in to talk with the president of an Umbanda federation, a retired general (white) with whom I was chatting, to ask for charity (in this case help in getting employment). In her presence, he immediately obliged by calling a friend on the telephone: "Eu tenho aqui uma pretinha. Ela é muito boazinha, precisa de um emprego. Você pode me ajudar?" The explicit reference to her color both suggests racial prejudice and paves the way for the job discrimination in employment that has remained at the very heart of Brazilian racial inequality.

Umbanda thus provided a microcosm of life in the Brazilian racial democracy: insistent statements of equality, in this case upheld by aspects of the rituals, which denied, and thus served to mask and perpetuate, the racial inequalities of the secular contexts within which they occurred. As has been pointed out by generations of Afro-Brazilians struggling against racism, the assertion of the myth, the denial of inequalities, serves to uphold them. Afro-Brazilians and their culture were symbolically integrated into modern Brazilian culture, though in the pacified, acculturated form represented in the figure of the Preto Velho, black, poor, humble, accepting of his fate, submissive, docile, helpful, curing the ills of Brazil. Though the dictatorship, which began in 1964, sharply reduced the political spectrum of Umbanda politicians, the state retained its patronage and state support for Umbanda, which continued to expand both in the major metropolitan centers and nationally.

Two further points must be made here concerning the limits of Umbanda's legitimacy and growth during this period. Despite its measure of public recognition as a religion, it still suffered from the prejudice of the elites, as I learned early in my research, when I described my topic to Brazilian academic colleagues. Most reacted with displeasure and many urged me to study some aspect of modern Brazil, not an Afro-Brazilian religion, which represented a sign of "ignorança" (ignorance), a "coisa do negro" (a black thing), a "símbolo de nosso subdesenvolvimento" (a symbol of our underdevelopment). One sociologist, when I told him I was discovering a large white middle-class involvement in Umbanda (which even at this time was often not distinguished from the Afro-Brazilian churches), claimed I was lying and threw me out of his office. These incidents illustrated the continuing stigma of these practices and the sense of shame and backwardness they evoked within the dominant classes (though in accord with the contradictory attitudes noted above, many of these same people often secretly practice these religions).

Moreover, while Umbanda made inroads among practitioners of ongoing "genuine" Afro-Brazilian traditions, many also consciously resisted its influence. An example of these attitudes is provided in the writings of a group of poor Afro-Brazilian leaders who in the early 1950s clearly expressed their contempt for middle-class white Umbanda, its wealthy centros, and its leaders' efforts to co-opt their African origins. They asserted their own pride in their African heritage, of which they considered their practice of Umbanda to be an integral part. But they sought autonomy, not racial activism, and rejected as well efforts by a new generation of racial politicians to enlist them in its activities.[6]

Thus, through the 1970s Umbanda developed as a religion based on alliances among sectors of the population with different class interests and with potentially significant differences in cultural background and identity. These were merged in, and obscured by, populism and patronage politics and were secured by the myth of racial democracy, which denied these class and racial differences, claiming them to be transitory and insignificant. This alliance occurred during a period when the urban sectors lacked cohesion as classes, when politicians had very limited means of access to lower class voters, and when the lower classes' access to resources such as Umbanda could serve the interests of both the Brazilian state and the rapidly expanding urban sectors of a developing nation.

ReAfricanization and Umbanda

Current expressions of racial consciousness and political activism, which form the context of reAfricanization, are part of a complex interplay of forces: continuing racial discrimination, fanned by worsening economic conditions and the dramatic growth of urban populations which have selectively affected Afro-Brazilians; greatly expanded transnational contacts with the Third World; and increased political freedom within which to develop and carry out both cultural and political ideas.

Racial discrimination against Afro-Brazilians in employment and education, long expected to diminish with development, remains active and has worsened as increased prosperity has heightened economic inequalities and accelerated impoverishment of the lower classes, within which most Afro-Brazilians remain as a result of past and present racial discrimination (Andrews 1991, 1992; Hasenbalg 1979; Hasenbalg and Silva 1988). Afro-Brazilians who were able to take advantage of expanded higher education during the 1970s, only to confront continuing discriminatory barriers in employment, were among the founders of the current racial activist groups (Hasenbalg 1979; Rufino 1988).

Persistent discrimination undoubtedly heightened interest in international currents of racial protest and cultural expressions of African identity that circulated among African diaspora populations during the 1960s and 1970s. Political and artistic themes and activities from Africa, the Caribbean, and the United States—soul music, reggae, negritude, black power, civil rights, pan-Africanism, and various images of insurrection and African indigenous movements and new nation states—furnished inspiration for the expression of Afro-Brazilians' growing discontent.

The strengthening of Afro-Brazilian identity and racial awareness has fed into what many observers regard as an increased self-conscious racial polarization of Brazilian society; more frequent use by Afro-Brazilians of the aggregate self-referential term "negro" ("black") in place of the former multiracial terminologies; and an increasing perception of opposition between "blacks" and "whites," or as phrased in the language of the dominant Brazilian culture, between "whites" and "non-whites" (Hasenbalg 1985; Silva 1985; Skidmore 1993; Andrews 1991). This situation represents a move toward the racial polarization that has prevailed in the United States and directly challenges Brazil's official claims to "multiracialism" and racial democracy.

Although these changes began during the repressive era of the 1960s, they have extended into the succeeding period of redemocratization that began in the mid-1970s, which has brought an extended period of relative freedom of political expression and has enabled racial activists to organize, mobilize, and express their ideas, though the state has continued to deny Brazilian racism and to strongly oppose any mobilization around racial issues. Changes in the international orientation of the Brazilian state have even provided indirect support for Afro-Brazilians' transnational interests. Since the late 1960s, successive Brazilian governments have become progressively disenchanted with Europe and the United States and have increased their economic, trade, diplomatic, intellectual, and artistic ties with Third World countries; established Third World research centers; and encouraged exchanges of personnel

(Dzidzienyo 1985). This shift has facilitated exchanges among the people and the politics of Africa and the African diaspora.

These changes have inspired a variety of Afro-Brazilian political and cultural movements in major Brazilian cities, ranging from the more politically oriented and militant groups of the Movimento Negro whose participants have been mainly black intellectuals, to the more culturally oriented groups. These latter include movements such as "Black Soul" in Rio, or "Blackitude Baiana" in Salvador, located principally among the youth in poor black suburbs and concerned with the expression of an African identity through music, dance, dress, and activities occurring within more traditional Afro-Brazilian cultural groups, such as carnival groups and Candomblé churches. These different forms show some regional distribution, with cultural forms dominating in the Northeast, where Afro-Brazilians' demographic predominance combined with the lowest national levels of economic development and the greatest poverty has created the most acute racial inequalities. It is here that until recently multiracialism has been most pronounced and racism most camou-flaged, partly through elite patronage and support for traditional forms of Afro-Brazilian cultural expression such as Candomblé. The more politically activist and militant groups have been centered in the cities of the center south, where lower proportions of Afro-Brazilians, combined with higher levels of economic development and more open competition in the labor market, have produced the greatest degree of overt racism. Here also, the presence of a European-oriented national industrial elite and extensive European immigration have produced a generally greater visibility of European cultural forms and the relatively lesser visibility of Afro-Brazilian culture.

The reAfricanization of traditional Afro-Brazilian cultural forms in Northeastern Brazil is exemplified in Bahian carnival. This large and pre-dominantly public participatory street celebration has throughout this century been controlled politically and culturally by the Bahian elite,[7] though the majority of its participants, like the population of Salvador, are poor Afro-Brazilians. Local Afro-Brazilian carnival groups (blocos and afoxés) date back to the nineteenth century, and at first prohibited from public participation in carnival, they were gradually assimilated within it. During the 1970s, however, these groups began to assert their own new interests in black pride, and featured representations of North American Indians drawn in the image of Hollywood westerns and floats presenting scenes from Portuguese colonial days now turned to portrayals of African political liberation and scenes and costumes drawn from African cultures. Samba music influenced by Afro-Caribbean reggae replaced the Portuguese folk-influenced musical style (*frevos*) of the *trios elétricos* (Dunn 1992; Risério 1981; Risério, Chapter 14, herein).

Afro-Bahian carnival groups, some of which admit blacks only, now contest the domination of carnival by Bahian elites and compete with them in carnival's public spaces. They challenge hegemonic control of carnival themes, commercialism, and efforts at exclusivity through prohibitive pricing of elite-controlled events. And similar examples of such challenges may be found among the samba blocos in Rio. Some of the major samba organizations (*escolas de samba*) have recently chosen Africanist themes (Moore 1988), and some local African-oriented samba groups have also rejected elite domination and commercialism in favor of an intimate neighborhood style and locale for the promotion of an Afro-Brazilian identity and solidarity (Rufino 1988). In Rio, however, the degree of control exercised by commercial interests over carnival's development as a highly lucrative international public spectacle makes its Brazilian image and identity far less accessible to challenge.

Bahian carnival groups have extended their activities into various forms of community activism, such as newspapers and theater productions, but so far they have generated little political activism and have had little electoral success (Dunn 1992). They thus represent what Hanchard (1993) has termed "culturalism," expressions of African consciousness and black pride that have so far remained centered on cultural expression and have not evolved secular political goals of countering racism.

Bahian Candomblé, the linchpin and most traditional expression of Afro-Brazilian cultural identity, provides another example of "culturalism." Its recent activities should perhaps be referred to as ongoing instances of "Africanization," rather than "reAfricanization," since it has long held a well-established reputation as a consciously Afrocentric Afro-Brazilian religion. Its leaders' concern with fidelity to their Yoruba religious ancestry, which has led them to travel to Nigeria in search of ritual knowledge and authentic ritual materials, places this religion at the opposite pole from Umbanda. The pursuit of African authenticity has been supported by the local Bahian elite, whose patronage of African orthodoxy presents a strong contrast to the efforts of Rio's dominant classes to whiten Umbanda and has been interpreted as a local patronage accommodation to the predominance of Afro-Brazilian populations and religious forms in this most African of Brazilian cities (Dantas 1988).

Nevertheless, recent changes reflect an intensification of Candomblé's ongoing dedication to African orthodoxy and, like Bahian carnival, the effects upon it of recent transnationalism and state-level interests in stimulating and promoting Third World intellectual and cultural exchanges. The Centro de Estudos Afro-Orientais at the Federal University of Bahia (one of several such centers formed with state support to represent and promote Third World intellectual and cultural exchanges) began to offer courses in the Yoruba language and religious culture. Taught by visiting Nigerians, these courses proved extremely popular among Candomblé personnel, thus greatly increasing the accessibility of "authentic" African source materials with which to pursue orthodoxy and in turn helping to promote the interests of Africanization.

In 1983, the Second Conference of the Tradition of the Orixás was held in Salvador under the sponsorship of the state of Bahia (the first took place in 1981 in Ife, Nigeria). A highly transnational event, the conference brought together worshipers in this West African tradition from Nigeria, the Caribbean, South America, and the United States (Veja 1983; Birman 1984; Fry 1984). Visiting African religious dignitaries were very impressed with the "authenticity" of Bahian religious practices, but they were equally disturbed by Candomblé's syncretism with Catholicism, especially by the strong associations between African orixás and Catholic saints, whose images adorned even the most traditional Candomblé houses. Their disapproval resulted in a proposal, supported by leaders of the most prestigious Candomblé houses, to banish the Catholic saints and all other aspects of Catholic practice and worship from Candomblé, which proved explosive at the conference and which has fueled an ongoing controversy within the Bahian Candomblé community (Birman 1984; Fry 1984; Veja 1983) where many continued to regard Catholicism as an essential part of Candomblé. But the most orthodox and influential Bahian Candomblé leaders' adoption of desyncretism has begun a trend within this religion that has gained momentum in Bahia and is also making itself felt in southern Brazil (Prandi and Gonçalves 1989). This encounter highlighted the constructed, Brazilianized aspects of even the most orthodox of Afro-Brazilian religious traditions, and at the same time it set in motion a process of further purification that went far beyond former concerns with preserving and perfecting African practices to attack what had previously been accepted as an integral part of Candomblé within its Brazilian setting, unquestioned by Brazilian practitioners. The transnational context of the encounter, which decontextualized Candomblé from its Brazilian setting, seems to have provided the new optic that identified Catholicism as an alien, European accretion and imposition.

The conference also sought to valorize African culture, or "africanidade"; to promote Candomblé and the Yoruba religion generally, as the highest form of African religious expression; and to gain for it international respect and recognition as a world religion (Birman 1984:48). Thus, in this setting, Candomblé itself became transformed into a transnational symbol of Africanness. Participants in the conference further expressed their determination to repudiate the efforts by local Bahian officials, politicians, and members of the elite to commercialize Candomblé through links to state festivities or tourism, or in any other way to attempt to control its practices (Birman 1984:48). However, Candomblé's reAfricanization has so far remained confined to cultural pursuits and has thus far resisted efforts to draw it into politics.

The cases of carnival and Candomblé thus offer examples of other dynamic inventions of tradition, but unlike the previous history of Umbanda, they are now moving to traditions based on closer ties to Africa: carnival with its appropriation of African themes; Candomblé through its preservation of African traditions and efforts to purify itself of European components. While Umbanda sought to reduce and to downplay its African identity, Bahian Afro-Brazilian cultural forms seek to reduce and to remove their Europeanness. Moreover, while Umbanda represented an appropriation by dominant sectors of society of an ongoing Afro-Brazilian tradition located within subordinate groups, both of these latter cases involve changes that these subordinate groups have applied to their own traditions. They reflect new processes of cultural/ traditional innovation, but not from the top down, not as forms of elite hegemony. Rather, they reflect resistance and identity formation from the bottom up.

These processes of Africanizing and de-Europeanizing found in Candomblé appear to have spread to southern Brazil and to be affecting Afro-Brazilian religions there, including Umbanda. I will first review the evidence of ritual changes and then return to the issue of underlying structural changes. Since the 1970s Candomblé has reportedly been expanding in Rio and São Paulo while Umbanda's growth has declined (Prandi and Gonçalves 1989; Concone and Negrão 1985).[8] Since Candomblé has until very recently been only a minor presence in southern Brazil, while Umbanda has proliferated, this new evidence suggests a reverse process, with more African-marked forms increasing at the expense of more "whitened," Europeanized ones. Candomblé's southward expansion has benefited from the migrations of Bahian Candomblé personnel to these southern capitals; from the proselytizing activities of Bahian Candomblé leaders who have traveled extensively to southern capitals, teaching orthodoxy and preaching "desyncretism" (Prandi and Gonçalves 1989); and from the same forms of academic transnationalism found in Bahia. Beginning in 1977, the University of São Paulo also offered a course in the Yoruba language. Taught by Nigerian students, it soon came to attract mainly Candomblé personnel (600 students in 10 years) and to serve as a contact point for teaching the ritual and religious background of Candomblé, through private lessons, and for obtaining African Candomblé products from Africa (Prandi and Gonçalves 1989).

Candomblé's Africanizing influence also appears to be invading Umbanda centros in Rio and São Paulo. Brief references to the defection of Umbanda personnel to Candomblé in recent studies (Amaral 1991; Dos Santos 1989; Prandi and Gonçalves 1989) suggest that some practitioners are exercising a preference for more Africanized rituals over more whitened ones. Some Umbanda leaders are adding new Africanized ceremonies to their regular practices, with the two forms now alternating on different days of the week, and others are apparently undergoing a reAfricanization of their rituals, purging European (Kardecist and Catholic) doctrines and teachings, and beginning to desyncretize Umbanda pantheons. Researchers have described celebrations of the spiritual retirement of Umbanda spirits, final spiritual farewells conducted within reAfricanizing centros, as Umbanda spirits are dispatched permanently to the spirit world, their "mission now completed" (Prandi and Gonçalves 1989). This suggests a process of selective deconstruction within Umbanda of its constituent parts.

These indications of the recent Africanization of Candomblé and Umbanda in southern Brazil require more systematic investigation. And they provide only tantalizing suggestions concerning the more important issues here—the degree to which such ritual changes may represent new assertions by Afro-Brazilians of African identities, like those just examined above in Bahian carnival and Candomblé, and what such assertions might mean for the future, which I will now consider.

I have argued that Umbanda's popularity and legitimacy have rested on the multiclass and multiracial alliances from which it was constructed, and the ideology of racial democracy that it has drawn upon and helped to sustain, and to which its ritual orientation, its "invented tradition" of "whitening," is integrally related. These now seem to me to be threatened. Current expressions of reAfricanization, with their assertions of black pride and identity and their challenge to European hegemony, systematically oppose and repudiate major features of Umbanda. They reject Umbanda's European-oriented ideology and its inclusion of Catholic and Spiritist rituals, along with its Freyrean notions of multiculturalism. The humble ex-slave Preto Velho, a central Afro-Brazilian symbol in Umbanda, bears little resemblance to the imagery of liberation employed by proponents of Africanization.[9]

These new forms, which consciously link cultural interests to racial ones, also explicitly reject the myth of racial democracy, centerpiece of the particular cultural configuration of Umbanda rituals and pantheon and the social creed of Umbanda practice. They show some evidence of racial as well as cultural separatism, and their explicit rejection of elite (white) domination, cultural hegemony, and patronage suggests the emergence of counterhegemonic consciousness among the oppressed and dominated groups of urban Brazil. These rejections of Umbanda's multiracial and multiclass composition and repudiations of political, commercial, and touristic forms of patronage strike directly at the structures that have to this point underlain Umbanda's development.

The cultural and political interests that lie behind current examples of Africanization and reAfricanization thus seem diametrically opposed to those represented in Umbanda's earlier history, and to the degree that followers of Umbanda are influenced by these new ideas I would expect them to reject Umbanda as it is presently constituted socially, politically, ritually, and ideologically. The examples of reAfricanization in southern Brazil discussed above may be evidence that this is already beginning to occur, that some practitioners and leaders are reAfricanizing Umbanda, replacing European influences with African ones, returning to or becoming part of the other, older, "ongoing" Afro-Brazilian traditions that resisted Umbanda all along, or defecting to join Candomblé, as the evidence previously described suggests.

These groups may then extend the reAfricanization process, creating Afro-Brazilian social groups that express and promote a new form of consciousness and identity. This pattern in turn would result in a tendency toward the creation of racial segregation within Umbanda, with Afro-Brazilian groups withdrawing from it to practice reAfricanized rituals, leaving Umbanda truly "whitened," a white religion for white Brazilians. This reduction of racial diversity would withdraw from Umbanda its strongest corroboration for the myth of racial democracy: the visual evidence of Afro-Brazilians and whites worshiping together. Such racial segregation in religious practice seems already to be the pattern in Porto Alegre, one of the most racially segregated of Brazilian cities (Oro 1988), and I believe that reAfricanization would encourage this tendency elsewhere. At the same time, it is important to emphasize that racial politics in Brazil today is still very limited in scope, and there are still a great many Afro-Brazilians who do not share an interest in heightened racial consciousness and continue to support the ideology of whitening (Hanchard 1993; Skidmore 1993). These may continue their attraction to "whitened" forms of Umbanda.

Even with reduced Afro-Brazilian participation, Umbanda would still remain ethnically diverse. Many European and Asian immigrants are adherents of Umbanda and leaders of its centros and federations, and researchers have noted Umbanda's role in integrating these ethnic groups into Brazilian national culture (Greenfield 1992; Oro 1988). Umbanda may thus remain as a potent symbol of Brazilian identity, though with fewer Afro-Brazilian practitioners it is not likely to retain as persuasively its current Afro-Brazilian identity.

Umbanda will probably remain a multiclass religion, since its white adherents are distributed through all social classes. But some degree of breakdown in class patronage alliances within it seems likely to occur quite independently of reAfricanization. In the years since Umbanda's founding, the social sectors involved in it have coalesced more consciously as social classes and have gained their own political representation, and increased political freedom has also produced many alternatives to Umbanda through which political mobilization can now occur.

Returning now to reAfricanization, and the deeper issue of its potential for creating new levels of racial awareness and political activism, the question is how effective can traditional forms of Afro-Brazilian culture such as those discussed here be in promoting racial awareness and stimulating racial activism? Hanchard (1993) has noted that while so far there has been no critical "moment" of open racial confrontation between Afro-Brazilians and the dominant sectors of Brazilian society, their recent activism has placed the issues out in the open as never before. Acknowledging that many of the barriers to more militant political activism are structural ones involving both the strength of racial hegemony (the myth of racial democracy) and the fragmentation and lack of self-identification among Afro-Brazilians, Hanchard also sees the pursuit of Afro-Brazilian cultural goals as a potential impediment to political activism, though he acknowledges they may be effective in consciousness raising and identity creation. Even when such culturally oriented groups are infused with new African identity and consciousness, Hanchard finds that their general tendency is to create and promote cultural expression as an end in itself, rather than as a means to greater levels of political activism. And he notes an additional barrier to activism posed by more traditional cultural forms, which have already become incorporated into the national culture as symbols of Brazilian identity, and in the process "deracinated," stripped of racial significance and content, and depoliticized (Hanchard 1993:59). In other words, these forms of traditional culture have been co-opted at the national level and have themselves become part of the "cultura do racismo" (culture of racism) (Rufino 1988:14), part of the denial of racism. To become racially meaningful, they must repudiate such co-optation, and must be revitalized by the infusion of new meanings to counter old ones, so as to become counterhegemonic forces. These processes seem to be occurring in carnival and Candomblé in recent years, with the rejection of elite domination, commercialism, patronage, and folklorization, and the welcoming and invention of new forms, as in carnival, or of new levels of African centeredness, as in Candomblé.

None of these seems likely to occur in Umbanda as it is currently constituted: despite the changes noted in my discussion, Umbanda still stands as a bulwark of racial hegemony and patronage, the denial of racism, and support for the myth of racial democracy. To the extent that the goals that lie behind current directions of reAfricanization are to succeed, Afro-Brazilians must either secede from or reinvent Umbanda.

NOTES

1. My use of "Afro-Brazilian" ("afro-brasileiro") follows common usage of this term by academics in Brazil to refer in the aggregate to Brazilians of African ancestry. Afro-Brazilians themselves are increasingly using the term *negro* ("black") as a self-referential term that connotes a common self-identity.

2. My research in Brazil on Umbanda was conducted in 1966, 1968–1969, and 1975–1976.

3. The term "genuine," employed by Hobsbawm and Ranger to refer to ongoing, historically continuous traditions, is useful contextually to distinguish from more recent, "invented" traditions. Nevertheless, the term is also problematic, since "genuine" implies an absence of appropriation or invention of traditions among groups within historically continuous traditions, and because it also implies a moral value judgment about traditions that are "genuine" and others which by implication must be "artificial."

4. This association ignores the Catholic Church's own tacit acceptance of witchcraft, and its widespread efforts throughout the Catholic world to exorcise the works of a Christian devil, and blames these activities on Africans and their cultures.

5. The *orixás*, central deities in Candomblé, have become largely otiose figures in Umbanda, powerful but distant spiritual personages who are paid homage in Umbanda ceremonies, but rarely descend to earth to possess Umbanda mediums, and are instead petitioned through their less powerful but more accessible spiritual intermediaries, the Cablocos and Pretos Velhos.

6. During the early 1950s, visits by members of the militant Teatro Experimental do Negro to black Afro-Brazilian religious leaders to urge that they practice racial and religious separatism provoked angry rejections (see Brown 1986:154–155).

7. The Bahian elite is here treated as part of the national "white" elite, though it has been pointed out that it includes many "brancos da Bahia" who might phenotypically be classified as mulattos (Azevedo 1955).

8. I am speaking here of the expansion of Candomblé *relative to Umbanda*. It should be kept in mind that Pentecostal forms of Protestantism are spreading very rapidly in urban industrial areas of Brazil, encroaching upon Catholicism and possibly, as well, upon Afro-Brazilian religions.

9. A recent researcher in Rio has observed another kind of transformation among the Pretos Velhos, from elderly and humble spirits, into young and vigorous ones, some of whom appear threatening, devious, and even dangerous. Change may signal another mode of the reAfricanization of Umbanda through the symbolic transformation of its spiritual personae (Lindsay Hale, personal communication on his own recent fieldwork in Rio, 1993)

REFERENCES

Amaral, Rita de Cássia. 1991. "O tombamento de um terreiro de Candomblé em São Paulo." *Comunicações do ISER* 10(41):89–92.

Andrews, George Reid. 1991. *Blacks and Whites in São Paulo, Brazil, 1888–1988*. Madison: University of Wisconsin Press.

_____. 1992. "Racial Inequality in Brazil and the United States: A Statistical Comparison." *Journal of Social History* 26(2):229–263.

Azevedo, Thales de. 1955. *As elites de côr: um estudo de ascenção social.* São Paulo: Companhia Editora Nacional.

Bastide, Roger. 1978. *The African Religious of Brazil.* Tr. by Helen Sebba. Baltimore: The Johns Hopkins University Press.

Birman, Patricia. 1984. "Comentários à propósito da II Conferência Mundial da Tradição dos Orixás." *Comunicações do ISER* 3(8):47–54.

Borges, Dain. 1993. " 'Puffy, Ugly, Slothful and Inert': Degeneration in Brazilian Social Thought 1880-1940." *Journal of Latin American Studies* 25(2):235–256.

Brown, Diana DeG. 1977. "Umbanda e classes sociais." *Religião e Sociedade* 1:31–42.

_____. 1979. "Umbanda and Class Relations in Brazil." In Maxine Margolis and William Carte, eds., *Brazil: Anthropological Perspectives.* New York: Columbia University Press.

_____. 1986. *Umbanda: Religion and Politics in Urban Brazil.* Ann Arbor: UMI Press.

Brown, Diana DeG., and Mario Bick. 1987. "Religion, Class and Context: Continuities and Discontinuities in Brazilian Umbanda." *American Ethnologist* 14(1):73–93.

Cavalcânti, Lauro. 1988. "Black-brêque: estudo de um grupo soul em relação a adeptos do samba." *Comunicações do ISER* 7(28):21–32.

Concone, Maria Elena. 1981. "Ideologia umbandista e integralismo." In Leôncio Martins Rodrigues et al., eds., *Trabalho e cultura no Brasil.* Vol. 1, pp. 379–395. Recife/Brasília: ANPPCS/CNPq.

Costa Eduardo, Octávio da. 1948. *The Negro in Northern Brazil.* Monographs of the American Ethnological Society, No. 15.

Costa Pinto, Luis. 1952. *O negro no Rio de Janeiro.* São Paulo: Companhia Editora Nacional.

Dantas, Beatriz Gois. 1988. *Vovô Nagô e Papai Branco: usos e abusos da Africa no Brasil.* Rio de Janeiro: Edições Graal Ltda.

Dos Santos, Jocêlio Teles. 1989. "As imagens estão guardadas: reafricanização." *Comunicações do ISER* 8(34):50–58.

Dossar, Kenneth. 1992. "Capoeira Angola: Dancing between Two Worlds." *Afro-Hispanic Review* 11(1–3):5–10.

Dunn, Christopher. 1992. "Afro-Brazilian Carnival: A Stage for Protest." *Afro-Hispanic Review* 11(1–3):11–20.

Dzidzienyo, Anani. 1985. "The African Connection and the Afro-Brazilian Condition." In Pierre-Michel Fontaine, ed., *Race, Class, and Power in Brazil*. Los Angeles: Center for Afro-American Studies, UCLA.

Fernandes, Florestan. 1978. *A integração do negro na sociedade de classes*. 2 vols. 3d ed. São Paulo.

Fontaine, Pierre-Michel, ed. 1985. *Race, Class and Power in Brazil*. Los Angeles: Center for Afro-American Studies, UCLA.

Freyre, Gilberto. 1946. *The Masters and the Slaves*. 1933. Tr. Samuel Putnam. New York: Alfred A Knopf.

Fry, Peter. 1984. "Reflexões sobre a II Conferência Mundial da Tradição dos Orixás e Cultura: de um observador não participante." *Comunicacões do ISER* 3(8):37–45.

Giacomini, Sonia. 1988. "Uma dupla leitura: macumba, cultura negra e ideologia do recalque." *Comunicações do ISER* 7(28):55–71.

Greenfield, Sidney M. 1992. "Descendants of European Immigrants in Southern Brazil as Participants and Heads of Afro-Brazilian Religious Centers." Paper presented at the meeting of the American Anthropological Association, San Francisco, December 1–6.

Hanchard, Michael. 1993. "Culturalism vs. Cultural Politics: Movimento Negro in Rio de Janeiro and São Paulo, Brazil." In Kay Warren, ed., *The Violence Within: Cultural and Political Opposition in Divided Nations*. Boulder, Colo.: Westview Press.

Hasenbalg, Carlos.1979. *Discriminação e desigualdades Raciais no Brasil*. Rio de Janeiro: Graal.

_____. 1985. "Race and Socioeconomic Inequalities in Brazil." In Pierre-Michel Fontaine, ed., *Race, Class, and Power in Brazil*. Los Angeles: Center for Afro-American Studies, UCLA.

Hasenbalg, Carlos, and Nelson do Valle Silva. 1988. *Estrutura social, mobilidade e raça*. São Paulo: Vertice and IUPERJ.

Herskovitz, Melville. 1966. *The New World Negro: Selected Papers in Afro-American Studies*. Ed. Frances S. Herskovitz. Bloomington: Indiana University Press.

Hobsbawm, Eric, and Terence Ranger. 1983. *The Invention of Tradition.* Cambridge: Cambridge University Press.

Hutchinson, Harry. 1952. "Race Relations in a Rural Community of the Bahian Recôncavo." In Charles Wagley, ed., *Race and Class in Rural Brazil.* Paris: UNESCO.

Landes, Ruth. 1947. *City of Women.* New York: Macmillan.

Lewis, J. Lowell. 1992. *Ring of Liberation: Deceptive Discourse in Brazilian Capoeira.* Chicago: University of Chicago Press.

Matta, Roberto da. 1991. *Carnivals, Rogues, and Heroes: An Interpretation of the Brazilian Dilemma.* Tr. John Drury. Notre Dame, Ind.: University of Notre Dame Press.

Moore, Zelbert. 1988. "100 Years of Abolition in Brazil or Carnival: It's as Real as It Gets." Paper presented at the National Council for Black Studies, 12th Annual Conference, Philadelphia, Pennsylvania.

Nina Rodrigues, Raimundo. 1935. *O animismo fetichista dos negros baianos.* 1900. Rio de Janeiro: Civilização Brasileira.

_____. 1945. *Os africanos no Brasil.* 1906. São Paulo: Companhia Editora Nacional.

Oro, Ari Pedro. 1988. "Negros e brancos nas religões afro-brasileiras no Rio Grande do Sul." *Comunicações do ISER* 7(28):33–54.

Ortiz, Renato. 1978. *A morte branca do feiticeiro negro.* Petrópolis: Vozes.

Prandi, José Reginaldo. 1991. *Os Candomblés de São Paulo: a velha magia na metrópole nova.* São Paulo: Editora HUCITEC.

Prandi, José Reginaldo, and Vagner Gonçalves. 1989. "Axé São Paulo." In Carlos Eugênio Marcondes de Moura, ed., *Meu sinal está no seu corpo.* São Paulo: EDICON/USP.

Ramos, Artur. 1934. *O negro brasileiro.* Rio de Janeiro: Editora Civilização Brasileira.

Risério, Antônio. 1981. *Carnaval Ijexá.* Salvador: Corrupio.

Rufino, Joel. 1988. "IPCN e Cacique de Ramos: dois exemplos de movimento negro na cidade do Rio de Janeiro." *Comunicações do ISER* 7(28):5–20.

Silva, Nelson do Valle. 1985. "Updating the Cost of Not Being White in Brazil." In Pierre-Michel Fontaine, ed., *Race, Class, and Power in Brazil.* Los Angeles: Center for Afro-American Studies, UCLA.

Skidmore, Thomas. 1974. *Black into White: Race and Nationality in Brazilian Thought.* New York: Oxford University Press.

_____. 1993. "Bi-racial USA vs. Multi-racial Brazil: Is the Contrast Still Valid?" *Journal of Latin American Studies* 25(2):373–386.

Veja. 1983. "Festa Nagô: santos de todo o mundo baixam em Salvador." July 27.

Willems, Emilio. 1966. "Religious Mass Movements and Social Change in Brazil." In Eric Baklanoff, ed., *New Perspectives on Brazil.* Nashville: Vanderbilt University Press.

13 | The Fall of a Black Prophet: Pentecostalism and the Rhetoric of Race in Urban Brazil

JOHN BURDICK

It is May, 1988. The Pastoral Negro of the Catholic Church is in full swing, commemorating the centennial of abolition with the Brotherhood Campaign, replete with neighborhood meetings and seminars, designed to raise consciousness about the falsity of abolition. I am standing on a street in São Jorge, a working-class town of 8,000 inhabitants, in the outer periphery of Rio de Janeiro, talking to Manuel, a member of the evangelical Assembly of God, a man who calls himself a *crente*.[1] A Catholic militant passes by and reminds me of an upcoming seminar on the history of slavery, to be held in the church. Despite the fact that my companion is black, the militant does not address him. After he leaves, I ask my companion if he would be interested in attending the seminar. "Oh yes, I'd like that," he replies. "It's good to learn these things, to know the truth about what happened." He has been hearing his neighbors talk about the Pastoral, and has even seen the guide booklet. "Very true, Isabel signed the papers," he says. "But she didn't free us. No, we are still slaves." I hope to see him at the seminar, I say. He becomes hesitant. "Well . . . no, I don't think so." But why not, Sr. Manuel? He pauses. "You saw that I was not invited. That is not a place for crentes. They do not want us to be part of it."

Later, I approach the Catholic militant who slighted my friend. Why, I ask, had he not invited him? His reply is remarkable in its clarity. "I don't have anything against crentes. Not for religion, you see. This is not about that. But they don't care about such things. It is a waste of time. They just sing, 'Holy, Holy, Holy.'" Do you really think you can raise the consciousness of a crente? He waves his hand in exasperation. "No, John, I don't

237

want the grief. You invite them to a meeting, and all they want to do is convert you."

I begin with this anecdote because it condenses a perspective and a problem which I would like to suggest are with us at this very conference. There is a sort of dismissal going on right here that resembles that of the militant of my story. We have contributions on Candomblé, Umbanda, black culture, and the black consciousness movement; yet what is undoubtedly the most demographically important social movement in Brazil today here remains (despite its embodiment in our keynote speaker)[2] unnamed and uninvestigated. Pentecostalism, now the religion of at least twelve million Brazilians, has from four to five times as many active members as do the Catholic Base Communities, and (relying on Damasceno's 1988 figures) some four hundred times as many active participants as does the black consciousness movement. A large proportion of these crentes are Afro-Brazilians.[3] In the towns of the periphery on which I have data, up to one-half are black—versus 15 percent for active Catholics.

The silence surrounding Pentecostals is, I submit, rooted in our mistrust of them. We view them as classic exemplars of political apathy and false consciousness. In particular, we tend to view Pentecostalism, in contrast to Afro-Brazilian religions, as a vehicle for ideological whitening and assimilationism. As Roger Bastide put it, "In this religion of mystic trance the most important factor for the man of color is . . . the effort to get out of the low class and into the bourgeoisie. At the very moment when he seems closest to Africa—shaking and trembling, speaking in tongues, possessed by the Holy Ghost—he is actually farthest from it, more Westernized than ever before."[4]

The anecdote at the start of this essay, however, should have suggested that there are reasons to be skeptical of this view. It should have alerted us to the possibility that the relationship of Afro-Brazilians to Pentecostalism is in fact far more contradictory than Bastide seems to allow.

Let me begin with what for many is the most obvious level of this relationship. There can be no doubt that Pentecostalism does indeed appeal to many Afro-Brazilians as a vehicle for entering into white society. São Jorge's Catholics and crentes recognize this appeal when they quip that "the black man wants to be a crente so he can call the white man 'brother.'" The quip seizes on a real social relation, between white proselytizer and black proselytized. "Let me tell you," said one convert, "they give so much attention to you, they invite you, it's really something. . . . The welcome they give, they come to you to shake your hand, you really feel at home. . . . Because, man, no one cares about the blacks, and there they greet you in the street, they give more attention in the street to black people."

Such statements certainly express an assimilationist impulse, the desire to establish a kinship relation with whites. "In the Assembly of God," said one convert, "the white man treats the black man kindly. There we are like members of a family." Yet these statements are also marked by an important inner tension: for in addition to expressing the desire to be treated *kindly*, they express the desire to be treated as an *equal*, effectively embodying an implicit challenge to the legitimacy of Brazilian race relations. Thus one convert could tell me that "the same treatment they give to whites they give to blacks. I'd go and see the opportunity they gave us, the black pastors, black children up there singing and all. And in society, no one does that."

Pentecostalism as harbinger of racial equality. Is it too good to be true? Probably. Indeed, as I will argue, black crentes encounter from lighter-skinned co-religionists a range of subtle, and not so subtle, forms of resistance to their aspirations to equality. Yet despite this resistance, blacks find in Pentecostalism an arena in which equality is at least conceivable; and an arena, in fact, in which it is possible to invert the racial hierarchy. Let me put the matter in even stronger terms: Pentecostalism provides blacks discursive resources with which to forge a powerful racial consciousness. I want to illustrate the nature of this consciousness, as it is formed in relation to that of light-skinned crentes, by reflecting on an episode of possession by the Holy Spirit that I witnessed in São Jorge's Assembly of God church.

It was a Sunday when the pastor (who is white) was absent. The highest authority present was Elias, the pastor's son, who had just taken possession of the office of vice-president the preceding week. The trouble began about halfway through the hymn-singing. In the row in front of me, a black man in his twenties stood up suddenly and rushed from the pews, down the center aisle and up to the presbyters' dais, all the while shouting in a high-pitched, unworldly voice. When he arrived and riveted himself in front of the pastor's son, a hush fell upon the congregation. With a voice that shook with rage, the young man spoke for several minutes, minutes that seemed an eternity. With hand outstretched above Elias's head and thunder in his voice, the prophet's attitude was unmistakably one of reproof. Then, in mid-shout, he fell in a heap. The church exploded into cries and prayer, the presbyters leapt from their seats to lay hands upon the prophet's crumpled body and prayed intensely for several minutes. Finally the young man regained consciousness, stood up shakily, and left the dais bent and weak, wiping his brow. Elias immediately seized the microphone and preached with towering indignation for several minutes about how to ascend the pulpit one must be prepared in the sight of God, that one could not climb to its heights in any way one liked. But though he thundered, the congregation thundered as well, and drowned him out. It was only when another presbyter led a mighty and spine-tingling hymn that everyone finally began to sing in unison. As soon as this show of unity had occurred, the presbyters hastily called an end to the service, half an hour before normal ending time. I left the church entirely drained.

In the following weeks I heard profoundly different interpretations of this event and, in particular, of the fall of the prophet, whose name was Alexandre. Some crentes claimed that the young man had fallen because he had been moved, not by the Holy Spirit, but rather by his own flesh. God had stricken him down before the multitudes. Others, meanwhile, suggested that because Alexandre had, they believed, a background in Umbanda, he had fallen owing to the influence of the Enemy. Whether the cause was flesh or the Devil, tellers of both these accounts emphasized what they took to be Alexandre's lack of humility before Elias. As one put it, "He ascended there in an exalted way, but he descended humiliated. If someone exalts himself, God himself humiliates him." Those who interpreted the prophet's fall in these ways tended to be lighter-skinned crentes within, or aspiring to enter, the authority hierarchy of the church. I will return to this point shortly.

A large number of the crentes who were present that night, however, insisted Alexandre had been moved neither by his own flesh nor by the Devil, but rather by the Holy Spirit. Here, the argument was that Alexandre had fallen quite simply because he had been overwhelmed by the power of God. I could distinguish two main groups holding this view. The first included lighter-skinned men and women with no pretensions of entering the authority hierarchy of the church. But this group's hold on the view proved rather tenuous. When, in particular, the pastor returned to his flock and responded to the event by preaching that Alexandre had been inspired only by his flesh—while, at the same time, and very significantly, refraining from disciplining Alexandre—some of these lighter-skinned crentes began to entertain doubts about their initially sympathetic position. Among the second group, the black crentes, I found no waverers: indeed, to this very day the black members of São Jorge's Assembly of God continue to declare that Alexandre was divinely inspired.

To shed light on these interpretations, on the pattern of who holds them, and on their consequences, I need to focus on the rhetorics of race and spirituality that blacks encounter in the Assembly of God and explore their multiplicity and inner tension.

Pentecostal doctrine proclaims that the more humble one is in the world, the more open one is to the Holy Spirit. I first realized the implications of this for collective understanding of black spirituality when a white woman invited me to accompany her to the house of a black prayer-healer. When I told her I could not go, she said, "No matter. There's a woman who prays for the sick on Thursdays. She's light, but her prayers are a blessing too." That little "but" spoke very loudly.

There is, it turns out, an image, widely shared among crentes, of all racial self-identifications of blacks as able to come "closer to God" than anyone else in church, as having "greater fervor," speaking in tongues, prophesying, having visions, curing, and expelling demons with greater frequency than their lighter-skinned co-religionists. This is partly why light-skinned crentes are receptive to black leadership in church. No other social arena offers blacks comparable opportunities to attain positions of visible authority: nearly half of São Jorge's presbyters are black, and many blacks are deacons and prayer-healers.

While the image of black spiritual specialness is fairly universal in the Assembly of God, light-skinned crentes offer different reasons for this specialness than blacks do. Sometimes they point to the fact that blacks know better than others how to "humble themselves." And sometimes they point to the fact that blacks "were once in Macumba." The widespread stereotype that blacks—one and all—have been at one time or another involved in Umbanda or Macumba allows light-skinned crentes to claim that every black in the Assembly is living proof of Christ's saving grace. "If He is willing to save a Macumbeiro," one white crente declared, "certainly He will forgive anything!" Blacks, in this view, are now especially committed to seeking God because they wish earnestly "to escape that evil." It should come as no surprise that these accounts are easily turned against blacks. As I will suggest in a moment, this is precisely what happened in some interpretations of Alexandre's prophetic fall.

Blacks, meanwhile, when accounting for their own fervor and spirituality, stress neither their own innate humility nor their dubious heritage of Macumba; instead, they emphasize the blues of being a black in a white-dominated society. As one black presbyter explained, "The black person has more desire, more hunger, more thirst for God. The Bible says 'Blessed are they who hunger and thirst for justice, for they will inherit the Kingdom of God.' Because sometimes, you know, they're not well looked upon, you know? They're left to the side, that's why they have more of that desire to seek God. And we are well received." Some blacks go even further, claiming their fervor is rooted in the history of slavery. "The black person understands spiritual liberation better," a black deacon told me, "because they were liberated once as a people." Another said, "We were once liberated materially, but it was a false liberation. We stayed as slaves. That is why we seek after a true liberation. Because we still suffer." Some even say *crença* was founded by the slaves themselves. "It was the blacks who founded the crente churches," an elderly black man reflected. "Crença began as a religion that the slaves liked, because they couldn't go to church. The Catholic Church, which was all white, was all there was. But after liberation, they started to support their own church, and that's how it started." Blacks thus became religious tutors to the whites: "The whites liked the lovely unity of the blacks," one black deacon declared, "so they went to join them."

Now, as I have intimated, for those with lighter skin, the image of black spiritual specialness has another, more problematic side. While not questioning blacks' claims to spiritual gifts, many lighter-skinned crentes still believe blacks to be more prone to backsliding and temptation than whites. As one of them said, "I think that *pretos* have to be a bit more vigilant than whites. Because they are weaker when faced with temptation, they can fall much quicker." Whites in positions of leadership do not hesitate to challenge the validity of black spiritual gifts. Here the reverse side of the Macumba coin reveals itself. "Look," said one white presbyter, "blacks were dedicated to that thing, that spiritism, that manifestation of the spirit. So, when they feel, you know, happy in the church, they already think they can prophesy." Not surprisingly, blacks bitterly resent such attitudes. "It's just when we speak against the white people there on the bench," one young black woman argued, "that's when they say it's

Macumba! If they like what they hear: 'Ah, let's go to brother so-and-so, he'll help us, he has great spiritual power!' But if they don't like it: 'Ah, brother so-and-so is a silly chatterbox, he's just a Macumbeiro!'"

Rhetorical battles over the connection between race and spirituality are especially intense between blacks and mulattos. Mulattos who aspire to move up in the ranks speak resentfully about how the pastor has accepted blacks into the presbytery as a concession to avoid accusations of racism and insist that there are no differences between the spirituality of lighter- and darker-skinned church members. Indeed, some mulattos go so far as to say that blacks are even less spiritual than either mulattos or whites because they are too "proud." As one mulatto put it, "Whenever they get any little office, they become proud. So it's hard for God to work through them." Blacks retort that, by trying to be "more than what they are," it is the mulatto who suffers from spiritual barrenness. A young black female crente complained that "a person who is ashamed of himself is ashamed of his race, he doesn't make room for the Holy Spirit. If he criticizes, laughs, is ashamed, God doesn't use him. The mulattos criticize.... For them to have a spiritual life like the blacks have, they have to stop wanting to humiliate others, wanting to be better than blacks."

This discussion of the intersection between racial and spiritual rhetorics should have prepared us to undertake an analysis of the events leading up to Alexandre's church-shaking performance. The story began the preceding spring, in a confrontation between Alexandre and Elias, who at the time was still a mere presbyter. During a choral rehearsal, Alexandre was recounting a vision when Elias interrupted him and said, "Shut up." As one eyewitness testified, "Everyone was pretty shocked." A few months later Elias was nominated to be the church's new vice-president. The nomination stirred controversy. Elias has been outside the church for nearly ten years and had returned to the fold only the preceding year. Many congregants of all races had felt that the speed with which he had been promoted smacked of nepotism. It was, in addition, general knowledge that not only did Elias lack the gifts of the Holy Spirit, but also that his profession—he was a policeman—required him to wear a firearm, something many crentes believe to be contrary to the Word of God.

Blacks, it seems, were particularly incensed by the nomination of Elias. With so many strikes against him, many blacks were deeply annoyed that another presbyter—a black named Oswaldo—had not even been considered. Oswaldo had been an active crente all his life and possessed the gifts of prophecy and vision. Yet the pastor had passed over him.

As the issue finally reached the public arena, it became clear that attitudes toward Elias were divided along racial lines. When the presbyters voted on his nomination, five of the six voting against him were blacks, and seven of those voting for him were whites or mulattos. The presbyters' decision was brought to the entire congregation for pro forma approval, with those opposing the result free to express themselves. Only one voice was raised against the nomination—the voice being none other than Alexandre's (he left in a huff). His voice no doubt resonated with the secret feelings of many in the congregation; but he was, it seems, the only one resentful enough to stand forth in protest. After that, the atmosphere among the presbyters became intensely strained, and the pastor took extraordinary measures to redress the situation. One crente recalled that "The presbyters were not getting along. So the pastor called for a week of prayer to bring unity again."

At the end of that week, a struggle that had been lost in the sphere of human words now entered the battleground of divine speech. For the Assembly's blacks, Elias represented authority rooted in whiteness, nepotism, and worldly privilege, rather than in the power of the Holy Spirit. Their resentment of Elias and all that he represented came to be articulated, I submit, through taking sides in the interpretation of Alexandre's prophecy.

I do not claim, however, to know why Alexandre fell to the floor that night. What I do claim is that the meaning of his fall went far beyond his own state of mind at that moment. The prophet and those who supported him were not participants of the official black consciousness movement; indeed, most had never even heard of it. Yet in rising up and feeling God speak through him in reproof of Elias, Alexandre was, I suggest, joining in a battle, part of the long, deep, tortuous struggle between the races in Brazil. In this battle, the pastor would claim victory, as he preached for weeks that Alexandre had succumbed to the flesh. Yet it was a victory profoundly limited both by the large number of blacks in the church and by the general acceptance of the rhetoric of black spiritual specialness. It is of great importance that the pastor simply could not, in the end, exclude or even discipline the very prophet who, he claimed, had sown anarchy in his church. The pastor's failure to discipline was worth a thousand words. He was, I believe, aware that he was encountering in Alexandre's performance an issue of monumental proportions, one that could easily threaten to divide his church. Indeed, to this day, blacks in the Assembly cite the pastor's unwillingness to discipline Alexandre as proof of the young prophet's divine inspiration. The pastor's refusal to discipline in effect ceded to the black prophets of São Jorge's Assembly of God another inch of ground.

The tale of Alexandre's fall illustrates the contradictory quality of blacks' experience in Brazilian Pentecostalism. If, on the one hand, this religion carves out discursive spaces in which blacks can enlarge their social power and develop racial consciousness, it provides, on the other, discursive resources that help lighter-skinned people in their efforts to maintain their domination. By themselves, black Pentecostals have little chance of bringing about greater racial democracy in Brazil. Yet their nuanced, dialectical discourse on race cannot be lightly dismissed. In alliance with other groups, they may yet help to crack the hegemony of whitening ideology and forge a new future for Brazilian race relations. It is, in fact, possible that in congregations that come to be dominated by Afro-Brazilians, a wholly new discourse of black spirituality will emerge and become socially empowered, perhaps in a way similar to the black Baptist movement of the U.S. South in the 1960s. Even if they have not yet attained this kind of social power, the black Pentecostals' sheer numbers alone suggest the importance of listening very carefully to them. The leaders of Brazil's black consciousness movement can hardly afford not to.

NOTES

1. Literally, a "believer." *Crente* is a term commonly used in Brazil to describe evangelical Christians or, in a broader sense, Protestants.—Ed.

2. Federal Deputy Benedita da Silva, a member of the Brazilian Assembly of God.—Ed.

3. For data, see *Comunicações do ISER* (October 1985), special issue edited by Maria da Graça Floriano and Regina Reyes Novaes.

4. Roger Bastide, *African Religions of Brazil,* tr. Helen Sebba (Baltimore and London: The Johns Hopkins University Press, 1978), p. 372.

Part	MUSIC, CARNIVAL, AND IDENTITY
Five	

The three essays in this section involve black Brazil's cultural practices, here centered on music. That the music and dance of black Brazil occupy a rather privileged position within Brazil should surprise no one. The extent to which black Brazilian musical and other expressive performative arts are themselves important manifestations of cultural resistance, black consciousness, and even political action, however, may surprise more than a few readers. In the first essay, Brazilian author, poet, lyricist, and social commentator Antônio Risério analyzes the "markedly black" character of today's Bahian carnival as a stage for protesting racial discrimination and denouncing social inequalities. No one who has attended Bahian carnival during the last ten years will dispute his observation. Additionally, rather than dismissing the recent assimilation of what he calls the "black-mestizo" carnival by the Bahian tourist industry as merely appropriation, he views the transformative effect of black-mestizo aesthetic values in today's Bahia as, in fact, hegemonic.

In his essay, Brazilian ethnomusicologist and anthropologist José Jorge de Carvalho presents a study of the ways in which blacks have been represented in commercial song texts over the past sixty years. Carvalho first analyzes the traditional fixation (from the white perspective) of black women as either sexual objects or as crazy and stupid, and black men as either old, poor, and humble or as romantic hustlers. Next he identifies the stereotyped identities of people of increasingly lighter skin: mulattas, morenas, and blonds. Finally, Carvalho deals with the complexity of contemporary racial identification presented in songs from the perspective of black Brazilians. The essay is provocative in asserting, at the national level, the cultural obsession Brazilian song writers have with racial identification.

Closing out this section, Zairean-born ethnomusicologist Kazadi Wa Mukuna discusses the history of the dramatic dance from Maranhão known as the Bumba-meu-Boi. Extant since colonial times, this folk drama performed by slaves and members of the lower class served as a collective statement of resistance, criticism, and ridicule against slave owners and members of the ruling class.

14 Carnival: The Colors of Change

ANTÔNIO RISÉRIO

Brazil is not, as the title of Jorge Amado's first novel would have it, "the country of carnival." Rather, it is a country of "many carnivals," as in the song by Caetano Veloso.

The most frequently analyzed contrast in Brazil's carnivalesque variety concerns carnival celebrations in Rio de Janeiro and Bahia. Carioca carnival is, above all, a spectacle. On one side, the stage; on the other, the public. This arrangement seems to contradict the "classical" model found in the history of Western carnival, from permissive Roman festivals in honor of Saturn to the carnivals of the Middle Ages, where the idea of a separation between stage and public, transforming festivities into theater, would simply be unthinkable. To paraphrase the Russian scholar Mikhail Bakhtin, it would have destroyed carnival, since "to live," not "to contemplate," was the central verb of carnivalesque ideology. From this perspective, Bahian carnival is typologically closer to saturnalia and medieval festivals than is that of Rio. Rather than being a spectacle for the public, Bahian carnival is a prodigious and frenetic festival experienced by all.

The opposition between spectacle and participatory festival is but one of the signs—albeit an extremely powerful one—of the difference between the carnivals of Rio and Bahia. One could point out many distinguishing features, but in this essay I prefer to concentrate on the markedly *black* character of Bahian carnival, which in a certain sense defines is physiognomy. In recent carnival history, the black dimension has been revived and has become predominant since the 1970s, to such an extent that a foreign observer, Sheila Walker, has compared the decade's significance to that of the 1960s for African-Americans in the

United States. Of course Walker was also referring to other phenomena, but only through lateral references. What she emphasized above all was what I classified at the time, with some linguistic reservations, as a "process of the re-Africanization" of Bahian carnival.

The reason for my caution was in the prefix "re," suggesting backward movement. What occurred was in fact a carnival with a new face. The so-called *afoxés* and *blocos afro* expanded. They were organizations comprising primarily black-mestizo youth, using African names and including waves of people dressed in smocks and playing music to the sound of songs that referred to other black cultures, especially the Yoruba tradition, which was transformed into a sort of central code of symbolic manifestations of black African roots. Although seeking support in the Bahian black-mestizo tradition, it was a carnival that pointed not toward the past, but toward the future of Brazilian race relations.

There was, however, a justification for using the term "re-Africanization." That moment of the blackening of carnival presented a conjunctural novelty, but it was not absolutely new in contextual terms. The history of Bahian carnival is not one that links us exclusively to the Latin world. Its roots are also, with equal force and clarity, in Africa. In fact, blacks and mestizos provided the tone, magnetizing and distinguishing Bahian carnival as a fundamental variant of great festivals.

Before carnival took its own form, the festivities that preceded Lent were limited to the Portuguese tradition of the *entrudo,* which was ultimately prohibited because of its anarchistic violence. After this prohibition, there was official encouragement of street festivals, organized as a carnival procession. The African influence is noticeable from the very beginnings of the transformation. Manoel Querino, for example, defended the thesis of the influence of the *damurixá* in the configuration of Bahian carnival. The damurixá was a masked festival that took place in January in Lagos, Nigeria. According to Querino, in 1897 this very same black carnival took place in Bahia, an "exact reproduction" of what occurred in Africa. More recently, Olábìyí Yái has raised the hypothesis of the influence of another Yoruba festival—*gueledé*—in the origins of Bahian carnival. Speaking of this period, in *Os africanos no Brasil,* a classic of Brazilian anthropology, Nina Rodrigues also emphasized the African character of the Bahian festival. The names of carnival groups of the period speak for themselves: African Embassy, Sons of Africa, African Warriors, and so on. An eyewitness to this history, Nina Rodrigues underlines the African themes and motifs of these groups.

In truth, once receiving permission to have the festival, nothing was more natural than for black-mestizos to turn to the aesthetic and cultural repertoire of Africa. It was then, in the final decades of the nineteenth century, that the Africanization of Bahian carnival took place.

Of course throughout this history of carnival one notes diverse configurations. For example, the first black-mestizo groups were encouraged to participate in the official carnival parade to reinforce the whitened elites' struggle against the clamor of the entrudo, which they wanted to wipe from the social map of a country aspiring to civilization. At the turn of the century, these same black groups became unsettling for the elitist civilizational dream and were converted into equivalents of the old entrudo because of their primitivist character. In other words, at a moment in which their culture was increasingly acquiring French manners, the elite saw something simianesque and dissonant in the colorful black groups. The struggle began, in the press, with the attempt to remove the black carnival entities from the streets. In the end, just the opposite occurred: the elite withdrew from the streets to private clubs. One should recall that even in the 1970s the Bahian elite hesitated to set foot in the streets. Rather, they would go from their living rooms to the clubroom. Caetano Veloso played with this theme when he sang: "todo mundo na praça / e manda a gente sem graça / pro salão" ("everyone in the plaza / and send the boring people / to the ballroom").

From the black-mestizo perspective, things were also changing. There is an ebb and flow in the Afro-carnival tide, depending on diverse ideological factors and on actions of the ruling elite: changes in blacks' self-image, their capacity for community organization, transformations in the country's imagination, and so forth. Nevertheless, when they do express themselves, the Afro-carnival groups express themselves with relative clarity, even though they may eventually be caught in a double bind between resistance and co-optation. The example of the afoxé Filhos de Gandhi is illustrative.

After an interregnum of almost twenty years, during which the afoxés almost disappeared, Gandhi emerged in 1949, founded by people associated with Candomblé and the dock workers union. Gandhi was rooted in Bahian black-mestizo soil and adopted an attitude opposed to European colonialism. The afoxé was named in honor of the Indian anti-colonialist leader a few months after his assassination and at a moment when the port of Salvador harbored British ships. Mahatma Gandhi had often protested the dominating presence of Europeans on the African continent. At the same time, the afoxé's discourse avoided the theme of racial conflict or tension. It was "integrationist." After an interval in which it almost disappeared, Gandhi reemerged in the 1970s, when the situation was quite different. Black-mestizo youth organized new afoxés and carnival groups with discourses and postures that had little to do with the explicit integrationism of the traditional afoxé. It was a moment of the affirmation of "being black," in a situation marked, from end to end, by an ideology of cultural pluralism.

Frantz Fanon used to say that every community segregates its own light. That is a beautiful metaphor for a communitarian alchemy which seems to resist attempts at empirical investigation. But, beyond this alchemy, which occurred in the broader context of Brazilian life, two things directly affected black-mestizo youth who, growing up in the midst of the "economic miracle" promoted by the military dictatorship, rushed to form new afoxés and blocos afro. On the one hand, they followed models provided by the aesthetic-political movements of North American blacks. On the other, they developed a new vision of Africa, born of the liberation of the last continental redoubts under white domination, most significantly colonies of Portugal, like Brazil in the previous century. New Portuguese-speaking countries dotted the international scenario, and this fact beat strongly on the drums of Brazil.

We should also note the energy of North American music. Black Soul was the magic password, a movement flourishing in the country's major cities: Black Rio, Black Sampa (São Paulo), and, with less intensity, Black Bahia. These movements comprised thousands of young people who, united around soul music, celebrated the greatness of the black race, called themselves "blacks" (in English), and thought rock was nonsense and that samba had sold out to whites. But things took another direction, from Black Soul to Brazilian "negritude." Consciousness came through fashion, a soul dancer once told me. And because of obvious cultural determinations, Bahia would be the passageway from "soul" to *ijexá*, from "black" to "afro," from "funk" to afoxé, styles which melded together in something that might warrant the name *black-ijexá*.

Also important during this time were the political movements of black North Americans, who were living through the intense period of black power and the radical Black Panthers. Although news about the black movement arrived in Brazil in fragmentary and distorted fashion, its impact on Brazilian black-mestizo youth is undeniable, as was that of the victories of African guerrilla movements in general. Closing the circuit, black leader Abdias do Nascimento returned from self-exile and the Movimento Negro Unificado emerged. In sum, Bahia's new Afro-carnival organizations—in a black-mestizo community marked by cultural forms and practices of African origin—grew out of this confluence of soul music, black power, and black revolutions.

Two general reflections are warranted here. On the one hand, it is important to discuss the traditional vision of the carnival universe as a space of confraternization, where daily routine is suspended and the ruling sociopolitical system relaxes its control, permitting an ephemeral dissolution of hierarchies. On the other hand, one must discuss the problem of the "appropriation" of realities that are distant in time and space, examining how this appropriation occurs in light of a well-defined social situation.

In relation to the first question, that of carnival as a "rite of inversion," we can use a Bakhtinian perspective to put in check the view of carnival that seems to predominate in Brazilian anthropology. This view, incapable of understanding the specificity of Bahian carnival, is no more than a transposition, to Brazil, of Bakhtin's reading of medieval carnival, mixed with the more recent spices of Victor Turner's symbolic anthropology and the concepts of "liminality" and "communitas."

Speaking of medieval carnival culture—including carnival festivities per se, comic spectacles, parodic verbal works, and so forth—Bakhtin stresses that these acts and rites were opposed to the official culture of those times, offering a different worldview, external to the church and the state. It was a world parallel to the official world, in which men and women of the Middle Ages participated only on predetermined occasions. Here we are in the vast and colored reign of "rites of inversion" which occur when routine is suspended with the creation of another world, which is lived, in its fullness, as long as carnival lasts. In Bakhtin's words, "during carnival it is life itself that represents and interprets . . . another form free from its realization." Life stages another life which is more egalitarian and ruled by better principles. For a certain time, this game is real—and all participate in it.

But the Russian theoretician draws a firm contrast between carnival and official festivals of the Middle Ages, promoted by the church and the state. These festivals "did not extract the people from order." They were festivals that consecrated the established regime. Festivals of stability, of the permanence of rules, of the immutability of values and norms. To the contrary, carnival festivities celebrated temporary liberation from the established regime, in the provisional abolition of hierarchies and taboos. That is, in sum, the carnivalesque view and perspective of the world, according to Bakhtin, to which would correspond a typically carnivalesque language, marked by a reversed logic, by parody, by cross-dressing, by profanation, and so on. Bakhtin speaks, therefore, of a triple ritual—whose poles would be in the people, in the church, and in the state—and, in the case of carnival, in a language of inversions.

These formulations have been simply transposed to Brazil by anthropologist Roberto da Matta. He focuses especially on carnival, on the one hand, and, on the other, the ceremonies of September 7, Brazilian Independence Day, also called the "Day of the Fatherland." In the latter, we find a hierarchical structure while, in carnival, hierarchies are "put in quarantine." Matta includes carnival among the rituals of inversion, which is generically correct, but he does not go beyond this, and he stays within the Bakhtinian orbit, with a pinch of Victor Turner, who draws a distinction between the two primary models of human inter-relationships. On one side, there is society as "a structured, differentiated, and frequently hierarchical system of political-juridical-economic structures." On the other, a model of society lived in a non-structured and relatively non-differentiated manner, which Turner designates with the Latin word "communitas." Matta appropriates this vocabulary. Thus, on the "Day of the Fatherland," groups mark their ritual positions "in homology" with the positions they occupy in daily life. In carnival, however, thanks to the mechanism of "inversion," we find an open social field, a space of reconciliation, of "communitas." In short, Matta introduces Turner's lexicon into Bakhtin's sentence structure.

What about Brazilian carnivals? Brazil is not a medieval burgh, nor an African village. No one is going to pretend to deny universal characteristics of carnival ideology, such as the dissolution of hierarchical order, for example. But this goes for all carnivals. We cannot stop there. Bahian carnival is not contained in the space of inversion, but rather dramatizes social inequalities. This is very clear in the case of race relations. It is evident that Bahian carnival, beyond the universal dimension of the carnivalesque view of the world, renders explicit and denounces socio-racial asymmetries, advancing on the terrain of protest. Festivities, yes. "Communitas," yes. But without excluding such issues as the misery of the black population, racial discrimination, and even South African apartheid. What is certain is that, since the political-cultural densification of the festivity, Bahia has never been the same.

In relation to the second question, that of the "appropriation" of distant realities, we must see the carnival phenomenon in the context of the Brazilian social and racial situation in the 1970s. There was a triple effort at "appropriation": the appropriation of the Brazilian past, the appropriation of the African present, and the appropriation of the American present. One should add, generally speaking, that what is of interest in this appropriation of distant realities is the appropriation that coincides with the interests of the living present. What happened in the 1970s in Brazil was a general questioning of the image of Brazil and Brazilians, with a view toward the construction of a democratic society in the tropics. In the black-mestizo movement, all efforts converged to establish a difference: that of "being black." I will point out some of the most acute moments of this process of affirmation.

To begin with, a good number of black-mestizos, especially the most well educated, had to appropriate the past experience of blacks in Brazil, with Candomblé as the basic point of reference. And here we can indicate two extremes in the demarcation of "being black." On the one hand was the old fable that only a black can truly understand the black experience. Using, out of context, an expression of Depestre, we see here a sort of "somatic metaphysics," with the implication that a black person would not be totally capable of understanding Buddhism, medieval scholastics, or quantum physics. On the other hand, the "vanguard" of Candomblé became involved in a campaign for breaking with the complex phenomenon of religious syncretism.

The slaves brought to Brazil from Africa were kept from professing the faith they brought with them and were introduced into Catholicism by force. But they managed to disguise their original religions, using Catholic saints to practice their own rites under a Catholic façade. Syncretism is the fruit, therefore, of an act of cultural violence. But no historical process is static. Today, when it is no longer possible to recognize religious imposition, numerous people are born into syncretism. Beliefs seem to exist simultaneously and separately, but there are also moments when it is impossible to distinguish between them.

The Catholic Church was the first to attempt the rupture, under the guise of a struggle to "purify" popular festivals in Bahia. The attempt failed. Then came the reaction from Candomblé. The historic importance of the gesture is undeniable. The Church attempted, with colonialist arrogance, to expurgate the *orixás*. The *iyalorixás* immediately demanded the status of an independent religion for Candomblé. But the people continued to be syncretic. The anti-syncretism stance is, in Brazil and other places, more an intellectual attitude than a popular one. It was not by chance that Candomblé's offensive occurred at a moment when the religion of orixás solidified itself in writing. And the positive result, in this case, must be seen in terms of the clear delimitation of a religious field, which for the first time in this history of religion in Brazil publicly affirmed itself with such intensity.

On the extrareligious terrain, the appropriation of the black Brazilian past generated another significant fact: the declaration of November 20 as the National Day of Black Consciousness, in honor of Zumbi dos Palmares. The political-chronological mark thus shifted to specifically black history, here centralized in the celebration of the *quilombo* rebellion. The official date of May 13, the day on which Princess Isabel signed the law that abolished slavery, was emptied of significance.

The appropriation of North American models, on the other hand, can be seen from two angles. Aesthetically, what happened was relatively simple. Black-mestizo youth appropriated its gestures and clothing, based on the idea that "black is beautiful." On the other hand, the subject became more complicated in the political sphere. Black-mestizo leaders became radicalized, attempting to apply, in Brazil, the racial dichotomy that existed in the United States. Fortunately, the myth of racial democracy finally died in Brazil, but the attempt to impose a descent rule was not exactly a success. In truth, the leaders adopted a curious posture, lamenting the fact that in Brazil racial classifications were not as well defined as in the United States: it was a pity that we had in our past the Lusitanian mess and not the drastic separation that the British imposed on their colonies. . . . Thus the difficulty of delimiting a "black being," even though at a propitious moment, when Brazilian society decidedly increased the volume of its discourse about cultural pluralism which, as numerous scholars have pointed out, then took the place of the Marxist-developmentalist paradigm.

Finally, a significant change took place in our way of looking at Africa. Examining the subject today, from the privileged perspective of the retrospective gaze, we know that what we saw was a mythical Africa, deriving from a sort of sanctification of a culturally unidimensional geographical space. Rather than being a living, plural continent, Africa came closer to suggesting the monolith that appears at the beginning of Stanley Kubrick's *2001: A Space Odyssey*, as if the vast African symphony were reducible to a one-note samba. Besides this monolithic perspective, there was also political ingenuousness, a naive pan-Africanism. It is true that, in the conjuncture we are discussing, this perception had a positive function, to increase black-mestizos' confidence in their own strengths. Seen from a distance, however, one cannot help but say that this monolithic beatification of Africa competed, in terms of ingenuousness and mystification, with the "somatic metaphysics" cited above, a perverse epidermic Verstehen that excluded blacks from participation in the human species.

It is in this "Africanizing" framework, furthermore, that the question of nomenclature should be seen. The fact that the participants of Black Soul referred to themselves as "blacks" and that Bahian blocos called themselves "afro" is part of the same movement. A flood of names and expressions of African origin came to the surface. And a syntagm took on airs of a magical password: "the-Africans-and-their-descendants-in-the-diaspora." The key sign: diaspora. The only things that did not occur in Brazil, on a noticeable scale, were the fashion of name changes that affected the United States and the insistence on exodus, which was so prevalent in Jamaican discourse. Nor was there an attempt at the collective renaming of descendants of slaves.

But let's examine this a little closer. A "black" has just joined Ilê Aiyê and defined himself in the sphere of the diaspora. What can one say? The answer seems obvious. We are dealing with an attempt to establish an identity of transnational perspective. The concept of diaspora points primarily to this transnational dimension. It is evident that an international black identity is clear in the self-denomination "black"—and here we are talking about an ethnic identity that is unconcerned with the borders of nation states. In the same fashion, a Yoruba expression such as Ilê Aiyê is a black-mestizo gesture with a precise African referent. But the concept of "diaspora" is broader and decidedly transnational. It crosses, like a firebreak, South America, the Caribbean, and North America and includes any place on the planet where people of black African descent happen to be.

Perhaps it is even correct to speak, in relation to the Brazilian black-mestizo movement from the mid-1970s and the early 1980s, of "black ethnocentrism." Or in "racialism" ("positive ethnocentrism"), to recall an expression so dear to Sheila Walker. Today, this may sound rather narrow, at a time when special treatment is given to the concept of "multiple identities," which recognizes that a single individual can have diverse relationships with the social body and carry a kaleidoscopic identity involving class, gender, age group, and so forth. But what is certain is that, in the period in question, "black ethnocentrism" was highly positive. Brazilian black-mestizos were concretely engaged in a struggle to blacken their "very real cultural specificity." This is what we see in the space toward which the new afoxés, the blocos afro, Black Soul, the campaign against syncretism, the pan-Africanist stance, the struggles of the Movimento Negro Unificado all converged. All of this is part of the same movement. It configures a "racialist" or "Afrocentrist" moment in the most lively and combative segments of the black-mestizo population (and its allies) in Brazil. It was along this road that black-mestizos managed to broaden, on an unprecedented scale, the mechanisms for having their voice heard in the life of the country. And they spoke loudly in Brazilian disputes, debates, and discursive confrontations of the period.

But let's return to carnival. The carnival festival was the primary channel for the affirmation of black-mestizo youth. And it substantially modified Bahian life in particular. Several scholars have already recognized this reality, underscoring the political importance of the new afoxés and blocos afro on the road toward blacks achieving full citizenship in Brazil. For this reason, it was necessary to pass through "racialism." Ideologically, an afoxé such as Filhos de Gandhi seems to be the child of the "black fronts" of the 1930s, defined by Florestan Fernandes as a puritan vanguard of liberal radicalism. What the fronts wanted was a decrease in socio-racial differences, a convergence of juridical reality and social reality, demanding as well the democratic possibilities of capitalist society for blacks. In a word, blacks wanted to be "accepted." This is the key word of "integrationism." In the 1970s and 1980s we were very far from that. The black-mestizo wants to be accepted, yes, but accepted in his/her difference, like a clearly marked card. This was the path to transformation. In the old reasoning of the Brazilian left, carnival was seen as an open parenthesis in social life: after the party, everything went back to the way it was before. But nothing is like it was before. Carnival exists in a real society and is lived by real people, affecting them and being affected by them. Using an expression of Max Weber, what occurs is a "game of reciprocal effects" between carnival and society. And no one escapes from this game.

Since then black-mestizo carnival has been duly assimilated by the public powers and primarily by the tourism and cultural industries. Today Bahian carnival is unthinkable, from the entrepreneurial point of view, without its showy black characteristics. Or else this industry would suffer a tremendous loss. But this assimilation is not the sign of defeat.

The blocos afro, before accused of being racist, managed to impose themselves, transforming the sociocultural atmosphere. And this is a very interesting point. Although they are not owners of the Bahian cultural industry, of the means of production and circulation of this industry, black-mestizos occupy almost all the space and time of the mass media. Their manifestations and their aesthetic products rule almost absolutely, to such an extent that, to borrow freely from well-known concepts of Gramsci, we can affirm with tranquility that in today's Bahia, black-mestizo culture is not "dominant," but it certainly is "hegemonic."

15 | The Multiplicity of Black Identities in Brazilian Popular Music

JOSÉ JORGE DE CARVALHO

Popular Music and Afro-Brazilian Identity

The frequent allusions to people's skin color in the lyrics of Brazilian popular music make it legitimate to refer to this practice as a cultural obsession. Since the beginning of this century Brazilian songwriters have employed a variety of terms to denote people of dark skin color (*nega, nego, crioulo, preto, mulata, preta, pretinha, neguinho, neguinha, morena*) in hundreds (even thousands) of commercial songs. Curiously, terms for white-skinned color (*branco, branca,* and *loura*) are almost nonexistent in song texts. Perhaps this in itself indicates the complexity and multiplicity of black identities in Brazil. In this essay I analyze a selected anthology of song texts chosen to reveal how black Brazilians have been alluded to and characterized in commercial recordings of Brazilian popular music over the last sixty years.

This study utilizes theoretical models I have been developing to analyze how black identities are constructed in a wide range of Brazilian song texts. In a previous essay (Carvalho 1994) I discussed four models of black ethnic identity involving the songs of several types of Brazilian musical traditions. The first model applied to the song texts of orthodox Afro-Brazilian cults (Candomblé, Xangô, etc.). In these texts, black identity is suspended in favor of a more universal identification with the *orixás* (African deities) who are placed above exclusionary racial, social, political, and sexual distinctions. These song texts (primarily in Yoruba) move entirely within a mythical world which is quite distinct from the historical experiences of the descendants of slaves in Brazil (Carvalho

261

1993). Thus, instead of offering a unique black identity, these songs assert that anyone, black or white, can be an African.

The second model is drawn from the songs of the danced folk dramas known as *congadas* which feature an African royal embassy and a dramatization of the historical opposition between blacks and whites in Brazil. These groups perform a ritual of inversion: for one single day of the year the blacks occupy the main streets of many traditional towns and small cities of the country while whites must watch from the sidewalk. Unlike the orthodox cult songs, congada song texts make explicit references to the unequal social positions of blacks and whites in Brazil and present an ideological solution by inverting the situation of everyday life.

The third model, found in the songs of the Macumba and Umbanda cults, asserts that social and racial hierarchies are mobile and interchangeable and constructs an identity in which anyone can be black. In these songs the spirits of slaves, Indians, prostitutes, mestizos, and other supernatural entities (relevant to the historical experience of Brazilians) are added to the pantheon of African orixás.

Finally, the fourth model of black identity is found in popular commercial music. In previous writings I have presented only a rough sketch of this model by examining a few black protest songs. In the present text I wish to focus on this fourth model of black identity by analyzing song texts of popular music of the last sixty years from a wide range of genres. I have selected popular songs that deal with race relations and that offer images and representations of blacks in Brazil. My discussion is guided by a simple question: How are blacks depicted in Brazil's popular commercial songs?

Contrary to claims that listeners of rock lyrics in English do not pay attention to the words (Frith 1987), in Brazilian popular music words are very important. The most elaborate texts come from the loosely connected genres labeled MPB (*música popular brasileira*) featuring well-known singer-songwriters such as Chico Buarque, Caetano Veloso, Gilberto Gil, Milton Nascimento, Djavan, and João Bosco. In MPB, the predominant mode of the song texts is lyrical and the words develop a sophisticated phenomenology of love relationships, intricacies of the emotions, desires, fantasies, and abstract ethical and philosophical considerations about the lives of the individuals involved in a particular relationship. The point to be stressed is that the subjects of these songs are individuals; and the dilemmas they face are typically individualistic, between the autonomy and the surrender of the self. The melodic, rhythmic, and harmonic materials are utilized to musically construct and reinforce the subtle and fluid landscape of feelings, visions, and ideas that are expressed in the words. With songs such as "Oceano" by Djavan, "Tigresa" by Caetano Veloso, or, above all, "Super-Homem a Canção" by Gilberto Gil, MPB can certainly be regarded as a classical song tradition.

Why do these sophisticated song genres of popular music rarely mention racial issues? It appears that these songs are intended, at least ideally, to treat the souls—not the bodies—of individuals. If the body is mentioned, it is usually the face (smile, eyes, lips, hair, head) or perhaps the hands, fingernails, arms, shoulders. The texture of the skin might be relevant, but hardly its color. In contrast, Brazilian dance genres—especially those associated with an African origin—are loaded with references to skin color. A musical genre itself can therefore set an interpretive framework which prepares the listener for the contents of the text. To illustrate, consider how the *lambada* is danced—the man's right thigh is thrust well into the woman's thighs as the couple move their hips together in a way that openly imitates sexual intercourse. Given these choreographic details, it is easy to understand why lambada song texts do not describe men and women as angels or disembodied souls!

Many genres of Brazilian popular music have clear African or Afro-American influence that can be detected in their names: *samba, pagode, batuque, lambada, fricote, samba-reggae, axé music, carimbó, funk, reggae, rap*, and so on. Associated with these genres are certain stereotypes, images, references, representations, and statements about the living conditions of blacks in Brazil. From a sample of some five hundred commercial songs, I have found certain fixations of identity that are extremely revealing, from an ideological point of view, about the traditional positions held by the blacks in Brazil and about the new perspectives on the changes and ruptures in those traditional roles. From this sample, I chose only the texts in which the issue of color is explicitly mentioned (I consciously avoided metaphors and euphemisms).[1]

I have organized the discussion around certain themes that run through sixty years of commercial songs and present these within a conceptual argument linking questions of ideology, values, and politics to the social, cultural, and political transformations that have occurred in Brazilian society. I present historical examples precisely to point out the continuities of these stereotypes and representations. Two more things: given the nature of the basic question underlying this work, my first

criterion for selecting a song was literary: regardless of its social importance or aesthetic efficacy, songs which did not refer explicitly to skin
color were not chosen. From those songs that fit this criterion, I further
selected (1) the ones which had the greatest social impact, (2) those
whose texts are most blatant or complex, and (3) those I find the most
satisfying musically. I have also selected examples from the widest variety of genres possible, precisely to emphasize the pervasive obsession
with skin color in song texts. I have not attempted to exhaust the many
possibilities of textual analysis. Rather, my analyses are intended as
points of departure for further research on text meaning and especially
on the difficult issue of determining what constitutes an expression of
racism and discrimination in songs.

Conceptualizing Brazil's Popular Music

My initial contention is that Brazil's commercial popular music presents a model of black identity radically different from the three models
of Afro-Brazilian musical identity discussed above. Primarily, it differs
on a fundamental expressive convention: popular music, broadcast by
the mass media, constructs an imagined community and addresses anyone who is able to listen to the radio, TV, cassette tapes, or other available
media. The other models, fixed and controlled by ritual, convey meaning
and experience within the sphere of a concrete, bounded, living community. This difference is crucial for any discussion, not only of ethnicity,
but also of identity: for the conditions of expression of popular music
make it necessarily more open, more easily taken for emblematic identification than any kind of ritual music. One must bear in mind the cultural and social revolution caused by the growth of commercial popular
music. All the genres created within the popular music industry helped
de-ritualize many styles of sacred music that previously had been confined within the bounds of religious or ethnic communities. In this
sense, it can be argued that in the three previous models of ethnic identity, the community controls the production and diffusion of its symbols
and also the efficacy of expressing its values and its ideology. In the case
of popular music, most of the constitutive elements drawn from ritual
are transformed into aesthetic elements. Through the musical arrangement and orchestration, for instance, the idea of a gathering or a reunion,
typical of the traditional models, can be conveyed. This is why examples

of parody, imitation, and even exact duplication of folk genres (secular and sacred) are so frequent in popular music. All of this celebrates, even if surreptitiously, the free movement of performance and structure of popular song over the rigid constraints of ritual conventions. For these reasons, popular music requires an analytical framework that differs considerably from the conceptual models developed for understanding ritual music.

Popular music de-ritualizes symbolic expression, breaks ethnic and other kinds of barriers, and, theoretically, addresses everyone. This raises complex issues of identity. Whereas most issues of identity in complex society are formed on the basis of constructing closed territories, the messages conveyed through popular music are open-ended. Popular music involves a double movement in which some listeners capture the music in order to stereotype its meaning (Carvalho and Segato 1990) while at the same time the musical material, the song itself, retains a residue of escape disallowing it to be reduced to the semantic meaning any group of listeners want to attribute to it. It is within this tendency to move between rigidity and fluidity that identities are formed and reformed, celebrated and rejected in popular music.

Another important feature is that, unlike cinema, theatre, painting, and even literature, popular song often presents itself as an unfinished object, incomplete and fragmented. What Frank Kermode theorizes as "the sense of an ending" (1967), and believes crucial to the structure of Western literary fiction, does not necessarily hold true for popular song texts. Popular songs are frequently partially heard or simultaneously heard with other public or social messages. On the radio, on TV, in live shows, in dance halls, in clubs, we often hear only a catchy phrase or a couple of words from which we then are able to establish a complex relationship with the song without even knowing the entire text, the singer, the songwriter, or the musical genre. In other words, popular songs are not always presented from beginning to end as unified wholes; they are often more like sections, or parts, without a conclusion.

Moreover, popular songs are frequently unfinished by virtue of their mode of presentation. Songs from many eras are played on radio programs: old songs, not so old, golden-oldies, rarities, not so new, recent hits, and many other temporal labels and categories that are created and manipulated all the time. As a consequence, old songs are not necessarily old: for the world of popular songs, especially as broadcast by the radio, is basically a world in which the past continues to be a perfect part of the present. This is extremely relevant for the stereotypes and images of blacks we shall discuss later on.

As Bakhtin has argued, psychic life is partly social and partly internal. The contact between individual psyche and the outside world is semiotic and, most often, is found at the linguistic level. It is in this sense that songs reveal the collective psychic life, for they tend to reflect individual experience as spontaneously as possible. Popular songs are usually immediate objects which express desire with less sublimation or rationalization than other artistic expressions. Some are easily composed from internal impulses. It may take no more than a couple of minutes for someone to compose a catchy sequence of verses, or a refrain that might sell hundreds of thousands, or even millions, of copies and might remain in people's memories for decades. I believe this explains, at least partially, the fact that the number of composers of popular music is much higher, proportionately, than the number of playwrights, novelists, film directors, videomakers, and even painters.

A Model for the Analysis of Popular Song Texts

I identify three levels used by listeners to fix the meaning in a popular Brazilian song text. These can be grasped as three "I's" which stand for the individual interpreted as enunciating the text.

Level 1: The singer as the "I."—The first aesthetic identification for the listener in popular music is, in my view, with the singer. Following Simon Frith (1987), I maintain that the singer in popular music is almost always singing to a second person singular who is listening. The singer reveals a particular accent, establishes a gender, plays a specific character, and exhibits a unique personality.

Level 2: The poetic subject as the "I."—The individual (or group of individuals) within the text is taken as the "I." This is sometimes clear, sometimes not; it is the locus of speech. This "I" should be investigated through strict discourse analysis. The various ambiguities, alternatives, choices, levels of indeterminacy, and incompleteness are all assets and possibilities available to the composer to construct or disguise the "I."

Level 3: The rhetorical "I."—This "I" is constructed by the listener, based on the specific rhetoric of the song: its genre (inasmuch as it is known and recognized by the listener), its metaphors, images, onomatopoeias, and so forth. The rhetorical "I" depends on the musical and literary critical abilities of the listener: his/her capacity to understand the allusions, irony, parody, and all the possibilities of indirect discourse of the text, on the one hand, and his/her ability to decode the metamorphoses of the poetic subject when fixed or displaced by the singer or singers, on the other hand.

To sum up, Level 1 deals strictly with performance: the song is always sung by someone at a particular point in time which affects the understanding of the listener. As Roland Barthes says, no human voice is neutral (1990). Of course, Barthes was talking about the impact of the song on the listener which is not exactly on the order of the linguistic meaning of the text, but that of the fruition of the language itself. Now, in popular music the singer usually forces an identification with the poetic subject; the first option is to follow the singer's idealized, or imagined, biography—his/her gender, age, skin color, sexual preference, and so on. This is quite different from erudite genres of music such as the classical lied, which Barthes discusses, where the singer is frequently ambiguous in terms of gender or other distinctions; he/she merely incarnates the romantic soul, the subject (man or woman) in love with another human being or with nature. While many romantic genres of popular music partially follow this kind of model, most popular Afro-Brazilian dance genres emphasize specific social and racial attributes.

Level 2 refers strictly to the text, to the words chosen to convey the message. Level 3 refers to the ideological implications of the song. Level 3 is where power lies, where influence on the life of others can be exercised, where struggles for hegemony take place, and where censorship, value judgments, blindness, identifications, rejections, the building of personal models, and so on, occur. The ideological subject is always a subject in the making, constructed through a combination of Levels 1 and 2. Theoretically speaking, there may be as many possible ideological "I's" as there are listeners to a song. Additionally, revisiting old songs is a common mechanism in Brazilian popular music to alter, consciously, the conventional subjectivity already constructed by them and thus proposing new ideological identifications.

Images of Blacks in Brazilian Popular Music

The Black Woman: Crazy, Ugly, Stupid

Historically, carnival songs provide an arena in which whites express how they view blacks, especially black and mulata women.[2] Since the 1930s, numerous carnival songs have mentioned both of these female images. Take the following song, made famous by the singer Linda Batista:

"Nega maluca"/"Crazy Black Woman"
Samba
Singer: Linda Batista
Composers: Evaldo Ruy and Fernando Lobo

Tava jogando sinuca	I was playing snooker
uma nega maluca me apareceu	[when] a crazy black woman came to me
vinha com o filho no colo	she was holding a baby in her arms
e dizia pro povo	and was telling everybody
que o filho era meu.	that the son was mine.
Não sinhô, tome que o filho é seu	No sir, take him, the son is yours
não sinhô, guarde que Deus lhe deu.	no sir, keep him, God gave him to you.
Há tanta gente no mundo	There are so many people in the world
mas meu azar é profundo	but my bad luck is deep
veja você meu irmão	you see, my brother
a bomba que estourou na minha mão	the bomb that blew up in my hand
tudo acontece comigo	everything happens to me
eu que nem sou do amor	I, who am not on the side of love
até parece castigo	it even seems like punishment
ou então influência da cor.	or else influence of color.

The poetic subject seems unconcerned with the black woman's feelings: from his point of view she and her child are a nuisance, a burden thrust on him because of his bad luck. While the *nega* is presented as crazy, preposterous, his real problem is with his fellow men and he is ashamed of admitting openly that he has had a relationship with a black woman. He laments to his colleagues, explaining that he is not involved in love. Moreover, the word "even" in the phrase "it even seems like punishment" sounds like an admission of bad luck, since, in his mind, sexually exploiting a black woman is a common and inconsequential social act.

As we will see in this and in other cases, it is not by chance that the last word of the song is surprisingly difficult to understand; the instrumental accompaniment partially masks the singer's voice. The singer appears to be saying *cor* (color), but the word might also be *dor* (pain, suffering). Influence of color? Does this mean the poetic subject is himself black, and therefore less fortunate than the rest, to the point that a black woman accuses him of having an illegitimate child with her? If that were so, we would then be facing a very special kind of discrimination, which is self-racism: because I am black, things are never easy for me. There is also the possibility that the subject is a white man who has gotten into this trouble because he was foolish enough to have an affair with a black woman. What lies behind this is the idea that if a white person mixes with a black, he/she is likely to wind up in trouble or with misgivings. Nonetheless, I believe it is more probable that the composer of the song is black. In other words, he is also the poetic subject. In such a case, the singer as the "I" (Level 1) is performing a double inversion in relation to the text: instead of a black man, a white woman is narrating this affair.

What kind of identity is being constructed here? The nega is an anonymous person, someone who offers herself to satisfy the sexual needs of a man, even those of a black man! He had forgotten all about her and now she reappears, claiming help for her baby with her assumed father.

The next song, sung by Emilinha Borba, deals with a crucial marker of black women in Brazil: their hair.

"Nega do cabelo duro"/"Black Woman with the Hard Hair"
Batucada
Singer: Emilinha Borba
Composers: Rubem Soares and David Nasser
(1942)

Nega do cabelo duro	Black woman with the hard hair
qual é o pente que te penteia	where is the comb that can comb you
teu cabelo ondulado	your wavy hair
não desmancha nem na areia	doesn't even untangle in the sand
toma banho e bota fogo	take a bath and put fire to it
qual é o pente que te penteia.	where is the comb that can comb you.

Here, the nega is ridiculed for not being able to find a comb that can untangle her hair. The expression "bota fogo" alludes to the common and painful practice of using a red-hot iron comb to straighten one's hair. The singer and the chorus seem to publicly make fun of the black woman in an almost sadistic manner. Hair is a revealing symbol of race relations in Brazil, and I have shown elsewhere (Carvalho 1994) that "bad hair" (the term used in Brazil for kinky hair characteristic of blacks) is an extremely frequent theme in popular songs. I want to pursue the issue a bit further by investigating the song "O teu cabelo não nega" ("Your Hair Can't Deny It"). This song, sung at virtually every carnival ball for the last fifty years, is considered one of the ten greatest popular songs ever written in the country.

"O teu cabelo não nega"/ "Your Hair Can't Deny It"
Marcha
Composers: Lamartine Babo, João Valença, and Raul Valença
(1932)

O teu cabelo não nega, mulata	Your hair can't deny it, mulata
porque és mulata na cor	because you're the color of a mulata
mas como a cor não pega, mulata	but since color doesn't rub off, mulata *your I ... by*
mulata eu quero o seu amor.	mulata, I want your love.

your color

What the poetic subject expresses openly here refutes the myth of racial democracy so widespread in Brazil. Since color does not "rub off," the poetic subject feels safe in asking the mulata for her love. Of course, "love" here is a euphemism for sex and to have an affair with a mulata is not a serious commitment but only a game. This perspective also helps explain the text of "Nega maluca": she is the crazy one because she wants to hold the man responsible for the pregnancy. Returning to the present example, blackness is treated as the symbolic equivalent of having a contagious disease. The subject addresses the mulata directly, as if they both should agree. It is interesting that many people sing the word "nega" instead of "pega" in the third line which changes the meaning to: "and since color can't be denied." This variant suggests the idealization of the mulata and could be a Freudian slip acting to soften the crudeness of the statement.[3]

The Black Woman as a Sexual Object

"O teu cabelo não nega" and "Nega do cabelo duro" are from 1931 and 1942, respectively. However, consider the more contemporary song "Fricote," by Luis Caldas, written in the 1980s.[4]

"Fricote"

Fricote

Singer: Luis Caldas

Composers: Luis Caldas and Jorge Drago

(1985)

Nega do cabelo duro	Black woman of the hard hair
que não gosta de pentear	who doesn't like to comb herself
quando passa na praça do Tubo	when she crosses the Tubo square
o nego começa a gritar	the black man starts to shout
pega ela ai, pega ela ai	grab her, grab her
pra que? pra passar batom	what for? to put lipstick on her
de que cor? de violeta	what color? purple
na boca e na buchecha	on the mouth and on the cheek
pega ela ai, pega ela ai	grab her, grab her
pra que? pra passar batom	what for? to put lipstick on her
de que cor? de cor azul	what color? the color blue
na boca e na porta do céu.	on the mouth and on heaven's door.

This song, which was quite a hit, continues the symbolism of the nega's "uncombed" hair. The first level of meaning in the text suggests a black perspective (contrasting with the white perspective of "Nega do cabelo duro"). But what is this black subject actually saying? The nega is crossing a public square and a group of men (probably blacks) catch her and paint her with lipstick. There is a double entendre in the text; when the singer rhymes *buchecha* (cheek) with *violeta* (purple), he doesn't really mean buchecha but *buceta*, a vulgar term for vagina (in live shows Luis Caldas sings buceta openly). And *porta do céu* (heaven's door) can be read as something equivalent to "cunt." One does not have to be Freud to realize that the lipstick here is a phallic symbol, evoking the image of a black man's penis.

This song provoked strong reactions from Brazilian feminists and members of the Black Movement, who accused Luis Caldas of both misogyny and racism. Indeed, lasciviousness, sadism, objectification of the black female body, and even rape are explicit in this text. Following our model of analysis, the song supports this interpretation, for the singer is black and, according to the musical conventions used in the performance, he is certainly not protesting the actions! The poetic subject of the text (Luis Caldas the singer, we assume) reports the action in the third person singular and hence is not directly implicated in the assault on the woman. It is "the black man" who runs after the black woman crossing the street. The subject's escape from direct responsibility is musically reinforced by the antiphonal singing of the song's central strophe. This is musically iconic with the dialogue, producing the image that not one person, but rather a group of people are chasing the woman, holding her down, and painting her face and genitalia. In other words, we've been given the picture of a gang rape.

Fricote is a dance genre, appropriate to express the frivolity of Bahian carnival. Very funny . . . for the black man, at least! We do not know if the nega, who does not like to comb her hair, took pleasure in being painted with that phallic lipstick. In the song she is not given a choice (or a voice) in the matter. However, some white middle-class women whom I asked about this song text expressed the opinion that the nega would take this sexual gang assault as a compliment: she is so attractive in her pure blackness (she keeps her hair natural, kinky) that the men run after her. This song follows a general pattern in popular songs: negas and mulatas are not given a voice or a point of view of their own; and they are never given a personal name.

In popular songs, the black woman is not only an object that men (black or white) use to exercise their sexual fantasies; many times she is also sadistically beaten up, punched, verbally insulted, and occasionally murdered. Take the following song, recorded by Germano Mathias in the 1950s, which Gilberto Gil seems to have taken special musical delight in re-recording in the 1970s:

"Minha nega na janela"/ "Black Woman in the Window"
Samba-choro
Singer: Gilberto Gil
Composers: Germano Mathias and Fio Jordo

Não sou de briga, mas estou com a razão	I'm not a fighter, but I'm right
ainda ontem bateram na janela	just yesterday they knocked on the window

do meu barracão
saltei de banda, peguei da navalha
  e disse:
pula, muleque abusado
e deixa de alegria pro meu lado.
Minha nega na janela
diz que está tirando linha
êta nega tu é feia
que parece macaquinha (vê só!)

olhei pra ela e disse:
vai ja pra cozinha
dei um murro nela
e joguei ela dentro da pia
quem foi que disse que a nega não
  cabia?

Spoken: A nega na janela/ no
barraco/ e vejam só de repente eu
peguei . . . a nega deve ter ido de
tarde no armazém e tal, o sol, a
Guanabara muito bonita,
luminosa, e ela ja entrou de papo
com aquele malandro. Pois não
teve conversa não, fui la dentro,
puxei a lamina, aquela, tá
entendendo?, alemã legítima, e
disse: Muleque descarado, tu tá
atrás da minha nega, miserável.
Vou te mostrar agora.

of my shack
I jumped to the side, grabbed my
  blade and said:
back off, you abused punk
and stop messing around with me.
My black woman in the window
says that she's taking down the line
boy, woman, you are ugly!
you look like a monkey (just
  look!)

I looked at her and said:
go to the kitchen right now
I slugged her
and threw her in the sink
who says she didn't fit?

Spoken: The black woman in the
window/ in the shack/ and, you
see, suddenly I took . . . the black
woman might have gone to the
grocery in the afternoon and
then, the sun, Guanabara bay so
beautiful, luminous, and she
already began to chat with that
scoundrel. Well, there was no talk;
I went inside the house, took my
blade, that one, you see, legitimate
German steel and said: shameless
crook, you're after my nega, you
son of a bitch. I'm gonna show
you now.

Here, the poetic subject is an incredibly jealous and violent man. It is not even clear if the black woman actually betrayed him. Her only guilt seems to involve her enjoyment of showing off. She cannot defend herself when he insults her, comparing her with a female monkey. The spoken words, at the end, masked by the instrumental accompaniment of the *samba de breque*,[5] are extremely violent. It is critical to disentangle the superimposition of the various "I's" present in the song.

First of all, Gilberto Gil, a black male, sings as if the nega were his woman—that is, his and Mathias's, the composer. Second, as far as discourse analysis is concerned, the poetic subject leaves no doubt: the nega deserves her punishment. But what of the listener, the constructed "I"? This text exemplifies the seductive character of popular song whereby the listener is seduced by an appealing rhythm, a smooth melody, or by the singer's voice (the "grain" of his voice, as Barthes would say). By focusing on the aesthetic nature of the performance, the listener is able to suspend his or her awareness of what is actually being sung. The listener's tendency is to identify with the singer rather than with the text: the common listener might not even agree with the idea of throwing a black woman in the sink, but can agree with the idea of Gilberto Gil expressing this desire. What a paradox for someone like Gilberto Gil, normally a champion of the black cause! Is he just teasing the listener by singing the song? Is he saying: listen to this preposterous song by Germano Mathias; isn't it funny?

We have now moved from an ideological critique of a song text to a critique of a singer; or rather, to a critique of the relationship between the poetic subject found in the text and the singer as the poetic subject. Gil uses the ironic mode here, in the sense outlined by Hayden White (1973). But using the symbolically loaded image of the black woman is somewhat risky in the Brazilian context, for the question remains to what extent the listener will catch the irony.

"Pungar"
Fricote
Singer and composer: Gerude

Se a pungada derrubar	If the pungada knocks you down
Apenas uma forma de amar	it's just one way of loving
Ai, ai, ai, ai,	Ah, ah, ah, ah,
Ai, ai, ai, ai, ai	Ah, ah, ah, ah, ah
Cafungar no cangote na nega	To breathe on the nega's neck
Um cheiro forte de pó	A strong smell of dust
Uma paixão vibração	A passion, a vibration
Da cabeça ao chamato	From head to toe
Se a pungada derrubar	If the pungada knocks you down
Apenas uma forma de amar	it's just a way of making love
Na pungada derrubou	The pungada knocked down
apenas uma cena de amor	just a love scene
na Casa da Mina tambo rufou	in the House of Mina the drum sounded

Oba	There it is
na Casa da Mina tambor rufa oba rufou	in the House of Mina the drum shall sound
eu vou falando mal	I will denounce it
tambor que não tem cachaça	a drum that doesn't have white rum
eu vou falando mal.	I will denounce it.

Here, the singer, Gerude, from São Luis, Maranhão, depicts one of the main African-derived traditions of his state: the *tambor de crioula*. In the song, the main dance step of the *tambor de crioula (pungada)* is described as just a way of making love. The central phrases are typical of the images of black women as hot and submissive lovers:

> To breathe on the nega's neck
> A strong smell of dust
> A passion, a vibration
> From head to toe

What he is in fact describing here, quite literally, is an orgasm. The 'ah ah ah' of the third phrase is quite clearly an expression of sexual pleasure. In short, the black woman is depicted as someone the man mounts, like an animal. And after she satisfies his sexual pleasure, he leaves. The text indicates no personal impact made by the black woman on the man who enjoys mounting her.

Two implicit associations with the terms *cafungar* and *pó* are used to convey the message of this text. The term *cafungar* (to sniff) is commonly associated with the act of inhaling cocaine. The poetic subject seems to regard the nega as an intoxicating drug, a substance that allows him to realize extraordinary trips. Additionally, *pó* (dust) can mean both cocaine powder and also the dust which has covered the nega's body because of the dance which is being performed in the open square during the tambor de crioula.

This song text illustrates how difficult it is to separate racial relations from sexual practices in Brazil. Since colonial days, stories have persisted regarding the fondness of Portuguese men for black women as sexual objects. Above all else, they were fond of the smell of black women, reportedly stronger than that of white women, who were thought to be odorless and tasteless. This hierarchical relationship between the nega and the man who mounts her from behind (ideologically, a white man) might certainly give rise to negotiations between the two parties involved, and the nega might even feel happy to provide a total orgasm to the man in exchange for certain benefits and privileges. Moreover, two white middle-class Brazilian women whom I asked about this text accepted it as realistic, on the grounds that "it describes a sexual power a white woman does not have, but would like to have." Finally, the poetic subject here is most likely a white man, but the constructed "I" could be a man of any skin color, either a white, a mestizo, or a black.

The Black Man: Old, Poor, Humble

Another strong image, common in many songs, is that of the old, poor, humble black man, who still carries the marks of slavery with him. The musical form often used to express his agonies and hopes is the lament. The following song, "Lamento Negro," sung beautifully by the Trio de Ouro, is a masterpiece of its kind.

"Lamento negro"/ "Black Lament"
Batuque
Singers: Trio de Ouro
Composers: Constantino Silva and Humberto Porto

Xango, Xango
Ogum dilode
Ogum dile Xango
Meu pai, Xango
Ja se foi la na Aruanda
Ja se foi, se vai
Cao o
Maleme, meu pai, maleme
Xango
o o o o
o o o o
Tete angoro corumba
Zi no samba no ta sarava
Zi mureque brada ponto
pra desce Oxum Mare
pra salvar nossa terera
cum dina maduna marere
Cao o
Maleme, meu pai maleme
Xango.

This song conveys a sense of pan-African-diaspora tradition combining musical and textual features from Macumbas, Juremas, and Candomblés de Caboclo. Musically, the song is performed as a *batuque*, a rhythm typical of the African traditions of the Rio de la Plata region such as the Uruguayan *candombe*. Textually, Yoruba culture is invoked through the naming of Xango and Ogum (deities of the Yoruba-based Candomblé). The word *maleme*, a Bantu word, means mercy and is used in Afro-Venezuelan traditions. The Portuguese portions of the text tell of the departure of the African deities, leaving the blacks in the Americas to suffer the pains of slavery and post-slavery: "já se foi la na Aruanda, já se foi, se vai" (he has already gone to Aruanda, he's gone, he is leaving). A pentatonic melody adds to the sense of sadness in this lament.

The last strophe of the song is elegantly constructed. The words alternate between Portuguese, Yoruba (Xango, Oxum), Bantu (samba, maleme), and Bantu-like words that sound like corrupt Portuguese (zi, mureque, terera). We have not been able to translate the expression "Tete angoro corumba," but the next phrase, "zi no samba não ta sarava" sounds like "if samba is not saved" and "zi mureque brada ponto" can be read as broken Portuguese "if the poor black sings his ritual song." He sings his ritual song so that "Oxum Mare can save our temple." "Cum dina maduna marere" is again an unknown expression which sounds Bantu. We are able to understand the basic intention of the subject, but he is not able to tell us clearly if his prayer was successful: whether Oshum Mare saved his faith we don't know, for in the last minute he lost himself in language and could not make his way through the African languages and broken Portuguese (or, to play with the title of an essay by Clifford Geertz, he got 'lost in translation'). This is poetically and conceptually sophisticated: the African *orixás* are never clear, they are not as talkative as local spirits and their message can only be deciphered by the initiates. In other words, the song itself seems to belong to the realm of the esoteric.

This song is paradigmatic, therefore, of an aesthetic strategy of using African words, phrases, and names of gods to imprint a black-African mood to popular songs. This strategy is present in the songs of Brazilian popular music luminaries such as Jorge Ben, Gilberto Gil, Gal Costa, Caetano Veloso, and Vinicius de Moraes. The overall feeling of the song is a bit like a Christian Negro spiritual. When the subject appeals to "my Lord, Xango" he seems to be addressing the One God who has hidden himself from men. Additionally, as a literary-musical genre, the lament belongs to the Western cultural tradition, not to the African, and it has been used in Brazilian popular music for whites to sing about the sufferings of the black people.

In this song it is difficult to define the ideological "I." While the poetic subject is a black, the text emphasizes an overt and formally unnecessary sympathy for blacks, apparently indicating the singer is taking the role of a black person. This means he or she is likely to be, existentially, a white. In other words, both black and white singers are singing qua whites a song lamenting the black people's social and spiritual condition. As we will see later, with contemporary Brazilian funk, reggae, and rap, it is easier to accuse and fight discrimination from the black point of view. The lament is rarely used because the subject shows himself/herself entirely autonomous. Nonetheless, this lament is perfect, using all the relevant materials and clichés and putting them together in a most efficacious way. The vocals are superb: the lead singer was the great Dalva de Oliveira and one of the two male members of the Trio de Ouro at that time was black.

"Cem anos atrás"/ "A Hundred Years Ago"
Choro serenata
Singer: Nelson Gonçalves
Composers: Benedito Lacerda and René Bittencourt

Sonhei que vivia cem anos atrás	I dreamed I lived a hundred years ago
e vi Pai João ainda rapaz	and I saw Father John still a boy
Viçosa e bonita eu vi Me Maria	I saw Mother Mary healthy and pretty
Se fosse verdade, que bom que seria!	If that was true, how good it would be!
Na grande varanda da vasta fazenda	In the large veranda of the big farm
eu vi Sinha Moça de bata de renda	I saw the farmer's daughter in a lace skirt
Na fria senzala eu vi os escravos	In the cold the slave house I saw the slaves
que foram na guerra exemplo de bravos	who were examples of bravery during the war
Meus olhos se abriram, tristonho acordei	My eyes opened, sadly I awoke

Voltando a verdade da vida, chorei	Returning to the truth of life, I wept
Não vi Pai João, que a guerra levou	I didn't see Father John, whom the war took away
Nem vi Me Maria, que o céu reclamou	Nor did I see Mother Mary, who was taken to heaven
Em vez do gemido tristonho das redes	Instead of the plaintive murmur of the hammocks
senti o siléncio das frias paredes	I felt the silence of the cold walls
não sei como um sonho tão bom se desfaz	I don't know how such a good dream is erased
viver eu quisera cem anos atrás.	I wish I could have lived a hundred years ago.

This song exemplifies the seductive power of singing in popular music. Nelson Gonçalves, one of the greatest singers in Brazil, beautifully renders the overall feeling of loss and longing explored in the text. Both the singing and the orchestration prepare the listener to identify with the author's dream. But what sort of dream is this? The text depicts Brazilian slave society as an era of happiness and promise: Mother Mary, the tender black woman, would be taking care of the young white lady, and Father John, the warm and faithful black man, would also be there to help the poetic subject. But the subject avoids the stark reality of slave existence while having the slaves even fight bravely during war to defend their master! The poetic subject wants to go back to the style of life of a hundred years ago, as a white slave holder!

It is worth noting that this song, first recorded in 1946, was reissued in 1988 in the LP *Abolição e Música* (Abolition and Music). This recording was released as part of the celebrations surrounding the centenary of the abolition of slavery in Brazil. What motivations were behind putting such a song text in circulation again?

The Black Man as the Romantic Hustler

The *malandro* is another fixed image of the black man that emerged in the 1930s and continues until today. The *neguinho* (little black man) is the happy black *malandro* (romantic hustler) who lives in the *favelas* (the hillside slums of Rio de Janeiro) and is frequently a composer of samba songs. A romanticized and mythical figure, he provides humor but does not threaten the whites, for he assumes the role expected of a black and operates within the established hierarchy.

"Olha o jeito desse nego"/ "Take a Look at the Style of That Black Dude"
Samba
Singer: Linda Batista
Composers: Custodio Mesquita and Evaldo Ruy

Lá vem chegando	There he comes
o neguinho que eu gosto	The neguinho whom I like
Que eu gosto, que eu me enrosco	I like, I turn around him
até fazer besteira	until I do a foolish thing
Reparem no seu passo	Look at his step,
marcando o compasso	following the beat
Pois quem é que não cai	For, who is he who does not fall
no laço de qualquer maneira?	into the trap anyway?
De terno branco todo engomadinho	Dressed with a white suit, so neat
De camisa azul-marinho	with navy-blue shirt
e gravata vermelha	and red tie.
Traz sob o braço um viola de pinho	He carries a wooden guitar under his arm
e faz um samba num instantinho	and he makes up a samba in a moment
se lhe der na telha.	if he feels like it.
E olha o jeito desse nego!	And look at the style of this nego
É pose so!	It's pure poise!
E olha a boca desse nego!	And see the mouth of this nego
É ouro so!	It's pure gold!
E olha a roupa desse nego!	And see the clothes of this nego
É seda so!	It's pure silk!
E olha a alma desse nego!	And see the soul of this nego
É ouro em po!	It's gold dust!
La na gafieira ele faz sucesso	There in the samba house he is a hit
não paga ingresso e bebe de graça	He doesn't pay to enter and drinks free
Se bebe não tomba,	If he drinks he doesn't fall,
se não bebe empomba	If he doesn't drink he blows up
Faz barulho e zomba,	He makes a fuss and laughs,
mas é boa praça.	But he is a nice guy.

The song is sung by a white woman, but she is possibly taking the role of a black woman in describing the malandro.

Preta or Nega as Any Woman

The four images we have seen so far belong to what I call the realm of images and stereotypes fixed by a white eye. They have lasted for more than half a century. We will now move from song texts that allude to concrete black women and men to texts that depict any woman qua preta, or nega. There are many song texts that use these two words in this broadest sense. I have chosen a *lambada* to expand the musical panorama here presented. Here is Beto Barbosa, arguably the best-known lambada singer in Brazil, singing to his lover, whom he calls preta (black woman).

"Preta"/ "Black Woman"
Lambada
Singer and composer: Beto Barbosa

Preta fala pra mim	Black woman speak to me
fala o que voce sente por mim	tell me what you feel for me
sera que você me quer	is it true that you love me
sera que você vai ser	is it true that you want to be
a minha mulher	my wife
diga o que será	tell me what will happen
quando o seu corpo	when your body
no meu se encontrar	meets mine
bateu legal bateu forte a capoeira	the capoeira felt good, felt strong
pintou virou varreu minha cabeça	turned my head over
preta fala pra mim	black woman speak to me
minha mulher.	my woman.

The terms nega and preta are also used as expressions of affection or intimacy between lovers or couples in Brazil. In other words, nega is a woman with whom a man can achieve a certain level of intimacy. When a man calls a fair-skinned woman nega, this means she is able to preserve for him, in that particular situation at least, something of the sexual mystery attached to the black woman. And most of the time the fair-skinned woman will take this treatment as a compliment. As a blond female friend of mine told me: "When your husband calls you 'minha nega' (my black woman) it means he still finds you attractive, in spite of the fact that you are his wife." The implication is that true sexual pleasure is achieved outside of marriage with a black woman. The black woman comes to represent total openness and sexual freedom, as opposed to the white wife, who represents controlled and conventional desire.

Of course, this is the transposition of a courtly sexual code that comes from the days of slavery. For a white man, especially one with a minimum of economic or social status in the hierarchy of slave-holding Brazil, the relationship with his wife was extremely formal and distant, and he would use black women sexually more often than his wife. Within this patriarchal, male-oriented framework, therefore, to call his wife nega might mean a compensation for the oppressed role she would play for him in the house. Moreover, nega might also imply the instinctual, free, and unlimited reins of desire that were expressed openly in the song "Pungar" previously discussed.

Another intriguing use of nega is found in the title of a song by Caetano Veloso, "Eu sou neguinha?" ("Am I a Little Black Girl?"). The text explores the vicissitudes of a poetical subject trying to escape from fixed identities—political, gender, sexual. The gist of the song is the oxymoron created by the text being sung by a male singer; if a female singer sings it, the greatest part of its aesthetic effect is lost.[6]

Forgetting the Nega: Morenas, Mulatas, and Blonds

We now leave fixed images and enter the sphere of relative and fluid identities. It is important to note that these images are still constructed primarily by a white eye. The image of the preta as any woman opens the door to a set of transformational images: mulatas, morenas, and blonds.

The mulata embodies all of the seductive feminine traits of the Brazilian woman who reigns during carnival. The following well-known song exalts the mulata's appeal and coquettishness.

"Mulata assanhada"/ "Restless Mulata"
Samba
Singer: Miltinho
Composer: Ataúlfo Alves

Ai, mulata assanhada	Ah, restless mulata
Que passa com graça	Who gracefully passes by
Fazendo pirraça	Playing roguish tricks
Fingindo inocente	Pretending to be innocent
Tirando o sossego da gente.	Taking away our tranquility.
Ai, mulata, se eu pudesse	Ah, mulata, if only I could
E se o meu dinheiro desse	And enough money I had
Eu te dava sem pensar	I would give you, without thinking
Essa terra, este céu e este mar.	This land, this sky and this sea.

Ela finge que não sabe	She pretends she doesn't know
Que tem feitiço no olhar.	That she's got bewitching eyes.
Ai, meu Deus que bom seria	Ah, my God, how nice it would be
Se voltasse a escravidão!	If slavery came back!
Eu pegava a escurinha	I would grab the little dark one
Prendia no meu coração.	and arrest her inside my heart.
E depois a pretoria	And afterward the justice
É quem resolvia a questão.	would settle the dispute.

As with the song "Cem anos atrás," here the poetic subject longs for the return of the days of slavery, when a white man could simply pick the mulata he desired.

The morena is a tan-skinned white Brazilian woman with dark hair. In the next carnival song the morena is described as someone who will take the carnival crown from the mulata.

"Linda morena"/ "Pretty Morena"

Marcha

Singers: Mário Reis and Lamartine Babo

Composer: Lamartine Babo

Linda morena, morena	Pretty morena, morena
morena que me faz penar	morena who makes me suffer
a lua cheia, que tanto brilha	the full moon, that shines so strongly
não brilha tanto quanto o seu olhar.	doesn't shine as much as your eyes.
Tu és morena, uma ótima pequena	You are a morena, an excellent girl
não ha branco	there is not a single white man
que não perca seu juizo.	who doesn't lose his mind.
Toda gente faz questão do seu sorriso	Everyone is fond of your smile
teu coração é uma espécie de penso,	your heart is like a guest house,
de penso familiar a beira-mar.	a familiar guest house by the sea.
Moreninha não alugues tudo não	Little morena, do not rent all the rooms,
deixa ao menos o poro para eu morar.	spare at least the basement for me.
Por tua causa	Because of you
já se faz revolução	revolutions are already being made

vai haver transformação	a transformation will take place
na cor da lua	the color of the moon
antigamente a mulata era rainha	in old times the mulata was the queen
desta vez oh moreninha	but this time, oh little morena,
a taça é sua.	the trophy is yours.

We should mention, first of all, the open reference to the white man. It is equally worth mentioning the idea of a woman whose heart is like a guest house, which means she is prepared to receive dozens of people (mostly men!) at the same time. The poetic subject seems so fond of her that he contents himself with the basement of the hotel. One wonders whether a certain sexual overtone is not present in this request to keep the "basement" for him; after all, Lamartine Babo wasn't exactly a prudish songwriter.

Loura (blond) is a light-skinned woman with blond hair; she is the type of woman least mentioned in song texts. This is understandable, for the white woman played the ontological role of the universal, in relation to which all the other "colored" women would be situated (the nega, the cabocla, the mulata, etc.). The next song text is important because it is one of the rare songs that does mention the loura.[7]

"Linda lourinha"/ "Beautiful Little Blond"
Marcha
Singers: Silvio Caldas and Os Diabos do Céu
Composer: João de Barro

Lourinha, lourinha	Little blond, little blond
dos olhos claros de cristal	of light crystaline eyes
desta vez em vez da moreninha	this time instead of the little morena
tu seras a rainha do meu carnaval.	you shall be the queen of my Carnival.
Loura boneca	Blond doll
que vens de outra terra,	who comes from another land
que vens da Inglaterra, ou vens de Paris	who comes from England, or from Paris
quero te dar o meu amor mais quente	I want to give you my love, hotter
do que o sol ardente	than the burning sun
deste meu pais.	of this country of mine.

Linda lourinha tens o olhar to claro	Beautiful little blond
deste azul tão raro	you have such light eyes
como um céu de anil	of this rare blue like a navy blue sky
mas tuas faces vão ficar morenas	but your cheeks will become brown
como as das pequenas	like those of the girls
deste meu Brasil.	of my Brazil.

Taken as a set, the last three songs illustrate the transformation from mulata to morena to loura. Initially, the mulata was conceptualized as a product of national pride and the perfect result of the country's practice of miscegenation. She was the natural queen of carnival, a festival officially touted for its racial integration. In the second song, however, Lamartine Babo asserts that times have changed and the morena will decrown the mulata and will reign over carnival. Just five years later comes this last song proclaiming that now, instead of the little morena (the mulata is not even mentioned!), it is the blond's turn to be the queen.

We are presented with a transformational chain of colors that works in one direction only: from darker to lighter. First, the mulata was worshiped; then, the morena came and showed that she could perform the role of the mulata too; finally, the blond proved able to act as a morena and, transitively, to take the place of the mulata. How does the blond accomplish this? Very simply: through tanning her skin in the sun!

There are two ideological consequences of this unidirectional chain of colors. First, it only works in the direction presented, that is, the mulata does not (can never) transform herself into the blond. Second, the black woman (preta or nega) has become an invisible part of the landscape; she is never even considered an option to be the queen of carnival.

The Carnival Black

"O canto da cidade"/ "The Song of the City"
Samba-reggae
Singer: Daniela Mercury
Composers: Tote Gira and Daniela Mercury

A cor dessa cidade sou eu	I am the color of this city
o canto dessa cidade é meu	the song of this city is mine
o gueto, a rua, a fé	the ghetto, the street, the faith

eu vou andando a pé	I am walking
pela cidade bonita	through the beautiful city
o toque do afoxé e a força,	the play of the afoxé and its strength,
de onde vem?	where does it come from?
Ninguém explica	Nobody explains
ela é bonita	it is beautiful
Uo o verdadeiro amor	Oh oh true love
uo o voce vai onde eu vou	you're going to where I am going
No diga que não quer mais	Don't say you don't want it anymore
eu sou o silêncio da noite	I am the silence of the night
o sol da manha.	the morning sun.
Mil voltas o mundo tem	The world has a thousand whirls
mas tem um ponto final	but it has a final stop
eu sou o primeiro que canta	I am the first to sing
eu sou o carnaval	I am the carnival
A cor dessa cidade sou eu	I am the color of this city
o canto dessa cidade é meu.	the song of this city is mine.

Daniela Mercury, singer and co-writer of this song, is one of the stars of axé music, a new Bahian popular music style which has spread throughout Brazil, from north to south. This song was a tremendous hit in the country for more than a year and it epitomizes the thrill of the Bahian carnival. The song contains a poignant paradox between the poetical "I" and the singer's "I." In the song, Daniela claims to be the same color as the city of Salvador, a city known as the most African city in Brazil. Although Daniela is certainly not black, she has been described by the media as "the blackest white woman in Bahia." By this is likely meant that she sings and dances like a black Bahian woman.

This is one of the most ideologically complex texts of this entire anthology and it exhibits the nuances and ambiguities of racial identification in Brazil. To start with, the tone of the narrative is romantic: through synecdoche the ego fuses itself with the nature, history, and culture of Bahia. There could be even a double synecdoche at work if we take the word color in this context to mean spirit—for she does not say "I have" but rather "I am" the color of the city.

In the first phrase of the text, we encounter an oxymoron because Daniela Mercury is a white woman whereas the city of Salvador is the blackest city of Brazil. Some listeners might interpret the text to mean

Daniela has become black by fusing herself with the city of Salvador and its African-related cultural traditions. This is a rather compromised reading, typical of the white tourists who come each year to enjoy carnival in Bahia. These tourists are what I call the "Carnival Black" (negro or negra) who purchase and don the costume of a black Carnival Club—like Olodum—in order to participate as a black during carnival.

Other listeners might read the song's paradox as bitterly ironic: since Daniela Mercury is a white woman, she has actually "whitened" Salvador by becoming the city's spokeswoman and carnival emcee. In any case, the idea of the Carnival black is a non-black idea and is a contemporary version of the myth of racial democracy.

Turning the Tide to Black Pride: Funk and Rap

None of the song texts examined thus far presents the self-esteem, pride, and sense of autonomy from the perspective of a black Brazilian. It was only in the early 1980s that transnational musical styles associated with black diaspora culture—such as reggae, funk, and rap—were introduced systematically into Brazil (Carvalho 1994). These styles have exerted a strong and steady influence on Brazil's urban black youth. The songs of these contemporary black musical styles differ from the earlier texts with respect to the perspective. Here, race relations in Brazil are viewed through a "black eye." These songs create a new group of images, or counter-images, to be more precise politically.

An example of this is the following funk song made famous by the singer Sandra de Sá and clearly inspired by Gilberto Gil's song "Sarara crioulo" which makes a pun on the blond hair of some blacks.[8]

"Olhos coloridos"/ "Colorful Eyes"
Funk
Singer: Sandra de Sá
Composer: Macau

Os meus olhos coloridos	My colorful eyes
me fazem refletir	make me think
eu estou sempre na minha	I'm always doing it my way
e não posso mais fugir	and I can no longer escape
meu cabelo enrolado	my curled hair
todos querem imitar	they all want to imitate
eles estão baratinados	they are perplexed
também querem enrolar	and also want to curl

você ri do meu cabelo	you laugh at my hair
você ri da minha roupa	you laugh at my clothes
você ri da minha pele	you laugh at my skin
você ri do meu sorriso	you laugh at my smile
a verdade é que você	the truth is that you
tem sangue crioulo	have black blood
tem cabelo duro	have thick hair
sarará miolo	blondish brains
sarará crioulo	blondish mulato
sarará crioulo	blondish mulato
sarará crioulo	blondish mulato
sarará crioulo.	blondish mulato.

The following rap song has been quite a sensation, both in Brasília, where it was recorded in October of 1993, and in São Paulo, the two main centers for rap in Brazil.

"Sub-raça"/ "Sub-Race"
Rap
Singer and composer: Câmbio Negro

Woman (spoken): É uma gente mal-educada, fica falando grosseria pra gente, é uma gente suja, é uma gente que você olha para as caras das pessoas e tem vontade de fugir, entendeu? Um horror, não são brasileiros não, cara, é uma sub-raça ...	*Woman (spoken):* It's a people with bad manners, they keep talking dirty street talk; for us, they're dirty people; a people who you look at their faces and you want to run away, you see? Horrible. They're not Brazilians, my friend, it's a sub-race ...
Chorus: É a puta que o pariu!	*Chorus:* It's you, son of a bitch!
Singer: Agora irmaos vou falar a verdade	*Singer:* Now brothers, I'm going to tell you the truth
a crueldade que fazem com a gente	the cruelty they do to us
só por nossa cor ser diferente	just because we are of a different color
somos constantemente assediados pelo	we are constantly bombarded by the
racismo cruel	cruel racism
bem pior que o fel	worse than gall
é amargo de engolir um sapo so por ser preto	it's bitter to swallow just because one is black,
isto é fato, o valor da própria cor	that's a fact, the value of one's color

não se aprende em faculdades ou colégios	is not learned in schools or colleges
e ser negro nunca foi um defeito	and being black has never been a fault
será sempre um privilégio	it shall always be a privilege,
de pertencer a uma raça	of belonging to a race
que com seu proprio sangue construiu o Brasil ...	which with its own blood built Brazil ...
Sub-raça é a puta que o pariu!	Sub-race it's you, son of a bitch!
Sub-raça é a puta que o pariu!	Sub-race it's you, son of a bitch!
Sub-raça sim, é como nos chamam aqueles que não respeitam	Yes, sub-race, that's how we're called by those who don't respect
as caras dos filhos dos pais	the faces of the sons of the fathers
dos ancestrais deles	of their ancestors
não sabem que seu bisavo, como eu era escuro	they don't know their great grandfather was dark like myself
e obscuro sera seu futuro	and his future is going to be obscure
se não agir direito	if he doesn't behave well
talvez sera encontrado em um esgoto	maybe he will be found in a gutter
da Ceilandia com tres tiros no peito.	in Ceilandia with three shots in his chest.
O papo é esse mesmo e a realidade é foda	That's the situation and reality is fucking hard
não de o bote mal dado senã o gangue te bola	don't miss the jump or else the gang will grab you
fique esperto, racista e se liga na fita	open your eyes, racist, and get in tune with things
somos animais mesmo,	we're really animals,
se foda quem não acredita.	fuck those who don't believe it.
Sub-raça é a puta que o pariu!	Sub-race it's you, son of a bitch!
Sub-raça é a puta que o pariu!	Sub-race it's you, son of a bitch!
É a puta que o pariu! Pode crer!	Son of a Bitch! Fuck you!

The band Câmbio Negro is part of the *rap consciência* (consciousness rap) movement. Like funk, although politically more radical, Brazilian rap seeks to construct a symbolism of reversion through accusation, condemnation, and black pride. The text of "Sub-Raça" was written in response to an insult against blacks by a young white woman who appeared on Brazilian national television. The poetic subject in the song mirrors the insulting words of the white woman and turns the label of sub-race back on her. Here, the singer decides to fight racism openly. One of the strong points of these lyrics is certainly the presence of the expression "puta que o pariu," probably the strongest curse in Brazilian Portuguese and the first time it has ever appeared in a song text. The song made an enormous impact, musically and emotionally, among young Brazilians of all colors.

In most of the examples of Brazilian reggae and rap, and in the more radical varieties of funk, the singer and the poetic subject are one in the same: the lyrical mode disappears and the I-Thou relationship becomes a conscious and controlled dialogue. The movement toward black pride has led to a greater fixation of the singer's "I." Inversions, ambiguities, and indirect language have given way to a clearer biographical profile as song texts are written from the perspective of, and must be sung by, blacks. Thus, the differences between Levels 1 and 2 of the model presented here are practically eliminated.

Radicalizing the Images of Blacks and Whites Even Further

The next song text presents the most radical picture of race relations in Brazil ever formulated through song text. I chose it because of the synthesis proposed by its title and also because it represents quite a distinct aesthetic and ideological voice.

"O preto e o branco"/ "The Black and the White"

Pagode

Singer: Bezerra da Silva

Composers: Carlinhos Russo and Zezinho do Valle

É, mas tem preto, compadre	Yes, but there exists a black man, pal
Que para num branco	Who sticks to a white
Tem branco que para	And there is the white
Num preto também	Who sticks to the black too
Mas para mim ta tudo certo	But for me it is all right
Para mim ta tudo bem	For me it is all very well
Eu disse pro preto que o branco da branco	I told the black that the white 'whitens' (goes haywire)

E o preto me disse que vai muito além	And the black told me he goes much further
Me disse que o preto apesar de ser preto	He told me the black in spite of being black
Quando é bom preto da branco também	When he is a good black he 'whitens' too
É por isso que o preto se amarra num branco	That's why the black sticks to a white
E o branco se amarra num preto também	And the white sticks to a black too
O preto e o branco são limpos e arregados	The black and the white are clean and well kept
São sempre tratados iguais a neném	They are always treated like a baby
Tem gente que aperta, tem outro que cheira	There are people who roll, there are others who snort
Tem até quem bate e da beijo de bem	There are even those who cut and kiss quite well
É por isso que o preto se amarra num branco	That's why the black sticks to a white
E o branco se amarra num preto também	And the white sticks to a black too
Até em cartório já ficou provado	Even in the notary it has been proved
A força que o preto no branco contém	The power that the black has on the white
Depois que mistura seu nome ao dela	After his name is mixed with hers
É difícil tirar esse nome de alguém	It is difficult to erase this name from someone
É por isso que o preto se amarra num branco	That's why the black sticks to a white
E o branco se amarra num preto também.	And the white sticks to a black too.

Contrary to funk, reggae, or rap, *pagode* is a local Brazilian musical genre, a variant of samba. Pagode is deeply rooted in the favela hillside slums of Rio de Janeiro. The words to "O preto e o branco" make reference to a secret code, unknown to most people outside of the favelas. In this context, the term *branco* means, alternately, white man and cocaine;

and *preto* means black man and marijuana. The poetic subject bases his statements on a representational code that separates the white and black worlds. The white world is one of cocaine and asphalt (urbanized Rio de Janeiro); the black world is one of marijuana and muddy hills. In the song, the poetic subject begins to fuse these two ideologically and affectively separate worlds by stating that there are blacks who also like cocaine and whites who also like marijuana.

In the second strophe, the poetic subject says to a black that cocaine "makes one white" (i.e., provokes an electric discharge in one's brains), to which the black replies that good marijuana "makes one white too." Later he will explain various ways of consuming and experiencing the drugs, mixing the two apparently separated worlds. Although Bezerra da Silva has made accusations of racial discrimination explicitly in another song, what he offers here is an absolutely cold, sharp, cynical picture of Brazilian society: there are corrupt people, crooks, dealers, liars, and hypocrites. All the social institutions found in the favelas (black and white) are criticized systematically: carnival, the *jogo do bicho* (an illegal form of gambling), drug traffic, smuggling, robbery, Afro-Brazilian religions (Candomblé, Umbanda), Protestantism, Catholicism, politics (he insists that black politicians can be as corrupt as white ones).

Given the degree of moral degradation that characterizes life in the favelas of Rio de Janeiro, this pagode song instructs blacks not to be deceived by anyone and not to take sides in this tough and violent world. From the poetic subject's perspective, everything is fine, cocaine as well as marijuana, whites as well as blacks. Bezerra does not offer a racial utopia but rather a set of Machiavellian ethics for blacks. This set of ethics, as Benedetto Croce explains, is an ethics which replicates life instead of affirming or denying it.

Epilogue: Teaching a Black Girl How to Dance

In March 1994, as I was preparing the final version of this essay, my five-year-old daughter proudly sang for me the following song she had just learned at her school in Brasília. As busy as I was for over two years, looking for recordings that circulate through the media, I had forgotten how strong the oral transmission of racial images (especially from adults to children) still is. Whatever doubts I might have had as to whether I was presenting an exaggerated picture through all of those racist examples from popular music disappeared as I listened to the song that had been taught to my own daughter at school. I close with this song, sparing the reader further comments.

"Dança pretinha"/ "Dance Little Black Girl"
Children's Song

Plantei uma florzinha	I planted a little flower
no meu quintal	in my backyard
nasceu uma pretinha	a little black girl was born
de avental	carrying an apron
dança pretinha	dance, little black girl
eu não sei dançar	I don't know how to dance
pega um chicote	pick up a whip
que ela vai dançar.	and she is going to dance.

NOTES

Author's Note: I want to thank Rita Segato and Leticia Vianna for the valuable suggestions in the building of this conceptual model. I also thank Manuel Alexandre Cunha and Nilza Mendes Campos for their help in the reading of some song texts; Ernesto Ignacio de Carvalho for helping me with writing song texts; and Nivio Caixeta for the search for some musical examples in the archives of the radios Nacional and Cultura FM of Brasília. I am especially thankful to Gerard Béhague for the opportunity to present this work to his students and colleagues at the University of Texas at Austin. I feel equally obliged to George Marcus (Rice University), Max Brandt (University of Pittsburgh), and Patricia Sandler (University of Illinois at Urbana-Champaign) for their kind invitations to share this essay with their colleagues and with themselves.

1. There are many black females and (not so many) black males represented in these songs. Some of the song texts are so insulting and negative to black women that one might ask how they could circulate so freely in Brazilian broadcast media for so long, especially if no equivalent examples in the popular music of other countries are found.

2. The mulata is the brown-skinned woman ideologically and aesthetically viewed as the "positive" result of miscegenation between blacks and whites.

3. While preparing this essay, I discussed the song text to "O teu cabelo não nega" with many Brazilian friends and colleagues who had sung the song at numerous carnival balls. Invariably they were shocked by the actual content of the text and said they had sung it believing they were praising the mulata!

4. Luis Caldas is a well-known musician from Bahia and *fricote* is one of the new variants of Bahian carnival rhythms.

5. *Samba de breque* is a genre of commercial samba popularized in the 1940s and 1950s.—Ed.

6. A question can be put to Caetano: why use the predictable image of the *pretinha* instead of being innovative in terms of color; using say, "Am I a little morena, or a little blond?"

7. This song is the only one I could find, among over five hundred songs, up to 1986 which mentions the *loura*. This, in itself, makes it extremely relevant.

8. For a further analysis of Gil's song, see Carvalho 1993.

REFERENCES

Bakhtin, Mikhail. 1990. *Art and Answerability*. Austin: University of Texas Press.

Barthes, Roland. 1990. "The Grain of the Voice." In Simon Frith and Andrew Goodwin, eds., *On Record: Rock, Pop and the Written Word*, pp. 293–300. New York: Pantheon.

Carvalho, José Jorge. 1993. *Cantos sagrados do Xango do Recife*. Brasília: Fundação Cultural Palmares.

———. 1994. "Black Music of All Colors: The Construction of Black Ethnicity in Ritual and Popular Genres of Afro-Brazilian Music." In Gerard Béhague, ed., *Music and Black Ethnicity: The Caribbean and South America*, pp. 187–206. Miami: North-South Center Press, University of Miami.

Carvalho, José Jorge, and Rita Segato. 1990. "Sistemas abertos e territorios fechados: para uma nova compreensão das interfaces entre música e identidades sociais." Paper read at the Symposium on Music, Knowledge and Power, International Council for Traditional Music, University of Santa Catarina, Florianópolis.

Frith, Simon. 1987. "Why Do Songs Have Words?" In Avron Levine White, ed., *Lost in Music: Culture, Style and the Musical Event*, pp. 77–106. London: Routledge and Kegan Paul.

Kermode, Frank. 1967. *The Sense of an Ending*. Oxford: Oxford University Press.

White, Hayden. 1973. *Metahistory*. Baltimore: The Johns Hopkins University Press.

SONGS CITED

1. "Nega maluca." From *Os Grandes Sucessos dos Carnavais*, vol. 2 (originally released 1950). RCA, 1987.

2. "Nega do cabelo duro." Sung by Emilinha Borba (originally released in 1942).

3. "O teu cabelo não nega." From *Lamartine Babo, Música Popular Brasileira* #06 (song originally released in 1932). RCA, 1970.

4. "Fricote." From *Magia* by Luis Caldas. Polygram 826 583, 1985.

5. "Minha nega na janela." From *Antologia do Samba-Choro* by Gilberto Gil/Germano Mathias. Philips 6349 361, 1978.

6. "Pungar." From *Gerude* by Gerude.

7. "Lamento negro." From *Abolição e Música* by various artists (song originally released in 1941). Revivendo, 1988.

8. "Cem anos atrás." From *Abolição e Música* by various artists (song originally released in 1946). Revivendo, 1988.

9. "Olha o jeito desse nego." From *Abolição e Música* by various artists (song originally released in 1944). Revivendo, 1988.

10. "Preta." From *Beto Barbosa* by Beto Barbosa. Continental 1.73.405.016, 1988.

11. "Mulata assanhada." From *Ataulfo Alves. Música Popular Brasileira* #7 (song originally released in 1961). RCA: Abril Cultural, 1970.

12. "Linda morena." From *Reminiscências* by various artists (song originally released in 1932). Moto Discos, 1988.

13. "Linda lourinha." From *Reminiscências* by various artists. Moto Discos, 1988.

14. "O canto da cidade." From *O Canto da Cidade* by Daniela Mercury. Columbia 177.287, 1992.

15. "Olhos coloridos." From *Sandra de Sá* by Sandra de Sá. RCA 103.0689, 1986.

16. "Sub-raça." From *Sub-Raça* by Câmbio Negro. Brasília: Discovery, 1993.

17. "O preto e o branco." From *Eu Não Sou Santo* by Bezerra da Silva. RCA, 1990.

18. "Dança pretinha." From *Ela* by Elis Regina (song originally released in 1971). Philips 836009, 1988.

16 The Rise of Bumba-meu-Boi in Maranhão: Resilience of African-Brazilian Cultural Identity

KAZADI WA MUKUNA

Race relations between blacks and whites in Brazil have been a source of research topics for social and political scientists in recent decades. In these studies blacks are often portrayed as weak members of society whose fate was left to the mercy of their masters. Closer examination of documents from the colonial period sheds light on a variety of subtle defense mechanisms devised by African slaves to protect their identity and ensure their survival in a hostile milieu. Most of these defense mechanisms were formulated as cultural manifestations celebrated yearly in conjunction with a religious and/or secular occasion. In them, music played a significant role in carrying out deep-seated mockeries, insults, and ridicules of the ruling class. Often, the struggle for assimilation of cultural manifestations became intertwined with the struggle for racial and cultural identity.

Elsewhere (Mukuna 1994), I have discussed theories surrounding the quest for the origin and authorship of Bumba-meu-Boi and have argued that, as conceptualized and celebrated in Brazil, it is a folk drama containing dialogue, music, and dance which depicts the interaction among social classes in colonial Brazil. Bumba-meu-Boi was created in Brazil during the so-called Leather Civilization period (ca. 1750–1840) by African slaves as a collective statement of retaliation by the oppressed members of the society against their oppressors and a means by which the lower class denounced slave owners and ridiculed the ruling class. The examination here of public opinion about Bumba-meu-Boi that appeared in local chronicles between 1850 and 1958 reveals that its rise in the state of Maranhão, from a banned slave manifestation to an accepted cultural manifestation of the state, not only documents these purposes but also illustrates the process of social change in Maranhão and in Brazil as a whole.

The earliest document to mention Bumba-meu-Boi that has reached us is an article titled "A estulotice do Bumba-meu-Boi," which appeared in *O Carapuceiro* in 1840 (Gama 1840). The author describes this folk drama as insipid, stupid, and foolish for making fun of the servant of God. Since that time, numerous accounts about Bumba-meu-Boi have been published in local chronicles throughout Northeast Brazil reflecting a variety of opinions concerning its assimilation. Examination of these opinions suggests several reasons why the presentation of Bumba-meu-Boi was persecuted in Brazil. One, often referred to in literature, is its identification with slaves, whose humanity and moral values were questioned by the ruling class during the colonial period. Closer study of the Bumba-meu-Boi story line corroborates that slaves used the drama as a defense mechanism to guarantee their survival in the face of hostile conditions. The story line of the Bumba-meu-Boi is as follows:

> On a ranch owned by a Portuguese master (referred to in the play as Amo) and his wife Dona Maria dwelt the slave Francisco (also called Nego Chico), his pregnant wife (Mãe Catarina), and other slaves. The Amo has a favorite ox referred to as "Boi Estrela" (the Star Ox), "Fama Real" (Royal Fame). One day, Mãe Catarina has an urge to eat of an ox's tongue. Making her desire known to her husband, Mãe Catarina specifies that the tongue must be that of the master's favorite animal. Concerned for the life of his unborn child, Pai Francisco leads the ox into the woods where he kills it and takes the tongue to his wife who cooks and eats it. The next day the Amo, realizing that his favorite ox is missing, summons all his cowboys and slaves together to ask if anyone has seen it. One of them informs him that he had seen Pai Francisco taking the "Star Ox" into the woods from whence minutes later a gunshot was heard. Searching the woods they encounter the remains of the ox. Infuriated by the sight of his dead animal, the Amo orders the Director of Indians to arrest Pai Francisco. Before undertaking such a dangerous mission, the Director of Indians seeks a blessing from the priest. Addressing Pai Francisco, the Amo orders him to bring his ox back to life or die. A Portuguese medical doctor enters the scene and makes several attempts to resurrect the ox but all are in vain. Finally, an Indian medicine man is summoned. He places a fresh leaf in the ox's mouth. The animal arises, and everyone dances joyfully through the night.[1]

A Bumba-meu-Boi troupe is a "cultural" entity often defined by the occupation of the majority of its members, or simply by geographic or administrative divisions such as a district, township, or quarter. In many communities in the state of Maranhão the population makes its living in such activities as fishing, cattle raising, and agriculture. The economy of Pindar, Maranhão, for example, is primarily agricultural, built around the sugarcane and rice industries, small-scale fishing on the Mirim River and the neighboring lakes, and cattle raising. Among members of this community the sense of belonging is vital to their identity. They take pride in their community and in their occupation. Until recently, this sense of belonging, especially in the interior of the state, has been demonstrated by minimal population mobility.

A Bumba-meu-Boi troupe helps construct cultural identity by creating a feeling of belonging and unity. According to José Ribeiro de Souza, "Members gather pennies and make tremendous sacrifices to maintain their existence as a group which thinks, acts, reacts, and feels" (1970:351). This phenomenon, on which the membership of Bumba-meu-Boi is founded, is rooted in the African philosophy of existence and identity which stresses the concept of belonging. Souza further asserts that "Bumba-meu-Boi arouses in its participants the feeling of existing as a cultural group and expresses its opinion about other entities" (1970:350). Each group boasts about the beauty of its ox and its community, praises its organization, and exalts the quality of its accompanying musical ensemble, while denigrating those of other troupes in *toadas* (songs) improvised during the performance according to prescribed but unwritten poetic rules of the *boiada*.[2] As a social group par excellence, a Bumba-meu-Boi troupe was compelled to protect that which belongs to it or that to which it belongs from criticism and verbal insults from outsiders. This practice of *desafio* (verbal challenge) became associated with the boiada.

In the Amazon, Eduardo Galvão (1951:276) records:

When Bumba-meu-Boi troupes encountered each other, members engaged in a poetic challenge of improvised verse and dance movements. A Boi from a small town was once ridiculed in such a four-line verse:

> There comes the Boi
> Behind the pepper plant
> Never have I seen an ugly Boi
> Such as this from Itaperêra.

When members of a particular group were incapable of formulating strong satirical responses to such mockeries, verbal challenges
invariably were transformed into physical ones aimed at destroying the
opponent's ox frame. This tradition of rivalry was not unique to Bumba-
meu-Boi in Brazil. It was also common practice among *capoeira*[3] groups
and samba schools, which for similar reasons received the same treatment from the ruling class in their quest for recognition and identity.
"Em capoeira, quando o pau comia, a gente usava o próprio berimbau
para se defender" (In capoeira, whenever the fight started, we used the
berimbau itself to defend ourselves).[4] In Bumba-meu-Boi, clubs, knives,
and other objects were hidden under the ox's frame for the same purpose
(Galvão 1970:276). *Sambistas* (performers of samba) also used their
musical instruments as defensive weapons.[5] Discussing the effect of the
concept of belonging on these confrontations, Caio Prado points out that
the "code of alliance in a relation of confrontation, be it rivalry or conflict, transforms itself into an expression of violence" and defines two
types of violence, physical and ideological, that can arise from these confrontations, depending on the nature of the enemy:

> Among equals, it is a "context of rivals"; among different classes, it is
> an object of repression activated by the dominating rule. . . . If, in the
> most restricted sense, the *boiada* represents original communities, it
> can turn itself, in a broader sense, into a language of defense of inter-
> est in a confrontation between classes. (Prado Júnior 1975:119)

An article published in *A Voz Paraense* (1850) urged authorities to
banish Bumba-meu-Boi from the city:

> The Boi Caiado, celebrated on the vesper of Saint Peter's Day, by more
> than 300 blacks, mulattos, and whites of different sizes who late at
> night trampled the rocks and grasses of the streets and squares in the
> city and countryside, resulted in stabbings and blows with sticks
> beside shouting that was offensive to moral decency and public secu-
> rity. Let us hope that those responsible in the Police Department
> would put an end to the Boi Caiado in a similar manner that Judas was
> finished with on alleluia Saturday.

In the same year, an anonymous citizen expressed resentment of the
Bumba-meu-Boi performance in the city:

> I would like those men, who promised twice to turn away Dr. Rego of
> the Police Department, to come and see the disdain and isolation in
> which their protégé exists; they should come to witness his madness;

they should also come to assist the presentation of the least deserved merrymaking for an authority, such as Dr. Rego practiced on the night of June 29, placing himself in front of a group of scamps with their "Bumba-meu-Boi" designating places where they were to dance, and had the impudence to threaten with prison a portion of the best young men from the city of Obidos, only because they were throwing small spools at the directors of the bumba who were his slaves Casemiro and Claudino. (*O Velho Brado do Amazonas* 1850)

What is not expressed in these opinions, in conjunction with the state of Maranhão, is that the intolerance of Bumba-meu-Boi was not only based on social and moral issues that constituted a predominantly secular character for which the folk drama was renowned, but also on the racial identity of those who were practiced it. Despite the harsh recommendations to abolish it, Bumba-meu-Boi continued to crystallize as a cultural manifestation with all its racial characteristics. Discussing the struggle of blacks for social mobility through musical expression, João Baptista Borges Pereira points out that the samba was:

Pejoratively associated with the black, poor, and promiscuous populations, with the centers of street roguery, with the *rodas de batuque*, with magico-religious or recreational practices condemned by the "respectable" customs of the times. The incipient musicality was also more than merely socially shameful and reprehensible, and precisely because of this, it was legally categorized as a "police matter." (Pereira 1967:214–215)

To the authorities, Bumba-meu-Boi was also a "police matter" and met a similar fate. Remarks about this assertion began to be chronicled in Maranhão in 1858. A short notice titled "O Boi" appeared in *O Globo* announcing the reappearance of the blacks' merrymaking called Bumba-meu-Boi which years earlier the police had prohibited, considering it uncivilized. Three years later, the São Luis newspaper *O Imparcial* published a statement by an author who identified himself as "Um Amigo da Civilização" (A Friend of Civilization):

When a large portion of the population takes upon itself to end with those deadly firecrackers, authorization is granted to the stupid and immoral merrymaking of slaves called Bumba-meu-Boi—the reason for the firecrackers. And it is astonishing that this is still happening when years ago the president ordered the police to no longer authorize this merrymaking for being detrimental to good order, to civilization and to morals. When, due to Bumba-meu-Boi, there are beatings with clubs and even stabbings, it is because of the enormous racket which breaks the silence and disturbs the quiet needed to sleep, silence that the police should maintain. We hope that the police reconsider the thoughtless step they have taken and become responsible to public opinion for what may happen because of the Bumba-meu-Boi. (*O Imparcial,* June 15, 1861)

This rather strong statement invited, the same year, a reaction from a columnist for *A Verdadeira Marmota* newspaper also in São Luis, who could not understand the reason for the prohibition against Bumba-meu-Boi in the state. The author writes that these negative reactions against the Bumba-meu-Boi are due to the population's ignorance of the story behind the merrymaking and concludes with a succinct description of the plot.[6] Once again, it is obvious that the real reason was not ignorance but racism which lies at the core of stigmatizing African Brazilians as immoral and lawless. This pronounced antagonism against Bumba-meu-Boi reached its apogee in 1861 leading to the total prohibition of the merrymaking in the following years.

The return of Bumba-meu-Boi in 1868 was hailed in a column by João Domingos Perreira do Sacramento in these terms:

In the last fifteen days, from June 12 to the present, this columnist has noticed a wise resolution by the police authority regarding the rebirth of an old practice which seems to have been prescribed by our customs.... Hurray! for the police and viva the Bumba! ... The columnist requests permission from those civilized spirits who have so much to fear for the rebirth of our old customs, to shout hurray! to Senhor Dr. Morato and viva the Bumba! (Sacramento 1868)

In spite of its acclaimed return, Bumba-meu-Boi was far from being accepted in Maranhão. The return did not end the antagonism, but marked the beginning of a period of denouement which continued for considerable time and which I have elected to identify for the sake of discussion as a "period of tolerance." Published announcements attest to the prevailing atmosphere of both sympathy for and hostility toward Bumba-meu-Boi. In 1869, for example, the newspaper *Paiz* published an open letter requesting that the Chief of Police deny permission to Bumba-meu-Boi troupes even for rehearsals. Three days later, *Publicador Maranhense* published still another open letter addressed to "His Excellency the Chief of Police" in support of Bumba-meu-Boi. Making reference to the earlier letter in *Paiz,* the author pleads to the authority to permit the performance of Bumba-meu-Boi that year, and continues:

> On the contrary, we remind everyone that this merrymaking has been held each year, and that even last year it ran through this city three times without causing these cases mentioned in the *Paiz*. We hasten to request His Excellency Mr. Chief of Police to act for the good and grant permission to this merriment which, taking place only once a year, does not bother good society, since some old slaves participate with their master's permission. This is one more guarantee for this distraction of the good youth. His Excellency, thus, in virtue you will attend to our request. (*Publicador Maranhense* 1869)

As the end of the period of tolerance neared, one senses from notices printed in newspapers that the antagonism toward Bumba-meu-Boi had begun to subside in Maranhão as well as in other states of Northeastern Brazil. The ruling class could now tolerate Bumba-meu-Boi when the presentation was held in restricted areas designated by the police. "In Fortaleza (Ceará), from about 1900, police allowed the Bumba-meu-Boi in closed areas" (Barroso 1949:219). In Maranhão, however, newspaper articles support the claim that Bumba-meu-Boi was not tolerated until early in the second half of the twentieth century. Until then, physical abuses were still common during confrontations between troupes. On June 30, 1915, an article titled "Polícia que dá e apanha" ("Police Dish It Out and Take It") appeared in the newspaper *A Tarde,* which contained an account of an event that occurred during the presentation of the Bumba-meu-Boi in the township of Mocajutuba. On that occasion a physical confrontation took place between a police delegate, whose brother was hit by a rock thrown during a Bumba-meu-Boi, and a participant of the Bumba-meu-Boi. On July 2 of that year, an anonymous letter to the editor in the same newspaper, titled "O Boi" ("The Ox"), requested the editor's intervention in lobbying the authorities to limit the space available for the presentation of the Bumba-meu-Boi:

> Mr. Editor of *A Tarde,*
>
> It seems incredible that in a capital such as ours, the police would allow the notorious Bumba-meu-Boi to roam freely in the main streets from nine o'clock at night until ten o'clock the next morning, as has been happening.

> This merrymaking (if such name should be given to it) should be permitted only in secluded areas; it is not right, it is not lawful nor proper that one observes such a sad and depressing event which lacks qualification. What awful times!
>
> Intervene for us, Mr. Editor, because it is already time for the police to rise from the sleep.

Similar requests to the authorities led to the restriction of Bumba-meu-Boi's mobility in the city. Some forty years after the above letter to the editor appeared, the author of an article in *O Globo,* titled "A morte do Bumba-meu-Boi" ("The Death of Bumba-meu-Boi"), is astonished at what he reads in the paper:

> I am reading in the newspapers that "it is prohibited for Bumba-meu-Boi groups to parade in the streets of the city, in demonstration of their characteristic dances, which will only be permitted in the suburban perimeter starting at the corner of Getúlio Vargas Avenue and Senator João Pedro Street." This is sad, you know? It is sad for us that the people of Pernambuco, Alagoas, and Rio de Janeiro will learn that it is a crime to celebrate a tradition in the streets of the city of São Luis in Maranhão. . . . Oh! you, cosmopolitan city that denies what is the most native in the veins of your people. I feel pity for you. For dark is the future of he who denies his past!

The author extends an invitation to the authorities of the state of Maranhão:

> To follow the example of their colleagues in other major cities such as Recife, in Pernambuco, where during the festive period, *maracatus*[7] are subsidized by the Mayor's Office and are permitted to roam the streets of the legendary city; in Maceió, Alagoas, where during the month of the *congada,*[8] the government helps buy clothing and other objects for the *lanceiros*[9] to assure the continuity of this folk expression in the chronicle of Maceió and in the middle of the capital of the United States of Brazil[10] (Rio de Janeiro) where Saint Barbara's day is celebrated by the police in uniforms and members of the local cults go to Copacabana beach to deposit flowers and gifts to the queen of the sea Yemanjá, singing "Saravá!"

The author concludes that in the future "it won't be necessary anymore to prohibit them [Bumba-meu-Boi troupes] from entering the streets. São Luis which had plenty (of cultural manifestations) will become the land which also had the most famous Bumba-meu-Boi in Brazil."

The "period of tolerance" was also a "period of adjustment" not only for the Bumba-meu-Boi as a cultural expression, but also for African Brazilian as a category of racial identity. During this period certain decisions and practices were being reassessed and new ones were being formulated. Confrontational behavior was no longer observed and Bumba-meu-Boi troupes from different localities could now dance in the same place without incident. Elder members in the Boi de Zé Vale troupe in Pindare still recall these events in their toadas:

> I blew my whistle
> In order to gather
> Oh! my Saint John
> Oh! come to bestow a blessing on us
> To deliver us from our enemies
> For those who wish to conquer us.

Examining a similar situation with the samba, João Baptista Borges Pereira indicates that different phases of the samba's process of acceptance—from the status of total inferiority to that of superiority which it continues to enjoy to the present—were attained through "a reformation of this new music according to the actual standards in the most exigent strata of Brazilian society, submitting it to a constant metamorphosis as a musico-choreographical expression, and exposing it before the general consensus as a socio-cultural element" (Pereira 1967:214). In Maranhão, Bumba-meu-Boi was also submitted to similar standards of "good society" in the form of racial persecution. Its response to these standards, resulting in the modification of its original objectives (i.e., to denounce and ridicule slave owners, to be a collective statement of retaliation against the ruling class, to become a mere vehicle of social control for the community), was also a defense mechanism to ensure its rise to the status it now occupies in the state. To observers of the Bumba-meu-Boi, this resilience marked a series of stages of social adaptation forced upon them by the ruling class as conditions for their social acceptance as a racial entity.

As with the acceptance of the samba, marked by the 1917 recording of "Pelo Telefone," the first song with the official title of samba, and the organization in 1932 of the first public parade contest in Rio de Janeiro,[11] the "period of tolerance" of Bumba-meu-Boi, which lasted nearly a century, ended in 1965 with the first competitive parade in São Luis on July 13. The success of this event, in which fifteen Bumba-meu-Boi groups from the capital and the interior participated, was celebrated with the publication of the results and praise for the winners in the July 17 issue of *Diário da Manhã*.

Although parade contests to stimulate and accelerate the acceptance of Bumba-meu-Boi were no longer organized in Maranhão after 1965, newspaper and journal articles continued to document the growing favorable public opinion and the shift from mere tolerance to total acceptance of the Bumba-meu-Boi. This feeling is voiced by Haroldo Moura (1966) who boasts that the organization and beauty of Bumba-meu-Boi in Maranhão make it superior to that of the entire Northeast of Brazil. In 1977 Bumba-meu-Boi received its first recognition in academic circles with Regina de Paula Santos Prado's master's thesis, titled "Todo ano tem: as festas na estrutura social camponesa" (Federal University of Rio de Janeiro).

In short, Bumba-meu-Boi came to be accepted by the ruling class as the most representative aspect of Maranhense culture. This recognition was corroborated by the selection of Bumba-meu-Boi to represent the state at the interuniversity sport competition in Brasília in 1977. A newspaper article reported that at the "IXth Brazilian School Games, Maranhão won a gold medal not through its athletes, but through its artists. Maranhense folklore, represented by Bumba-meu-Boi in the style of the island of São Luis, was considered the original."[12] Continuing his comments about the Boi at the games, the reporter reproduces a section of a column from *O Bicho* expressing admiration for the Bumba-meu-Boi from Maranhão. Concluding the article, the writer proudly elevates Bumba-meu-Boi to the national level:

> The folklore of Maranhão, which was one of the most requested presentations here at the IX Brazilian School Games, gave a true "show" when it was presented at the tower. The place, frequented often, was too small for those who wanted a closer look at the Bumba-meu-Boi *de matraca*, and there, without regard to states, everyone joined in the contagious sound and dance of the young folklorists.... This folkloric wonder, which affirmed itself definitively at the Brazilian Student Games, should be included on Brazil's calling card to the world.[13]

The creation by the authorities of the Federation for the Defense of Folklore Groups in Maranhão further validated Bumba-meu-Boi and confirmed its ascension to a paramount position in the cultural life of the state. In time, Bumba-meu-Boi became one of the major tourist attractions in Maranhão. To some, the rather rapid elevation of the

Bumba-meu-Boi hindered the recognition of other cultural manifestations which had coexisted with it through the years. Virgílio Pinto laments this phenomenon:

> In the vast cultural tradition of Maranhão, Bumba-meu-Boi has without doubt gained high diffusion and recognition. Perhaps it is because this manifestation has its strongest expression in this state. It is such that when one arrives in Maranhão, regardless of the month, he goes straight to ask where one could see the "Boi." If this exaltation of the Boi emphasizes the manifestation of traditional folklore of Maranhão to the point of identifying it with Maranhão, giving reason for people to come and see it, on the other hand, it detracts from other popular manifestations existing herein. It is important to underline that these others are as creative and expressive as Bumba-meu-Boi. . . . But if tourists want to see only Bumba-meu-Boi, the local people also see it as the only form of expression. It is true that there is a little exaggeration in this affirmation. Tambor de Crioula also draws people, but without a doubt, it does not attract the majority of the population. Then, it is necessary that the Maranhense turns his attention to other manifestations. Better yet, they should stimulate them. Thus, the folklore of our land would be deeply rooted, and Bumba-meu-Boi, in spite of its frequent presentation, would not run the risk of losing the authenticity as appears to have happened to many. (Pinto 1977)

Despite conceptual and stylistic changes, pertinent to the assimilation and the continuity of Bumba-meu-Boi in Maranhão, and existing regional variations, certain basic features of Bumba-meu-Boi persist. Among others, its satirical nature serves as a reminder of the shameful past from which the plot was conceptualized. This satirical nature, however, represents only one of the functions fulfilled by Bumba-meu-Boi. Others, such as the use of Bumba-meu-Boi as a mechanism for social control and the observance of the boiada as an occasion for religious devotion allowing individuals to renew their covenant with the adopted saints and to fulfill promises made to the saints in exchange for divine protection and favorable answers to their prayers, resulted from its resilience to a changing time and society. Together these functions constitute a deep-seated defense mechanism designed and utilized by African Brazilians in their struggle for identity. In this form of defense, music played a vital role by becoming a vehicle through which deep-seated insults and mockeries were carried out. These social mockeries were and continue to be expressed in refrains and verses sung during the

boiada. They contain "signs of social order" and provide what Alan Merriam has called the "ethos" of the culture which helps to comprehend
those behind the expression and their society (1978:201). Although the
context of Bumba-meu-Boi has changed, the struggle for racial harmony
persists, justifying its continued practice.

NOTES

1. This version of the story line was recorded in 1981 as told by José Vale
and his colleagues of "Rei da União" group in Pindaré, Maranhão.
2. The term *boiada* refers to the actual performance of the Bumba-meu-
Boi drama. It is also a generic term in Maranhão designating the period during
which the performance of the folk drama is observed (June 24–January 6).
3. *Capoeira* is a form of choreographed self-defense which originated
among slaves in Bahia and Pernambuco. It is performed to the accompaniment
of songs and rhythmic background of musical bows (*berimbau*), basket rattle
(*caxixi*), and hand drums (*pandeiro*). For more on capoeira, see Rego (1968).
4. Personal interview with Master Noronha in Salvador, Bahia, August 16,
1976.
5. Personal interview with Paulinho da Viola, Rio de Janeiro, June 11,
1976.
6. This article was republished in *O Estado do Maranhão,* July 1, 1979.
7. A dramatic dance/procession in which the characters represent,
through songs and dances, the coronation of the King of the Congo.
8. A set of quadrilles performed with sticks accompanied by songs representing the fight between the Moors and the Christians.
9. Participants of the *congada*.
10. The ancient name of Brazil. This appellation was changed in 1964 to
the present name of the Federative Republic of Brazil.
11. This parade contest, organized by the newspaper *Mundo Esportivo,*
established the Praça Onze carnival tradition.
12. *O Imparcial,* July 31, 1977.
13. Ibid.

REFERENCES

Barroso, Gustavo. 1949. *Ao som da viola.* 2d ed. Rio de Janeiro: Departamento de
    Impresa Nacional.

Galvão, Eduardo. 1951. "Boi Bumbá: versão do Baixo Amazonas." *Anhembi*
    3(8):276–291.

Merriam, Alan. 1964. *The Anthropology of Music*. Chicago: Northwestern University Press.

Mukuna, Kazadi wa. 1994. "Sotaques: Style and Ethnicity in a Brazilian Folk Drama." In G. Béhague, ed., *Music and Black Ethnicity: The Caribbean and South America*, pp. 207–224. Miami: North-South Center Press, University of Miami.

Pereira, João Baptista Borges. 1967. *Cor, profissão e mobilidade: o negro e o rádio de São Paulo*. São Paulo: Editora da Universidade de São Paulo.

Prado Júnior, Caio. 1975. *História econômico do Brasil*. São Paulo: Editora Brasiliense.

Prado, Regina de Paula Santos. 1977. "Todo ano tem: as festas na estrutura social camponesa." Master's thesis, Federal University of Rio de Janeiro.

Rego, Waldeloir. 1968. *Capoeira Angola: ensaio sócio-etnográfico*. Salvador, Bahia: Itapua.

Souza, José Ribeiro de. 1970. *Brasil no folclore*. Rio de Janeiro: Gráfica Editora Aurora.

Signed Popular Press Articles

Gama, Padre Lopes. 1840. "A estulotice do Bumba-meu-Boi." *O Carapuceiro* (Recife), no. 2 (January 11).

Moura, Haroldo. 1966. *Journal Pequeno* (São Luis), June 23.

Pinto, Virgílio. 1977. *O Estado do Maranhão* (São Luis), August 12.

Sacramento, João Domingos Perreira do. 1868. "Chronica interna." *Semanário Maranhense* (São Luis) 1:45 (July 5), 7–8.

Unsigned Newspaper Articles

"A morte do Bumba-meu-Boi." *O Globo,* June 21, 1955.

"O Boi." *O Globo,* June 2, 1958.

"O Boi." *A Tarde* (São Luis), July 2, 1915.

O Estado do Maranhão (São Luis), June 9, 1974; August 5, 1977; May 17, 1979; June 10, 1979; July 1, 1979.

O Imparcial (São Luis), June 15, 1861; August 5, 1976; August 12, 1977; May 17, 1979; June 10, 1979.

"Pelo desenho do couro eu sei se o Boi vai ganhar." *O Estado do Maranhão* (São Luis), June 30, 1976.

"Polícia que dá e apanha." *A Tarde* (São Luis), June 30, 1915.

Publicador Maranhense (São Luis), July 9, 1869.

O Velho Brado do Amazonas, September 27, 1850.

A Voz Paraense (Belém), July 3, 1850.

Part Six

BLACKS IN THE VISUAL MEDIA

The final section of *Black Brazil* presents three views on the representation of blacks in Brazilian film and television. In his essay, NYU film and media scholar Robert Stam discusses cinematic portrayals of Afro-Brazilian religions within Brazil's national film tradition. After reviewing prejudicial representations typical of a Eurocentric vision, Stam examines the more sympathetic view which often characterizes Brazilian cinema, discussing such films as Anselmo Duarte's *O Pagador de Promessas* (1962), Glauber Rocha's *Barravento* (1962), and Nelson Pereira dos Santos's *O Amuleto de Ogum* (1974). He concludes that aesthetic recasting of religious traditions in film and other art forms may serve the purposes of a collective agency in the present.

Sociologist Denise Ferreira da Silva analyzes the stereotyped portrayal of blacks in Brazilian *telenovelas* and their symbolic absence from television's notion of modernity. Through her examination of the telenovelas *Corpo-a-Corpo* and *Vale Tudo*, Silva reinscribes race and racial dynamics in discussions of modern Brazilian society as transmitted by the telenovela, concluding that the telenovela actualizes the hierarchical and exclusionary beliefs of Brazilian racial culture, which continues to be based on the ideology of "whitening" and the myth of racial democracy.

Finally, telecommunications scholar Michael Leslie shows, through an empirical analysis based on the theory of cultivation effects, how commercial television in Brazil helps sustain the myth of racial democracy and cultivate modern racism by failing to deal with issues affecting the black population such as racial discrimination, economic deprivation, and social limitations.

The Flash of Spirit: Cinematic Representations of Afro-Brazilian Religion

ROBERT STAM

Afro-diasporic religions such as Candomblé, Vodou, and Santería are almost invariably caricatured in dominant media. The affiliation of such Hollywood "voodoo" films as *Voodoo Man* (1944), *Voodoo Woman* (1957), and *Voodoo Island* (1957) with the horror genre already betrays a viscerally phobic attitude toward African religion, linked, perhaps, to the shock waves generated by the role of Vodou in the Haitian revolution. But more recent films show little if any progress in this regard. *The Believers* (1986) presents the Afro-Caribbean religion Santería as a cult dominated by ritual child-murderers, in a manner reminiscent of the "unspeakable rites" invoked by colonialist literature. Other films eroticize African religion in a way that betrays ambivalent attraction and repulsion. *Angel Heart* (1987) has Lisa Bonet, as Epiphany Proudfoot the voodoo priestess, thrash around with Mickey Rourke in a sanguinary love scene. Another Mickey Rourke vehicle, *Wild Orchid* (1990), exploits the religious atmosphere of Candomblé as what Tomás López-Pumarejo calls an "Afro-dysiac." And the Michael Caine comedy *Blame It on Rio* (1984) stages Umbanda as a frenetic beach orgy in which the priestess (*mãe de santo*) doles out amorous advice in English to tourists while all the celebrants take off their clothes and jump into the sea.

Brazilian films are less likely to portray African religions in a caricatural way, although here too prejudicial representations are not unknown. In *As Noites de Iemanjá* (Nights of Iemanjá, 1981) a bored housewife (Joana Fomm) witnesses a Candomblé ceremony devoted to Iemanjá, the goddess of the sea, goes into trance, and becomes more and more sensual and destructive. She becomes Iemanjá, seducing a series of men into the sea during the act of love. The promotional materials for the film reflect a process of diabolization: "Diabolic! Seductive! Loving all men in search of herself. . . . Possessed by forbidden rites, she emerges from the waves to destroy men." Iemanjá becomes conflated with a whole series of misogynistic myths—Eve, Pandora, the sirens, the Lorelai, and Iara, the voracious seductress of the Amazon.

Palimpsestic Prejudices

More generally, however, Brazilian films treat African religions with a certain amount of respect. The specific subject of this essay is the representation of African religious practices within Brazilian cinema, especially within the fiction feature film. But since the dominant media generally relay a Eurocentric vision of African spirit religions as superstitious cults rather than as legitimate belief systems, we may begin by clearing away some sedimented prejudices. These prejudices are enshrined in the patronizing vocabulary ("animism," "ancestor worship," "magic," "fetishes," "cults") used to speak about African religions.[1] Within Eurocentric thinking, superimposed Western hierarchies work to the detriment of African trance religions. First, the religions are seen as oral rather than written, and therefore as lacking the scriptural authority and cultural imprimatur of the religions of the book. In fact, however, the "text," in the very inclusive semiotic sense of that word, simply takes distinct semiotic form, whether performative or verbal-musical, as in Yoruba praise songs dedicated to the spirits (*orixás*). Second, spirit religions are mistakenly seen as polytheistic rather than monotheistic, in any case a debatable hierarchy and a misrepresentation of most African religions. In Yoruba religion the figure of Olorum, Master of the Skies, refers to an overarching divine principle or vital force reigning over the specific orixás with their anthropomorphic personalities. Third, African spirit religions are seen as superstitious rather than scientific, a view deriving from the positivist genealogy of religion as historically moving from myth to theology to science—a secularization of earlier notions of religious providence, now sublimated into the more "scientific" idea of "progress." But religions are not arranged in hierarchies of relative rationality; all religions involve a leap of faith, whether in the form of a belief in the Virgin Birth, the resurrection of Christ, or simply trust in an invisible yet all-powerful supreme Being. African trance religions might even be said to be more open to scientific thinking in that they insist less on rigid dogmas than on practical questions of energy and power of realization (*axé*). For Muniz Sodré (1989), African religions are radically "ecological," promoting a spirit of "confraternization" with plants, animals, and minerals. If on one level extremely pragmatic, African religions can be seen on another as theoretical and speculative; in Nigeria, Karin Barber (1984) of the University of Ife has discerned common elements in deconstruction and Yoruba *oriki* praise poetry, specifically indeterminacy, intertextuality, and constant variability. Fourth, African trance religions are belittled as corporeal and ludic (danced) rather than abstractly and austerely theological, a prejudice rooted in Manichean ideas of the flesh as inherently evil and in puritanical hostility to bodily pleasures. Fifth, the African religions are seen as insufficiently sublimated in that they involve literal animal sacrifice rather than symbolic or historically commemorative sacrifice. This hierarchy posits more abstract religions as superior, yet many scholars (for example René Girard) see the scapegoating mechanism as common to all religious cultures. Sixth, the trance religions are seen as wildly gregarious, drowning the individual personality in the collective and transpersonal fusions of trance, rather than respecting the unitary, bounded consciousness. The Christian ideal of the *visio intellectualis*, which Christian theology inherited from the Neo-Platonists, flees in horror from the plural trances and visions of the trance religions of Africa and of many indigenous peoples.[2]

African religions are as diverse as the cultural complexes (Yoruba, Bantu, Hausa) that gave them birth, and even more diverse because they historically syncretized not only with Christianity, Judaism, and European Spiritism but also with indigenous religions and with one another. Some African religions are relatively "pure" or traditional, while others are highly, and multiply, syncretic. Syncretism with Catholicism has sometimes led to a double system of rough equivalences between orixás and saints. Oxala is often associated with Christ, although in African terms Oxala is androgynous, so that Oxala is elsewhere identified with a woman saint, Saint Anne. Iemanjá, as a water goddess, is sometimes identified with the Virgin Mary. In *O Pagador de Promessas* (The Given Word, 1962), Iansã, a goddess of the River Niger and of storms, is linked to Saint Barbara, seen in popular Catholicism as a saint who protected people from storms and lightning. In any case, Brazilian films proliferate in the traces of such syncretism. A sequence in *O Pagador de Promessas*, for example, shows women in ritual clothing washing the steps of a church, a practice that mingles a Portuguese custom with the African custom of washing sacred objects and shrines. The time has passed, we should add, when "syncretism" can be used as a pejorative; all religions are syncretic (European Christianity, for example, borrowed many elements from so-called pagan pre-Christian religions, such as the ritualized use of trees to celebrate Christmas).

The Centrality of Trance

The core of most of the West African religions practiced in Brazil is the notion of trance or divine possession, the idea of a spirit that "rides" or takes possession of a human being, a takeover expressed in dance and gesture. The phenomenon of Spirit possession—by which the responsibility for a person's ritual behavior is assumed by a spiritual entity—has existed everywhere in the world, including in Europe, but in Western society it has generally come to be seen as aberrant behavior. (The substratal memory of such practices is betrayed, however, in such expressions as "What got into you?" or "What possessed you?" and their aura still lingers around words like "charm," "spell," "hex," and "enchantment.") In West African religions, each orixá appears and manifests him or herself in the bodily behavior of the adept of the religion. The sacred rhythms of the drums, as Mabille puts it, "reach the depths of their being and make them the playthings of the gods who possess them" (Walker 1975:29). Rather than an anguished, guilt-ridden, quasi-private dialogue with God à la Puritanism, African religion is gregarious, based on collective participation. In contrast with a Christianity which emphasizes humble submission to God in postures of respect and subservience and "looking up," and the effacement of the body within a dualistic metaphysic which subordinates the body to the mind, African religions see the body as gloriously manifesting the divine. In spatial, metaphorical terms, human beings do not painfully "ascend" toward God; rather, the gods "descend" into human beings. Spirit possession is in this sense the supreme religious act expressing the fundamental nature of the relationship between human beings and their deities. The difference between Afro-American religious practices, for example in the gospel church, and Afro-Brazilian religious practices, is that the personalities of the individual orixás have been preserved in Brazil, and not just the general spirit of trance and possession. Like the members of the Greek pantheon, the orixás are seen as having very human characteristics: they marry, have children, quarrel, and have distinct preferences in terms of colors, foods, drink, and rhythms.

In terms of sexual politics, the existence of male and female deities, and the fact that men can be possessed by female deities and vice versa, can be considered a "feminist" advance over Judaism and Islam, with their very patriarchal conceptions of God, and over Christianity with its masculine triad of Father, Son, and a sexually ambiguous Holy Ghost expressed in phallic symbols like birds and tongues of flame. (Vera Figueiredo's film *Samba da Criação do Mundo* [Samba of the Creation of the World, 1979] deploys Rio's Beija Flor samba school to tell the story of the mating of the orixás to create the world, while her current project *Pomba Gira: Deusa do Amor* [Pomba Gira, Goddess of Love] plans to offer a feminist interpretation of a figure in Umbanda, the "pomba gira" who embodies female mischievousness and creativity.) Candomblé priestesses (*iyalorixás*) of the kind that appear in *O Pagador de Promessas* and *Barravento* (both 1962), furthermore, are very powerful, even venerated figures; they are mothers (*mães*) not of a nuclear family but of a community.[3] Nor is Candomblé repressive toward homosexuality. In the 1940s, Ruth Landes noted that although women dominated the traditional *terreiros*, homosexual men dominated the others. Analysts speculate that homosexual men saw Candomblé as a way of identifying with women and also note that the metaphor of the "divine horsemen" who are "mounted" by the saints easily takes on a sexual dimension. The initiates, furthermore, are called the "wives" (*iaô*) of the saints.[4]

Geraldo Sarno's documentary *Iaô* (1978) records the successive phases of initiation rites into a Gêge-Nagô terreiro in Bahia. The film follows the slow transformation of three young women (*abians*) into *iaôs* or brides of the spirit. The duty of the abians is to "seat" their orixás, to bring them into their lives. The film shows the *catulagem* or cutting of the abians' hair. The priestesses chant as they cut the hair close to the scalp. Each abian is given armlets, bracelets, anklets, and necklaces. Their heads become the mediums open to the orixás; the blood of a dove is poured over consecrated heads and feathers are placed in the drying blood. A shallow cross is cut in the center of the head, opening up a point of connection between the inner and outer worlds. Finally, the iaôs publicly emerge three times before the community, each time wearing different costumes and following different drum rhythms, and finally appearing in full regalia.

I do not mean to idealize Afro-Brazilian religions. Like all religions, they are not immune to charlatanism, mundane power struggles, or commercial exploitation. But the world of the orixás is not the fossilized or disappearing or provincial world that the patronizing vocabulary of "survivals," "vestiges," and "reminiscences" would suggest, but rather an evolving and cosmopolitan one. Of the hundreds of orixás of which the African tradition speaks, only a small proportion survived slavery and the Middle Passage, and the signification of those who have survived has changed with dislocations in time and space. If Ogum was associated with the spread of iron-making technology in sub-Saharan Africa over two millennia ago, he is now recoded, in films like *O Amuleto de Ogum* (Amulet of Ogum, 1974), as a New World symbol of the struggle against social oppression. Tânia Cypriano is currently making a film called *Odo Ya! Fighting Aids*, a documentary about AIDS education programs in Rio, São Paulo, and Bahia which use the language, symbols, and culture of Candomblé for purposes of AIDS education and prevention. Under the rubric *Odo Ya*, a salutation to Iemanjá as a symbol of life and hope, these programs have developed manuals, pamphlets, and a newsletter. The campaigns stress the positive nature of sexuality as a form of axé while emphasizing the need to preserve life. As poetic figures, meanwhile, the orixás now play an artistic role in Africa and the diaspora akin to the role of the classical deities of the Greek pantheon within literature, painting, and sculpture. For Henry Louis Gates, Jr., the Yoruba trickster figure Exu-Legba provides the germ of the deconstructive "signifying" aesthetic of African-American literary narrative. The orixás permeate the sculpture of "Mestre Didi" (Deoscoredes M. dos Santos), the photography of Pierre Verger, the painting of Carybé, the plays of Wole Soyinka, and the music of Olodum, Ilê Aiyê, and Timbalada, not to mention Paul Simon and David Byrne.

From Religion to Film

Prior to Cinema Novo, Afro-Brazilian religion was not a frequent theme in Brazilian cinema. One 1950s light comedy, Maria Basaglia's *Macumba na Alta* (Macumba in High Society, 1958), uses Afro-Brazilian religion as a plot gimmick, much as Molière used Turkish culture in *Le Bourgeois Gentilhomme*. The opening credits combine terreiro music with high society imagery. The surprise effect of the title obviously depends on the notion that Afro-Brazilian religion is incompatible with upper-class life. The film is largely set among São Paulo socialites, including "the doctor," a charlatan who feigns knowledge of psychoanalysis, and Pinta, a white composer and samba singer. The "doctor" speaks about "transference" at the same party where an Afro-Brazilian dance group performs. The interesting point, which the film never explores, would be the similarities and differences between fashionable upper-class notions about mediums and transference and the Africanized mediumship of trance religions, a connection later explored in the 1980s film *A Prova de Fogo* (Trial by Fire). A comic *chanchada* from the same period as *Macumba na Alta*, *Samba em Brasília* (1960), also touched on the theme of the infiltration of Macumba into the realm of high society, whether carried by black characters or not. In the film, Heloísa Helena wants to fire her maid because the maid ruined her party by preparing inedible food. She changes her mind when the maid says she doesn't mind losing her job, since her "saint" (i.e., orixá) is powerful. The mistress exclaims: "So you know macumba!" Instead of firing her for this knowledge, the mistress contracts her services as a *macumbeira*, in hopes that the maid's *despachos* (hexes) will get her cited in the social columns as one of the "ten most elegant." Thus mistress and maid, both white, make common cause around African ritual practices. And, even more surprising, the despacho works and the mistress is indeed cited in the social columns.

The "Bahian Renaissance"

It was only in the 1960s that Brazilian cinema began to speak seriously of Afro-Brazilian religion, and even then with a highly ambiguous attitude. The Cinema Novo directors, speaking generally, either ignored Afro-Brazilian religion completely or regarded it as something to be tolerated or reformed by well-meaning secular leftists. These attitudes begin to change with the "Bahian Renaissance"—the cinematic rediscovery of the cultural riches of Salvador, Bahia, in the early 1960s, a movement that generated such films as Triguerinho Neto's *Bahia de Todos os Santos* (Bahia of All Saints, 1960), Anselmo Duarte's *O Pagador de Promessas* (The Given Word, 1962), Glauber Rocha's *Barravento* (The Turning Wind, 1962), and Roberto Pires's *A Grande Feira* (The Big Market, 1962). A city at once Portuguese, Bantu, and Gêge-Nagô, Bahia is the center of both Catholicism, with hundreds of churches, and Candomblé, with hundreds of terreiros. Yoruba religion is particularly strong there because the Yoruba arrived constantly during the latter decades of slavery, entering into an urbanized lifestyle in many ways reminiscent of that from which they came, and because Bahia maintained close cultural and commercial contact with West Africa (Risério 1993:111).

Bahia de Todos os Santos heralded the movement and formed a landmark film both for the history of Brazilian cinema and for the representation of black Brazilians. The film is set twenty years before the film's making, in the time of Vargas's Estado Novo (1937–1945), a regime which was repressive toward black political movements—it banned the Frente Negra—and toward black cultural practices like Candomblé. The film's protagonist, Tônio, is the man "in between"—between black mother and white father, between Candomblé and nightclub, between traditional communitarianism and urban individualism. Most interesting for our purposes here is the film's treatment of the police repression of Candomblé. When Vargas's soldiers find Mãe Sabina (Tônio's grandmother and a mãe de santo) without her religious license, which they know she as a priestess cannot get, they sweep the Candomblé statues off the altar, destroying everything they can find. When a soldier lectures her on proper social order—"You portray yourselves as victims, but you're all just parasites"—Mãe Sabina reacts with dignity. A scene of the Candomblé faithful scattering before the onslaught of the cossack-like mounted police has a poignancy reminiscent of the portrayal of police repression in Eisenstein's films. The Estado Novo officers are as cruelly impersonal, and as artistically depersonalized, as the cossacks in *Potemkin*. The actions of those who claim to represent law and order only sow disorder and panic. Mounted policemen lash into women and children simply because they practice a different religion. The Candomblé congregation reacts with dignity as the officers destroy their objects of worship in a barbarous display of Inquisition-like violence: "They think we have to live exactly like them," says Mãe Sabina, "they can wipe out everything, but they can't wipe out what we have in our souls." Glauber Rocha picked up on this theme in his review of the film: "Where is freedom of religion for blacks," he asked, "when police invade macumbas in Rio and blacks in Bahia are exploited as part of the industry of the picturesque?"[5]

O Pagador de Promessas

Two other "Bahian Renaissance" films, *O Pagador de Promessas* and *Barravento*, also focus on the issue of Afro-Brazilian religion. Based on the stage play by Dias Gomes, *O Pagador de Promessas* centers on the vow of its peasant protagonist Donkey Zé to bring a cross to the Church of Saint Barbara in gratitude for the miraculous cure of his donkey. The Catholic priest refuses him entrance because the vow was proffered in a Candomblé shrine. Zé does not give up, however; he remains on the church steps. Inexorably, the whole town becomes involved with his dilemma. Zé becomes the victim of a tragicomedy involving diverse people and institutions. *Cordel* poets write about him, while the press turns him into a political symbol, manipulating his naive words to portray him as a left-wing revolutionary. The official Church, meanwhile, denounces him as a heretic, while the common people project him as the incarnation of their hopes and dreams. Zé becomes a kind of Christ-figure; he sacrifices himself and resists temptation. The people of Bahia, largely black and mulatto, support his struggle. When he is killed by the police, they solemnly carry him into the church, borne on the very cross that he carried for such a long distance.

Aesthetically, *O Pagador de Promessas* represents what Glauber Rocha called "coconut milk in a Coca-Cola bottle," that is, the film packages Brazilian cultural practices like samba and *capoeira* in a form largely derivative of Hollywood. Like the films of Vera Cruz, *O Pagador de Promessas* uses conventional Hollywood devices, including classical framing, elaborate lighting, fluid cutting and camera movement, emotionally manipulative commentative music, and shot-reverse-shot for dialogue, all in the name of fluid well-conducted entertainment. But it is the presence of Afro-Brazilian religion that really gives the film its popular flavor. Anticlerical rather than anti-Christian, the film contrasts Zé's sincere Christ-like faith with the ossified hierarchical Christianity of the priest. Father Olavo "diabolizes" African religions; he sees them as the work of the devil. In the background of the film, of course, is the historical repression of African religions in Brazil, of Xangô in Alagoas in the 1920s and in Pernambuco in the 1930s, and of Candomblé throughout the first half of the twentieth century. On one level, then, the film satirizes official Catholicism, which led to the film being banned by the Church in both Italy and Spain. The "galego" barman and the cordel poet in the film both see the Church as chiefly interested in protecting its "business" against its more popular rivals. On another level, the film deploys elements of Christian allegory. Donkey Zé is associated with Christ; he rides into town on a donkey, he carries his cross, he is tested by temptation, and he is called a "new Christ" by the media. The Monseigneur, meanwhile, is associated with Pontius Pilate; "Bonitão" with Judas; Marli with Mary Magdalene.

Although Candomblé serves as the main motor of the plot in the sense that the entire film flows from the fact that Zé's vow was made in a terreiro, in another sense Candomblé is peripheral, in that the film deliberately never brings us into its world. In the opening sequence, Duarte already underlines Zé's separation from Candomblé by showing him alone, kneeling in a posture of Christian humility before a Catholic-style altar featuring an icon of Saint Barbara, while the collectivity sings and dances. The suggestion, from the outset, is that Zé "is really a Christian at heart," an impression reinforced by his repeated refusals of the mãe de santo's invitations to the terreiro. (The film too refuses the mãe de santo's invitations.) His discourse, as Ismail Xavier points out, is double and contradictory (1983:56–57). To Padre Olavo, he insists that Iansã and Saint Barbara are the same; but to the mãe de santo he argues the opposite; they aren't the same. In social terms, the film evokes a kind of microcosmic revolution by having the people take over a prestigious institution, yet the "revolution" consists, ultimately, only in gaining entrance to a more ecumenically tolerant Catholic Church, not in adherence to Candomblé, for example, nor in the inauguration of a revolutionary alternative. (The film was made in the liberal period of Pope John XXIII and the Ecumenical Council.) Although it portrays the official Church as authoritarian, formalistic, and intolerant, the film is, in the end, integrationist. Zé catalyzes a larger struggle whose goals are ultimately apolitical. His sacrifices energize the masses who come to legitimate a Catholic vow which happened to be made in a terreiro. Thus the real choice presented is not between Catholicism and Candomblé, or even between Catholicism and revolution, but rather between a dogmatic Catholicism and a humane and ecumenical Catholicism.

Barravento

The style of Glauber Rocha's *Barravento* is completely antithetical to that of *O Pagador de Promessas*. While *O Pagador de Promessas* featured well-known actors from theater, television, and film, *Barravento* featured mainly nonprofessional or beginning actors. If *O Pagador de Promessas* was a quasi-industrial production, *Barravento* was artisanal, improvised, collaborative, using minimal equipment. If *O Pagador de Promessas* is full of "pretty effects," *Barravento* deliberately eschewed picturesqueness, with Rocha asking Tony Rabatony, his director of photography, to avoid all aestheticism. While *O Pagador de Promessas* clarifies spatial and temporal relations at all times, *Barravento* is purposely ambiguous about such issues. If the structure of *O Pagador de Promessas* is unified, with clear causality—everything revolves around the vow and its realization—*Barravento* is characterized by rupture and discontinuity. If the style of *O Pagador de Promessas* is Hollywoodean, redundant, conventional, that of *Barravento* is elliptical, obscure, discontinuous. While *O Pagador de Promessas* uses conventional European-style commentative music guiding our feelings at every turn, *Barravento* uses Afro-Brazilian music—ritual chants, work songs, sambas, percussion—as a structuring device.

If *O Pagador de Promessas* implicitly condemns Candomblé from the point of view of a renovated Catholicism, *Barravento* would seem to critique Candomblé from the standpoint of historical materialism. But any evaluation of the film's ideological stance must take into account the film's complex and conflictual production history. The first script was by Luis Paulino dos Santos, a Bahian whose background was largely in documentary filmmaking. Brought up in Pelourinho, the traditional black quarters of the center of Salvador, dos Santos's family was intimately linked to Candomblé. The script was relatively apolitical and completely sympathetic to the religion, but the film's producer, Rex Schindler, asked for a more critical attitude. For diverse reasons, Luis Paulino dos Santos left the film and was replaced by Rocha, then twenty-one years old,[6] who gave the following version of the changes he made in the script: "I reorganized black mythology according to the dialectics of religion/economy. Religion as the opium of the people. Down with the Father! Long live human beings fishing with nets. Down with prayers! Down with mysticism!" (Rocha 1981:307). Rocha's stated goal in *Barravento* was to show that "underneath the forms of exoticism and decorative beauty of Afro-Brazilian mysticism there dwells a hungry, illiterate, nostalgic and enslaved race" (1981:13).

Barravento does show the oppression inflicted on poor black fishermen, and apparently critiques Candomblé as a distraction from this oppression. The protagonist Firmino (Antônio Pitanga), just back from the city, tells his brothers and sisters to forsake religion and to organize against oppression. In the village, the fishermen rent a net from an absentee capitalist; Candomblé seems to legitimate the system in that the fishing master (*mestre*) negotiates with the net's owner, who takes the lion's share of the profits while the fishermen remain poor. Although the mestre complains that the fishermen are going hungry, he does not push his demands with sufficient energy.[7] Meanwhile, Firmino confronts Aruã, a young man protected by Iemanjá destined to inherit the mestre's role. Firmino, the self-proclaimed agnostic, paradoxically tries to cast a despacho (hex) against Aruã, but it is ineffective. Then Firmino cuts the net as a provocation. But when the boss comes to take back the damaged net, the fishermen simply return to the old life-threatening days of the *jangadas*. Firmino decides to demystify Aruã once and for all by having his girlfriend Cota seduce him. Parallel montage juxtaposes the stages in the ritual preparation of Aruã's girlfriend Naína, a shy white girl frightened by her own mediumistic powers, with the story of Cota's seduction of Aruã. The initiatory blood ritual is made to alternate with the sexual initiation at the beach, while both series of images are underlined by Candomblé drumming. The next day, a *barravento* comes up, leading to the mysterious deaths of Naína's stepfather and of Cota herself. Firmino and Aruã fight via capoeira, but at the end of the fight Firmino tells the community to follow Aruã as the new leader. The flame of political leadership passes from Firmino to Aruã. Firmino disappears from the scene as magically as he first came, while Aruã plans to go to the city, buy a net, and come back so the community will not be so exploited.

Barravento's prefatory intertitles offer a Marxist perspective on religion as a kind of "opium of the people" which prevents the fishermen from mobilizing for change:

> The seacoast of Bahia is the home of black fishermen whose ancestors came from Africa as slaves. There they still worship the African gods and are dominated by a tragic and fatalistic mysticism. They accept misery, illiteracy, and exploitation with the passivity typical of those who await the coming of the Kingdom of God.

> Iemanjá is the queen of the waters, the lady of the sea who loves, protects, and punishes the fishermen. The barravento is the moment of violence, the moment when land and sea are transformed; when love, life, and the social world undergo sudden exchanges.

The preface, then, clearly denounces Candomblé as an obstacle to social progress.[8] It arbitrarily links Candomblé to the idea of fatalism and passivity, while the phrase "still worship" implies that the people will some day abandon their obsolescent and historically condemned affection for the gods and inscribe themselves within the telos of modernity. The prefatory titles give voice, in short, to a Eurocentric vision of African religions.

The impression created by the preface is further reinforced not only by Rocha's own statements about his intentions, but also by much of

Firmino's dialogue. Firmino repeatedly exhorts the fishermen to leave religion and organize to fight the system. Yet in other ways the film affirms the power and beauty of Candomblé. This ambiguity doubtless derives partially from the ambivalences of the director himself as a white Protestant, yet who as a Bahian inevitably imbibed the ambient respect for Afro-Brazilian religiosity. The ambiguity also derives from the film's conflictual production history and the fact that the original director, who had partial African ancestry (a black grandfather), was more sympathetic to Candomblé than the white Marxist Rocha. To what extent, then, does this ambiguous sympathy for Candomblé derive from Rocha's own attitudes and to what extent does it represent the "trace" of the earlier work by Luis Paulino dos Santos? A comparison of the completed film and the original script suggests that Rocha politicized the script by "framing" it with a Marxist critique of religion and by introducing the "revolutionary" character Firmino, but without completely discarding the core feeling of the original.

The opening intertitles would seem to close off ambiguities and the "undecidables" of interpretation, and most critics have followed the intertitles' lead in seeing the film as a critique of Candomblé. If we go by the logic of "trust the tale, not the teller," however, we can see that the surface condemnation of Candomblé is contradicted by a number of the film's epidermic characteristics as well as by its deep structural features. First, the film has the "feel" of authenticity, owing to the care taken to respect the ceremonies themselves; the woman (Dona Hilda) who plays the Candomblé priestess, for example, was in fact an important figure in the Gantois terreiro. Second, although Firmino speaks a racially inflected materialist discourse—"You're just working to fill white men's bellies! . . . Millions of blacks are suffering in the world"—his actions imply that he also believes in the religion. Firmino is a liminal, borderline character sharing many characteristics with Exu; he too is a messenger between two worlds; he too is associated with alcoholic drink, and with "vital strength, with the libido and the dynamic principle of individuation."[9] Firmino perfectly fits Abdias do Nascimento's definition of Exu as "the god of dialectical contradiction."[10] At diverse points, Firmino is musically and rhythmically associated with Exu. His spying at Cota's seduction of Aruã, for example, coincides with a chant of exaltation to Exu. We are led to wonder if Firmino proposes the seduction of Aruã in order to demystify him in the eyes of the community or because he himself believes that Aruã's defloration will destroy Aruã's charismatic power:

the question is left open. Nor can we assume that simply because Firmino verbally criticizes the alienating role of Candomblé that he is therefore speaking for the author, although Xavier speaks of a kind of "homology" between the convulsive behavior of the character and the eruptive, discontinuous style of the film itself.[11] In fact, like most Rocha protagonists, Firmino is driven by contradictions. His words mingle the discourses of the civil rights movement, of Brazilian populism, and of Marxist dialectics. He is a catalyst for mobilization, yet many of his individual decisions backfire. Like the barravento itself, he appears suddenly and brings turmoil in his wake. He cuts the net as a provocation, but the fishermen merely return to the old, dangerous ways.

The film's mise-en-scène, furthermore, as Xavier points out, underlines Firmino's isolation from the community. His oratorical style, his direct address to the camera, even his white suit, seem out of place. When he harangues the fisherman, the editing places him and his interlocutors in completely different spaces. Although the community is socially oppressed, it is also the locus of art, spirituality, and solidarity. The depiction of the work of the *puxada de rede* (pulling in the net) evokes a Utopian world where work is transformed into rhythmic, musical play. The film sacralizes communal labor, finding it expressive of cosmic harmony, and thus conforms to a very African notion of collective labor, evoking a world where art, religion, and everyday life are vitally interwoven, even under conditions of oppression. The Candomblé music, furthermore, pervades the entire space of the community. The music, the lyrics of which thank Iemanjá for a good catch, facilitates the work and links it to the world of the sacred, in a blurring of the material world of the *aiyê* and the spiritual world of *òrun*. While the film denounces poverty, then, it also portrays a communal style of life in some ways more attractive than that which Firmino proposes.

Moreover, *Barravento* offers a celebration, affectionate and exalted, of Candomblé's sensuous mise-en-scène; the imagistic core of the film is thus supportive of the religion. While excoriating religious alienation, it paints a beautiful picture of the religiously oriented life. The camera movements, the sound, the drums highlight the beauty of the rituals— the *iyalorixás* wielding her *adja* over the trembling body of Naína in trance; the iaô (initiates) with their shaved heads; the mãe de santo summoning Ifa by throwing cowrie shells (*búzios*) on a lace cloth on the ground. Rather than the conventional portrayals that showed such religious practices as a meaningless frenzy, Rocha presents a religion that is dignified, complexly codified, and efficacious for its practitioners. *Barravento* is thus open equally to a spiritualist or a materialist reading. The despacho against Aruã as Iemanjá's protected son can be seen as ineffective either because Candomblé has no worldly efficacity, or because Firmino does not perform the ceremony correctly; the fishermen die because Aruã, who is supposed to remain virgin, has been profaned through Firmino's machinations, or they die of natural causes. The film's title already evokes some of these ambiguities since it can refer literally to a tropical storm and figuratively to revolution, but it can also refer to a specific moment in the Candomblé ritual, the moment just before the medium goes into trance. Thus the film itself goes in and out of trance. It performs a distanced, exotopic analysis of the social oppression of a community; at the same time it incorporates into its own structure the religious vision of that community.

If Rocha at the time of the film's making took a distant, critical attitude toward Candomblé, in subsequent years he moved toward a more approving and identificatory attitude. In a statement made in 1971 in New York, Rocha's language of magic links African spirituality to artistic revolution, while completely inverting the Eurocentric view of African religion as "witchcraft":

> Revolutionary art should constitute a kind of magic which can enchant people to the point that they can no longer live in this absurd reality. Borges, going beyond this reality, wrote the most liberatory irrealities of our time. His esthetic is that of dream. For me, his work provides a spiritual illumination which helps dilate my Afro-Indian sensibility in the direction of the original myths of my race. This race, poor and apparently without a future, elaborates in mysticism its moment of freedom. The Afro-Indian combats the colonizing mysticism of Catholicism, which is nothing more than the witchcraft of repression and the moral redemption of the rich. (Rocha 1981:111)

Barravento made a dramatic rupture with the racial conventions of casting and plotting within Brazilian cinema, in that Afro-Brazilians dominate the film, while the Euro-Brazilians are "visitors" like Naína, or oppressors like the owner of the net, and in that its very structure is impregnated by Afro-religious values. Much as writers like Alejo Carpentier were inspired by African religion to create "lo real maravilloso," *Barravento* creates a "magic realist" world where characters can call on the orixás to conjure up a storm. Rather than simply praise or condemn

Candomblé, the film sees religion in a Jamesonian manner as "a master code" in which competing discourses fight it out.

Slow Fade to Afro: The 1970s

The films of the 1970s reveal a dramatic transformation in the attitude of Euro-Brazilian directors toward Afro-Brazilian culture. Whereas 1960s Cinema Novo films tended to ignore or question the legitimacy of Afro-Brazilian culture, many of the films of the 1970s make that culture the source of all that is most vital in Brazilian life. Nelson Pereira dos Santos's *O Amuleto de Ogum* (Amulet of Ogum, 1974) celebrates the syncretic Afro-Brazilian religion called Umbanda. Founded in the late 1920s, Umbanda has a following estimated at between 20 and 30 million. São Paulo reportedly had 90,000 Umbanda temples, Rio 60,000 ("O Boom Umbandista").[12] Umbanda combines African elements—the orixás, the centrality of spirit-possession (including the Bantu traditions of receiving spirits of the dead)—with Catholicism, Kaballa, indigenous symbology, and the spiritism of Alain Kardec. The term Umbanda refers to a wide spectrum of practices, from those which emphasize Kardecist spiritism, to those which emphasize the historical links to African religions. The color breakdown in Umbanda varies from group to group, but even when whites are in the majority, Africa, in Roger Bastide's phrase, "still casts its great black shadow over umbanda." Umbanda is often said to be *the* Brazilian religion in that it incorporates cultural elements from the major groups constitutive of Brazilian identity. At the same time, Umbanda, like every religion, forms a "master code in which competing discourses fight it out." Some *umbandistas* tend to de-Africanize the religion, while others try to re-Africanize it. Umbanda is above all an open process, in which entities are constantly "reinvoiced." Umbanda cosmology has recently incorporated Zumbi, the leader of the maroon community of Palmares, as spiritual mentor for the *pretos velhos* (old blacks) and some foresee a similar incorporation for Anastácia, the popular black female figure popularly credited with putting an end to slavery.

In *O Amuleto de Ogum*, Dos Santos strives to be "popular" not only in his choice of subject matter but also in perspective, discarding all vestiges of superiority and wholeheartedly affirming the values of the umbandista audience to whom the film hopes to appeal. *O Amuleto de Ogum* introduces a frame-story, in the style of popular ballads, in which the narrator-singer himself, named Firmino (perhaps after the black protagonist of *Barravento*), introduces, concludes, intervenes, and comments on the action. As the blind singer, played by Jards Macalé, walks down the street with a guitar slung over his shoulder, he is jumped by three street hoods, who force him to sing. After the frame-song, the singer's tale recounts the trajectory of Gabriel (played by Nelson's son Ney Sant'ana), a young Northeasterner whose body has been magically "closed"—made invulnerable to bullets—by an umbandista at his mother's request. Ten years later, protected by Ogum's amulet, Gabriel moves to Caxias, a notoriously lawless Rio *subúrbio* known for its vigilante violence, for its *bicheiros* (bookies), and for its vibrant popular culture. In Caxias, Gabriel joins the town's underworld, ultimately becoming a gunman in the service of his uncle Severiano (Jofre Soares), who is criminal head of a numbers racket. When the criminal gang discovers Gabriel's closed body during a gun battle, Gabriel becomes extremely famous. He starts to enjoy himself, spending long hours in Madame Moustache's nightclub. But he also annoys Severiano by his refusal to kill gratuitously, and especially by taking up with Severiano's lover Eneida (Anecy Rocha).

Severiano begins to set traps for Gabriel. While buying him sports cars and fancy clothes, he also tricks him into killing the president of the Red Cross. When Severiano discovers Gabriel and Eneida together, the couple is obliged to disappear. Subsequently, Gabriel leads a rival group against Severiano, a conflict that turns Caxias into a war zone. Severiano kills all of Gabriel's companions one by one, but reserves a secret weapon for Gabriel—the despachos of Gogo, a mercenary *pai de santo*—who tries to get at the alcohol-loving Gabriel's liver. One night, Gabriel's enemies find him drunk, weigh him down with stones, and throw him into the sea. Nearby, however, Pai Erlei, an Umbanda priest, is paying homage to Iemanjá. Pai Erlei rescues Gabriel, recognizes his amulet, and brings him to the terreiro, where he is initiated into Umbanda.

In revenge, Severiano has Pai Erlei sequestered, then tries to buy him off by offering him money in exchange for making Gabriel vulnerable. Pai Erlei refuses and defends the principles of Umbanda. Then Severiano pays Eneida to find Gabriel; she finds him at an Umbanda children's festival. After she and Gabriel make up, Gabriel tells Eneida the secret of the amulet, that his mother had offered her own life as a guarantee for his closed body. When Eneida passes on this information to Severiano, the latter orders his thugs to kill Gabriel's mother. In a bloody confrontation, Gabriel and Severiano kill each other, but Gabriel falls into Severiano's swimming pool, just as Gabriel's mother arrives at the Rio bus station. (Severiano's thugs had killed Gabriel's mother's maid by mistake.) Gabriel is magically resurrected, not in the pool, but in a boat at sea, with six-guns blazing as the frame-story ends. The blind singer finishes his story, but the bandits don't like its conclusions. They decide to kill him, but discover that he too has a closed body. If they don't like his story, Firmino tells the bandits, then they "can go to hell."

The character Gabriel is partially based on a real-life prototype from Caxias (Tenório Cavalcânti), a local Robin Hood style mobster/ politician who became a popular hero with a reputation for having a closed body. In the film version, Nelson retains the idea of a popular criminal with a closed body, but he gives the figure a religious base in Umbanda. (The prototype, Tenório Cavalcânti, complained that Nelson had turned him into a mystic.) The film's Gabriel is naive and manipulable. He begins to grow only when he allies himself with Pai Erlei. Gabriel learns the mysteries of Umbanda, discovers his saint Ogum Beiramar (Ogum by the Sea), and having his offering to Iemanjá accepted, grows in stature and earns the right to represent the people. In his final incarnation, he has become the warrior Ogum.

O Amuleto de Ogum is not just *about* Umbanda; it is impregnated with the values of Umbanda. The narrative itself, as the director himself pointed out, is structured by three Umbanda cycles.[13] The first concerns the ceremony of closing the body and Gabriel's protection by Ogum. The second concerns the *pomba-gira*, an Umbanda figure representing woman at her most capricious, here in the form of Eneida as Gabriel's temptress. The third cycle belongs to Exu. Here Severiano deploys Umbanda against Gabriel, asking Exu to make Gabriel an alcoholic. When Severino visits Pai Erlei, he is possessed by Exu, throws himself on the ground, screams and giggles, and starts aggressing himself. Pai Erlei receives a preto velho and recommends that Severiano redeem himself by performing a *trabalho* or duty. At another point, Severiano talks like an astonished child. He at first seems quite disturbed for having shown vulnerability, for allowing the religion to "soften" him. Brief as this moment is, it is hard to imagine another like it when one thinks of cinematic criminals. The film is also bathed in the purifying presence of water. Pai Erlei's terreiro is near a waterfall. Gabriel falls into Severiano's pool and emerges from the sea, just as he makes an offering to Iemanjá, goddess of the sea.

Although not a believer, Nelson shows respect for Umbanda as a religion, a respect reflected even in his methods of filming. A pai de santo, José de Carvalho, head of the "Xangô Spirit Tent," was consulted on all religious questions. One of the actors, Zé Indio, also an adept of Umbanda, kept a protective eye on the filming process. In the case of the Cosme and Damião feast, the pai de santo had to authorize the filming of the feast out of season. Many of the participants were believers. Pai Erlei is a real *babalaô*; the dancers celebrating Iemanjá are umbandistas. Furthermore, *O Amuleto de Ogum* virtually *requires* the spectator to become an umbandista, at least for the duration of the film, if only to understand the narrated events. The film simply assumes umbandista values, without explaining them to the uninitiated. A Catholic audience, the director points out, need only see a priest raising the host to know a mass is being celebrated. An umbandista audience, similarly, easily recognizes the ceremony which "closes" the protagonist's body, recognizes his protection by Ogum, the warrior divinity and symbol, in Brazil, of the struggle for social justice. It recognizes Gabriel's amulet as being made of steel—since Ogum is god of metals—and recognizes the sword evoking Ogum and the trident evoking Exu. When Gabriel is shot but does not die, the audience recognizes the song "Ogum é de lei" (Ogum Is the Law) and the image of Saint George to be seen behind Gabriel. The audience recognizes the hoarse voice of the preto velho (the old hunched slave who possesses mediums of all colors) and the provocative manners of the pomba-gira. At the same time, the film does not idealize Umbanda; one Umbanda priest in the film works for popular liberation; the other is a greedy charlatan and opportunist.[14]

Afro-Brazilian religions interweave the world of aiyê and òrun together; the sacred penetrates the quotidian. The symbiology of the orixás, for example, pervades everyday life, in that what one eats, what one wears, encode references to the orixás. Everyone knows that Ogum likes beer and that the Exus like rum. The Afro-informed audience knows also the family relations between the orixás, that Ogum is Exu's brother, that both are sons of Iemanjá, and that the pomba-gira is Exu's wife, much as the audience at a Greek tragedy would know that Zeus is the son of Chronos. Iberê Cavalcânti's *A Força de Xangô* (The Force of Xangô, 1979) assumes this kind of popular knowledge to construct a plot which interfaces the orixás and their protégés in the everyday world. The protagonist Tonho (Geraldo Rosa), son of Xangô, is an inveterate drinker, capoeirista, and womanizer who falls in love with Zulmira (Ivone Lara), daughter of Iansã, on Wednesday of Carnival, a day dedicated to both Iansã and Xangô. Tonho promises to be forever faithful and take care of their innumerable children. But time passes, Tonho's enthusiasm wanes, Zulmira ages and gets fat, and Tonho regresses to his earlier ways. Enraged, Zulmira invokes Exu, and on the third Friday of the seventh month, a blond gypsy Iaba (Elka Maravilha) arrives on a boat from Itaparica, along with her assistant Beicinho (Grande Otelo) and a loquacious parrot. Tonho falls in love with this transparent embodiment of a spiritual entity. The former layabout begins to work tirelessly to buy her clothes and jewels, ultimately losing all his friends and falling into a sad, lonely life. Then he meets Rosinha de Oxum, as sweet and understanding as Iaba is capricious. He goes to a terreiro for an exorcism, since what Exu gives, Exu can also take away. Xangô comes to the rescue and teaches him how to escape from Iaba's clutches.

A Força de Xangô is based on a story by Carybé about Xangô and his three wives: Iansã, Oba, and Oxum. The characters in the film are inseparable from their protective saints. They embody their myth, and the myth, in turn, catalyzes their behavior. Even their clothes reflect their links to the orixás: the red of Xangô and Iansã, the yellow of Oba and Oxum, the black of Exu. While the basic premise is brilliant—few films have used Afro-Brazilian religion to emplot films—and although the director's goal was to thoroughly mingle reality and dream, the orixás and the characters, the film is not always successful in this goal. The opening sequence, a stylized dance to Xangô complete with Xangô's ax, gives way to banal magic-less realism, while the acting leaves much to be desired. Elke Maravilha overacts as a pomba-gira, diabolizing the role in a way alien to the religion, and there is a tension between the Bahian locale and the Carioca speech dominant among the actors.

A year after A Força de Xangô was released, another film about Umbanda was released: Marco Altberg's Prova de Fogo (Trial by Fire, 1980). The film's source is an autobiographical book by Nívio Ramos Sales (renamed Mauro in the film and played by Pedro Paulo Rangel), a Carioca journalist and Umbanda priest who leaves the Northeast for Rio. As a child, Mauro is precociously spiritual, demonstrating rare sensibility and intuition. On the advice of his friend Vanda, he visits an Umbanda center where he confirms his vocation as a medium. Becoming completely dedicated to the life of the terreiro, he discovers that he can "incorporate" very different orixás, for example the virile Boiadeiro and the very feminine Ciganinha, who wears women's clothing and brightly colored skirts. A more experienced pai de santo, João, takes charge of the terreiro and assigns a woman, Sandra, as *mãe pequena*. While João is in love with Sandra, Sandra is more interested in Mauro, especially when he is possessed by the masculine *boiadeiro*. Parallel to his religious activities, Mauro works in a bank and studies business administration. In the end he returns to his native Alagoas where he becomes a well-reputed pai de santo, and, alongside his wife and son, follows his spiritual guide: the *ciganinha*.

Unlike *O Amuleto de Ogum*, *Prova de Fogo* does not mix religiosity with violence and crime; rather, it concentrates on the religious vocation per se. Indeed, most of the scenes are set in the terreiro. Umbanda in the film is portrayed as an amalgam of religion, psychoanalysis, and art—religion because it involves the sacred and trance, psychoanalysis because it fosters the personal growth of "clients," and art because it involves performance and staging. The film illustrates the conceptualization of Umbanda as the "poor man's couch," the popular view that Umbanda is often effective where psychoanalysis or conventional therapy fail.[15] In *Prova de Fogo*, Umbanda is pragmatic, quotidian; it is neither exotic nor purely spiritual. It is more couch than altar, less about African traditions, although they are present, than about individual cure.

Despite its "magical" side, *Prova de Fogo* is based on phenomena either lived by Nívio Ramos Sales or observed by Marco Altberg during his pre-production research. Altberg himself witnessed the gender-bending whereby men can be possessed by female entities and vice versa. In a form of religious cross-dressing, Mauro wears feminine clothes, while his wife encourages him and speaks to the female entity as if it were her friend and neighbor. Nor does the film shy away from the issue of homosexuality. At one point the ciganinha advises a homosexual "client" to place candy in his lover's anus and then give it to him to eat. The source biography describes a time in the history of Candomblé when men were just beginning to head Candomblé terreiros, and when "it was expected that the men would be gay; if they were not, there was general disappointment" (Sales 1981:13). The film portrays Umbanda as nurturing of bisexuality and the feminine in men and the masculine in women. African-derived religions, speaking more generally, often display a high tolerance for ambiguities of all kinds, whether sexual, intellectual, or spiritual. One orixá, according to the author of the source text, spends half of the year as a woman and half as a man. Mauro is possessed at first by a masculine entity, but as he grows within Umbanda he becomes more open to the side represented by the ciganinha, and learns how to mold his own sensibility with her help. *Prova de Fogo* also portrays the capacity of many Brazilians to live simultaneously in two socio-ideological worlds, two mental universes. Mauro is involved with the spiritual in one of his lives, but he studies the quintessentially modern subject of administration in the other, showing critical distance toward both worlds.

Conclusion: Cultural Counterpoint as Aesthetic Resource

In some Brazilian films, cultural counterpoint involving Afro-Brazilian religion becomes an absolutely crucial thematic and aesthetic resource, at once a theme and a formal strategy. *O Pagador de Promessas* evokes the conflicting values of Catholicism and Candomblé through the manipulation of cultural symbols, setting in motion a cultural battle, for example, between *berimbau* (an African instrument consisting of a long bow, gourd, and string) and church bell, thus synecdochically encapsulating a larger religious and political struggle. Dos Santos's *Tenda dos Milagres* (Tent of Miracles, 1977) counterposes Catholicism and Candomblé as part of the larger conflict between Bahia's white elite and its subjugated mestizos, between ruling-class science and Afro-inflected popular culture. Brazilian cinema often does more than merely reflect a preexisting syncretism; it actively syncretizes, counterpointing cultural forces in non-literal ways. Rocha's *Terra em Transe* (Land in Anguish, 1967) uses Candomblé to evoke the trance of the title, while inverting its conventional associations to suggest that the truly superstitious, those "in trance," are not the impoverished black practitioners of Afro-religions but rather the mystical power-mongers of the white political elite.

What is interesting in aesthetic terms is the link between African religions and "magic realism." In their attempts to forge a liberatory film language, Brazilian artists, like African artists, have drawn on the most traditional elements of their cultures, elements less "pre-modern" (a term that embeds modernity as telos) than "para-modern," elements such as popular religion and ritual magic. The performing arts are at the very center of African spirit religions. Without dance and song and spectacle, they do not exist. If the drums don't play, the gods don't come. Thus there is a kind of affinity between African religion and the cinema as "performing arts," just as there is an affinity between religious magic and the "magic" of montage. In African films such as *Yeelen* (1987), *Jitt* (1992), and *Kasarmu Ce* (This Land Is Ours, 1991), and in Brazilian films like *Macunaíma* (1969) and *O Amuleto de Ogum*, magical spirits become an aesthetic resource, a means for breaking away, often in comical ways, from the linear, cause-and-effect conventions of Aristotelian narrative poetics, a way of defying the "gravity," in both senses of that word, of chronological time and literal space. The values of African religious culture inform not only Nigerian cinema but also a good deal of Brazilian cinema. Nigerian director Ola Balogun's *A Deusa Negra* (The Black Goddess, 1978), the first Brazilian-Nigerian co-production, treats the historically close links between Nigeria and Brazil. A kind of *Roots* in reverse, the film concerns Babatunde (Zózimo Bulbul), a Nigerian who goes to Brazil to look for long-lost relatives and find out more about Oluyole (Jorge Coutinho), an enslaved ancestor brought to Brazil. At a Candomblé session, he interrogates a priestess (Lea Garcia) about his mission. He meets Elisa (Sônia Santos), who is possessed by Iemanjá, whose statue Babatunde carries. He discovers that Elisa is the same person as Amanda, with whom Oluyole had fallen in love centuries before. Elisa suggests that Babatunde go to Vila Esmeralda, in Bahia; he invites her to accompany him. In Bahia, he gives his Iemanjá statue to a terreiro and discovers that Elisa is the relative whom he was seeking all the time. In a sense an African film that happens to have been made in Brazil, *A Deusa Negra* continues the Yoruba cultural strain already marking Balogun's earlier films. *A Deusa Negra* synthesizes the modern and the traditional through an Afro-magical Egúngún aesthetic, that is, an aesthetic that invokes the spirits of the ancestors as embodiments of a deep sense of personal and collective history.[16] The film's transgenerational approach mingles the past (slavery, the quilombos) and the present. The question of cinematic "magic" illustrates the pitfalls of imposing a linear narrative of cultural "progress" in the manner of "development" theory, which sees people in traditional societies as mired in an inert preliterate past, incapable of change and agency. In the arts, such films suggest, the aesthetic reinvoicing of tradition can serve purposes of *collective* agency in the present.

NOTES

1. For a critique of Eurocentric language concerning African religions, see Mbiti (1969). The term "African religions" is on one level a misnomer, since virtually all religions—Christianity, Judaism, Hinduism, Islam—are represented in Africa.

2. For a brilliant analysis of the confrontation between Catholicism and Tupi-Guarani religion, see Bosi (1992).

3. A Bahian popular saying has it that a normal mother "has" children but a mother of the saints "makes" children, that is, the children of the saints. See Risério (1993:97).

4. For a discussion of homosexuality within Candomblé, see Matory (1988).

5. The review was published in the Salvador newspaper *Diário de Notícias* and is held in the files of Rio de Janeiro's cinemateque (File 188).

6. José Gatti (1987) offers a thorough account of the production process of *Barravento*. He takes up the same issues in his doctoral dissertation (1995).

7. Actor Antônio Pitanga, who plays Firmino in the film, recalls that the fishermen were so worried about the real-life boss–net owner that they were careful not to pronounce any rebellious words from the script when he was nearby (Gatti 1995:29).

8. The promotional literature for the film had a slightly different emphasis, placing less stress on the alienating role of religion and more on the slave-like conditions in which the fishermen live. The notes begin, "After the abolition of slavery, black Brazilians still remain in a certain sense slaves."

9. See Gatti (1995). See also Juana Elbein dos Santos (1986).

10. Abdias do Nascimento offers this definition in an interview in Raquel Gerber's documentary *Ori* (1989).

11. For an excellent analysis of *Barravento*, see Xavier (1983).

12. See "O Boom Umbandista" (1981). Diana DeG. Brown (1994:xvi) gives somewhat lower estimates.

13. See Nelson Pereira dos Santos (1975).

14. When I was teaching on a Fulbright Fellowship at Federal University in Niterói, one of my students, André Luiz Sampaio, presented a paper (and a videotape) which consisted of an Umbanda pai de santo (Ogum Jessi Jessi Patecuri) interpreting specific sequences from *O Amuleto de Ogum*. Such an exercise reveals that Umbanda is a hermeneutic system like any other.

15. One often hears in Brazil of people with problems who tried psychoanalysis or conventional therapy to no avail, but who resolved their problems through Umbanda.

16. Egúngún, as practiced in Brazil, calls up representations of male ancestors. It was founded, interestingly, as a response to the preponderant role of

women in Candomblé. For a documentary presentation of Egúngún, see the Carlos Brajsblat film titled, simply, *Egungun*.

REFERENCES

Barber, Karin. 1984. "Yoruba Oriki and Deconstructive Criticism." *Research in African Literature* 15:4 (Winter).

Bastide, Roger. 1978. *The African Religions of Brazil: Toward a Sociology of the Interpenetration of Civilizations*. Tr. Helen Sebba. Baltimore: Johns Hopkins University Press.

"O Boom Umbandista." 1981. *Veja* (January 7), pp. 40–41.

Bosi, Alfredo. 1992. *Dialética da colonização*. São Paulo: Companhia das Letras.

Brown, Diana DeG. 1994. *Umbanda: Religion and Politics in Urban Brazil*. New York: Columbia University Press.

Gates, Jr., Henry Louis. 1988. *The Signifying Monkey*. New York: Oxford.

Gatti, José. 1987. *Barravento: A estréia de Glauber*. Florianópolis: Editora da Universidade Federal de Santa Catarina.

_____. 1995. "Dialogism and Syncretism in the Films of Glauber Rocha." Ph.D. dissertation, New York University.

Jameson, Fredric. 1981. *The Political Unconscious: Narrative as a Socially Symbolic Act*. Ithaca: Cornell University Press.

Matory, J. Lorand. 1988. "Homens montados: homosexualidade e simbolismo da possessão nas religiões afro-brasileiras." In João José Reis, ed., *Escravidão e invenção da liberdade*. São Paulo: Brasiliense.

Mbiti, John S. 1969. *African Religions and Philosophy*. Oxford: Heinemann.

Risério, Antônio. 1993. *Caymmi: uma utopia de lugar*. São Paulo: Perspectiva.

Rocha, Glauber. 1981. *Revolução do Cinema Novo*. Rio de Janeiro: Alhambra/ Embrafilme.

Sales, Nívio Ramos. 1981. *A prova de fogo*. Rio de Janeiro: Esquina.

Santos, Juana Elbein dos. 1986. *Os nagô e a morte*. Petrópolis: Vozes.

Santos, Nelson Pereira dos. 1975. "O cinema e a cultura popular." *Jornal do Brasil* (February 23).

Sodré, Muniz. 1989. *Cultura negra e ecologia*. Rio de Janeiro: CIEC.

Walker, Sheila. 1975. "Spirit Religions in Brazil and the United States." *Black Scholar* 8 (September).

Xavier, Ismail. 1983. *Sertão/mar: Glauber Rocha e a estética da fome*. São Paulo: Brasiliense.

18 The Drama of Modernity: Color and Symbolic Exclusion in the Brazilian *Telenovela*

DENISE FERREIRA DA SILVA

> If you had stayed in your place none of this
> would have happened! You had no right to get
> involved with my son! We try to be liberal, I am
> liberal! I have tried all my life to be liberal, and
> I treat you people well! But trying to mix your
> blood with mine is too much, it had to turn
> out like this! I don't have a son anymore. But I
> will have one consolation for the rest of my life!
> Black blood will never flow in the veins of a
> Fraga Dantas!
> —Alfredo, Cláudio's father, shortly
> before the accident. *Corpo-a-Corpo*,
> episode 153, scene 23

Day after day *telenovelas* (soap operas) show chapters in the lives of characters who suffer in their search for "true love." Like the first spectators of *Romeo and Juliet*, the telenovela public follows couples in their attempts to overcome the barriers put in their way by (real or symbolic) modern Capulletos and Montecchios. This is only possible because, like Shakespeare, telenovela authors write their stories of impossible love at a given historical moment, and through the lovers' drama they describe modern Brazilian society's beliefs and values. In this essay I examine the hierarchical and exclusionary beliefs of Brazilian racial culture which form the foundation of the idea of modernity transmitted by the telenovela.

The two main theses of Brazilian racial culture, "whitening" and "racial democracy," provide the bases for Brazil's predominant "myth of modernization." Both propose that the modernization of Brazilian

339

society is possible only through the exclusion (or dilution) of the black component of the population. For whitening theorists this represented a project for a more or less distant future, while for Gilberto Freyre, in contrast, it was the primary factor in the formation of the Brazilian nation in the past. In both cases, however, the link between modernization and whitening is fundamental.

The ideas of this "nationalist" phase of Brazilian racial thought were not the only ones to enter the discourse of the average Brazilian. The conclusions of studies undertaken by the "Paulista school" were also incorporated into the repertoire of Brazilian racial culture. Although critical of the idea of racial democracy, the studies produced under the UNESCO project also suggested a link between modernization and race. For these authors, however, the scheme is inverted. Florestan Fernandes (1978), for example, suggests that the development of capitalist forms of production would lead to the destruction of the archaic elements inherited from slavery which were responsible for the subordinate position of the black population.

In truth, after the 1950s, the idea of "racial democracy," combined with São Paulo's economic explanation, was consolidated as the primary belief of Brazilian racial culture. An example of this combination is the view that the subordination of blacks had purely economic causes and had nothing to do with racial discrimination. In the period after the 1950s both blacks, as a specific social group, and the racial question itself are practically absent from representations of Brazilian modernity. In this essay, I seek to reinscribe racial thematics in discussions of modern Brazilian society.

In the discourse on Brazilian modernity analyzed here, the perception of coexisting modern and traditional aspects in Brazilian society stands out. Taking a modern perspective, it is postulated that the traditional aspects are remnants of an earlier phase that imposes limits and promotes conflicts in the social experience of modern Brazilians. The notion of individual is central to the view of modernity that appears both in studies of urban middle sectors and in the discourse of the telenovela texts and authors analyzed here.

In the case of the telenovela, the emphasis on the subjective experience of social life is constitutive, since its primary focus is the love story. The modern conception of love introduces at least two aspects of the notion of individual. On the one hand, it points toward freedom in the choice of the person loved. Love is placed above family interference in the choice of personal and amorous relations. On the other hand, love is a purely subjective experience. The dramas presented in telenovelas are centered basically on this conflict between love (modernity) and family impositions (tradition). This conflict, however, is resolved by the characters as individuals starting from transformations that take place on the level of subjectivity.

The reinsertion of race into the discourse on modernity transmitted by the telenovela has revealing results. Both in the words of the authors and in the telenovela texts one sees a certain difficulty in representing blacks as part of this modernity. This will become clear in the last part of this essay, where I analyze four love stories, one of which includes a black character. We will see that the only black character to be involved in a love story (out of twenty telenovelas analyzed in a broader study) does not experience the conflicts that characterize the drama of modernity in the same way that white characters do. In this regard, I will demonstrate that the telenovela actualizes the hierarchical and exclusionary beliefs of Brazilian racial culture.

Between Love and Family

Telenovelas narrate love stories, tales of love as it is lived and thought of in the West: "fatal love . . . threatened and condemned by life itself." However, they are more than just "romances of fatal love." The scenario of the lovers' dramas is daily life in contemporary Brazilian society. In this context, themes such as the family, internal conflicts, emotion, personality, work, ambition, machismo, and racism are articulated in narratives which, through love stories, reflect the daily life of the telenovela public.

Anthropological studies on urban culture that proliferated in the 1970s and 1980s demonstrate that individualism and the family occupy important positions in the symbolic universe of the urban Brazilian middle sectors.[1] Starting from the significance of the family for the construction of those studied, the authors distinguish between two types of urban middle sectors. For traditional sectors, kinship and neighbor relations have a central role in their view of the world, in the construction of identity, and in the sociability of the agents who recognize and value kinship ties. For modern sectors, in contrast, the sociability of actors and the role of the family are determined by "personal choices and affinities." The members of this group emphasize the autonomy and freedom of the individual while the family is seen as limiting. At any rate, both among the modern and the traditional sectors the family is the central reference point for the construction of the subject's identity: in the traditional sector identity is constructed through similarity and among the moderns it is constructed through contrast (Salem 1985).

In fact, these studies reveal that neither of the two systems of values is completely dominant. Both among the modern and the traditional sectors one observes the presence of the opposing model that generates tension even when it is of secondary importance. According to Salem (1985), different authors interpret this coexistence in the symbolic universe of the *modern segments* in distinct manners: (a) as the result of "a discontinuity between symbolic systems which are internalized at different moments of the subject's biography"; (b) as a typical phenomenon of modern societies, given the "coexistence of competing world views and the relative autonomy of social dominions"; (c) as a question which is constitutive of individualist ideology; and (d) as a result of the difficulty of implementing egalitarian values in a hierarchized society such as Brazil's (1985:24).

In the analysis of love stories we will see that in the telenovela, a product of modern Brazilian culture, the characters, as members of modern middle segments, are torn between love and family, between individual choice and traditional values.

Mirror of Modernity

Scholars, critics, and television professionals unanimously point toward the late 1960s as a crucial moment for the Brazilian telenovela. The creation of TV Globo in 1965 introduced a new, entrepreneurial mentality which invested in technical perfection and in the professionalization and specialization of personnel. This fact led to the improvement in the quality of telenovelas and propitiated a radical transformation in its dramaturgy, which until then comprised Brazilian and Latin American (Mexican, Cuban, Argentine, etc.) melodramas and literary adaptations. With the absorption of writers and directors from the theater and the cinema there occurred a change in the concept of telenovela and "the definitive Brazilianization of the genre" through the nationalization of texts and the introduction of "realism" (Ortiz 1988; Fernandes 1987).

Literature on the telenovela in Brazil presents two distinct visions of the meaning of these transformations. Critics who analyze the production pole see the telenovela as a product and a vehicle of the new mentality promoted by the process of industrialization and modernization of Brazilian society. According to them, the Brazilian state and private enterprises invested as much in technological perfection as in the creation of a consumer public for industrially produced culture (Caparelli 1986).

For Ortiz, Borelli, and Ramos (1988), for example, the "Brazilianization" of telenovelas resulted from the modernization of Brazilian society. The country's industrialization not only guaranteed the technical conditions demanded by realism but also created a more demanding public for the cultural industry. Kehl (1986) discusses the ideological impact of these transformations, suggesting that the modernization of telenovelas in the 1970s introduced "Brazilian reality" into the texts, thus "inserting the telenovela into Brazilian reality." The primary objective of this strategy would be the promotion of "national integration via the desire to consume." For Kehl, the telenovela was the primary instrument for the production of the ideal image of the Brazilian people. Prime-time telenovelas exhibited by the Globo network "offered, in the 1970s, the uprooted Brazilian [uprooted by industrialization and urbanization] ... a 'glamorized' mirror, closer to the reality of desire than to the reality of life, and for this reason [they served] as a conforming element of Brazilian identity" (1986:289).

Audience studies have a different viewpoint. Starting from the presupposition that television viewers reelaborate the messages transmitted by television in accordance with their own social experience, these authors relativize the thesis that the telenovela is merely an instrument for the imposition of the beliefs and values of modern society.[2] Leal (1986) has undertaken research involving families of both the dominant and working classes, observing that both the stories and the very act of watching the telenovela assume different meanings for each group analyzed. Whereas families of popular classes reveal a total involvement with the plot, viewers of the dominant class, in contrast, have a more distant relationship with the stories. Leal observes that "television is extremely attractive to the popular group, above all because it transmits a modernity and a kind of speech recognized as belonging to the symbolic universe of another [dominant] class" (1986:35).

From this same perspective, Prado (1987) analyzes the way in which women of Cunha (a town in the interior of São Paulo) reelaborate messages transmitted by the female characters of the eight o'clock

telenovela. The author observes that female viewers, on referring to telenovela characters, make explicit aspects related to their experience as
women in a small town. According to Prado, the telenovela is a "mirror"
in which the women of Cunha see recurring issues of their daily life,
and for these women the telenovela is a "field of symbolic projection,
where [they can] rediscover society, social relations, and [themselves]"
(1987:124).

The authors mentioned above implicitly or explicitly associate the
telenovela with the modernization of Brazilian society. Those who study
their production emphasize that the changes undertaken in the process
of production of the telenovela are part of the modernization of society
itself. Technological improvements in telecommunications are part of
the broader processes of the consolidation of capitalism in the country
and of rupture with the traditional forms of business organization. Case
studies suggest that the telenovela can be conceived as a mirror which
reflects the tensions inherent to a culture in which diverse and contradictory beliefs and values coexist. For these authors, the introduction of elements of "Brazilian life" transformed the telenovela into a
cultural artifact that "reflects" the tensions and questions introduced by
modernity.[3]

I do not intend to enter a discussion about the role of the telenovela
as a vehicle for the imposition of the dominant sectors' view of the world.
In truth, an interpretive vision of the meaning of the telenovela in the
Brazilian cultural scene indicates that it is only consolidated at a moment
when the forms of life and beliefs and values of modern industrial society are disseminated throughout society. At the same time, I do not
believe that these beliefs and values totally dominate the cultural scene.
The recurrence of "projects of modernization" reveals not only the existence of concrete differences but also of different visions of Brazilian
reality. Nonetheless, being a product of the modernization of society—
and a "modern" vision of that society—the telenovela is a privileged site
for analyzing the dominant conception of race relations in *modern*
Brazil.

Chronicle of Daily Life

Like any product of the culture industry, the making of the telenovela follows the rhythm of industrial production. To guarantee production quality, its elaboration requires highly specialized technicians

and a high degree of fragmentation in its production (see Ortiz, Borelli, and Ramos 1988). Among all the professionals involved in the telenovela, authors and directors are the ones with greatest autonomy and a more global view of the product. But even direction has become increasingly fragmented: direction of actors, direction of interior scenes, direction of exteriors, and so forth. In fact, the only professional who remains outside of this sophisticated production scheme is the author. He or she is the only one with a broad vision of the final product.

In fact, although the author initiates the process by writing the synopsis and the initial chapters, as soon as the story goes on the air each chapter written is influenced by the reaction of the public, television critics, and the competition. In effect, the telenovela is a product whose elaboration is complete only with the exhibition of the final episode. Up to this point authors are subject to diverse influences.

> I tried my best not to be Manichaean, separating the good from the bad, dividing my characters into good guys and the villains. Life is not like that. We all make mistakes, even though we have many virtues.... My characters ... are flesh and blood people who do good and bad things, and they are often quite contradictory. That is reality. (Manuel Carlos)[4]

For the authors, plots and themes are *realistic* when they deal with questions that are significant for the *individual* in accordance with modern society's universe of beliefs and values. This vision appears in their definition of "real characters," that is, those whose psychological dimension is emphasized.

> In an open-ended work, the author generally does not have the whole story in mind, but rather merely the central story line which is vaguely developed and which has an ending that is even more vague. As he or she writes, the story develops. It is an open work subject to wind and storms and all sorts of pressures. For this same reason it is also fascinating. (Dias Gomes)

The telenovela is a *collective work:* its development is shaped primarily by the reactions of the public and by the interests of the network and its affiliates. While some critics point toward the market as the primary source of restrictions on creative freedom, others identify the reactions of the public as determinant in story development.

For the authors, the telenovela must respond to the demands of the different groups that compose Brazilian society. Conceived as a conjunction of diverse social representations, the telenovela should be made with elements that form part of a symbolic universe that is common to all groups. But where do authors find the elements that, according to them, are common to all Brazilians and to all human beings in general?

> I like dramas that take place in daylight, a mixture of sun and sea, comedies of everyday life. . . . *Sol de Verão* (Summer Sun) is like that, as was *Baila Comigo* (Dance with Me). In fact, the two *novelas* give continuity to what I would like to have called "Scenes of Daily Life" or "Everyday Things" numbers 1 and 2. . . . That's how I write my novelas: with real human types who are common to almost all Brazilian families and who are, for this very reason, universal types the whole nation knows and can identify on the street, in their neighbor's house, in the corner bar, or on the bus. . . . (Manuel Carlos)

> I am certain that the suburban aspect will appear frequently in the *novela*, pleasing the public, because it brings with it a special flavor, the face of Brazil. We are going to take advantage of this to show what is really happening in Rio's Zona Norte: *chorinho*, samba, discos, and, obviously, the animal game [numbers racket]. (Aguinaldo Silva)

> My *novelas* never tell the story of just two characters. They are works involving the entire cast. Everyone is important, because they deal with people's everyday life and family. (Manuel Carlos)

The plots' realistic nature is guaranteed by the fact that the dramas, real or not, are lived out in a contemporary setting by characters who are very similar to the "common people." Nonetheless, although both rich and poor are included in the range of types created by the authors, contemporary telenovelas typically portray the world of the middle class. At the same time, authors claim they are dealing with problems and issues that are part of the daily life of all people, regardless of socioeconomic differences.

Stressing dramatic or humoristic aspects, the telenovela author believes that he or she is talking to people about themselves and about the things they experience and would like to see discussed and experienced by characters who are "universal types" and who live through the common dramas of everyday life in Brazil. In this sense, belief in the characters' universality is guaranteed by belief in the universality of the individual's internal dimensions.

The telenovela is a *chronicle of daily life:* the characters are common, contemporary, universal *individuals.* For the authors, the stories are universal because they are elaborated with elements that make up part of their, and their audience's, social experience. For this reason, emphasis is on questions associated with people's private life: on the one hand, the everyday experience of domestic life, friendship, and family, and, on the other, the subjective side of this experience manifested through emotions and fantasies: laughter and tears are the most basic expressions of this inner world.[5] The telenovela narrates these experiences by way of the conflict between subjectivity and social rules (Maggie 1981). As a *chronicle of modern Brazilian society*, it represents the quotidian of Brazilian life from a modern perspective, but privileging subjectivity, that is, the subjective experience of social life. In love stories, the key element of the telenovela, traditional values are generally represented by the family and modern values by the choice of the person loved.

Color in the Telenovela

Black television professionals and activists of the black movement have levied two primary criticisms at the Brazilian telenovela: the limited presence of black actors and actresses and the fact that those who do appear by and large play stereotypical roles (poor people, criminals, and domestic servants).[6] In this section I analyze the response of telenovela authors to these criticisms.

The most common argument used to justify the limited presence of blacks in the telenovela is the supposed lack of talented black actors and actresses. According to some authors, this lack is due to the absence of a black theater for training professional actors. This argument is significant because it presupposes an unthinkable differentiation in a society that claims to be egalitarian in racial terms. Assuming that there is a specific dramaturgy and a need for different professional training for blacks and whites, the argument suggests that blacks and whites have incommunicable social experiences.

Another critical point is the superficiality and the stereotypical nature of the roles played by black actors. Authors respond to this criticism with the argument of the supposed lack of talent of black actors. If this argument exists—and it does—how does one overcome it?

> Of course there is prejudice in reality, and of course it can be transmitted in fiction. But ... I think it is absurd that blacks do not exist as intensely in fiction as they do in real life. In Brazil blacks have absolute

participation. I even told you that they don't have a greater participation because of the lack of opportunities, but they represent an enormous number of people. Blacks and whites in Brazil are absolutely
normal, no one in Brazil thinks it is odd for a black man to be with a
white woman or vice-versa. At least I don't think anyone finds it
strange. It's so common in Brazil! [Blacks] are more Brazilian than the
whites, so I don't see why they are not represented in fiction on TV
and even in the theater. In our literature they are admirably portrayed
by Jorge Amado and so many other writers . . . Machado de Assis, for
example. So is it a discrepancy associated with romantic fiction? For
example, who earns more than black singers in Brazil? And who performs as much? Do you know any singer who is more respected than
Milton Nascimento? He may not be more respected than Chico Buarque and Tom Jobim, but he is no less respected. And what about black
singers like Alcione? They sing throughout the world, and in Brazil
they sing at foreign embassies, houses of millionaires, and for the
president. And what about soccer players and athletes in general? And
musicians? At the same time, there is a very serious problem, primarily in Rio de Janeiro: black actors and actresses are not being trained.
There are very few of them: Milton Gonçalves and Ruth de Souza,
among others whose names you will recall. But basically there are just
these few. The Teatro Experimental do Negro used to exist, but I don't
know if it still does. So the problem is the lack of training and opportunity for blacks, who are very talented. Because blacks know how to
sing, they have a good voice, and there are many talented ones! If you
want to make a novela with a lot of black actors, there just aren't any.
You have to use them as extras, but not give them speaking roles. . . .
Besides, it is evident that blacks have few opportunities in Brazil, and
for this reason they always appear as maids and the like. . . . I remember that Janete Clair once put Milton Gonçalves in the role of a psy-
choanalyst in *Pecado Capital.* I thought it was a good thing, and I don't
recall that there were any problems or social pressures.[7]

This testimonial, taken from a personal interview with the author, is very
rich because it reveals the contradictory beliefs of Brazilian racial culture: "blacks are more Brazilian than the whites," "blacks have few opportunities in Brazil, and for this reason they always appear as maids." Talent
is what allows them to break the vicious circle of scarce opportunities. In
reality, music and sports are both forms of expression in which success—
at least in terms of common sense perception—requires innate talent;
romantic fiction requires more than that. In fact, the compensatory argument which emphasizes natural talent for certain kinds of activities

brings with it the implicit belief that color (race) in itself favors certain kinds of abilities which are thus "natural." For telenovela authors, romantic fiction requires precisely those abilities that race or color cannot provide, abilities which, besides not being natural, are counterposed to nature. In other words, the flip side of the racist discourse which links certain abilities to phenotype characteristics also identifies those abilities which the so-called *natural* characteristics of blacks do not favor.

The idea that the telenovela represents the reality of modern Brazilian society is revealing. The argument of the lack of good black actors suggests that to act in the telenovela and represent characters with psychological depth it is necessary to attain a level of perfection that is possible only through the kind of professional training that blacks are lacking (because of the limited social opportunities available to them). Authors admit that blacks, although a numerical majority, occupy a disadvantaged social position in modern Brazil, and they thus lack the economic ability to invest in professional training (at all levels). For this reason, since the telenovela represents the reality of modern Brazil, when black actors and actresses appear as domestic servants (or as the unemployed or as delinquents) they are merely representing their disadvantaged social position. In this sense, the argument based on socioeconomic conditions finds support in reality.

This does not, however, answer the second criticism. The problem is not only the fact that the majority of characters played by black actors and actresses occupy disadvantaged social positions. The real issue is that these characters have no psychological depth, as do the majority of the other characters who are "white."

Here we come back to the argument of the need for a black theater to solve the problem of blacks' deficient professional training. If the telenovela deals with universal questions common to all individuals, why couldn't it also be a space for the improvement of black actors? Why the need for a specific dramaturgy for blacks? Telenovela authors do not explore this question, and they become ill-at-ease when it is brought up. The belief in equality, one of the basic principles of modern culture, impedes them from pursuing the question. In a certain sense, for these authors the specificity of the black actor cannot be expressed in dramas that the telenovela narrates, that is, blacks' social experience is not universal.

At this point we can return to the primary belief of the myth of modernization: the thesis that modernization would only be possible with the exclusion of blacks and browns from the Brazilian population. In this sense the difficulty with which telenovela authors discuss the "specificity" of the black actor suggests a difficulty in thinking about blacks in relation to modernity (beyond their disadvantaged social position, which is explained by the existence of slavery, by the past). Thus the argument that emphasizes the natural talent of blacks in forms of artistic and professional expression which require innate qualities and not training and/or vocation (in the modern sense of the term).

   Color is the mark that identifies those who, according to the myth of modernization, naturally lack the attributes of the modern individual: rationality and an interior life. In this sense, the racist postulates that attribute an insurmountable inferiority to blacks and indicate that the social experiences of blacks and whites are incommunicable impede thinking of blacks as being totally integrated in modernity. One consequence of this is the impossibility of conceiving the black empirical subject as an individual. This is clear in the following explanation, taken from a personal interview with a telenovela author who compares interracial love relationships in *Baila Comigo* and *Corpo-a-Corpo*.

> The placement was very different in the two novelas. With Zezé Motta and Marcos Paulo there was a tremendous sensuality. A great passion and a great love that was perfectly valid, possible, and acceptable within the novela.
>
> In my novela, however, it was a crystallized and crystalline situation, a great love and respect that she had for that marvelous, dignified, honest, straightforward, hardworking black man. She liked him and it was good for the children. She fulfilled herself with him. She was a widow, and he was an honorable man. She had no place to live, and she went to live in a house that she shared with him. This was more or less the situation. Beatriz's marriage to Milton was a good solution.
>
> In the case of Marcos Paulo and Zezé, on the other hand, it was a handsome man passionately in love with a sexy black woman. Zezé was a pretty woman, and what man does not look at pretty black women? Blacks, whites, blonds, Swedes, Americans, Englishmen, all men look at pretty women, whether they are blond or black, it doesn't matter. Zezé Motta is some woman; any man, no matter how prejudiced, would have said: "Even I would go out with her."

   In modernity, the idea of love is associated with the belief in individual choice. Love emerges from the individual's sovereign will, despite traditional social rules (Viveiros de Castro and Benzaquen de Araújo 1977). In the above comment, one notes that the author, on comparing two couples, emphasizes the attributes necessary for blacks to concretize an interracial marriage. Love is not sufficient to justify relationships between members of different racial groups, and both the black man and the black woman must possess certain attributes (physical for her, moral for him) that justify the attraction of the white partner, indisputable qualities that compensate for the negative mark of color and separate them from other members of the racial group, that is, from blacks without qualifications.

The qualities attributed to black characters involved in love stories are charged with values that communicate social rules that justify the joining of blacks and whites. In one case they remit to the classical theme of the white man's sexual attraction to black women and, in the other, the black character possesses qualities that transform him into an *exceptional human being*. Love does not emerge exclusively from the subject's will, but rather is mediated by socially positive attributes that the black man and woman possess.

But what is the significance of color? The explanation of Gilberto Braga, the author of *Corpo-a-Corpo*, is revealing:

> I find this extremely complex.... Several times in my novelas we have assigned black actors to roles that were not written specifically for them. [Question: What kind of roles?] Roles that involve racism, I believe. The only novela I remember having written that indicated race in the description of characters was *Corpo-a-Corpo*, because it had a racist theme *[sic]*. It was funny, because I felt bad when I began writing it because I would say, "Sônia, pretty, 30 years old, black." But why am I writing "black"? I would feel bad. Then I would think: "Well, the only way to stop feeling bad is to indicate the color in the description of all characters. . . ." I had to give the color of each character to avoid being a racist. (Personal interview)

In fact, the naturalized discourse that uses differences in color as a criterion should be hidden. Why? When the author recognizes herself/himself as a racist by indicating the color of a character, he/she perceives the exclusionary nature of color. Telenovela characters have no color because the telenovela tells stories and dramas that are common to all human beings, universal experiences. Thus, in accordance with the myth of modernization, by indicating the color (black) of a character, the author identifies him or her with the exclusionary beliefs and values that the color symbolizes and that establish an insurmountable inequality (insurmountable because it is natural) at the heart of a representation of a Brazilian reality that claims to be founded on the egalitarian and universal beliefs of modernity. Nonetheless, since the exclusionary nature of color is the basis of Brazilian modernity, the indication of the color white in relation to other characters actualizes the contradiction that underlies the integrationist version of modernization: racial democracy.

In modernity, the dynamics of relations between objective black and white subjects has color as the defining element of their different social experiences. If modernity presupposes the absence of color (the absence of exclusion), those who lack that mark—white characters—symbolize those who possess the attributes of the modern individual. However, those whose color is determinate—black characters—have their social experience circumscribed to the postulates that color actualizes in the Brazilian social imaginary: exclusion from modernity. For this reason, the argument of the lack of talent owing to the disadvantaged social position of blacks dominates the perspective of the authors, even of those who recognize the existence of racism in Brazilian society. Thus, they do not question the fact that the "universal characters" they create cannot be—and, in fact, are not—portrayed by black actors.

In the next section, I analyze four love stories taken from the telenovelas *Corpo-a-Corpo* (Eloá and Osmar, Sônia and Cláudio) and *Vale Tudo* (Raquel and Ivan, Solange and Afonso) in order to demonstrate how the telenovela describes the tension provoked by the coexistence of traditional and modern values in the symbolic universe of the urban middle sectors. Through the analysis I intend to show how the exclusion of blacks from modernity is actualized in the representation of the conflicts of modern Brazilian society, pointing toward a specific social experience for those characters for whom color is a determinant factor in their social experience.[8]

Tales of Mortal Love: Dramas of Modernity

Corpo-a-Corpo

The central plot of *Corpo-a-Corpo* (Gilberto Braga, 1978) is the story of the couple Osmar and Eloá, both of whom are engineers. They work in similar positions in the same firm—Fraga Dantas. One day a mysterious man, whom all think to be the devil, begins to help Eloá move up in the firm. This leads to a crisis in the marriage which culminates in the couple's separation. In the middle of the story they discover that everything was a plan involving the company's vice president and Osmar's former lover, Tereza. The vice president wants to murder company owner Alfredo Fraga Dantas, and Tereza seeks the separation of Osmar and Eloá. While the vice president helps Eloá move up in the firm, Tereza gains Alfredo's confidence (the plan is to marry him and later kill him). The mysterious man is unmasked as an instrument of Tereza and the vice president's pact.

Besides this central plot involving the theme of machismo, other love stories are also developed. The relationship between Sônia and Cláudio (Afredo Fraga Dantas's son) deals with the theme of racism. Alfredo does not accept the couple's relationship and blackmails Sônia, who separates from Cláudio. The imposition of the father's interests over his children's freedom and the problems caused in relationships between people of different social classes is represented in the relationship between Bia (Alfredo's youngest daughter) and Rafael. Another important subplot is the relationship between Lúcia Gouveia and Amauri (Osmar's brother). In it the themes of ambition and unhealthy passion are discussed.

"Osmar and Eloá"

The crisis in this couple's marriage begins when Eloá becomes upwardly mobile in professional terms. Humiliated by his wife's success, Osmar reveals the extent of his machismo. In a citation of a classical theme of Western literature, Eloá moves up in the company thanks to the help of a mysterious man whom, during a large part of the story, both the public and the characters believe to be the devil (Fausto). However, near the middle of the story, all discover that the "devil" was created by the sweet and angelical Tereza to take revenge on Osmar, who had abandoned her twenty years earlier for Eloá. Even knowing that everything was the work of Tereza, Osmar, his machismo bruised, decides not to stay married to Eloá.

Midway in the story, the mysterious man reappears to Tereza and proposes a pact to win back Osmar. With the mysterious man's help Tereza creates situations that nourish Osmar's feeling of inferiority. Two things happen so that Osmar finally decides to return to Eloá. First, the tragic end of his brother Amauri's morbid passion for Lúcia Gouveia. Amauri had been responsible for the second appearance of Fausto. To get Osmar back, Tereza should kill Alfredo, Cláudio's father. The ambitious Lúcia would thus become wealthy and free to live her adolescent passion for Amauri, whom she had always rejected because of his poverty. The second episode, similar to the story of Osmar and Eloá, occurs with the young couple Bia and Rafael. In a contest, Bia reveals herself to be much more competent than Rafael in an area that he had until then dominated. Rafael enters into crisis, but manages to overcome his competitiveness. In the case of Amauri and Lúcia, Osmar sees the destructiveness that determines unhealthy and unequal relationships—such as the one he had with Tereza—and in Bia and Rafael he sees an example in which relations between men and women can be established on more equitable grounds.

"Sônia and Cláudio"

The meeting of Sônia and Cláudio marks the beginning of a great love. In love from the first moment, the couple is compatible in every aspect, with the same tastes, dreams, and worldviews. Their separation occurs only because, in a plan elaborated by Lúcia Gouveia, Alfredo leads Sônia to believe that because of her Cláudio was giving up his professional fulfillment. Sônia gives in to the blackmail and breaks up with Cláudio. The event that makes their reconciliation possible occurs moments after the revelation of the blackmail. When Sônia is leaving the ranch, Alfredo tells her that he will never permit her marriage with Cláudio and that black blood would never flow in his family. Soon thereafter, he is involved in a horse accident, lies between life and death, and urgently needs a blood transfusion. Under those circumstances, Sônia, the only person who possesses the rare type of blood he needs, donates her blood and saves Alfredo's life.

When he discovers that Sônia had saved his life, Alfredo goes through a series of transformations. He not only asks that she and Cláudio forgive him and accept the ranch but also insists on getting to know Sônia's family. Besides that, he also assumes a different attitude in relation to the black servants Odete and Vanderley. Proving the transformation, Alfredo makes a stinging speech when Sônia is discriminated against by the doorman of an upper middle-class building. Furthermore, challenged by Cláudio, who claimed that he had protected Sônia only because she was his daughter-in-law, Alfredo reveals the depth of his change when he reacts indignantly to the racist attitude of one of his employees in relation to an applicant for a secretarial position in the company.

Vale Tudo

The central story line of Vale Tudo (Gilberto Braga, 1988) revolves around the discussion of possible strategies of social ascension. Raquel and her daughter, Maria de Fátima, represent the two extremes. While the former takes honesty to a paroxysm, the latter represents ambition and dishonesty taken to its ultimate consequences. The central love story is that of Raquel and Ivan. Ivan's ambition leads to a point of conflict in the couple's relationship, but the action of Maria de Fátima carries their crisis forward and keeps them separated through most of the story.

The telenovela's characters lives are focused on the aviation company TCA, owned by the family of Odete Roitman. Ivan, Fátima, and, indirectly, Raquel have close relations with the company and the members of the Roitman family. When he separates from Raquel, Ivan marries Heleninha, the alcoholic daughter of TCA's owner, and Fátima marries Afonso (the youngest son) as part of Odete's plan to separate him from Solange and force him to live in Europe. In the following analysis we will see that the main conflicts in the love stories between Ivan and Raquel and Solange and Afonso are caused by family relations.

"Ivan and Raquel"

The relationship between Ivan and Raquel is shaken when they discover dollars in Rubinho's suitcase. Raquel insists that they give the suitcase to the police, while Ivan wants to use the money to leave the country and improve their life. Odete, on discovering that Raquel is the only obstacle to getting Ivan and Heleninha together, proposes an agreement with Fátima: she promises to support Fátima's marriage with Afonso if she (Fátima) will promote Raquel and Ivan's separation. The ambitious Fátima creates a farce that leads Raquel to believe that Ivan had robbed the suitcase filled with money. Ivan denies the charge and blames Fátima (who, at the time, lived with them) for the money's disappearance, but Raquel does not believe him and the two separate. New lies and schemes by Fátima lead Raquel to suspect that Ivan was right and that Fátima had been responsible for the theft of the dollars. Pressured by her mother, Fátima confesses everything that she had done and the two break off their relationship definitively. After some time, Ivan and Raquel begin to meet secretly. Once again, Odete separates them, inventing a case of blackmail against Ivan which she uses as a tool to keep Raquel away.

Raquel gives in to Odete's blackmail and distances herself from Ivan, who nonetheless separates from Heleninha. Angry, Odete fires him from the company and uses her powers to keep him from finding a job in the field of civil aviation. Some time later, Raquel finds Ivan working as an assistant hotel manager and decides to reexamine the evidence Odete has against him.

Odete is murdered. Fátima, who had decided to help her mother and Ivan by reexamining the evidence in the blackmail case, becomes the primary suspect and is arrested. Knowing that Fátima could not use her alibi because it would incriminate Ivan, Raquel goes to the police station and confesses to the crime. Learning that Raquel is in jail to protect him, Ivan decides to confess to the crime of blackmail.

"Afonso and Solange"

Fátima provokes the separation between Afonso and Solange by making him believe that Solange was using her job as an excuse to be with her lover. Despite Solange's denials, the insecure and extremely jealous Afonso prefers to believe in Fátima's farce. After some time, Fátima begins to approach Afonso, pretending to be interested in helping his reconciliation with Solange. In reality, Fátima is plotting with Odete, who does not accept Afonso's relationship with Solange. The two create an image of Fátima as the perfect (traditional) woman, completely different from the independent Solange. But what is necessary for their reconciliation? Three events contribute to Afonso freeing himself from his mother's domination. First, Raquel and Fátima reveal Odete's strategies to separate him from Solange, the farce they prepared to get him to marry Fátima, and the plans to separate Ivan and Raquel and have him marry Heleninha. Second, Afonso discovers that Odete has an affair with César Ribeiro, Fátima's former lover and accomplice. Finally, the family's former maid, Ruth, reveals that it was not Helena, as all had believed, but rather Odete who was responsible for the death of Leonardo (the oldest and favorite son).

The Drama of Modernity

As we have seen, the conflicts between the couples originate in the fact that one of them identifies with the values of traditional culture. A hierarchical conception of the world, characterized by machismo, kinship ties, parents' authoritarianism, and racism, is opposed to a modern worldview that values individual freedom and social relations with an egalitarian base (Dumont 1966).

Love, the symbol of individual will, exists despite these differences, which are exacerbated by the actions of agents of separation who represent traditional rules. These agents render explicit the couples' contradictions, reaching particularly the one identified with the universe of traditional values, and leads to the inviability of the amorous relationship. Resolution occurs when the ambivalent member of the couple overcomes his or her contradictions. In the case of Eloá and Osmar, for example, the story shows that for a relationship to work out, it must be based on egalitarian grounds. To be happy in modern life, individuals should break with the traditional rules that they internalized in the course of growing up: Raquel rethinks her total dedication to her son; Afonso must free himself from his mother's authoritarian power.

The specificity of the solution found for the drama of Sônia and Cláudio points toward the special place that the racial question occupies in modernity. It was the fact that Sônia is black that unleashes the conflicts leading to the breaking off of the relationship. It is not a question of a difference in social experience (subjectivity), but rather of a difference conceived as natural (phenotype features).

Sônia's color brings into play the signifieds that explain both the separation and the reconciliation. Being black, she was forced to separate from the man she loved; by donating her blood to Alfredo, she made him rethink his values and conduct and see blacks in an "egalitarian" manner. The solution was of the same order as the initial contradiction: Sônia donates her blood to Alfredo who, hours earlier, had said there would never be black blood in his family (Matta 1981).

When compared with the other cases, this solution is revealing. Since Sônia is the one identified with traditional values, she would have to change. But how? Becoming white? In a certain sense this solution—"social whitening"—exists in the Brazilian imaginary, but not strongly enough to overcome the impediments to an interracial marriage and disqualify racist beliefs. Because the *whitening thesis* is based on highly naturalized beliefs, the idea of "social whitening" does not have the ideological strength to eliminate the marks of black "origin." Since it is impossible to whiten Sônia, the solution found is that with a greater ideological power because it actualizes the naturalized contents of racial culture: blacken Cláudio. As in the *myth of racial democracy*, whites should become mestizos in order for the relationship between the two (black and white) to be possible. Sônia does this when "she mixed with him in the past," donating her blood to Alfredo (Cláudio's father).

With Sônia and Cláudio's story, we see that the beliefs of racial culture do not contradict the values of modern culture. Overcoming racism demands not only its recognition, but also the deconstruction of the natural bases on which the hierarchical and exclusionary beliefs of Brazilian racial culture are founded. In the telenovela, however, this only occurs through recourse to an allegory that actualizes these beliefs and their exclusionary bases.

In fact, this solution is the only one possible because in the telenovela, as in the Brazilian social imaginary, Sônia does not exist as an individual. Why? Because her "individuality" is totally subordinated to the natural fact of color. In the other love stories, the conflicts are overcome because the individuals change the way they conceive of their social experience. With Sônia and Cláudio, in contrast, the conflict originates not only because she believes in her own inferiority and recognizes racism as an active and efficacious rule, but primarily because Sônia has no free will in face of the fact of nature that has marked her as unequal. Her color suggests her submission to the rules of nature and her natural incapacity to enjoy the attributes characteristic of the individual. In fact, the solution of donating blood reveals that this limitation cannot be overcome even in modernity. For this reason, the only option is to transform the bearer of the rules (an artifice of mythical tales), in this case the white, racist father.

The telenovela incorporates the exclusionary contents of racial culture when it resolves the conflict through a naturalized allegory—the symbolism of racial mixing—which actualizes the exclusion of blacks from modernity. Modern culture, however, values precisely the opposite: free will, the superiority of individual will over all (social or natural) determinations which are presented as prior to and/or contrary to the demands of individual subjectivity. In this mirror of the native version of modernity, the only black personage to live a love story does not participate in the drama of modernity because she is imprisoned by the rules of nature. At no time does Sônia, the black personage, have her social experience described in the same way as the other couples because in the Brazilian social imaginary blacks do not possess the qualities that are characteristic of the modern individual.

Final Comments

The above analysis sought to reinscribe racial thematics in discourses on Brazilian modernity. The point of departure was to identify the representation of Brazilian modernity present in a cultural production of contemporary Brazilian society, the telenovela. It began with the presupposition that the question of race, although hidden, is at the base of the formulation of any representation of Brazilian modernity because it has been at the source of the primary theories about the modernization of Brazilian society since the middle of the last century.

Within a more general perspective, this study discusses the bases and contents of this view of modernity and assumes that it is present, in different forms, in the diverse representations of modern Brazilian society. In this sense, on analyzing the limits of the black presence in the telenovela, I indicate the possibility of explaining the absence of blacks in other representations of contemporary Brazilian society.[9]

In truth, privileging not the fact of their absence, but rather the manner in which blacks are present in the telenovela, causes the reemergence of the exclusionary (racist) beliefs which, although repressed in contemporary discourses on modernity, are at the base of the myth of modernization. That is, the reinscription of the racial question in discourses on modernity reveals the persistence of beliefs that symbolically reinforce blacks' exclusion from the opportunities offered by contemporary Brazilian society.

NOTES

1. This discussion is based on works by Tânia Salem (1985) and Gilberto Velho (1985), one of the pioneers of this current.

2. Besides the works cited, see also Maggie (1981, 1987) and Fischer (1984).

3. I do not believe that these different visions among those who study the telenovela in Brazil can be explained merely in terms of the distinction between the "apocalyptic" and the "integrated" proposed by Eco (1979). These different conceptions about the telenovela are related to the focuses, methodologies, and conceptual frameworks used. One characteristic of this study is that I analyze an aspect associated with production with a focus similar to that of case studies.

4. The passages in this section were taken from interviews published in the Globo network's Boletins de Divulgação (press releases) at the time the novelas were initially broadcast.

5. It is important to call attention to the fact that the similarity of social experience is sought primarily in the private sphere and not in the public aspects of modern life; in public life, in the world of work, similarities and differences are products of forces beyond the control of individuals, which in fact contradict the demands of their subjectivity, and which, at the same time, impede the experience of this same subjectivity. Thus the similarities of modern life can be found only in an emphasis on the meaning that private (and public)

life has for individuals and not in performance of the tasks of public life. To avoid the contradiction characteristic of modern culture, the existence of social inequalities, the social only has meaning in telenovelas through the personal.

6. For this study I analyzed twenty telenovelas broadcast during prime time (8:00 P.M.) between 1978 and 1988. I counted the participation of 1,780 actors and actress, including supporting roles and extras. Of this number, only 72 were black. The majority of the characters they represented were domestic servants (21), delinquents (12), or had no defined occupation (7).

7. The passages in this section were taken from recorded interviews granted to the author, who has respected desire for anonymity when requested.

8. These two telenovelas were chosen for two reasons. First, because they were written by Gilberto Braga, a writer who, in the late 1970s, inaugurated a new phase in the history of the Brazilian telenovela when he incorporated themes considered to be characteristic of the intellectualized middle class, such as women's liberation, psychoanalysis, and so forth, and began to discuss current political and social issues. The second reason is that *Corpo-a-Corpo* was (and remains) the only novela to present a black protagonist as a participant in one of the main love stories and also the only one to deal with racism as a theme.

9. One of the characteristics of the development of Brazilian social sciences, for example, is that, after the work of the Paulista school of sociology, the study of race relations practically disappeared from most general analyses and became an unprivileged niche in Brazilian social sciences.

REFERENCES

Caparelli, Sérgio. 1986. *Comunicação de massa sem massa*. São Paulo: Summus.

Dumont, Louis. 1966. *Hommo Hierarquicus*. Paris: Gallimard.

Eco, Umberto. 1979. *Apocalípticos e integrados*. São Paulo: Perspectiva.

Fernandes, Florestan. 1978. *A integração do negro na sociedade de classes*. São Paulo: Ática.

Fernandes, Ismael. 1987. *Memória da telenovela brasileira*. São Paulo: Brasiliense.

Fischer, Rosa M. 1984. *O mito na sala de jantar: leitura interpretativa do discurso infanto-juvenil sobre televisão*. Porto Alegre: Movimento.

Freyre, Gilberto. 1987. *Casa grande e senzala*. Rio de Janeiro: José Olympio.

Kehl, Maria Rita, et al. 1986. *Um país no ar: história da TV brasileira em 3 canais*. São Paulo: Brasiliense/FUNARTE.

Leal, Ondina F. 1986. *A leitura social da novela das oito*. Petrópolis: Vozes.

Maggie, Yvonne. 1981. "A quem devemos servir? Impressões sobre a novela das oito." Mimeograph.

_____. 1987. "O diabo na sala de jantar." *Religião e Sociedade* (Rio de Janeiro) 12(2).

Matta, Roberto da. 1981. *Relativizando: uma introdução à antropologia social.* Petrópolis: Vozes.

Ortiz, Renato. 1988. *A moderna tradição brasileira.* São Paulo: Brasiliense.

Ortiz, Renato, Silvia Helena Simões Borelli, and José Mário Ortiz Ramos. 1988. *Telenovela: história e produção.* São Paulo: Brasiliense.

Prado, Rosanne M. 1987. "Mulher de novela, mulher de verdade." Master's thesis, Museu Nacional, Rio de Janeiro.

Salem, Tânia. 1985. "Família e camadas médias: uma revisão da literatura recente." *Boletim do Museu Nacional* (Rio de Janeiro) 54.

Velho, Gilberto. 1985. *Subjetividade e sociedade.* Rio de Janeiro: Zahar.

Viveiros de Castro, E., and R. Benzaquen de Araújo. 1977. "Romeu e Julieta e a origem do estado moderno." In Gilberto Velho, ed., *Arte e sociedade.* Rio de Janeiro: Zahar.

19 | The Representation of Blacks on Commercial Television in Brazil: Some Cultivation Effects

MICHAEL LESLIE

McConahay, Hardee, and Batts (1981) argue that a new attitude toward racial problems in the United States called "modern racism" is developing. According to this perspective, most U.S. whites now believe that blacks and other minorities no longer require social intervention programs to compensate for the effects of racism and discrimination in our society because these unjustices have already been remedied by legislation. According to this view, minorities have already been overcompensated for any suffering or harm that may have come to them owing to historically unfair treatment at the hands of their fellow Americans, and everyone is now on an equal footing and anyone can succeed, regardless of race. Thus, there is no need for affirmative action or compensatory educational programs directed toward minorities in our society.

Matabane (1988) and Gray (1989) have suggested further that in societies where racial inequality and discrimination exist, television may function to *reduce* awareness and sensitivity to the plight of blacks. For example, the fact that the popular situation comedies rarely deal with issues of racial conflict, economic exploitation, and class relations may lull viewers into thinking that such problems no longer exist.

Gerbner, Signorielli, and Morgan (1986) claim that television plays a key role in shaping our image of social reality by providing a constant flow of images of the society in which we live. They say that television's fictional and nonfictional programming is at variance with the facts of social reality, that is, that television presents a distorted image of society. They describe the impact of heavy viewing of television on the viewer's worldview as the "cultivation effect." Using U.S. data, the researchers have shown the cultivation effect to operate regardless of the educational level

of viewers. That is, being well educated does not immunize heavy viewers against acquiring a distorted perception of the world or mainstream
political views (Gerbner, Gross, Signorielli, and Morgan 1980). A review
of knowledge gap research (Gaziano 1983) suggests, however, that those
with less education would probably be more cultivated by television than
those with more education.

In summary, heavy viewing of U.S. television programming has
been shown to positively correlate with distorted views of social reality
and social problems and their origins. In addition, people who watch a
lot of television may be deceived into believing that social problems are
less severe than they actually are (Volgy and Schartz 1988), or that they
do not require any form of ameliorative government or public action.
The educational level of the viewer moderates the effects of cultivation,
influencing both its intensity and direction.

Television and Racial Attitudes in Brazil

Brazil, like the United States, has a history of black slavery and marginalization (Fernandes 1969; Degler 1971; Wagley 1977) and has a substantial black and brown population. Asians make up less than 7 percent.
U.S. research suggests a strong correlation between attitudes about people of African origin and their portrayal on television (Jeffries-Fox and
Signorielli 1978; Berry and Mitchell-Kernan 1982; Matabane 1988). Is
there a similar correlation between television viewing and attitudes
toward blacks in Brazil?

Some 95 percent of the Brazilian population has access to television, which attracts 60 to 80 percent of the available audience during
prime time (Kottak 1990; Nielsen 1990). Recent research (Leslie 1992;
Subervi-Velez and Oliveira 1991) on the content of Brazilian television
indicates that Brazilian television reflects both the invisibility and powerlessness of black and brown Brazilians: they are seldom seen on Brazilian television programs or advertising—less than 10 percent of all air
time. When they do appear, it is predominantly in stereotypical roles.

In testimonies to researcher Haroldo da Costa (1988), a broad
cross-section of Brazilian blacks said they felt psychologically marginalized and stereotyped in the mass media and in Brazilian cultural, political, economic, and social life: some identified television as a prime
source of unfavorable portrayals. Abdias do Nascimento (1978), a noted
Brazilian playwright, politician, and social activist, has used the term

"cultural genocide" to describe the impact of Brazilian television's portrayals (and nonportrayals) of the black Brazilian population. The Brazilian historian Joel Rufino dos Santos (1988) and the anthropologist Sodré (1979) say blacks and browns are "invisible" on Brazilian television.

Nonfictional treatment of racial issues in Brazil can best be described as episodic and historical. Racial issues have been dealt with centrally in some *telenovelas,* such as *Escrava Isaura* and *Corpo-a-Corpo,* or during a special commemorative period such as the centenary of the abolition of slavery in May 1988. But while the centenary produced a temporary outpouring of books, documentaries, and discussion of the issues (Subervi-Velez and Oliveira 1990), the subject of race, and the position of blacks in Brazilian society, has been studiously neglected on Brazilian television. There are no serious, ongoing programs on Brazilian television in which the condition of blacks (and browns) in Brazilian society is examined and problematized (Kottak 1990).

Brazilian society is infused with the myth of racial democracy, according to which discrimination based on skin color does not exist in Brazil; everyone, it is said, has an equal chance to succeed (Freyre 1987). This myth contrasts sharply with Brazilian economic, political, and social reality (Wood and Carvalho 1988; Hasenbalg 1979; Oliveira, Porcario, and Araújo 1981; Moore, 1988; IBGE 1990) but is deeply ingrained in Brazilian social thought (Viana 1933; Nina Rodrigues 1957; Silva 1989). Brazil thus offers a good opportunity to test the cross-cultural robustness of the empirical relationships observed by Gerbner and Matabane between television viewing and the cultivation of racial attitudes.

Research Question

Recalling that Gerbner and others say television plays a key role in helping construct our image of social reality, one might ask how heavy viewing of Brazilian television correlates with viewers' attitudes toward Brazilian blacks. Do heavy viewers of television have different social attitudes about blacks than light viewers? Do they have a distorted perception of black Brazilian political potentialities? Do Brazilian heavy viewers' perceptions of social reality tend to be more at variance with sociological fact than light viewers' perceptions? How does the cultivation effect differ for each of the four major ethnic groups in Brazil?

Finally, to what extent does the level of education of the Brazilian viewer moderate the cultivation effect?

Methodology

To answer these questions, a study of the television viewing habits and attitudes toward blacks was conducted in Brazil in the summer of 1991. The survey was conducted by the leading Brazilian public opinion polling organization, IBOPE. The universe from which the sample was selected consisted of voters in the most recent national elections. A national proportional quota sample of 3,650 persons representing both urban and rural residents was drawn, using such demographic criteria as sex, occupation, race, geographic location, age, and education, as reported in the 1980 census.

The data were collected through personal interviews administered by a team of IBOPE-trained interviewers. Interviews were conducted in the home, in the street, or at the workplace. The raw data were processed at IBOPE headquarters in Rio de Janeiro and analyzed at the University of Florida, Gainesville, using the Statistical Package for the Social Sciences.

Four statements, adapted from a validated scale published by Shaw and Wright (1967), were used to measure Brazilian attitudes toward blacks. Using a 4-point scale, with 1 representing complete agreement and 4 representing complete disagreement, respondents were asked to indicate to what degree they concurred with each of the following statements:

1. I consider marriage between persons of different races natural.
2. Racial discrimination exists in Brazil, but few would admit it.
3. If there were a black candidate who was qualified to be president of Brazil, he/she could be elected.
4. If one of my best friends married a black, I would stop inviting him/her to my house.

The predictor variables were race, education, and daily television viewing hours. Low education was defined as less than a sixth grade education while high education was defined as having completed college entrance examinations or gone to college. Light television viewing was defined as less that two hours per day of exposure and heavy viewing was defined as more than six hours per day. Values for the racial variable were black, white, brown, and yellow (Asian). The respondents were divided into groups, composed of high and low scorers on the predictor variables, level of education, and daily television viewing hours. Means were then calculated for each group on each of the four dependent measures, controlling for race. Finally, the observed difference in means was tested for statistical significance. The results are shown in Tables 1 and 2.

Results

Effects of Light versus Heavy Television Viewing, by Race

As shown in Table 1, the average score for statement 1, concerning interracial marriage, was 1.3. Heavy viewers agreed most (1.2) while light viewers agreed least (1.4). Black heavy viewers registered almost complete agreement (1.1). In response to statement 2, about racial discrimination, heavy viewers tended to agree more with this statement than light viewers (1.5 and 1.9, respectively), with heavy white viewers showing the most agreement (1.4). While the average score in response to statement 3, which asked whether a black could be elected president of Brazil, was 1.3, heavy viewers averaged 1.2 while light viewers averaged 1.4. Yellow light viewers were least likely to agree (1.7) while heavy white viewers were most likely to agree (1.1). There was virtually no difference in the amount of disagreement with statement 4. Both heavy and light viewers averaged 3.6. The strength of Asian disagreement was somewhat lower, however, at 3.4.

The difference in the mean response to statements 1, 2, and 3 for heavy and light viewers was significant at the .001 level. There was no significant difference in the mean for heavy and light viewers with respect to statement 4. Thus, heavy television viewing appeared to be positively correlated with opinions regarding the social acceptability of Brazilian blacks.

Effects of Level of Education, by Race

As shown in Table 2, the majority of respondents strongly agreed that interracial marriage is natural (statement 1), with a mean score of 1.3. However, respondents with higher levels of education showed more agreement (1.1) than those with lower levels of education (1.5). Blacks with little education were more likely to agree with the statement (1.2) than whites with little education. Educated Asians agreed with the statement more than any other group (1.0). The mean score of 1.7, in response to statement 2, indicates that there was less agreement, with the

TABLE 1

Effects of Light versus Heavy Television Viewing, by Race

Statement 1. I consider marriage between persons of different races natural.

| | TV Viewing | | | |
| | Light | | Heavy | |
	Mean	Respondents	Mean	Respondents
Total	1.4570	1,499	1.2398	855
Black	1.3918	171	1.1310	84
White	1.4610	744	1.2575	466
Brown	1.4809	551	1.2447	282
Yellow	1.3030	33	1.2174	23

Total sample: Mean 1.3781; respondents 2,354.
$t = 5.78, p < .000$

Statement 2. Racial discrimination exists in Brazil, but few would admit it.

| | TV Viewing | | | |
| | Light | | Heavy | |
	Mean	Respondents	Mean	Respondents
Total	1.9493	1,499	1.5099	855
Black	2.0117	171	1.5238	84
White	1.9113	744	1.4227	466
Brown	1.9855	551	1.6383	282
Yellow	1.8788	33	1.6522	23

Total sample: Mean 1.7897; respondents 2,354.
$t = 8.80, p < .000$

Statement 3. If there were a black candidate who was qualified to be president of Brazil, he/she could be elected.

| | TV Viewing | | | |
| | Light | | Heavy | |
	Mean	Respondents	Mean	Respondents
Total	1.4089	1,499	1.2222	855
Black	1.4854	171	1.3214	84
White	1.4140	744	1.1760	466
Brown	1.3575	551	1.2553	282
Yellow	1.7576	33	1.3913	23

Total sample: Mean 1.3411; respondents 2,354.
$t = 5.19, p < .000$

Statement 4. If one of my best friends married a black, I would stop inviting him/her to my house.

| | TV Viewing | | | |
| | Light | | Heavy | |
	Mean	Respondents	Mean	Respondents
Total	3.6618	1,499	3.6643	855
Black	3.5731	171	3.6190	84
White	3.7124	744	3.6717	466
Brown	3.6316	551	3.6844	282
Yellow	3.4848	33	3.4348	23

Total sample: Mean 3.6627; respondents 2,354.
$t = -.06, p < .000$

TABLE 2

Effects of Level of Education, by Race

Statement 1. I consider marriage between persons of different races natural.

| | Level of Education | | | |
| | Low | | High | |
	Mean	Respondents	Mean	Respondents
Total	1.5922	944	1.1889	969
Black	1.4091	132	1.0545	55
White	1.6288	361	1.2289	651
Brown	1.6159	427	1.1266	237
Yellow	1.6250	24	1.0385	26

Total sample: Mean 1.3879; respondents 1,913.
$t = 9.11, p < .000$

Statement 2. Racial discrimination exists in Brazil, but few would admit it.

| | Level of Education | | | |
| | Low | | High | |
	Mean	Respondents	Mean	Respondents
Total	2.2383	944	1.3230	969
Black	2.2045	132	1.2182	55
White	2.2604	361	1.3333	651
Brown	2.2248	427	1.3376	237
Yellow	2.3333	24	1.1538	26

Total sample: Mean 1.7747; respondents 1,913.
$t = 16.23, p < .000$

Statement 3. If there were a black candidate who was qualified to be president of Brazil, he/she could be elected.

| | Level of Education | | | |
| | Low | | High | |
	Mean	Respondents	Mean	Respondents
Total	1.5148	944	1.2384	969
Black	1.5227	132	1.4904	55
White	1.5069	361	1.2104	651
Brown	1.4941	427	1.2532	237
Yellow	1.9583	24	1.2692	26

Total sample: Mean 1.3748; respondents 1,913.
$t = 6.25, p < .000$

Statement 4. If one of my best friends married a black, I would stop inviting him/her to my house.

| | Level of Education | | | |
| | Low | | High | |
	Mean	Respondents	Mean	Respondents
Total	3.5678	944	3.7534	969
Black	3.5455	132	3.8727	55
White	3.5983	361	3.7343	651
Brown	3.5621	427	3.8017	237
Yellow	3.3333	24	3.5385	26

Total sample: Mean 3.6618; respondents 1,913.
$t = -4.25, p < .000$

highly educated agreeing most (1.3) and the lower educated agreeing least (2.2). Highly educated blacks (1.2) and Asians (1.1) agreed most that this was the case. In response to statement 3, whether a black could be elected president in Brazil, the average agreement was 1.3, indicating generally strong agreement, with the highly educated averaging 1.2 and the lower educated 1.5. Highly educated blacks (1.4) and lower educated Asians (1.9) agreed least with this statement; highly educated whites agreed most (1.2). The mean score for statement 4 was 3.6, indicating generally strong disagreement. Asians, however, regardless of education, were more likely to *agree* with the statement than other ethnic group, averaging 3.3.

Means differences in the responses given by highly and lower educated Brazilians were significant at the .001 level. In other words, education had a consistent effect on attitudes toward blacks, with highly educated persons expressing more favorable attitudes toward Brazilian blacks than the less educated persons.

Discussion

It is clear that the level of education of Brazilian voters in this sample correlates positively with the favorableness of their *manifest* attitudes toward blacks, both socially and politically, as measured by this survey. The more highly educated the voter is, the more positive his/her manifest attitude appears likely to be. This finding concurs with U.S. research, which has found that manifest racial prejudice is strongest among the least educated American citizens.

A caution is in order, however, since the expression of overt prejudice is socially unacceptable in both Brazil and the United States. Thus educated and aware respondents may have been inclined to give the politically correct response, rather than to express their true feelings about blacks in response to each of these statements. The fact that the data were gathered from interviews, rather than anonymous questionnaires, may have further contributed to such an effect.

Also interesting is the finding that poorly educated Brazilians are least likely to recognize the presence of racism in Brazilian society. This denial has historical parallels in the United States, where a substantial portion of the population also denies that racism toward blacks and other minorities exists. The fact that highly educated Brazilians are more likely than less educated Brazilians to recognize the persistence of racial discrimination against Brazilian blacks lends support to the knowledge gap hypothesis.

It should be noted that the amount of social and political acceptance of black Brazilians appears to vary by ethnic group, with yellows appearing to be the least accepting of interracial marriage and blacks the most accepting. This may be an indication that blacks have accepted or find it expedient to give lip service to the racial democracy myth more than other minority groups in Brazilian society.

Lower educated Asians and blacks regardless of education had more difficulty believing that a black candidate could be elected president of Brazil. Considering the 1993 experience of black politician Benedita da Silva (Herscovitz 1993), who was the target of racial epithets and insults while campaigning for mayor of Rio de Janeiro, they had grounds for this belief. The fact that educated browns are more likely to believe a black candidate can be elected also points to their relatively greater acceptance of the racial democracy myth.

Heavy exposure to Brazilian television correlates positively with belief in the racial democracy myth. Heavy television viewers are more likely than light viewers to express liberal social attitudes toward black Brazilians. However, they also seem to be more aware of the persistence of racial discrimination in Brazilian society. Thus, heavy television watching in Brazil seems to both sensitize viewers to black social reality while intensifying belief in (or longing for) the democratic racial myth.

Limitations

Given the large sample size and relatively small difference in observed means, the possibility of Type I error in this study is significant. Also, the use of 4-point rather than 5-point scales may have induced directionality in measurement, as would the social desirability of scale content. However, the fact that differences between groups could be observed despite these methodological flaws would indicate fairly robust effects for the predictor variables. A better-designed future study could re-test these tentative observations.

Conclusion

Brazilian television helps sustain the myth that in Brazil a racial democracy exists by neglecting to acknowledge, examine, and discuss the generally unfavorable political, economic, and social conditions within which the majority of black Brazilians live. While ethnicity, education, and television viewing habits moderate television's impact, heavy, less educated television viewers are more likely than light viewers to be cultivated to view Brazil, erroneously, as a racial democracy. Thus, Brazilian television content may be a cultivator of modern racism in Brazil.

NOTE

Author's Note: An earlier version of this article, titled "Representation of Blacks on Prime Time Television in Brazil," appeared in *Howard Journal of Communication* 4 (Summer/Fall 1992).

REFERENCES

Berry, Gordon L., and Claudia Mitchell-Kernan. 1982. *Television and the Socialization of the American Child.* New York: Academic Press.

"O Boom Umbandista." 1981. *Veja* (January 7), pp. 40–41.

Costa, Haroldo da. 1988. *Fala, crioulo: depoimentos.* 2d ed. Rio de Janeiro: Editora Record.

Degler, Carl. 1971. *Neither Black nor White: Slavery and Race Relations in Brazil and in the United States.* New York: Macmillan.

Fernandes, Florestan. 1969. *The Negro in Brazilian Society.* New York: Columbia University Press.

Freyre, Gilberto. 1987. *Casa-grande e senzala.* Rio de Janeiro: José Olympio.

Gaziano, Cecile. 1983. "The Knowledge Gap: An Analytical Review of Media Effects." *Communication Research* 10(4):447–486.

Gerbner, George, Larry Gross, Nancy Signorielli, and Michael Morgan. 1980. "The 'Mainstreaming' of America: Violence Profile No. 11." *Journal of Communication* 30(3):11–29.

Gerbner, George, Nancy Signorielli, and Michael Morgan. 1986. "Living with Television: The Dynamics of the Cultivation Process." In Jennings Bryant and Dolf Zillman, eds., *Perspectives on Media Effects,* pp. 17–40. Hillsdale, N.J. and London: Lawrence Erlbaum Associates.

Gray, Herman. 1989. "Television, Black Americans and the American Dream." *Critical Studies in Mass Communication* 6(4):376–386.

Hasenbalg, Carlos. 1979. *Discriminação e desigualdades raciais no Brasil.* Rio de Janeiro: Graal; São Paulo: IBEAC.

Herscovitz, Heloiza G. 1993. "Benedita da Silva, uma estrela negra brilha na política do Brasil." *Informativo do Instituto Brasil/Florida* 9 (Spring/Summer).

IBGE (Instituto Brasileiro de Geografia e Estatística). 1990. *Pesquisa nacional por amostra de domicílios,* 1987: *cor da população.* Rio de Janeiro.

Jeffries-Fox, Suzanne, and Nancy Signorielli. 1978. "Television and Children's Conceptions of Occupations." In Herbert S. Dordick, ed., *Proceedings of the Sixth Annual Telecommunications Policy Research Conference,* pp. 21–38. Lexington, Mass.: Lexington Books.

Kottak, Conrad P. 1990. *Prime-Time Society: An Anthropological Analysis of Television and Culture.* Belmont, Calif.: Wadsworth Publishing Co.

Leslie, Michael. 1992. "Representation of Blacks on Prime Time Television in Brazil." *Howard Journal of Communication* 4(1–2):1–9.

Matabane, Paula A. 1988. "Television and the Black Audience: Cultivating Moderate Perspectives on Racial Integration." *Journal of Communication* 38(4):21–31.

McConahay, J. B., B. B. Hardee, V. Batts. 1981. "Has Racism Declined? It Depends on Who's Asking and What Is Asked." *Journal of Conflict Resolution* 25(2):563–579.

Moore, Zelbert. 1988. "Reflections on Blacks in Contemporary Brazilian Popular Culture in the 1980s." *Studies in Latin American Popular Culture* 7:213–226.

Nascimento, Abdias do. 1978. *O genocídio do negro brasileiro: processo de um racismo mascarado.* Rio de Janeiro: Paz e Terra.

Nielsen, Servicios de Midia. 1990. *LEDA Investimento Publicitário 89.* São Paulo: Dunn and Bradstreet Corporation.

Nina Rodrigues, Raimundo. 1957. *As raças humanas e a responsabilidade penal no Brasil.* Salvador: Livraria Progresso Editora.

Oliveira, Lúcia Garcia de, Rosa Maria Porcario, and Tereza Cristina N. Araújo. 1981. *O lugar do negro na força de trabalho.* Rio de Janeiro: IGBE.

Santos, Joel Rufino dos. 1988. "Invisibilidade e racismo." *Intercambio* (Rio de Janeiro) 1(1):31–36.

Silva, Denise Ferreira da. 1989. "Revisitando a 'democracia racial': raça e identidade nacional no pensamento brasileiro." *Estudos Afro-Asiáticos* (Rio de Janeiro) 16 (March).

Sodré, Muniz. 1979. "O negro e os meios de informação." *Revista de Cultura Vozes* 73(3).

Subervi-Velez, Federico A., and Omar Souki Oliveira. 1991. *Blacks (and Other Ethnics) in Brazilian Television Commercials: An Exploratory Inquiry.* Los Ensayistas: Georgia Series on Hispanic Thought, nos. 28–29. Athens: University of Georgia.

Viana, Oliveira. 1933. *Evolução do povo brasileiro.* São Paulo: Cia. Editora Nacional.

Volgy, Thomas, and John E. Schartz. 1988. "TV Entertainment Programming and Socio-Political Attitudes." *Journalism Quarterly* 57:150–154.

Wagley, Charles. 1977. *An Introduction to Brazil.* New York: Columbia University Press.

Wood, Charles H., and José Alberto Magno de Carvalho. 1988. *The Demography of Inequality in Brazil.* New York: Cambridge University Press.

Xavier, Ismail. 1983. *Sertão/mar: Glauber Rocha e a estética da fome.* São Paulo: Brasiliense.

Contributors

Jeferson Bacelar is Adjunct Professor of Anthropology and Director of the Centro de Estudos Afro-Orientais at the Universidade Federal da Bahia. He is the author of *A família da prostituta*, *Galegos no paraíso racial*, *Ser negro em Salvador*, and numerous articles in specialized journals.

Júlio Braga, former Professor of Anthropology and former Director of the Centro de Estudos Afro-Orientais at the Universidade Federal da Bahia, is the author of *Ancestralidade afro-brasileira: o culto de Baba Egum*, *O jogo de búzios: um estudo da adivinhação no candomblé*, *Sociedade Protetora dos Desvalidos: uma irmandade de cor*, and *Na gamela do feitiço: repressão e resistência nos candomblés da Bahia*, along with many articles on diverse aspects of Afro-Brazilian religions.

Diana DeG. Brown teaches anthropology at Bard College in New York. Her publications include *Umbanda: Religion and Politics in Urban Brazil* and articles and book reviews in such journals as *American Anthropologist*, *American Ethnologist*, and *Religião e Sociedade*.

John Burdick is Associate Professor of Anthropology at Syracuse University. His research focuses on religious and political movements in Latin America, particularly Catholic Base Communities, Pentecostalism, and African religious movements in Brazil. He is the author of *Looking for God in Brazil: The Progressive Catholic Church in Urban Brazil's Religious Arena*.

Cultural anthropologist José Jorge de Carvalho teaches at the Universidade de Brasília. He has done extensive research on African-derived ritual and popular music. He is the author of *Culto Xangô em Recife, Brasil* and *Estética da opacidade e da transparência*. He is also organizer of *O Quilombo do Rio das Rãs*.

Larry Crook is Associate Professor of Music and Co-director of the Center for World Arts at the University of Florida. An ethnomusicologist and a performing musician, he has carried out research projects in Brazil and Nigeria and has received a variety of grant awards for artistic collaborations with musicians and dancers from Brazil, Ghana, Guinea, India, and the United States. His research into musical traditions from Brazil and the Caribbean is published in books, journals, and encyclopedias. He is currently researching the history and contemporary manifestations of the *maracatu de baque virado* carnival tradition from Recife, Pernambuco.

Henry John Drewal is Professor of Art History at the University of Wisconsin. One of the leading American scholars of the survival of African art and cultural forms in the Americas, he is author of *African Artistry: Technique and Aesthetics in Yoruba Sculpture, Gẹlẹdẹ: Art and Female Power Among the Yoruba*, and *Yoruba: Nine Centuries of African Art and Thought*.

A native of Ghana, Anani Dzidzienyo is a sociologist at Brown University. He has worked on comparative race relations in Brazil and on the connections between political formations in Brazil and Africa. He is the author of *The Position of Blacks in Brazilian Society*.

Maria José do Espírito Santo França is a *filha-de-santo* (initiate) in the terreiro of Ilê Iyá Omin Axé Iyá Massê, the terreiro of Mãe Menininha do Gantois. A social activist, she works in the Conselho de Desenvolvimento da Comunidade Negra of Bahia's Secretaria da Justiça e Direitos Humanos.

Originally from Argentina, Carlos Hasenbalg is Professor of Sociology at the Instituto Universitário de Pesquisas of the Universidade Cândido Mendes in Rio de Janeiro and an internationally recognized specialist on race relations in Brazil. Among his many publications are *Discriminação e desigualdades raciais no Brasil, Estrutura social, mobilidade e raça* (with Nelson do Valle Silva), and *Race Relations in Post-Abolition Brazil*.

Randal Johnson is Professor of Brazilian Literature and Culture at the University of California, Los Angeles. Among his books are *Cinema Novo x 5: Masters of Contemporary Brazilian Film* and *The Film Industry in Brazil: Culture and the State*. Together with Robert Stam, he co-edited

Brazilian Cinema. He also organized and edited Pierre Bourdieu's *The Field of Cultural Production: Essays on Art and Literature.*

Michael Leslie is Associate Professor of Telecommunication in the College of Journalism and Communications at the University of Florida. His research examines modern communications technologies in intercultural contexts.

Kazadi wa Mukuna, a native of Zaire, is Associate Professor of Music and Co-director of the Center for the Study of World Musics at Kent State University, Kent, Ohio. He has a Ph.D. in ethnomusicology from the University of California, Los Angeles and in sociology from the Universidade de São Paulo. He is best known for his contributions on traditional African music on the continent and in the diaspora and on urban music in Zaire and Brazil.

Femi Ojo-Ade, originally from Nigeria, is Professor of French at St. Mary's College in Maryland. Among his books are *Of Dreams Deferred, Dead or Alive: African Perspectives on African-American Writers, On Black Culture, Being Black, Being Human: More Essays on Black Culture,* and *Colour and Culture in Literature.*

Since the early 1960s, Antônio Pitanga (born Antônio Sampaio) has been a leading actor in Brazilian film and television, starring in such films as *Barravento, Ganga Zumba, A grande cidade, A mulher de todos, A idade da terra, Ladrões de cinema,* and many others. He also directed *Na boca do mundo* (1978). A member of the Partido dos Trabalhadores, in 1992 he was elected to Rio de Janeiro's City Council, where he continues to serve.

Antônio Risério, who lives in Salvador, is a writer, poet, and lyricist. His books include *Carnaval Ijexá, Caymmi: uma utopia de lugar, Cores vivas, O poético e o político e outros escritos* (with Gilberto Gil), *Textos e tribos: poéticas extraocidentais nos trópicos brasileiros,* and *Fetiche.*

A leading figure in Brazil's black movement, João Jorge Santos Rodrigues is President of the bloco afro Olodum. He previously served as Director of the Fundação Gregório de Matos in Salvador and member of the Comissão Nacional do Centenário da Abolição. He is the author of *Olodum: Estrada da Paixão.*

Since 1987 Thereza Santos, long an activist in the black movement in Brazil, has served in the São Paulo state government's Office of Afro-Brazilian Culture. Trained as a sociologist, from 1973 to 1978 she lived in Guinea-Bissau and Angola, where she worked in the cultural area. She is co-author of *Mulher negra*.

Benedita da Silva, the first black woman elected to congress in Brazil, is currently a senator from Rio de Janeiro. She is a member of the Partido dos Trabalhadores. During the last decade she has been a major figure in the black movement and the women's movement in Brazil.

Denise Ferreira da Silva is Assistant Professor at the University of California, San Diego. She writes on global cultural politics and on race, gender, and class in Brazil, the United States, and South Africa.

Robert Stam is Professor of Cinema Studies at New York University. He is co-editor, with Randal Johnson, of *Brazilian Cinema* and author of such works as *Subversive Pleasures: Bakhtin, Cultural Criticism and Film*, *Reflexivity in Film and Literature: From Don Quixote to Jean-Luc Godard*, and *Tropical Multiculturalism: A Comparative History of Race in Brazilian Cinema and Culture*. He is also co-author, with Ella Shohat, of *Unthinking Eurocentrism: Multiculturalism and the Media*.

Index

Abolição e Música album, 279

abolition: atrocities following, 176; in black consciousness movement, 2, 32–33; Brotherhood Campaign and, 237; effects of, 19, 59–60; history of, 32–33; race and class structure at centenary of, 65–83; race and class structure following, 61–65, 116; status of Salvador blacks following, 85–96

Abranches, Carlos Dushee de, 123

Abreu, Hugo, 115–116

actors, blacks as, 347–349

administrative workers, racial distribution of, 81–83

affirmative action programs, 363

afoxé, 7, 46, 60, 224, 250; commercialization of, 152; in contemporary Bahia, 164–165; of Filhos de Gandhi, 251–252, 258; persecution of, 45

Africa: in Adão Ventura's poetry, 184–185; black slaves from, 17–18; and Brazilian culture, religion, and politics,130–133; Brazilian initiatives toward, 109, 113–122; colonization of, 204; commercial relations between Brazil and, 126–127; foreign relations between Brazil and, 110–113, 124–128, 128–130, 133–138; influence on Brazilian music, 277–278; influence on Brazil of, 1–3, 8–9, 103–104, 105–139, 143–145, 187, 192–195, 256–259; influence on contemporary Bahia, 96–98; influence on Olodum of, 48; return of Afro-Brazilians to, 112–113; roots of

Umbanda in, 216–217; state religions in, 203–204. *See also* Yoruba

African-Americans: musical influence of, 252–253; situation of, 106, 108–109, 110–111; situation of Afro-Brazilians versus, 117

African blocs. See *blocos afro*

African-Brazilian relations, 110–113

African films, 335

Africanisms: in Brazilian art, 154–158

Africanos no Brasil, Os (Rodrigues), 203, 250–251

Afro-Braziliana, study of, 109

Afro-Brazilian Chamber of Commerce, 124

Afro-Brazilians (*see also* blacks), 231*n*; Black Movement and, 26–27, 29–30; in Brazilian film, 313–336; Candomblé and, 53–58; cosmology of, 147–153; cultural situation of, 1–3, 103, 105–139; foreign policy initiatives of, 113–122; history of, 43–51; invisibility of, 31–32; negritude of, 175–197; and Nelson Mandela's visit to Brazil, 133–134; Pentecostalism and, 237–245; political abuses of religion of, 130–132; return to Africa of, 112–113; sacred art of, 155–158; self-affirmation of, 38, 201–211; television viewing and attitudes toward, 366–371; Umbanda among, 213–232; Yoruba deities in religion of, 147–150; Yoruba influences on, 143–172

Afro-Brazilian university students, in Black Soul movement, 5

Agle, Maron, 133
agriculture: income in, 68; labor structure in, 62–65; racial distribution in, 70–83
AIDS education, 318
Alagoas state, religious persecutions in, 207
Aleijadinho, 154
Algeria, 128
All Africa Peoples Conference, 110
Altberg, Marco, 332, 333
Alves, Ataúlfo, 282
Alves, Henrique, on Adão Ventura, 183
Amado, Jorge, 40, 126, 176–177
amarelo race category, 38, 83*n;* Brazilians classified in, 4
ambulatory workers, racial distribution of, 77, 89
Amerindians: backwardness of, 33; as slaves, 18
"Am I a Little Black Girl?" ("Eu sou neguinha?"), 282
Amuleto de Ogumo, O, 311, 318, 328–331, 335, 336*n*
Ananias, Marcos Francisco, 127
ancestors: in Afro-Brazilian religion, 150–152; in Yoruba cosmology, 146–147
Andrade, M. C. de, 63
Andrews, George Reid, 62
Angel Heart, 313
Anglophone Africans, 178; Brazil and, 108; end of colonialism and, 128
Angola: African-Brazilian foreign relations and, 118,121–122, 129; black slaves from, 17; Brazilian relations with, 129–130
anti-African prejudice: in film portrayals of African religions, 314–316; in Latin American foreign relations, 119–120
Apache do Tororó, 46
apartheid, 136, 192; Brazilian attitude toward, 122, 126, 128; in contemporary Bahia, 100, 134; Nascimento's condemnation of, 179
Apolônio, 46
ara, in Afro-Brazilian religion, 153

Ara Ketu, 166
Aratu Industrial Center, 95
Araújo, Emanoel, 156, 159,162
Araújo, Manuel, 40
Araújo, Tereza Cristina de, 37
architecture, Africanization of Brazilian, 154–155
art: Africanization of Brazilian, 154–155; Afro-Brazilian sacred, 155–158; Carioca, 23–24; Catholic, 158; Christian, 154–155; festival of black, 193; Yoruba influences on Afro-Brazilian, 158–164
àse: in Afro-Brazilian art, 159, 163; in Afro-Brazilian religion, 152–153; in Yoruba cosmology, 147
Assembly of God (*see also* Pencostalism), 237, 239–245; sermons in, 239–240
atabaques, suppression of, 207
Atlantic Ocean, as Yoruba river, 145–146
autos, in contemporary Bahia, 166
axé, 54, 171; in Afro-Brazilian religion, 152–153
axé music, 9, 39, 286; in Afro-Brazilian religion, 152–153; in contemporary Bahia, 99
axexé ceremony, in Afro-Brazilian religion, 152
ayé: in Afro-Brazilian religion, 150–152; in Yoruba cosmology, 146
Azeredo, Albuino, 39
Azevedo, Durval Rosário de, 189
Azikiwe, Nnamdi, 112; on Nigerian foreign policy, 110

Baba Egun, in Afro-Brazilian religion, 150, 151
Babalaô, 331
Babo, Lamartine, 270, 283, 284
Badauê, 46
Bahia (*see also* Salvador da Bahia): African themes in carnival of, 164–165; black carnival organizations in, 8, 39; Candomblé and Umbanda in, 130–131, 225–229; elite of, 232*n;* in films, 319–328; Mário Gusmão in, 180; music

in, 247–248; negritude of, 185–192; race and class structure in contemporary, 95–102, 185–192, 201–211; in reAfricanization of Brazil, 43–51, 104, 201–211, 213–232, 250; religious practices in 1930s in, 208; Rio de Janeiro carnival versus carnival of, 249–251; Yoruba language taught in, 194

Bahia de Todos os Santos, 319–320

Baila Comigo, interracial love relationships in, 350–352

Bakhtin, Mikhail, 249, 253–254, 266

Bandeira, Manuel, 185

Banjo (McKay), 182

Bantu, influence on Brazilian music, 277–278

Barão do Rio Branco, 114–115

Barber, Karin, 315

Barbosa, Beto, 281

Barbosa, Rui, 41

Barravento, 311, 317, 319, 320, 322–328

Barro, João de, 284

Barros, Alexandre de S. C., on Brazilian foreign policy, 114–115

Barthes, Roland, 267

Basaglia, Maria, 318

Bastide, Roger, 238

Bate-Folha, in Afro-Brazilian art, 162–164

Batista, Linda, 268, 280

batuque, 277, 301

"Beautiful Little Blond" ("Linda lourinha"), song text and analysis of, 284–285

Beija Flor samba school, in film, 317

Believers, The, 313

Ben, Jorge, 277

Bittencourt, René, 278

black (*preto*) race category, 25, 83*n;* average income of, 38; in Brazilian popular music, 290–292; Brazilians classified in, 4–5; in labor market, 70–83; in post-abolition Salvador, 85–96

"Black and the White, The" ("O preto e o branco"), song text and analysis of, 290–292

black athletes, Brazilian, 108

Black Bahia music, 252

Black Brazilian Front: Bahian carnival and, 164; racial protests by, 2

black carnival organizations, 8, 45–46, 224–225, 250–251

Black Consciousness Day, 189

black consciousness movement (*see also* negritude), 1–12, 238; abolition in, 2; black Brazil in, 8–9; Candomblé and, 57; contemporary forms of, 5–8; culturalism and, 3–5; cultural practices in, 9–11; events of 1988 and, 2–3; origins of, 1–2, 43–51; participants in, 224; Pentecostalism and, 245; racism and, 3, 4–5; Rastafarianism in, 8; in Salvador da Bahia, 85–102, 201–211; statements of issues in, 11–12

"blackening." *See* reAfricanization of Brazil

"black ethnocentrism," 258

Black-ijexá, 252

"Black Lament" ("Lamento negro"), song text and analysis of, 276–278

black liberation, negritude in, 177–185

black magic, Umbanda as, 216

black men, in Brazilian popular music, 276–280, 285–287

Black Movement, 15–16; contemporary organizations in, 40; future of, 29–30; history of, 25–26; immobilization of, 26–27; militancy within, 181; and Nigerian state visit to Salvador da Bahia, 132–133; objectives of, 27–28; open letter to Nelson Mandela from, 136; organizations in, 33–34; political action by, 28–29; politics and race in, 24–25, 32–33; racism and, 32–33, 38–39; women in, 27. *See also* Movimento Negro Unificado (MNU)

Black Power movement, 6; in contemporary Bahia, 165; musical influence of, 252–253

black press, emergence of, 33
Black Rio music, 252
blacks (*see also* African-Americans; Afro-
    Brazilians): in Bahia, 185–192, 201–211;
    on Brazilian commercial television,
    363–372; in Brazilian diplomatic
    positions, 117; Brazilian foreign policy
    and, 107–109, 122–124; as Brazilian
    majority,
    18, 24–25, 41–42; in Brazilian
    modernization, 339–341; in Brazilian
    politics, 19–21, 26–27; in Brazilian
    popular music, 261–294, 290–292; on
    Brazilian television, 195*n;* as Brazilian
    wage slaves, 18, 32–34; Bumba-meu-Boi
    and, 297, 300; carnival and, 249–259;
    contemporary social stratification of
    Bahian, 95–102; crime among, 18–19;
    division by color of, 25; executions of,
    44–45; folklorization of religions of,
    55–56, 167–168; future of whites and,
    42; Haitian, 119–120; history of
    Brazilian, 43–51; intermarriages
    between whites and, 27, 182; invisibility
    of, 31–32,
    41–42, 106, 127, 133–138, 194, 365; in
    labor market, 33, 35–36, 61–62;
    marginalization of, 55–56; music of,
    247–248; oral traditions of, 44–45;
    Pentecostalism and, 237–245; police
    murders of, 27, 29; in popular
    commercial music, 267–292;
    Portuguese betrayal of, 44; in post-
    abolition occupational stratification
    (tables), 90–94; poverty of, 18–19, 56;
    resistance to oppression of, 201–211; in
    Rio de Janeiro during 1940s and 1950s,
    64–65; in Salvador after abolition,
    85–102, 201–211; in São Paulo during
    1940s and 1950s, 63–64; self-
    affirmation of, 38, 201–211; state
    genocide against, 27–28; in *telenovelas*,
    347–358; terms denoting, 261;
    Umbanda and, 213–232; versus
    immigrants in Rio de Janeiro, 62–63;
    versus immigrants in São Paulo, 62;

violations of rights of, 18–19, 181–182;
    whites versus, 223
Black Sampa music, 252
Black Skin, White Masks (Fanon), 176
Black Soul movement: Afro-Brazilian
    university students in, 5; anti-racist
    agenda of, 6; music of, 252–253; origins
    of, 6
black votes, debasement of, 28
"Black Woman" ("Preta"), song text and
    analysis of, 281–282
"Black Woman in the Window" ("Minha
    nega na janela"), song text and analysis
    of, 272–274
"Black Woman with the Hard Hair"
    ("Nega do cabelo duro"), song text and
    analysis of, 269–270
black women: in Brazilian popular music,
    267–276, 281–285, 293*n;* sexual
    freedom with, 281–282
Blame It on Rio, 313
blocos afro, 5, 8–9, 16, 39, 60, 224, 250,
    257, 259; in contemporary Bahia,
    97–99, 164–165, 166; formation of,
    46–47
"blocos de trios," in contemporary
    Bahia, 99
blocos índios, 46, 51*n*
blond women, in Brazilian popular music,
    284–285, 294*n*
boiada, 299, 300, 307–308, 308*n*,
    336*n*
Bonet, Lisa, 313
Borba, Emilinha, 269
Bosco, João, 262
Bourgeois Gentilhomme, Le, 318
Braga, Gilberto, 351, 354, 360*n*
Braga, Júlio, 103, 136–137, 199
branco race category, 83*n;* average income
    of, 38; in Brazilian popular music,
    290–292; Brazilians classified in, 4–5; in
    labor market, 70–83; in post-abolition
    Salvador, 85–96
Brasília, 178
Brazilian crown, black claim to, 28–29
Brazilian Independence Day, 254

Brazilian Press Association, on community of Portuguese-speaking nations, 129

Brazilian rap, 8, 287–290

Brazilian society, 1; racism in history of, 20; in *telenovelas*, 344–347; Yoruba influences on, 143–145

British Commonwealth, end of African colonialism within, 128–129

Brito, Edvaldo, 189, 196*n*

Brizola, Governor, 134–135

Brotherhood Campaign, 237

brown (*pardo*) race category, 83*n;* average income of, 38; as blacks, 5; Brazilians classified in, 4–5; growth of, 35; in labor market, 70–83; in post-abolition Salvador, 85–96; in Rio de Janeiro during 1940s and 1950s, 64–65; in São Paulo during 1940s and 1950s, 63–64; whitening of Brazil and, 25

Buarque, Chico, 262

Bumba-meu-Boi, 7, 297–308; acceptance of, 306–308; in Afro-Brazilian religion, 150, 248; competitive parades in, 305–306; earliest mention of, 298; in Maranhão, 297–308; origin of, 297–298; samba and, 305–306; story line of, 298; suppression of, 298, 300–305; troupes performing, 299–300

Bush, George Herbert Walker, 128

Caboclo spirits, in Umbanda, 219

Cabral, Amílcar, 46, 48, 111

Cacique de Ramos, 45–46

Cacique do Garcia, 46

café com leite race category, 25

cafuso race category (table), 91–92

Caine, Michael, 313

Caldafé, Santos, 40

Caldas, Luis, 270–272, 293*n*

Caldas, Silvio, 284

Camaçari Petrochemical Complex, 95

Camargo, Adalberto, 125–126; founding of Afro-Brazilian Chamber of Commerce by, 124

Câmbio Negro, 288, 289–290

camelôs, racial distribution of, 77

Campo da Pólvora, execution of blacks at, 44–45

Candomblé, 7, 9, 15, 16, 24, 192, 194, 213, 224, 231, 238; in Afro-Brazilian art, 162–164; art and, 158; in Bahian carnival, 255–256; beliefs of, 54; as black ethnic identity model, 261–262; in Brazilian films, 313–314, 317, 320–328, 333–334; and community, 53–58; in contemporary Bahia, 97; in Hollywood films, 313; Islam and, 44; liturgical calendar, 211*n;*Olodum and, 47; persecution of, 45, 54–55, 130–131, 199, 201–211; in reAfricanization, 225–229; in Salvador da Bahia, 186–187; symbolism in, 167; Umbanda and, 232*n;* Yoruba influences on, 145

Candomblé Nagô, 160

Cape Verde, 111, 129

capitalism: in contemporary Bahia, 96; in contemporary Brazil, 66; racism of, 194; social effects of, 35

capoeira, 7, 24, 213, 336*n;* rivalries among, 300

Cardoso, Carlos, 48

Cardoso, Fernando Henrique, 121

Carioca: art, 23–24; carnival, 249

Carlos, Manuel, 346

Carneiro, Edison, 204

Carneiro, Nelson, on death of Mãe Menininha do Gantois, 131

carnival (*see also* black carnival organizations), 7, 8, 19, 136, 177, 231, 249–259; in African-Brazilian foreign relations, 119; attempts to suppress, 251; *blocos índios* and, 46; in contemporary Bahia, 97–99, 99–101, 172*n*, 224–225, 227, 249–254; Olodum and, 47–48; Yoruba themes in, 164–168

carnival blacks, in Brazilian popular music, 285–287

carnival literature, medieval, 253

carnival songs, black women in, 267–276

Carpentier, Alejo, 327

Carvalho, José de, 331
Carybé, 40
Casa d'Água, A (Olinto), 138*n*
Catholic art, Yoruba influences on
  Brazilian, 158
Catholic Base Communities, 238
Catholic Church, 211*n*, 232*n*; African
  religions versus, 205, 208, 216; in
  Brazilian films, 321–322; money and,
  168; Pastoral Negro of, 237; suppression
  of carnival by, 255–256
Catholicism: in Bahian carnival, 255–256;
  Pentecostalism and, 237–239;
  syncretism of Afro-Brazilian religions
  with, 315–316; syncretism of Umbanda
  with, 219, 226
Catholic lay organizations, 144
Cavalcânti, Iberê, 331–332
Cavalcânti, Tenório, 330
censuses, racial statistics in, 65
Center for Black Resistance, 28–29
centro, in Umbanda, 217–218, 220–221,
  228
Centro de Articulação de Populações
  Marginalizadas (CEAP): anti-racist
  agenda of, 5–6
Centro de Estudos Afro-Asiáticos, 59
Centro de Estudos Afro-Orientais
  (CEAO), 136–137, 189, 199, 226
CEPAL, 69
Césaire, Aimé, 176, 178, 193, 195*n*
Chamber of Commerce, Afro-Brazilian,
  124
child mortality, among Brazilian blacks,
  18–19
children's songs, 292–293
Christ, Assembly of God and, 241
Christian art, Yoruba/Moslem influences
  on Brazilian, 154–155
Christianity: African religions versus,
  187–188, 314–315, 316–318; in
  Brazilian films, 321–322
churches, 56–57. See also *centro*
Church of Lapinha, Yoruba/Moslem
  architectural influences on, 154–155

Cinema Novo, 40–41; Afro-Brazilian
  religion in, 318–328
class structure: in contemporary Brazil,
  65–83; post-slavery Brazilian, 61–65
Cliff, Jimmy, 39
Clifford, James, 143
cocaine. *See* drug abuse
coffee plantations, 19, 32, 61, 63
Cole, Patrick, 126
Collares, Alceu, 135
color: absence of public data concerning,
  61–62; in Brazilian popular music, 269,
  285; Brazilians classified by,
  4–5, 25; as determinant of human
  condition, 177; in *telenovelas*, 347–352,
  357–358
"Colorful Eyes" ("Olhos coloridos"), song
  text and analysis of, 287–288
commercialization, of Bahian blacks,
  98–100
commercial relations, between Africa and
  Brazil, 126–127
Communist Party, 181, 194, 195–196*n*;
  racial problems and, 35, 36
"communitas," in carnival, 254
Conceição, Jônatas, 137
congada, 304, 308*n*; in Afro-Brazilian
  religion, 150; as Brazilian popular song
  model, 262; in contemporary Bahia, 166
"conservative modernization," of
  contemporary Brazil, 66
Cor da pele, A (Ventura), 183
Corpo-a-Corpo, 311, 350–354, 339, 360*n*,
  365
cosmology: Afro-Brazilian, 147–153;
  Yoruba, 146–147
Costa, Araújo, 27
Costa, Gal, 277
Costa, Haroldo da, 364
Council of Black Organizations, 133
"Crazy Black Woman" ("Nega maluca"),
  song text and analysis of, 268–269
creation myth, of Yoruba, 168–170
crente, 237–238, 240–241, 245*n*
Croce, Benedetto, 292

crossroads, in Afro-Brazilian religion, 146
Cruz e Sousa, João da, 196*n*
Cuba, 114, 115, 117
culinary service, of black women, 34–35
"cultivation effect," of television, 363–364, 366
culturalism: in Brazilian politics, 229–231; Candomblé as, 227; racism and, 3–5
cultural nationalism, 219
cultural practices: Afro-Brazilian, 7–8; defined, 143; social and political power and, 9–11; Yoruba, 145–146; Yoruba influences on Afro-Brazilian, 143–172
culture, 9; in African-Brazilian foreign relations, 119, 129–130; Brazilian commercial television and, 364–365; in Brazilian politics, 130–133, 223–225, 229–231; in Brazilians films, 334–335; in contemporary Bahia, 95–102; history of Brazilian, 20, 43–51; in post-abolition Salvador, 85–96; in *telenovelas*, 339–360, 357–358; Umbanda in Brazilian, 213–232; of Yorubas, 145–146
"culture of work," of contemporary Bahia, 95
Cunha, Manuela Carneiro da, 112
Cypriano, Tânia, 318

Damas, Léon, 180
damurixá festival, 250–251
dance, in Yoruba religion, 146
"Dance Little Black Girl" ("Dança pretinha"), song text of, 292–293
Degler, Carl, 12*n*
desafio, in Bumba-meu-Boi, 299
despacho, in Afro-Brazilian religion, 148, 319
desyncretism, of black and white religions, 228–229
Deusa Negra, A, 335
Diabos do Céu, Os, 284
diaspora: African religion in, 187–188; Brazilian blacks as part of African, 7, 8–9, 48–49, 104, 257; in Brazilian

popular music, 277; Yorubas in, 170–171
Diop, Cheikh Anta, 48
"Diretas-Já" campaign, 37
discrimination. *See* anti-African prejudice; racial discrimination
Djavan, 262, 263
domestics: black women as, 34–35; income of, 68; racial distribution of, 76–77
Drago, Jorge, 270
Drake, St. Clair, 119
Drewal, Margaret Thompson, 171*n*
drug abuse, in Brazilian popular music, 274–276, 290–292
Duarte, Anselmo, 311, 319
Dunn, Christopher, 119

economic miracle, 35–36, 66–67
economy: blacks in Brazilian, 18, 49–50; blacks in First Republic, 85–96; of contemporary Bahia, 95; of contemporary Brazil, 66–67
education: blacks and, 36, 56, 222–223; correlation of racism with, 371–372; occupational stratification and, 72, 79–80, 81–82; racial inequalities in, 67–68, 70–83
egun, in Yoruba cosmology, 146
Egúngún (*eégún*) masking, 150, 157–158
Eisenberg, P. L., 63
employment: in contemporary Brazil, 66–67; racial discrimination in, 222–223
entrudo tradition, 250–251
eré, in Afro-Brazilian religion, 153
escola de samba, 7, 225; in São Paulo and Rio de Janeiro, 23–24
Escrava Isaura, 365
Espírito Santo, Dem do Zamborim do, 53
Estado Novo, 218, 219, 320; Frente Negra curtailed by, 33–34. *See also* Vargas, Getúlio (dictatorship)

388   *Index*

Estatuto do Trabalhador Rural, 63
Èsù: in Afro-Brazilian religion, 147. *See
  also* Exu
Èsù-Elégba: in Afro-Brazilian religion,
  148. *See also* Exu-Legba
Europe: in African foreign relations,
  116–117; Brazilian protests against,
  251–252; religion of, 217
European immigrants: in labor market,
  33, 61–62; into São Paulo, 62; as tenant
  farmers, 32
European migration, whitening of
  Brazilian society through, 32
European Union (EU), Portuguese
  membership in, 129
Exu, 331–332; in *Barravento*, 325; in *O
  Amuleto de Ogum*, 330. *See also* Èsù
Exu-Legba, 318. *See also* Èsù-Elégba

Fanon, Frantz, 48, 176, 194, 252
favelas, 39, 126; blacks in, 32, 33; in
  Brazilian popular music, 279–280;
  music of, 291–292
Federação Baiana do Culto Afro-
  Brasileiro (FBCAB), 167–168
Federation for the Defense of Folklore
  Groups, 306–307
Felicidade, Vera: on death of Mãe
  Menininha do Gantois, 130–131
feminism, Black Movement and, 27
Fernandes, Florestan, 62
Fernandes, Gonçalves, 207
fetishism, Umbanda as, 216–217, 219
Figueiredo, Vera, 317
filha-de-santo, 53
Filhos de Gandhi *afoxé*, 258; origin and
  history of, 251–252
filhos de santo dance, 146
film: African, 335; Afro-Brazilian religions
  in, 313–336; blacks in, 311. *See also*
  Cinema Novo *and titles of individual
  films*
First Republic: abolition and, 33; blacks
  during, 85–96
First World Festival of Black Art, 193

folklorization: of black cultural practices,
  7; of Bumba-meu-Boi, 306–307; of
  Candomblé, 55, 167–168, 206
Fomm, Joana, 313–314
football, Brazilian, 108
Força de Xangô, A, plot and analysis of,
  331–332
foreign policy: African-Brazilian,
  109–122; race relations and, 106–109
França, Aline, 176–177, 191
Francophone Africans, 178; Brazil and,
  108; end of colonialism and, 128
free labor: in post-abolition Salvador, 86;
  slavery versus, 63
French community, end of African
  colonialism within, 128–129
Frente de Libertação de Moçambique
  (FRELIMO), 46, 51n; in contemporary
  Bahia, 165
Frente Negra Brasileira (FNB), 320; origin
  of, 33–34; racial protests by, 2
Freyre, Gilberto, 3, 34–35, 176, 340;
  Umbanda and, 219–220
Friandes, Mestre Manoel, 154–155
"Fricote," song text and analysis of,
  271–272
fricote, 271–272, 293n
Frith, Simon, 266
Fundação Cultural Palmares, 183
funk, 287–290

Gadotti, Moacir, 57
Galvão, Eduardo, 299–300
Gandhi, Mahatma, 48, 251–252
Garcia, Januário, 126
Garvey, Marcus, 165
Gates, Henry Louis, Jr., 318
gbàlà, 172n; in creation myth, 168–170
Geertz, Clifford, 277
Gêge-Nagô culture, 54, 144, 209, 211n,
  317
Geisel regime, 113, 115
GELEDES, anti-racist agenda of, 6
Genocídio do negro brasileiro, O
  (Nascimento), 176, 179–180

geometry, in Afro-Brazilian art, 160–162
Gerude, 274, 275
Ghana, relations between Brazil and, 127–128
Gil, Gilberto, 152, 262, 263, 272, 273–274, 277
Gira, Tote, 285
Girard, René, 315
Global Forum of Nongovernmental Organizations, 40
gods: in Yoruba cosmology, 146–147, 158. See also *orixá*
Golden Law, the, 19; as anti-racism focus, 39; effects of, 32–33
Gomes, Dias, 320
Gomes, Duílio: on Adão Ventura, 183
Gonçalves, Nelson, 278, 279
González, Lélia, 37
Goulart, João, 113, 116; overthrow of, 122
Gouveia, Lúcia, 353–354
Grande Feira, A, 319
gueledé festival, 250–251
Guerreiro, Ramiro Elysio Saraiva, 124–125
guerrilla warfare, Olodum as, 48–49
Guinea, 111
Guinea-Bissau, 129; black slaves from, 17
Guinea-Conakry, 128
Gusmão, Mário, 180, 195*n*

Haitian blacks: in African foreign relations, 119–120
Haitian religion, 171*n*
Hall, Stuart, 9
Hamenoo, Charles Kwami, 127–128
Hanchard, Michael, 3, 6, 10
Hirst, Monica, 115–116
Hobsbawm, Eric, on tradition, 215–216
Holy Spirit: in Pentecostalism, 238, 239, 240, 241, 243
horror films, Afro-diasporic religions in, 313
"Hundred Years Ago, A" ("Cem anos atrás"), 283; song text and analysis of, 278–279

Iaba, 332
Iansã, 332; Saint Barbara and, 315
iaô, 317
ìbejì: in Afro-Brazilian sacred art, 156, 157
IBOPE, television surveys by, 366–371
identity: black, 261–294; Bumba-meu-Boi and cultural, 299–301; loss of black, 18, 23–25, 27
identity politics: among Black Brazilians, 10–11, 54–55; in contemporary Bahia, 97
Iemanjá. *See* Yemanja
Ifa: in Brazilian films, 326
Ife Portuguese program, 196–197*n*
Ilê Aiyê: in Afro-Brazilian religion, 150–152; in *Barravento,* 326; Black Soul movement and, 5; in contemporary Bahia, 97–99, 136, 165–167; in Curuzu, 39; influence on Olodum of, 48; origins of, 8, 46
Ilê Axé Omin Dá terreiro, 53
Ilê Axé Opó Afonja Candomblé, 130
Ilê Iyá Omin Axé Iyá Massê terreiro, 53
illiteracy, 71–72, 135
immigrants: as tenant farmers, 32
Ince, Basil, 107
income: occupational stratification of, 73; racial inequalities in, 68, 70–83
independence: of European colonies in Africa, 128–130
Indio, Zé, 331
industrialization: blacks and, 34, 35, 205–206; in contemporary Bahia, 95; in post-abolition São Paulo, 61–62
industrial working class, racial distribution within, 74–76
inequality. *See* racial discrimination; racial inequality
Institute of Research into Black Culture (IPCN), 126
Instituto Brasileiro de Geografia e Estatística (IBGE), 25, 37, 38, 136
Instituto de Pesquisa das Culturas Negras, 32

Instituto Rio Branco, Senegalese students at, 124

Integralistas, 218

"integrationism," 258

intelligentsia: Bahian, 47, 98–100; negritude and, 175–176

intermarriage, whitening of Brazil through, 27

International Congress of Orixá Tradition, 187

international relations: African-Brazilian, 110–113; race in, 107. *See also* foreign policy

interracial love, in *telenovelas*, 350–352, 357–358

irmandade, 144

Islam: African religions versus, 187–188; architectural influences of, 154–155; in Brazilian independence, 44–45; influence on Brazil of, 1, 144

Itamaraty, 114–115, 121, 127

ìwà, in Yoruba cosmology, 147

iyalorixá, 53, 186; described, 54; in films, 317

Ìyá Màpó, in Afro-Brazilian religion, 148

Jackson, Richard, 119–120

Jetonir, 53

jogo do bicho, 292

Jordo, Fio, 272

José, Fernando, on Nelson Mandela's visit to Brazil, 135–136

journalism: in Bahia, 204–205; in suppression of Bumba-meu-Boi, 300–304

Judeo-Christian concepts, in Afro-Brazilian religion, 24, 144, 315–316

Kaolin, in Afro-Brazilian religion, 167

Kardec, Alain, 328

Kermode, Frank, 265

Keto nation, 53

King, Martin Luther, Jr., 48, 181

"King Zulu," 29

"King Zumbu," 29

labor: education and, 67–68; free versus slave, 63

labor market: blacks in, 33, 35–36; blacks versus immigrants in, 61–62; European immigrants in, 33; in post-abolition Salvador, 85–96; racial structure of, 69–83; size and composition of, 37–38; urban, 68–69

Lacerda, Benedito, 278

Lacerda, Carlos, 122

lambada, 263, 281–282

Lampreia, Luiz Felipe, 121

lanceiro, 304, 308n

Lapinha Church, Yoruba/Moslem architectural influences on, 154–155

Lara, Ivone, 332

Latin America: anti-African prejudice in foreign relations of, 119–120; racism in history of, 20

Law of the Free Womb, 19

Law of the Sexagenarians, 19

Lazinho, 48

Leather Civilization period, 297

Levy Organizations, 127

Lewu, Yaiyeola Joseph, 132

Liberdade neighborhood, 97–99; racial protests originating in, 46

Licutã, Pacífico, 45

Lima, Arnaldo do Rosário, 189, 190

Lima, Eliana de, 23

Lincoln, C. Eric, 138n

Lobo, Fernando, 268

love, in *telenovelas*, 340–341, 341–342, 350–352, 352–356, 356–357

L'Overture, Toussaint, 180

Lusophone Africans, 178; Brazil and, 108, 115, 118, 122–124, 128–130

Macalé, Jards, 329

Macau, 287

Machado, Sérgio, 195n

Machel, Samora, 46, 48

machismo, in *telenovelas*, 353, 356

Maciel-Pelourinho neighborhood, 49

Macumba: Assembly of God and, 241–242; in films, 318–319; influence on Brazilian music, 262
Macumba na Alta, 318
Macunaíma, 335
Magalhães, Antônio Carlos, 40, 133; on Nelson Mandela's visit to Brazil, 135
"magic realism," in Brazilians films, 334–335
malandros, romantic black men as, 279–280
maleme, in Brazilian popular music, 276–277
Malês, the, revolt of, 44–45
Maluf, Paulo, 125
mameluco race category: post-abolition occupational stratification of (table), 93
Mandela, Nelson, 39, 49, 106, 180, 181; visit to Brazil by, 133–138
manual workers, racial distribution of, 70–83
maracatu, 7, 304, 308*n*
Maranhão, Bumba-meu-Boi in, 297–308
"March against the Farce of Abolition," 38
Marijuana. *See* drug abuse
Marley, Bob, 39
Marli, 29
Marx, Karl, 194
Marxism: in *Barravento*, 324–325; racial problems and, 35, 43
masking traditions, 171*n*, 250–251; in carnival, 164; Yoruba influences on Brazilian, 157–158
Masters and the Slaves, The (Freyre), 219
Mathias, Germano, 272, 273–274
Matta, Roberto da, 254
May 13th Society, creation of, 87
McKay, Claude, 182
media: and commercialization of Bahian blacks, 98–100; religion and, 56–57
Médici regime, 113; on Portuguese-speaking Africa, 122–123
Mendes, Dom Lucas, 135

Mendonça, R., 150–151
Menininha do Gantois, Mãe, 53, 189, 190–191; death of, 130–131
mercantilism, in Salvador, 85–86
Mercury, Daniela, 99, 285, 286–287
Mesquita, Custodio, 280
mestizos: in Bahian carnival, 250, 251–253, 255–256, 257–259; in Olodum, 47; in post-abolition Salvador, 85–86; in *telenovelas*, 357–358
metaphysics, in Afro-Brazilian art, 160–162
Middle Ages, carnivals in, 253–254
middle class: in contemporary Brazil, 66, 69; in post-abolition Salvador, 86; rural, 68
migrant workers, 72
military: loss of political control by, 2, 36; repression of blacks by, 2, 38, 45, 48
Miltinho, 282
Mimito, 149
Minas Gerais, Yoruba architectural influence at, 154
Ministry of External Relations, 114
miscegenation, politics of, 34–35. *See also* "whitening"
misogyny, in Brazilian popular music, 271–272
Moa, 46
Modernism, Umbanda and, 217
modernization, myth of, 339–341, 349–352
money, whitening effects of, 168
Montilus, Guerin, 119
Moraes, Vinicius de, 277
moralization, of Candomblé, 208
morena, in Brazilian popular music, 283–284
moreninho, as black epithet, 18
moreno race category, 25
Moslem *See* Islam
Motion pictures. *See* film
Motta, Zezé, 350
Moura, Haroldo, 306

Movimento Negro Unificado (MNU) (*see also* Black Movement): anti-racist agenda of, 5–6; musical influence of, 252–253; Nascimento's support of, 179; on Nelson Mandela's visit to Brazil, 137; origin of, 36–37; participants in, 224; political influence of, 258

Movimento Popular de Libertação de Angola (MPLA), 46, 51*n*, 165

Mozambique, African-Brazilian foreign relations and, 118, 129

mulata, in Brazilian popular music, 267–269, 270, 282–283, 293*n*

mulatto (*pardo*) race category, 83*n*; average income of, 38; as blacks, 5; Brazilians classified in, 4–5; in labor market, 70–83; in post-abolition Salvador, 85–96; whitening of Brazil and, 25

"mulatto escape hatch," 3

mulattos: as blacks, 18; Bumba-meu-Boi and, 300; discrimination against, 12*n*; in labor market, 61–63; Pentecostalism and, 243, 244; in post-abolition occupational stratification (tables), 90–94; in Rio de Janeiro during 1940s and 1950s, 64–65; in São Paulo during 1940s and 1950s, 63–64

multiculturalism, of Brazil, 219–220

multiracial society, Brazil as, 219–220

music: in *Barravento*, 323; black identities in, 261–294; in Brazilian culture, 247–248; Olodum and, 49, 188; racial politics of, 223, 224–225. See also *axé* music; Brazilian rap; Olodum; popular commercial music; reggae; samba

Música de Olodum, A, 49

Muslims. *See* Islam

Nagô. *See* Yoruba

Nascimento, Abdias do, 33–34, 36, 104, 175, 187, 193, 194–195, 325, 364–365; on Bahia, 185; as example of negritude, 177–185

Nascimento, Edson Arantes do. *See* Pelé (Edson Arantes do Nascimento)

Nascimento, Elisa L., 182

Nascimento, Milton, 262

Nascimento, Wagner, 121–122

Nasser, David, 269

national congress, blacks in Brazilian, 20–21

National Day of Black Consciousness, 39, 256

National Household Survey, 4, 67

Nazaré, Maria Escolástica de, 53

Nazário, Olga, 113, 116

negritude: in Africa and Brazil, 192–195; of Bahian blacks, 185–192; black liberation and, 177–185; as ideology, 175–177. *See also* "new negritude"

Neninho do Baluolê, Ogã, 28–29

Neto, Agostinho, 46, 48, 121–122

Neto, Calasans, 40

Neto, Triguerinho, 319

"new negritude," 104, 175–197, 252

Nigeria: absence of Brazilian cultural links with, 193; films of, 335; foreign policy of, 110; state visit to Salvador da Bahia from, 132

Nkrumah, Kwame, 48, 110, 112

Noites de Iemanjá, As, 313–314

non-manual workers: income of, 69–70; racial distribution of, 70–83

non-whites. *See* black (*preto*) race category; brown (*pardo*) race category; mulatto (*pardo*) race category; yellow (*amarelo*) race category

"Now" (Ventura), 184–185

Obà: in Afro-Brazilian religion, 147; in Yoruba cosmology, 147

Obalúayé, in Yoruba cosmology, 147

Obàtálá: in Afro-Brazilian art, 161–162; in Afro-Brazilian religion, 147, 148, 149; in Yoruba cosmology, 147

Obisakin, Lawrence, 196*n*

occupations: post-abolition racial stratification of, 88–96; racial structure

within, 70–83. *See also* professional
occupations
Odo Ya! Fighting Aids, 318
Odùduwàa, in Yoruba cosmology, 147
Ogum Beiramar, 330
Ògún (Ogum): in Afro-Brazilian art, 159;
in Afro-Brazilian religion, 147, 148; in
Brazilian popular music, 276–278; in
films, 311, 318, 328–332; in Yoruba
cosmology, 147
"Old Black" spirits, in Umbanda, 219–220
Olinto, Antônio, 130, 138*n*
Oliveira, Dalva de, 278
Oliveira, Lúcia Helena Garcia de, 37
Olodum, 10, 15, 16, 39, 43–51, 56, 192; in
Bahia, 188; Black Soul movement and,
5; executive directors of, 50; influence
of North American blacks on, 48; on
Nelson Mandela's visit to Brazil,
136–137; organization of, 49–50; origin
of name of, 196*n*; origins of, 8, 47–48;
purpose of, 49–51
Olodumare, 196*n*
Olókun, in Yoruba cosmology, 147
Olórun (Olorum): in creation myth,
168–170; in Yoruba religion, 314
Olósà, in Yoruba cosmology, 147
Omólù, in Afro-Brazilian religion, 167
oral traditions, among blacks, 44–45
Ordem Terceira de São Francisco,
Yoruba/Moslem architectural
influences on, 154–155
"Origin" (Ventura), 184
òrìsà (see also orixá): in Afro-Brazilian
art, 163; Afro-Brazilian images of, 158;
in Afro-Btrazilian religion, 147–150;
female, 148–150; Salvadoran devotees
of, 167–168; warrior, 148; in Yoruba
cosmology, 146–147
Orisanla: in Afro-Brazilian art, 161–162;
in Yoruba cosmology, 147
orixá, 53, 54, 56, 57, 130, 220, 232*n*; in
Brazilian music, 262; in carnival, 170; in
films, 314, 317–318, 326–328; spiritual
possession by, 316

Orleans de Bragança family, 28
Ortiz, Renato, 203
òrun: in Afro-Brazilian religion, 150–153;
in *Barravento*, 326; in Yoruba
cosmology, 146–147
Òsanyìn, in Yoruba cosmology, 147
Ositola, Kolawole, 158
Òsòosì, in Afro-Brazilian religion, 147,
148
Òsun (Oxum), 332; in Afro-Brazilian
religion, 147; in Yoruba cosmology, 147
Otelo, Grande, 195*n*
Oxala: in Afro-Brazilian art, 161–162; in
Afro-Brazilian religion, 147, 148, 149;
Christ and, 315; in creation myth,
168–170; in Yoruba cosmology, 147
Oya: in Afro-Brazilian religion, 147; in
Yoruba cosmology, 147
Òyó, in Yoruba cosmology, 147

"pact of silence," in Salvador racism, 88
padê ceremony, 148
Pagador de Promessas, O, 311, 315–316,
317, 319, 334; *Barravento* versus,
322–323; plot and analysis of, 320–322
pagode, 290–292
Palmares, kingdom of, 28–29
paradà: in Afro-Brazilian religion, 150; of
masking, 164
parade contests, 308*n*; of Bumba-meu-
Boi, 305–306
Paranhos, José María da Silva, Júnior,
114–115
pardo race category, 83*n*; average income
of, 38; as blacks, 5; Brazilians classified
in, 4–5; growth of, 35;
in labor market, 70–83; in post-
abolition Salvador, 85–96; whitening of
Brazil and, 25
Partido Africano da Independência da
Guiné e Cabo Verde (PAIGC), 46, 51*n*
Partido Comunista do Brasil (PCdoB), 26
Pastoral Negro, 237
paternalism: toward blacks, 1, 10, 53, 125;
in post-abolition Salvador, 87

Paula, Felício de, 126–127
Paulo, Marcos, 350
Pedro I, Emperor, 44
Pelé (Edson Arantes do Nascimento), 19, 112–113, 182–183
"Pelo Telefone," 305–306
Pelourinho, 98; Olodum in, 39, 47–49
Pentecostalism, 199, 200, 237–245
Pereira, João Baptista Borges, 301
performing arts, Yoruba influences on Brazilian, 157
Pesquisa Nacional por Amostra de Domicílios; survey, 67
Pessoa, Epitácio, 88
Pierson, Donald, 86, 88; on Bahian sects, 208; occupational stratification tables compiled by, 90–94
Pinto, Virgílio, 307
Pires, Roberto, 40, 319
Pitanga, Antônio, 16, 26, 41, 323
Plantel, 127
Poetas baianos da negritude, 189
poetic subject as "I," in popular commercial music analysis, 266, 267
poetry: of Adão Ventura, 183–185; of Aline França, 191; of Arnaldo Lima, 190; of Cruz e Sousa, 196n; of Yoruba creation myth, 169
police: murders of blacks by, 27, 29, 36; persecution of Apache by, 46; persecution of blacks by, 45, 48, 87–88, 199, 202–210, 210–211n; raids in Bahia by, 205; suppression of Bumba-meu-Boi by, 300–304
political repression, of blacks, 1, 2, 27–28, 29, 172n, 201–211
politics: abuses of religion in Brazilian, 130–132; within black consciousness movement, 5–6; blacks in Brazilian, 19–21, 26–27, 28–29, 106, 177–185; black women in Brazilian, 27; in Brazilian films, 320–328; in contemporary Bahia, 96–98; cultural practices and, 9–11, 229–231; culture in Brazilian, 130–133, 223–225; of Nelson Mandela's visit to Brazil, 133–138;

Umbanda in, 218, 220; Yoruba influences on Brazilian, 144–145
Pomba Gira: Deusa do Amor, 317
pomba-gira, 330, 331
popular commercial music, 261–294; analysis of, 266–267; analyzing texts of Brazilian, 266–267; as black ethnic identity model, 262; black images in, 267–292, 292–293; conceptualizing Brazilian, 264–266; de-ritualizing effects of, 264–266; genres of, 263, 264–265, 265–266; old men in, 276–278; sacred music versus, 264–265; writers and characteristics of, 262–263
Porcaro, Oliveira, 27
Porcaro, Rosa Maria, 37
Porto, Humberto, 276
Porto Alegre, segregation in, 230
Portugal: Brazilian relations with, 122–124, 128; colonialism of, 111; independence of Brazil from, 44
Portuguese-speaking countries in Africa, 178, 252; Brazilian relations with, 108, 115, 118, 122–124, 128–130
"positive ethnocentrism," 257–258
poverty, 135; of Brazilian blacks, 18–19, 55–56; among rural manual workers, 71–72; of rural population, 68
povo-de-santo community, 202; persecutions of, 207
Prado Júnior, Caio, 300, 300
Prandi, Reginaldo, 207
Predicament of Culture, The (Clifford), 143
prejudice. *See* anti-African prejudice
Preston, George, 159
preto doutor, 45, 51n
preto race category, 25, 83n; in Assembly of God, 242; average income of, 38; in Brazilian popular music, 290–292; Brazilians classified in, 4–5; in labor market, 70–83; in post-abolition Salvador, 85–96
Preto Velho spirits, 221, 229, 232n; in Umbanda, 219–220

"Pretty Morena" ("Linda morena"), song text and analysis of, 283–284
Prieswerk, Roy, 107
primitive cults, African religions characterized as, 205–206
professional occupations: blacks and whites in, 38, 66–67; income in, 68; racial structure within, 77–83
proletariat, 69
Protestantism, 58*n*; evangelical, 200
Prova de Fogo, A, 319, 332–334
public administrators, racial distribution of, 78
"Pungar," song text and analysis of, 274–276
Puritanism, Afro-Brazilian religions versus, 316

Quadros, Jânio, 113–114, 116
Querino, Manoel, 250
Quilombo de Palmares, 39, 256
quilombo: in contemporary Bahia, 166; history of, 43–44; resistance to oppression within, 207–208

Rabatony, Tony, 322
Raça Negra, 23
race: classifications of, 4–5; in international relations, 107, 117–118, 122–124; Brazilian foreign policy and, 106–109; in Brazilian popular music, 290–292; in contemporary Brazil, 65–83; images of in children's songs, 292–293; social context of, 4, 8–9; in *telenovelas,* 347–358; television viewing and attitudes toward, 366–371. *See also* black (*preto*) race category; brown (*pardo*) race category; mulatto (*pardo*) race category; white (*branco*) race category; yellow (*amarelo*) race category
"racial democracy," 3, 117, 127, 134, 176, 214; in Brazilian modernization, 339–341; Gilberto Freyre and, 219–220; heavy television viewing and, 371–372; myth of, 34–35, 37, 96, 219, 270, 365;

origins of, 87–88; Pentecostalism and, 245; in *telenovelas*, 357–358
racial discrimination, 1, 3, 18, 20–21, 24, 59–60; African image of Brazilian, 108–109; in Bahia, 185–192; Black Movement and, 27–28, 32–33; Candomblé and, 55; *centros* and, 220–221; in contemporary Bahia, 95–102; in labor market, 79–83; Nascimento on, 179–180; and Nelson Mandela's visit to Brazil, 133–138; official statements on Brazilian, 124–128; origin of MNU and, 36–37; in post-abolition Salvador, 85–96, 201–211; in São Paulo, 33, 36; Umbanda and, 220–221, 222–224. *See also* black consciousness movement; Black Movement
racial "exceptionalism," 3
"racial homogeneity," in contemporary Bahia, 100
racial inequality, 3; *centros* and, 220–221; in contemporary Brazil, 67–83; Pentecostalism and, 238–239; in Salvador after abolition, 85–102
"racialism," 257–258
racial "whitening." *See* "Whitening"
racism: toward African diplomats, 117–118; American versus Brazilian, 50–51; black consciousness movement and, 2–5; Black Movement and, 15–16, 32–33, 38–39; in Brazilian modernization, 339–341; in Brazilian popular music, 271–272; as Brazilian problem, 195; of capitalism, 194; correlation of education with, 371–372; culture of, 231; effects of, 38; in Latin America, 17; Pentecostalism and, 237–245; in post-abolition Salvador, 87–96; in São Paulo, 23–24; television and, 363–364; Umbanda and, 230–231
Ramos, Artur, 147, 171*n*
Ranger, Terence, on tradition, 215–216
rap. *See* Brazilian rap
rap consciência, 289

Rastafarianism, 8, 9, 39; in contemporary Bahia, 165

reAfricanization of Brazil, 43–51, 104, 199, 201–211, 213–232, 257–259

Recôncavo, 201, 210*n*; atrocities against slaves in, 176

reggae, 8, 9, 49, 285–287, 287–290; in contemporary Bahia, 165

Reis, João, 171*n*, 207

Reis, Mário, 283

religion: Afro-Brazilian, 7, 23–24, 53–58, 89, 144, 186–188, 199–200, 201–211, 218–219, 314–316; Afro-Brazilian in film, 313–336, 316–318, 318–319; in black ethnic identity models, 261–262; black versus white, 216–217; Brazilian political abuses of, 130–132; licensing and registration of ceremonies, 206; in persecution of blacks, 44–45; in Salvador da Bahia, 186–187; traditional African versus foreign, 204, 216–217; trance in Afro-Brazilian, 316–318; and Yoruba cosmology, 146–153. *See also* Candomblé; Catholic Church; Pentecostalism; Protestantism; Umbanda

reparations, following abolition, 33

Repensando a mulher negra (Porcaro and Costa), 27

repression. *See* political repression; social repression

resistance, culture of, 20

"Restless Mulata" ("Mulata assanhada"), song text and analysis of, 282–283

rights: activism to obtain, 19–20; violations of, 18–19

Rio de Janeiro, 16, 59, 177, 178, 192; Bahian carnival versus carnival of, 249–251; blacks in, 32; black slavery in, 17; blacks versus immigrants in, 62–63; in Brazilian independence, 44; Bumba-meu-Boi in, 304; establishment of Umbanda in, 216; mayoral candidacy in, 21, 26–27; military repression of blacks in, 38; Movimento Negro

Unificado (MNU) in, 37; Nelson Mandela's arrival in, 134; occupational structure during 1940s and 1950s, 64–65; Pentecostalism in, 200; racial protests in, 2; samba schools in, 225; Teatro Experimental do Negro in, 33–34; as Umbanda center, 218

"rites of inversion," 253

"River of Culture" metaphor, of Yorubas, 145–146

Rocha, Anecy, 329

Rocha, Fausto, 121–122

Rocha, Glauber, 40, 311, 319, 320, 321, 334; and *Barravento*, 322–328

rock lyrics, Brazilian popular music and, 262

Rodrigues, João Jorge Santos, 10, 15, 16, 103, 139*n*; on Nelson Mandela's visit to Brazil, 136–137; Olodum and, 188

Rodrigues, Raimundo Nina, 171*n*, 210–211*n*, 250–251; on police repression of blacks, 203–205

Roitman, Odete, 355–356

Rosa, Geraldo, 331

Rosário dos Pretos Church, 131

Rosinha de Oxum, 332

Rourke, Mickey, 313

rural workers: income of, 68; racial distribution of, 70–83

Russo, Carlinhos, 290

Ruy, Evaldo, 268, 280

Sá, Sandra de, 287

Sacramento, João Domingos Perreira do, 302

sacred art, Afro-Brazilian, 155–158

Sales, Nívio Ramos, 332, 333

Salvador da Bahia, 16, 177; African-Brazilian foreign relations and, 118; African impressions of, 106, 118; black consciousness movement in, 85–102, 185–192, 201–211; in Brazilian independence, 44; in Brazilian popular music, 285–287; Candomblé in, 167–168, 199; culture of, 144; history of, 43–45, 144; mercantilism in, 85–86;

Nelson Mandela's visit to, 133–137; post-abolition occupational stratification in (tables), 90–94; race and class structure in contemporary, 95–102; racial protests in, 2, 39; state visit from Nigeria to, 132

samba, 6, 7, 39, 49, 285–287; Bumba-meu-Boi and, 305–306; in contemporary Bahia, 165, 225; and creation myth, 168–170; rivalries among, 300. See also *axé* music

Samba da Criação do Mundo, 317

samba de breque, 273, 294*n*

Samba em Brasília, 319

Samba School, in carnival, 168–170. See also *escola de samba*

sambistas, rivalries among, 300

Sampaio, André Luiz, 336*n*

Sàngó (*see also* Xangô): in Afro-Brazilian art, 161–162; in Afro-Brazilian religion, 147, 148, 153; in Yoruba cosmology, 147

Sanni, 45

Santana, Hédimo Rodrigues, 131–132

Santana, Oscar, 40

Santería, in Hollywood films, 313

Santiago, Silviano, on Adão Ventura, 183

Santos, Joel Rufinodos dos, 365

Santos, José Lopes dos, 134–135

Santos, Luis Paulino dos, 323

Santos, Nelson Pereira dos, 311, 328–331, 334

São Jorge, Assembly of God in, 239–245

São Luis, Bumba-meu-Boi in, 303–304

São Paulo: in Brazilian independence, 44; Carioca artists in, 23–24; coffee plantations in, 32; displacement of black workers by immigrants in, 61–62; occupational structure during 1940s and 1950s, 63–64; racial discrimination in, 33, 36; rap music in, 288

São Tomé and Príncipe, 129

"Sarara crioulo," 287

Savimbi, Jonas, 121–122

Schindler, Rex, 323

sculpture, Yoruba influences on Brazilian, 157

Second Conference of the Tradition of the Orixás, 226–227

secular traditions, Afro-Brazilian, 7

Selcher, Wayne, 113–114

self-employed businessmen: income of, 69; racial distribution of, 80–81

self-employed manual workers, racial distribution of, 76

self-racism, in Brazilian popular music, 269

Senegal, Brazilian relations with, 122–124

Senghor, Henri, 123

Senghor, Leopold Sedar, 176, 182; state visit to Brazil by, 122–124

"serious play." See *siré*

Serra da Barriga, 42

service workers, racial distribution of, 75–76

sexual experiences: among Afro-Brazilian deities, 317; between blacks and whites, 34–35, 46, 275–276

sexuality: in Brazilian dance, 263; in Brazilian films, 318; in Brazilian popular music, 267–269, 271–272, 274–276, 281–282, 282–283, 283–284, 284–285

shanty slaves, 34, 207–208

Sharp Prize, 188

signs: in Afro-Brazilian art, 162; in Afro-Brazilian religion, 167–168

Silva, Aguinaldo, 346

Silva, Benedita da, 15, 26–27, 39, 134, 181, 245*n*, 371–372

Silva, Bezerra da, 290, 292

Silva, Constantino, 276

Silveira, Azevedo, 113

singer as "I," in popular commercial music analysis, 266, 267

siré: in Afro-Brazilian art, 163; in Afro-Brazilian religion, 153; carnival as, 164; Yoruba religion as, 146

slavery, 61; abolition of, 2, 19, 59–60; in Adão Ventura's poetry, 184–185; Black Movement and, 32–34; in Brazilian history, 43–44, 176; in Brazilian popular music, 278–279, 282; brutality of, 176;

Bumba-meu-Boi as arising from, 297–298; in children's songs, 292–293; free labor versus, 63; history of Brazilian, 17–18, 59–60, 112; influence on Brazilian music, 261–262; manual labor and, 82–83; race and class structure following abolition of Brazilian, 61–65; religion during, 203–204; in post-abolition Salvador, 85–96; "whitewashing" of, 191–192; Yorubas and, 170–171
slaves: military exploitation of, 42*n*; negotiations between masters and, 207–208; Portuguese betrayal of, 44
soap opera. See *telenovela*
Soares, Rubem, 269
social change, in contemporary Brazil, 66–67
social grouping, in contemporary Bahia, 99–101
social mobility: in contemporary Brazil, 66–67; in post-abolition Salvador, 86
social movements, 36
social power: black acquisition of, 20–21, 23–25, 201–211; in contemporary Bahia, 96–98; cultural practices and, 9–11; of popular commercial music, 265–266; in post-abolition Salvador, 86; Umbanda and, 213–232
social repression, of blacks, 1
social stratification: in contemporary Brazil, 65–83, 95–102; in post-abolition Salvador, 85–96
Sociedade Protetora dos Válidos, 132
Sodré, Muniz, 315
"Song of the City, The" ("O canto da cidade"), song text and analysis of, 285–287
songs. See *titles of individual songs*
SOS Racismo, anti-racist agenda of, 5–6
South Africa, 192; similarity of Brazilian apartheid to that in, 126
Souza, José Ribeiro de, 299
Soyinka, Wole, 178
spirit possession, in Afro-Brazilian religion, 316

spirits: in Afro-Brazilian religion, 316–318; in Yoruba cosmology, 146–147
spiritual otherworld: in Afro-Brazilian religion, 150; in Yoruba cosmology, 146–147
stereotypes, in *telenovelas*, 347–349
sterilization, of black women, 28
student movement, 36
"Sub-Race" ("Sub-Raça"), song text and analysis of, 288–290
suicide, in Afro-Brazilian religion, 148, 149
superstition, African religions portrayed in film as, 314–316
syncretism: of black and white religions, 213, 226, 228–229; of carnival and Catholicism, 255–256

"Take a Look at the Style of That Black Dude" ("Olha o jeito desse nego"), song text and analysis of, 279–280
tambor de crioula dance, 275, 307
Tambor de Mina, 7
Teatro Experimental do Negro, 33–34, 180, 232*n*
Teixeira, Cide, 171*n*
telenovela, 311; audiences for, 343–344; blacks in, 347–358; criticism of, 342–343; modernity and symbolism in, 339–360; production of, 344–347; superficiality in, 347–349; universality of, 346–347
television: blacks in, 311, 363–372; correlation of audience attitudes and viewership of, 365–372; surveys of, 366–371. See also *telenovela*
tenant farmers, abolition and, 32
Tenda dos Milagres (Amado), 126, 334
Terciliano Jr., art of, 162–164
Terra em Transe, 334
terreiro, 53, 54–55, 56, 199, 210*n*; black resistance movements in, 202–211; in films, 317; functions of, 57; licensing and registration of, 206; Umbanda in, 220

texturaafro (Ventura), 183, 184–185, 195
theater. *See* performing arts
Tosta, Maria Dionísia de Santana, 189,
  190–191
totemism, in Umbanda, 219
"Totem Ogun" (Araújo), 159
Toure, Sekou, 48
traditions, invention of, 199, 215–216. *See
  also* masking traditions;oOral
  traditions; religion; secular traditions
"Trajetória" (Azevedo), 189–190
trance: in Afro-Brazilian religions,
  316–318; in Brazilians films, 334–335
transformation, in Afro-Brazilian
  religion, 150
"tree of life," in creation myth, 168–170
Trindade, Solano, 33–34
Trio de Ouro, 276, 278
trios elétricos, 225
Troca de Cabeça (Gusmão), 195*n*
Turner, J. Michael, 5
Turner, Victor, 253, 254
TV Globo, 342
twins, in Afro-Brazilian sacred art, 156,
  157

ufanismo, 210*n*; inaccuracies of, 202
Umbanda, 199, 203, 213–232, 238;
  Assembly of God and, 241–242;
  Candomblé and, 225–229, 232*n*; in
  films, 328–332, 332–334; in Hollywood
  films, 313; influence on Brazilian music,
  262; invention and origin of, 216–218;
  as multiclass religion, 230;
  reAfricanization of, 222–231; whitening
  of, 213–222, 228–231; as white religion,
  229–230
union movement, in contemporary Bahia,
  97
United Nations Fourth Committee
  (decolonization committee), 111
United States: Abdias do Nascimiento in,
  36; in African foreign relations,
  116–117; Black Power movement in, 6;
  Brazilian foreign policy and, 114;
  influence on Brazil of, 256; influence on

Olodum of blacks from, 48; "modern
  racism" in, 363–364; racial classification
  in, 5; racism and television in, 363–364;
  situation of blacks in, 106, 108–109,
  110–111, 138*n*
universe: in Afro-Brazilian religion,
  150–152; in Yoruba cosmology, 146;
  Yoruba myth of creation of, 168–170
urban centers, blacks versus immigrants
  in, 61–63
urbanization: in contemporary Bahia, 95;
  labor market and, 68–69; Umbanda
  and, 222
urban workers, income of, 68–69
U.S.S.R., Brazilian foreign policy and,
  114, 115

Valença, João, 270
Valença, Raul, 270
Valentim, Rubem, 162; art of, 159–160,
  161
Vale Tudo, 311, 352; plot and analysis of,
  354–356
Valladares, Clarival do Prado, 191–192
Valle, Zezinho do, 290
Vargas, Getúlio (dictatorship), 320;
  Umbanda during, 220. *See also* Estado
  Novo
Veloso, Caetano, 249, 251, 262, 263, 277,
  282, 294*n*
Ventura, Adão, 104, 195; as example of
  negritude, 177–185
Verger, Pierre Fatumbi, 139*n*, 144, 171*n*
Vieira, Hamilton de Jesus, 189–190
violence: against women, in Brazilian
  popular music, 272–274; Bumba-meu-
  Boi and, 300–301, 301–302
Voodoo Island, 313
Voodoo Man, 313
Voodoo Woman, 313
Voudou, in Hollywood films, 313
Vovô, Antônio Carlos, 46, 136, 167

Wafer, Jim, on culture and politics in
  Brazil, 131–132
Walker, Sheila, 249, 257

Watts, Ernie, 152
Weber, Max, 258
Wetherell, James, 144
white (*branco*) race category, 83*n*; average
    income of, 38; in Brazilian popular
    music, 290–292; Brazilians classified in,
    4–5; in labor market, 70–83; in post-
    abolition Salvador, 85–96
White, Hayden, 274
"whitening," 3, 25, 176, 182–183, 199, 311;
    abolition of slavery and, 32–33; in
    Brazilian modernization, 339–341;
    money and, 168; in post-abolition
    Salvador, 86; in *telenovelas*, 357–358;
    through intermarriage, 27; Umbanda
    and, 213–232
whites: average income of, 38; blacks
    versus, 223; in Brazilian popular music,
    290–292; Bumba-meu-Boi and, 297,
    300; in contemporary Bahia, 99–101;
    employment of black women by, 34–35;
    future of blacks and, 42; history of
    persecution of blacks by, 43–51;
    involvement in Umbanda by, 220 222;
    in Olodum, 47; Pentecostalism and,
    238–240, 242–243; in post-abolition
    occupational stratification (tables),
    90–94; in post-abolition Salvador, 86; in
    Rio de Janeiro during 1940s and 1950s,
    64–65; in São Paulo during 1940s and
    1950s, 63–64; sexual experiences
    between blacks and, 34–35, 181–182,
    275–276; in *telenovelas*, 347–352,
    352–356, 357–358; terms denoting, 261;
    as worthless, 46–47
Wild Orchid, 313
witchcraft, African religions characterized
    as, 205–206, 327
women: in Afro-Brazilian religion,
    148–150; in black families, 89; in Black
    Movement, 27; in Brazilian popular
    music, 267–276, 281–285; Brazilian
    social status of, 15–16, 20–21, 23;
    employment of black, 34–35; in
    industrial working class, 75;

occupational distribution of, 70–83; in
    professional occupations, 77–79; as
    service workers, 75–76; sterilization of
    black, 28; violence against, 272–274
Workers' Party (PT), 16, 28
world image, in Yoruba cosmology, 146
worship: in Afro-Brazilian religion, 153;
    in Yoruba religion, 146. *See also* religion

X, Malcolm, 48
Xangô (*see also* Sàngó), 7, 207; as black
    ethnic identity model, 261–262; in
    Brazilian film, 331–332; in Brazilian
    popular music, 276–278
"Xangô Spirit Tent," 331
Xuxa, 182

Yâi, Olábìyí, 170, 172*n*, 194, 250
Yansan, in Afro-Brazilian religion, 147
yellow (*amarelo*) race category, 38, 83*n*;
    Brazilians classified in, 4
Yemanja: in Afro-Brazilian religion, 147;
    in Brazilian films, 313–314, 327; Virgin
    Mary and, 315
Yemoja, in Yoruba cosmology, 147
Yetunde, 171*n*
Yewa, in Yoruba cosmology, 147
Yoruba: cosmology of, 146–147; creation
    myth of, 168–170; influence on
    Brazilian art, 154–155, 155–158,
    158–164; influence on Brazilian music,
    261–262, 277–278; influence on Brazil
    of, 103–104, 143–172, 227; language
    taught in Bahia, 194, 226, 228; religion
    of, 314, 315, 319–320; in Salvador da
    Bahia, 186; themes in carnival,
    164–168, 250–251
Yourcenar, Marguerite, 201
"Your Hair Can't Deny It" ("O teu cabelo
    não mega"), song text and analysis of,
    270

Zappa, Italo, 120–121
Zumbi dos Palmares, 28–29, 42, 180, 188,
    256, 328; death of, 39